Too Jewish or Not Jewish Enough

Museums and Collections

Editors
Mary Bouquet, University College Utrecht, and
Howard Morphy, The Australian National University, Canberra

As houses of memory and sources of information about the world, museums function as a dynamic interface between past, present, and future. Museum collections are increasingly being recognized as material archives of human creativity and as invaluable resources for interdisciplinary research. Museums provide powerful forums for the expression of ideas and are central to the production of public culture: they may inspire the imagination, generate heated emotions and express conflicting values in their material form and histories. This series explores the potential of museum collections to transform our knowledge of the world, and for exhibitions to influence the way in which we view and inhabit that world. It offers essential reading for those involved in all aspects of the museum sphere: curators, researchers, collectors, students and the visiting public.

Recent titles:

VOLUME 17
Too Jewish or Not Jewish Enough: Ritual Objects and Avant-Garde Art at the Jewish Museum of New York
Jeffrey Abt

VOLUME 16
Museum Times: Changing Histories in South Africa
Leslie Witz

VOLUME 15
Museum, Place, Architecture and Narrative: Nordic Maritime Museums' Portrayals of Shipping, Seafarers and Maritime Communities
Annika Bünz

VOLUME 14
Contested Holdings: Museum Collections in Political, Epistemic and Artistic Processes of Return
Felicity Bodenstein, Damiana Oţoiu, and Eva-Maria Troelenberg

VOLUME 13
Transforming Author Museums: From Sites of Pilgrimage to Cultural Hubs
Ulrike Spring, Johan Schimanski, and Thea Aarbakke

VOLUME 12
Exchanging Objects: Nineteenth-Century Museum Anthropology at the Smithsonian Institution
Catherine A. Nichols

VOLUME 11
Extinct Monsters to Deep Time: Conflict, Compromise, and the Making of Smithsonian's Fossil Halls
Diana E. Marsh

VOLUME 10
The Witness as Object: Video Testimony in Memorial Museums
Steffi de Jong

VOLUME 9
Visitors to the House of Memory: Identity and Political Education at the Jewish Museum Berlin
Victoria Bishop Kendzia

VOLUME 8
Museum Websites and Social Media: Issues of Participation, Sustainability, Trust and Diversity
Ana Luisa Sánchez Laws

For a full volume listing, please see the series page on our website: https://berghahnbooks.com/series/museums-and-collections

Too Jewish or Not Jewish Enough

Ritual Objects and Avant-Garde Art at the Jewish Museum of New York

Jeffrey Abt

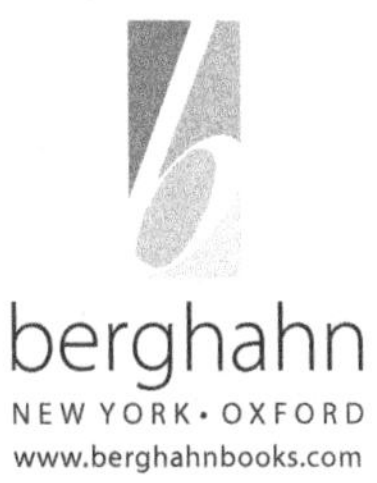

NEW YORK • OXFORD
www.berghahnbooks.com

First published in 2024 by
Berghahn Books
www.berghahnbooks.com

Library of Congress Cataloging-in-Publication Data

Names: Abt, Jeffrey, author.
Title: Too Jewish or Not Jewish Enough: Ritual Objects and Avant-Garde Art at the Jewish Museum of New York / Jeffrey Abt.
Description: 1st. | New York: Berghahn Books, 2024. | Series: Museums and collections; volume 17 | Includes bibliographical references and index.
Identifiers: LCCN 2023058363 (print) | LCCN 2023058364 (ebook) | ISBN 9781805392774 (hardback) | ISBN 9781805392781 (epub) | ISBN 9781805392798 (web pdf)
Subjects: LCSH: Jewish Museum (New York, N.Y.)—History. | Museums—New York (State)—New York—History. | Jews—Identity.
Classification: LCC N7414.75.N48 J482 2024 (print) | LCC N7414.75.N48 (ebook) | DDC 069.09747—dc23/eng/20240103
LC record available at https://lccn.loc.gov/2023058363
LC ebook record available at https://lccn.loc.gov/2023058364

British Library Cataloguing in Publication Data

A catalogue record for this book is available from the British Library

ISBN 978-1-80539-277-4 hardback
ISBN 978-1-80539-278-1 epub
ISBN 978-1-80539-279-8 web pdf

https://doi.org/10.3167/9781805392774

To Jules Kirschenbaum
1930–2000
artist, mentor, and non-Jewish Jew

Contents

Illustrations

Abbreviations

AAA	Archives of American Art
AF	Administrative Files
AJHS	American Jewish Historical Society
AK	Avram Kampf
AKatz	Arthur Katz
AM	Alexander Marx
ARC	Archival Collection
ARC MS	Archival collection manuscript
AS	Alan R. Solomon
BH	Ben Heller
CA	Cyrus Adler
CAP	Cyrus Adler Papers
CUL	Rare Book and Manuscript Library, Columbia University Libraries
DCK	David C. Kogen
DF	David Finn
FSW	Frieda Schiff Warburg
GS	Guido Schoenberger
JU	Joy Ungerleider (later Ungerleider-Mayerson)
JM	Jewish Museum
JMA	Jewish Museum Archives
JR	Joan Rosenbaum

JTS	Jewish Theological Seminary of America
KK	Karl Katz
LJTS	Special Collections, The Library of the Jewish Theological Seminary
LKCAJS	Library, Herbert D. Katz Center for Advanced Judaic Studies, Kislak Center for Special Collections, Rare Books and Manuscripts, University of Pennsylvania
LF	Louis Finkelstein
MS	Meyer Schapiro
MSC	Meyer Schapiro Collection
PR	Paul Romanoff
RG	Record Group
SI	Smithsonian Institution
SIA	Smithsonian Institution Archives
SG	Simon Greenberg
SH	Sam Hunter
SSK	Stephen S. Kayser
UJA-FNYC	United Jewish Appeal-Federation of New York Collection
VL	Vera G. List

Prologue

"The basic questions must be asked. Is there a dishonesty implied by the very name Jewish Museum? That is to say, can one link a religious or ethnic group with a museum in its proper sense as a place of the muses? And if so, how can it perform its function?" So wrote a loyal donor of the Jewish Museum of New York in 1971, less than seventy years after its origin as a collection of ritual objects and a decade after it began exhibiting avant-garde art that lacked visible Jewish content, often by non-Jews.

Displays of Jewish ritual objects in public, nonreligious settings by Jews were still a comparatively recent phenomenon at the time. So too was their institutionalization with the establishment of Jewish museums. Both initiatives occurred with growing frequency in the late nineteenth and early twentieth centuries, first in Europe and then the United States. Fruits of the Enlightenment and emancipation, they were created for various reasons that entailed differing ways of explaining the objects. Most often organizers used ritual objects to secure the advances of emancipation by interpreting Judaism to non-Jews and to nourish pride among fellow Jews in the richness and history of their material culture. As a result, the objects were deployed as evidence of religious observances, ethnological specimens, historical artifacts, or works of art. The Jewish Museum of New York, because of its age and prominence, exemplifies nearly this entire story. Seeded with a modest Judaica collection donated to the Jewish Theological Seminary in 1904, it grew into one of the world's leading and oldest continuously serving institutions of its kind and possesses the largest Judaica collection outside Israel. During the 1960s, however, the museum expanded its purview and building to present a series of exhibitions featuring avant-garde art devoid of Jewish content and created mostly by non-Jews. The exhibits were celebrated in the art world, and many are still renowned today, but they were also attacked by Jewish community members objecting to what they considered mystifying, provocative, and sometimes profane works of art. How was it, Jews asked, that a museum established to preserve and display Jewish ritual objects, and associated with a rabbinic seminary, had strayed so far from its founding mission?[1]

Studies have addressed that question by starting with brief reviews of the museum's origins in 1904, its relocation off the seminary campus in the late 1940s, or the advent of the avant-garde era per se in the late 1950s. Though most are excellent, these studies share certain oversights. For example, they bypass the profound changes in Jewish life during the late eighteenth and early nineteenth centuries brought about by the Enlightenment and emancipation that made possible the first public displays of Jewish ritual objects arranged by Jews. This omission is important for three reasons. First, because the nature of those changes, and the displays they enabled, set the terms for how such objects and, later, artworks created by Jews, might be presented and interpreted down to the present. Second, there is a direct lineage from those earliest displays to the museum's founding and early development. Third, the advent of the avant-garde era is made to appear as an anomalous product of immediate circumstances rather than as a logical and inevitable outcome of the prior eight decades of cultural history. Presenting a more extensive or accurate account of that story is not, however, the only objective of this book. Rather, it is also to unpack the values and concerns of the individuals who organized exhibits, supported and helped guide the museum, and commented on its programs over the years. From them, it is possible to glean insights into the sociocultural circumstances of the museum and its antecedents during a period of significant change in Jewish history. The story of the museum's avant-garde era is about a museum, to be sure, but it also about the people for whom it was a locus, with all the inconsistencies, contradictions, and disagreements of the community they comprised. Giving voice, in their own words, to as many of them as possible—be they rabbis or lay persons, museum professionals or visitors, scholars or the less well-educated, cultural critics or the casual observer—is a priority throughout this book. So too, is understanding the broader and evolving historical, cultural, and social contexts of what they said.[2]

There are several throughlines in the following narrative that are approached from the perspective of those responsible for arranging displays or leading the museum: a concern for audiences and what, today, would be called "stakeholders" and how exhibits might best serve them; the aims of exhibits as expressions of organizers' beliefs and perceptions; questions over what things to display; options for how best to arrange and interpret those things; and—as this study proceeds through the twentieth century—issues of governance, policy, personnel, facilities, and finances as the work of exhibitions and museums were professionalized.

Having worked for over a decade in museums and collections and then teaching museum studies, I view these sites as places where history, ideology, theory, and practice intersect. One cannot write responsibly about the subject of this book without acknowledging these interpenetrations. While museums express an array of sociocultural ideals, and the Jewish Museum is no exception, it would be unjust to those associated with it over the years to ignore the instances in which those ideals ran aground in the practical problems any such organization confronts daily. When, in the early 1970s, the Jewish Museum terminated its avant-garde exhibitions, it was a fiscal crisis that tipped the balance against them even though other policy concerns remained undecided. To capture these nuances, primary published sources, previously unpublished archival records, and oral histories are used to illuminate the perceptions and desires of the individuals participating in policy debates and practical day-to-day decisions. At the same time, this evidence is set in the context of studies that illuminate the historical circumstances, social and cultural theories, and broader critical debates underway throughout the period encompassed by this book. Finally, although it culminates in a case study of an emblematic institution and the developments that brought it about, this book is informed throughout by salient concerns within the Jewish community during the era: tensions between religion and secularism, particularism and universalism, and ethnicity and assimilation. These questions surface in museum debates over what objects most fully express Jewish values, its nature as a cultural history or art institution, and ultimately whether it should prioritize Jewish solidarity, or service to non-Jews as a means of promoting relations between them and the Jewish community.

This story begins with the earliest presentations of Jewish ritual objects, or Judaica, in three late-nineteenth-century public exhibitions. Each display was arranged by Jews to address somewhat different communal objectives, but all shared an interest in helping secure the social gains of Jewish emancipation. The exhibits also modeled for other Jews the appeal of Judaica collecting and the value of creating Jewish museums. The one begun at the Jewish Theological Seminary in 1904 grew into the Museum of Jewish Ceremonial and Historical Objects by 1931, and evolved into the Jewish Museum in 1947. The last step, which entailed a reconceptualization of its collections as art, set the stage for the museum's turn to the avant-garde beginning in 1957, a daring experiment that culminated in 1971. By starting with the origins of Judaica collecting and display among Jews as these activities accelerated in the late nineteenth century, I draw into focus social and cultural changes that transformed Jewish ritual objects from sacred accouterments for synagogue and home observances into collectibles for expositions and museums. Those changes evolved in similar ways in different locations, but it was in New York that they first coalesced into the ideas that propelled the museum's avant-garde experiment. There were other influences, to be sure, especially New York's intelligentsia, the city's art world, and the Jewish community's rapid assimilation and relative prosperity during the post–Second World War period.[3]

Fidelity to these matters demands attention both to the Jewish community's sociocultural circumstances during this period and to the granularity of their expression through the museum. Evidence resides not only in the face the museum presented to its public through collections, exhibits, catalogues, and educational programs, but in internal records of its debates over mission, budget priorities, opportunities and risks, and actual and desirable audiences. As the following narrative proceeds from the late nineteenth century into the early and then middle decades of the twentieth, there is a gradual shift in emphasis from secondary accounts and interpretations to primary sources. The latter increasingly include correspondence among key figures and their recollections captured in oral histories thanks to an increasing abundance of archival records as the story progresses. When the avant-garde program became a reality, different opinions emerged, and passions were aroused among people most closely associated with the museum. Those documents reveal the sometimes-counterintuitive beliefs that drew advocates, critics, and others into conflict, convictions that published accounts often obscure or oversimplify. The beliefs that led the Jewish Museum into the avant-garde were deeply held and urgent for their advocates who, as Jews, felt they were fulfilling Judaism's destiny in modern society. Jewish collectors and curators discovered profound meaning in new art, something they wanted to share with a larger public via the Jewish Museum, in part as an expression of Judaism's humanitarian values. That the art had nothing to do with Judaism per se and was often made by non-Jews did not matter to them. That the Judaica in the museum's collection, or works created by Jewish artists on Jewish topics, were far less meaningful for those collectors and curators than they were for other Jews was, for a time, a troubling but manageable issue. Though the museum subsequently backed away from its once-unqualified commitment to the avant-garde, it never entirely moved on from debates over how to balance contemporary art with its treatment of traditional Jewish visual culture, especially its vast collection of ritual objects. The Jewish Museum continues to be haunted by the question of what it ought to do just as the Jewish community struggles with questions of assimilation, religious solidarity, and, ultimately, survival.

The earliest public Judaica displays arose from the spread of secularism, starting with the Enlightenment, which fundamentally altered Jews' relationships with the surrounding societies in which they resided, the nature of Judaism itself, and Jews' understanding of their sacred objects. One result, toward the end of the nineteenth century, was the advent of Jewish collecting and public display of those objects—at an exposition in Paris, a historical exhibition in London, and a world's fair in Chicago—most rescued from declining synagogues or waning domestic use. Significantly, the displays were mounted to secure Jewish standing in societies where it remained tenuous. When these practices were institutionalized in museums, the Jewish Museum became the longest lived and leading example. There, the uses of ritual objects to inform non-Jews evolved into showing modern art by Jews exploring Jewish themes. This effort occurred during the immediate post–Second World War period when—between the Holocaust and the Cold War—the hopeful cultivation of universal fellowship, mutual understanding, and freedom called for new ways to promote interfaith dialogue. The turn to modern art was encouraged by the rabbi heading the Jewish Theological Seminary at the time who already had initiated programs to advance his vision of Jewish participation in and leadership of intergroup discourse on topics of concern for all Americans. He viewed the museum as playing a useful role in pursuit of these ideals and gave his blessing to efforts that enlarged its purview to art devoid of Jewish subjects and art by non-Jews, opening a door to the avant-garde.

This brief narrative, while seemingly about Jewish objects and the sites where they were collected and shown, is more accurately about the uses of such objects to navigate Jewish relations with a non-Jewish world. When the objects featured in the Jewish Museum's exhibits expanded from ritual accouterments and contemporary Jewish art to avant-garde works by non-Jewish artists, art-world denizens and the Jewish community took note. But the rationale for the avant-garde shows was not substantially different than it was for the ritual-object displays nearly a century prior. Ideally, the public presentation of such works might foster better relations between Jews and the societies in which they live. The various stages in this story correspond to the evolving circumstances of Jewish life in the times and places where Jews dwelled. Underlying these developments was the secularizing ethos of modernity both outside and within the Jewish community. A rabbinic seminary's acceptance of a museum within its precincts might be read as indicative. In adopting the institutional form of the museum for its ritual-objects collection, the seminary inadvertently acquiesced to museums' history of desacralizing religious objects and fostering their "resocialization" for nonreligious purposes. For these reasons, it will be helpful to explore the museum culture Jews entered, its secularizing machinery, and how notions of sacredness concerning Jewish ritual objects might function within it.[4]

Museum Culture

The notion of "museum culture" gained currency with an anthology edited by Daniel J. Sherman and Irit Rogoff that situates studies of museums and exhibitions in the broader contexts of cultural history, theory, and criticism. Their approach led them to conceive of these sites as comprising an "intricate amalgam" of historical narratives, display strategies, and the demands of governing ideals as a way of relating them to other cultural discourses. Their formulation invites us to understand a museum and its exhibits as forms of cultural expression and, from that vantage point, to see how the Jewish community used them to communicate its values and aims. Yet, as with other languages, museum culture possesses its own syntax. Sherman and Rogoff discern within it four components: collections and their classification, the spheres of interest collections represent, the audiences museums aim to serve, and the ways in which museum audiences receive or understand what those institutions do.[5]

Starting with collections and their taxonomies, a museum's classification of a given thing as a ritual object, historical evidence, or work of art might seem to arise naturally from the thing per se. But that determination might just as easily be shaped by an institution's self-identification. Applicable here may be "the law of the instrument" derived from the adage "If one's only tool is a hammer, one will regard everything as if it were a nail." Thus, an art museum will treat all objects coming its way as works of art regardless of their original uses or makers' intentions. This observation is relevant for Jewish ritual objects because, from their earliest public displays, organizers chose among one or more classifications and interpretive frameworks. Those choices reveal useful clues about the organizers' aims. Moreover, just as the categorization of objects is variable, so too are the purposes of the repositories in which they are housed. The predecessor of the Jewish Museum, which began as a religious-historical institution, was changed to an art orientation when it moved from the seminary campus to a separate site, even though the objects in the collection remained unchanged.[6]

Also relevant is Sherman and Rogoff's understanding of museum culture as invoking "notions of community." Embedded in the notion of community is a tendency to regard an institution's audience as an undifferentiated whole. While a museum convenes an intended audience for its exhibits, the nature of the actual audience for, and the variety of responses within it to, such exhibits is by no means assured. The dynamics governing the reception of exhibitions afford insights into the unacknowledged assumptions museums make about their constituencies and vice versa. They can also reveal differing responses of audiences or, more accurately, the varied responses of separate interest groups within a museum's audience. There is also a two-way street along which a museum's professional and lay leadership—such as collectors and donors—attempts to satisfy its own desires, as though proxies for a larger whole, that run headlong into the differing yearnings of one segment or another of the institution's presumed community. Just as a museum can form a community around its mission or exhibitions, those same activities can fragment a museum's community. Either way, the give and take of a museum and its community offers rich veins of information about both the institution and its audience.[7]

When Jews began exhibiting their ritual objects in public, it was not in a museum, but rather in a nineteenth-century international exposition and subsequent similar displays in extra-institutional contexts. That fact requires us to zoom out from museums per se to consider the larger context of public exhibits in which museums participated. Tony Bennett coined "exhibitionary complex" to capture the many sites and interests whereby objects are collected, organized, displayed, and viewed. For Bennett, those sites include temporary ones such as world's fairs as well as more permanent settings such as museums; and among the interests associated with these are not only intellectual questions arising from anthropology, art history, and natural history but also economic and political ones. International expositions, less ambitious local-history exhibitions, and museums differ from one another, and at many points those differences included display mechanics, taxonomies for arranging objects, and publics. Understanding the wider context of the exhibitionary complex is thus helpful when tracing the uses of artifacts over time and across multiple venues, such as Jewish ritual objects as they were taken up in one setting after another. Over the course of nearly a century, it is possible to track the journey of an individual piece of Judaica from an international exposition to a national historical exhibition, and eventually a museum (Figures 2.4, 2.5, 3.10). As the sites and circumstances of their display changed, the concerns Judaica embodied for succeeding generations of Jews also shifted, even—and sometimes particularly—when those objects were withdrawn from view in favor of things Jews valued more highly. In those circumstances, the exhibitionary complex also serves as a framework within which the absence of objects becomes apparent and can be as consequential as their presence, perhaps even signifying their neglect.[8]

Integral to the exhibitionary complex is the role of secularization in its formation. "We live in a secular age and museums are deemed secular institutions," Carol Duncan and Alan Wallach have observed. This view holds that the exhibitionary complex reifies the secularizing ethos of modernity during which museums became a prominent feature of society. By "modernity," I mean the period starting in the seventeenth and eighteenth centuries in Europe during which Enlightenment values of reason, equality, and freedom were articulated, disseminated, and enacted. The Enlightenment heralded the ascent of rationality and empiricism over religion as the best methods for understanding the world—a fundamental reorientation in Western thought that sparked revolutions in knowledge production and society. Just as the role of religion in society began to be cordoned off, so too religions' objects came to be regarded separately from their sacred purposes, primarily as materials for collecting and learned inquiry. Secularization was a handmaiden of the exhibitionary complex and, as such, warrants particular scrutiny as it applies to Judaism's ritual objects.[9]

The Contours of Secularization

Jews' presentations of their ritual objects in world's fairs, historical exhibitions, and museums both reflected and helped foster the secularization processes transforming Jewish life during the period of this study. The movement of Judaica from sacred to secular contexts, however, did not so much drain the objects of their sacral potency as periodically suspend it. Over time and in different places, the sacral aura of Judaica could paradoxically be reactivated. A museum storing away and neglecting ritual objects, thereby arousing latent religious sensitivities, exemplifies the instability of secularization. Recognizing secularization's nature and flows is no easy matter, however, especially within Judaism. "The secular and the religious," Irving Howe notes, "are in Jewish experience, hopelessly interwoven." Additionally, as Todd Endelman argues, secularization is but one aspect of a complicated and multidirectional process of the Jewish community's transformation that he separated into four components: emancipation, acculturation, secularization, and integration. Even so, the centrality of ritual objects here, and the contrast between their sacrality and the secular environments in which they are deployed, demands a focus on the dynamics of secularism. Before continuing, however, a digression on secularism and secularization is necessary.[10]

"Secular," in common usage, means temporal or worldly, essentially the opposite of religious. The differences in outlook represented by the two terms have hardened into what Larry Shiner calls a "secular-religious polarity" that manifests throughout modern society. As a social phenomenon, secularism is approached by Ari Joskowicz and Ethan B. Katz as an ideology aimed at suppressing religion in general and, in political practice, for separating church and state because of religion being perceived as uninformed, stifling, or at minimum antimodern. Such views are often grouped as "secularization theory." Sociologists of religion critique the concept, however, for doing little more than, as Shiner put it, serving "partisans of controversy"—advocates of secularism and their opponents in organized religion. William H. Swatos and Kevin J. Christiano attribute the dispute to a widely shared conviction among the secularists that in an era of scientific advances, religion's value is in decline, a position vigorously opposed by religionists. Shiner urges that secularization theory be abandoned as evidence accumulated of the mutability of both secularism's and religion's influence in contemporary society. Swatos and Christiano, for example, found scant evidence of an inexorable shriveling of religion's influence, perhaps because of its adaptability and penetration in all spheres of life including cultural and social systems as well as personal beliefs. Despite the seemingly overpowering nature of secularism, religion has refused "to go quietly—or even to go at all." This flux in the comparative sway of secularism and religion is evident as an underlying social phenomenon in Europe and the United States during the period leading up to the Jewish Museum's formation and in the decades following as the avant-garde era unfolded.[11]

Within the Jewish community, the secular | religious opposition can also be misleading. David Biale points out that as categories of personal belief they obscure actual behavior. Some Jews may retain religious beliefs but manifest secular behavior insofar as they do not observe Jewish law or participate in worship practices; others are fully observant and attend synagogues but abide by secular beliefs. Joskowicz and Katz also see in the Jewish community an ideological divergence with some embracing secularism and others opposing it, but within a broader debate over whether acculturation and assimilation are endangering Judaism's survival. That split originated in the nineteenth century following the French Revolution, when Jewish intellectuals welcomed a transformation of Judaism from an all-inclusive way of life into one religious denomination among several within a newly secularized France. This transition occurred because Jewish emancipation accompanied the secularization of France during the revolution. There was a price to be paid, however, and according to Joskowicz and Katz, one long-term result was a change among many Jews' practices and beliefs, from public manifestations of faith through ritual observances and religious attire to private spiritual pursuits.

While some might attribute to those changes the beginnings of assimilation and a withering of the Jewish community, Judaism did not fade away but rather evolved and survived. One tangible result of secularization, however, was the rendering of Jewish ritual objects less essential for religious purposes, releasing them to drift ever farther out of the orbit of sacral use, but without wholly stripping them of religious significance, with some landing in museums.[12]

Secularizing Sacred Objects

The first public displays of Jewish ritual objects by Jews followed a history of the sacred artifacts of other groups being presented in museums and expositions. The process, which often entailed their apparent desacralization, was an aspect of a broader phenomenon of deracination or "musealization" whereby objects were relocated from the contexts of their origins. This shift dates to the Renaissance, when voyages of discovery returned with the sacred artifacts of Europe's others acquired by scholars and monarchs collecting objects for learned inquiry or amusement. The acts of deracination and desacralization were not critically scrutinized, however, until the turn from the late 1700s to early 1800s, paradoxically concerning artworks created in the West. Questions arose in France amid debates over the Louvre. The collection of the soon-to-be-public museum was assembled during the French Revolution with art confiscated from the monarchy, church, and aristocracy within France, and from neighboring countries it subsequently conquered. Opening the Louvre to all French citizens signified the revolutionaries' egalitarian and nationalist ambitions. But pursuing those goals conflicted with another revolutionary aim, stamping out lingering monarchism and Catholicism after the revolutionaries deposed the king and suppressed the church. Among the artistic riches seized by the revolutionaries were portraits of former monarchs—that threatened to "reawaken royalist sentiments"; and depictions of religious miracles and martyrs—that undercut the government's aim of supplanting religious fanaticism with the "Cult of Reason." Purging the Louvre of inimical works was difficult, however, because too many were venerated masterpieces, the absence of which would draw into question the revolutionaries' stewardship of France's artistic patrimony. A rationalization for displaying them was found, according to Andrew McClellan, in the Enlightenment method of marshaling works into a "visible history of art." This endeavor entailed arranging paintings by chronology and artistic school, resulting in a reconceptualization of the major works as art objects rather than as royal or religious symbols, thereby shifting the basis of their societal value from the subjects depicted to the aesthetic mastery of their depiction. This method of "eliding original meanings" by aestheticizing and thereby secularizing the works became an essential feature of museums as engines of modernity. It was not without criticism, however, from those opposing the seizure of religious works for museums because doing so meant ripping objects from their meaning-conferring contexts. "Yes, you have transported the physical matter," one critic declared, but "have you also . . . transported the interest and charm that they drew . . . from the religious atmosphere that surrounded them, from that sacred aura that added to their luster? . . . All these objects have lost their effect in losing their purpose."[13]

In truth, that kind of relocation was not as decisive as first appears. As Judith Porter notes, there can be a gradient of effects depending on how an object is subsequently interpreted: "transposition," when religious meanings are translated from the contexts of sacred use to daily experience; "desacralization," when sacred meanings are ignored; and "differentiation," when original religious meanings are distinguished from the beliefs of outside observers. Porter also underscores the permeability of each category, adding that these types of secularization do not effect the complete elision of an object's religious significance, but rather an altered one. As a result, the secular and religious are in reality "differentiated but interrelated spheres" that continue to inform each other. This fluidity in the status of religious objects in museums, shifting from "sacred to profane and back again," is mirrored in visitors' responses. Many might be in accord with a curator's secular interpretation of such objects while others find contemplation of the objects to be, regardless of curatorial intent, "truly a worship experience." The indeterminate nature of secularization as it applies to sacred objects is no less applicable to Judaica and forms a useful context for this book.[14]

Also relevant is the phenomenon of visitors regarding museums as akin to religious sanctuaries, places where even ordinary objects acquire a sacral aura. Crispin Paine, attempting to tease apart the elements of what he calls "museumification," observes that the entry of such works into museums can have "a striking parallel with 'sacralization'—the making of an object sacred." Scholars like Joan R. Branham and Paine evince an aesthetics of sacralization, such as "sanctifying spotlights" highlighting objects on display. These phenomena led Ivan Gaskell to ask "'When is the sacred?' rather than 'What is the sacred?'" The potential for visitors to identify museums with religious settings concerned Helena Wangefelt Ström, who, viewing the matter as a subversion of museal secularism—especially among faith-community visitors, proposed display strategies to manage the dynamism and unpredictability of viewers' perceptions. These issues are yet more complex in museums of religion, exemplified by the St. Mungo Museum of Religious Life and Art in Glasgow, Scotland. Some, like St. Mungo, attempt to survey the beliefs and practices of many religions, while others represent—and are often sponsored by—individual religious groups. Relevant to the Jewish Museum is Paine's observation that when museums present a religion, they often imply "a unity of practice and belief" that is nonexistent among that religious community's faithful. How might, for example, a Jewish museum in the United States adequately represent the differing beliefs of Orthodox (including Haredi and Hasidic), Conservative, and Reform Jews? Another concern is the museological handling of religious traditions in which, as Chris Arthur points out, "concrete representation" of deities or other religious subjects are prohibited. Judaism's Second Commandment prohibition against graven images (see below) is a recurring issue in discussions about the comparatively modest scale and nature of its ritual objects, one often coupled with questions about whether the objects possess sufficient visual appeal and variety to merit exhibition at all.[15]

At the outset, I mentioned that the very first Judaica exhibits were designed partly to explain Judaism to non-Jews. Those projects were not unique, though they may have pioneered uses of sacred objects to promote mutual understanding in secular societies or among different religious communities. That aim was taken up by the Jewish Museum and pursued throughout the period of this study. The Jews who led these efforts were mobilized by the recurring dangers of antisemitism and the hopes that by informing others they could cultivate social harmony, religious acceptance, or at least tolerance. This challenge never went away. When Paine introduced his 2013 book *Religious Objects in Museums* with the observation that "To our surprise, religion is once again challenging the secular world," he was flagging a resurgence of religious advocacy in civic affairs, including an increase of religion-based conflicts between nations and within nations home to diverse religious communities. There is a deep historical resonance in the use of museums to ameliorate tensions fueled by religious differences. After all, the advent of the public museum is a feature of the secularizing ethos of the Enlightenment, which, itself, was born of a longing to eliminate the causes of religious wars in Europe by, as in the French Revolution, curtailing the power of religious institutions in civil society. What may seem at first paradoxical—that the Jewish community would voluntarily submit its sacred objects for secular scrutiny in expositions and museums, is less so when understood in the context of the benefits Jews hope to reap.[16]

Ritual Objects and Art

When Jews began displaying their ritual objects outside the contexts of religious observances in synagogue and home, they did not face obstacles in Jewish law or tradition. But there are differences in sacral standards that could affect how certain things might be displayed that would have been taken for granted by observant Jews whose activities are recounted in this book. Those standards vary according to two broad categories in relation to which the objects are understood. The first covers intrinsically sacred objects (*tashmishey kedusha*); the second concerns less sacred religious accouterments (*tashmishey mitzvah*). All are used to honor commandments or perform duties (*mitzvot*, plural of *mitzvah*) set out in the Torah, which contains the first five books of the Old Testament, Judaism's most sacred text. *Tashmishey kedusha* include Torahs that are hand-inscribed on parchment scrolls, other similarly made texts, and printed works containing entire biblical books or excerpts—any containing the name of God. Also falling into this category are things that come into physical contact with Torahs, such as wrappings or covers. *Tashmishey mitzvah* are the several kinds of objects used in other ritual observances such as cups for blessings over wine, spice containers for marking the Sabbath's conclusion, or nine-branch menorahs for observing Chanukah.[17]

These distinctions both reflect and have a bearing on the objects' physical appearances. Consequently, they can also influence which objects are collected and displayed by museums. For example, despite their absolute centrality in explaining Judaism, Torahs are less likely to be displayed—or displayed less frequently—due to their sacral nature and the religious stipulations governing their handling in preparation for and during display in secular settings. Accordingly, depending on the *minhag* (tradition) of a community, people might be asked to stand when a Torah is moved for an exhibit installation; and if it were displayed so that one could see the sacred text within it, viewers might be asked to wear head coverings out of respect. A museum might also avoid displaying Torahs in groups for want of visual variety from one to the next because their construction is governed by strict rules concerning materials and facture, the only variations coming in their sizes and letterforms used in their inscription. Thus, people unfamiliar with Torahs would be hard pressed to distinguish among different ones based on physical appearance. For all these reasons, Jewish exhibitors might prefer other religious objects to inspire Jews and/or inform non-Jews about Judaism.[18]

The objects categorized as *tashmishey mitzvah* are not subject to the same kinds of strictures regarding their facture and use. To the contrary, not only is wide latitude given for creating *tashmishey mitzvah*, but Jews are also encouraged to embellish these ritual objects based on the Torah verse "This is my God and I will glorify Him" (Exodus 15:2). Evidence shows that, indeed, throughout history Jews adorned them to the extent permitted by economic means, sociopolitical circumstances, and traditions. The results are often beautiful and worthy of display, although—because the objects were created for specific ritual purposes—not dramatically different one from another in form or size. Jewish communities often commissioned non-Jewish artisans to create their ritual objects or, if there were Jewish artisans available, the latter usually adopted the decorative materials and styles of surrounding cultures. The resulting objects are readily displayed as ethnographic specimens, historical artifacts, art, or all of the above. Given the nature and circumstances of their creation, however, aesthetic interpretation is typically in the context of decorative-art traditions of the eras and places Jews dwelled. These modest objects did not lend themselves to display as "high art" on a par with the paintings and sculptures created by non-Jews in Europe during the same periods. Not until the mid- to late-nineteenth century, thanks to the Enlightenment and emancipation, was there an efflorescence of creativity among Jews in painting, sculpture, and other media, some but not all addressing Jewish themes. Over time, their work furnished a larger context for scholars to conceive of a "Jewish art" comprised of a continuum of Jewish visual culture extending from ritual artifacts to modern paintings.[19]

The notion of "Jewish art" was advanced despite a history of thorny questions about the impact of the Second Commandment prohibition, specifically the use of figurative representations in Jewish ritual objects and art: "You shall not make for yourself a sculpted image, or any likeness of what is in the heavens above, or on the earth below, or in the waters under the earth" (Exodus 20:4). The issue arose both in non-Jewish speculations about Judaism's scarce visual-art contributions to Western civilization—in comparison to those of Christendom—and in Jewish apologia on the same topic. Adherence to the Second Commandment was frequently cited by all parties as explaining the scarcity of figurative representations, the paucity of works—other than ritual objects—in Judaism's material culture, and the visual clumsiness of those that *were* created. Only in recent decades have scholars shown that fidelity to the Second Commandment was not as strict as had been assumed and, to the contrary, rabbinic interpretations and community consensus welcomed visual expressions of Jewish beliefs. To the extent that Jewish output was limited, other factors such as oppression, exclusion from craft guilds, poverty, and periodic expulsions or pogroms were more likely to blame. Proof of those constraints, one might argue, is the flowering of Jewish visual arts and their reception in the wake of emancipation, what Richard I. Cohen called a "visual revolution in Jewish life." Yet, as individuals gained the freedom and means to express themselves artistically, as well as entrée to larger cultural worlds, they increasingly turned away from subjects presumably meaningful for the Jewish community such as depictions of biblical stories or religious scenes in homes and synagogues.[20]

This trend complicated matters when Jews gravitated from exhibiting ritual objects only, to featuring other works. With the creation by Jews of artworks that, visually, had nothing to do with Judaism came the "vexed question" of what qualified as Jewish art. While it was easy enough to discern the characteristics of Jewishness in ritual objects, related folk arts and crafts, or images depicting Jewish themes, it was not so obvious in works created by Jewish artists when they explored matters not visibly Jewish. Scholars' attempts to address that phenomenon have been tortured at best and at worst confusing. Should an artist's output be called Jewish based solely on her or his genealogy? What about works by non-Jewish artists on Jewish topics? For the purposes of a Jewish museum, would it be acceptable to display works without visible Jewish content by non-Jewish artists if they are nonetheless meaningful for Jewish curators or collectors? Though seemingly theoretical, these very questions arose as Jewish participation in museum culture shifted from an emphasis on displaying ritual objects to one on exploring avant-garde art. This book offers no new answers to that "vexed question." Rather, it instantiates the many ways Jews thought, or—perhaps more accurately—made assumptions, about the kinds of things appropriate for display in a Jewish museum. As the institution evolved and grew, and its historical and cultural contexts changed, that sense of appropriateness played out in unpredictable ways. Each step in this evolution was well-reasoned in the moment. After the museum's plunge into the avant-garde, however, fellow Jews began to question the judgment of the museum's leaders, sparking fierce debates that continue to this day. While they sometimes devolved into either/or disputes, pitting a fealty to Judaica or Jewish themes against a vision that appealed to underlying Jewish values or cultural aspirations, more often the clashes were over questions of balance. Was the museum "too Jewish" when it focused on Judaica and Jewish subjects? Or was it "not Jewish enough" when pursuing new art that spoke to Jewish art-world denizens? Though this story is centered on one emblematic museum, its telling reflects fundamental changes and formative debates in Jewish life from the mid-nineteenth to late-twentieth centuries. At stake is what a Jewish museum ought to exhibit and for whom. Like the "basic questions" that open this prologue, these concerns are suffused with nearly a century of struggles over religion and secularism, parochialism and universalism, and ethnicity and assimilation.[21]

Notes

1. For a worldwide historical survey of Jewish museums, including non-Jewish institutional collections of Judaica and related phenomena, a good starting point is still Fred Skolnik, ed., *Encyclopaedia Judaica*, 2nd edn., s.v. "Museums," by Grace Cohen Grossman and Avram Biran (Farmington Hills, MI: Macmillan Reference USA, 2007).
2. On the JM's prehistory, see Emily D. Bilski, "Seeing the Future Through the Light of the Past: The Art of The Jewish Museum," in *The Jewish Museum of New York*, ed. Vivian B. Mann with Emily D. Bilski (New York: Scala Books, 1993), 8–21. For its avant-garde era, see Julie Miller and Richard I. Cohen, "A Collision of Cultures: The Jewish Museum and the Jewish Theological Seminary, 1904–1971," in *Tradition Renewed: A History of the Jewish Theological Seminary*, ed. Jack Wertheimer, 2 vols. (New York: Jewish Theological Seminary of America, 1997), II:310–61; and Matthew Israel, "A Magnet for the With-It Kids," *Art in America* 95, no. 9 (October 2007): 73–83. See also, Hsiao-Ning Tu, "The History of the Jewish Museum in New York with an Emphasis on 1963–1971" (master's thesis, City College of New York, 1996).
3. For brevity's sake, I employ "Judaica" here and throughout the book for Jewish ritual objects used in synagogue and home religious observances. I recognize, however, that the term is also used more broadly for texts and material culture associated with Jewish history.
4. On "resocialization," see Philip Fisher, *Making and Effacing Art: Modern American Art in a Culture of Museums* (Oxford: Oxford University Press, 1991), 3–19.
5. Daniel J. Sherman and Irit Rogoff, "Introduction: Frameworks for Critical Analysis," in *Museum Culture: Histories, Discourses, Spectacles*, ed. Daniel J. Sherman and Irit Rogoff (Minneapolis: University of Minnesota Press, 1994), ix–xii.

6. On the law of the instrument, Abraham Kaplan, *The Conduct of Inquiry: Methodology for Behavioral Science* (San Francisco: Chandler Publishing Company, 1964), 28. For a more accurate use of the adage, see Abraham H. Maslow, *The Psychology of Science: A Reconnaissance* (New York: Harper & Row, 1966), 15–16.
7. Sherman and Rogoff, "Introduction," xii. The concept of community is itself problematic and warrants more investigation than is practical here. For a helpful exploration, though done in the context of nationalism rather than religion or ethnicity, see Benedict Anderson, *Imagined Communities: Reflections on the Origins and Spread of Nationalism* (London: Verso, 2006).
8. Tony Bennett, *The Birth of the Museum: History, Theory, Politics* (London: Routledge, 1995), 59–88.
9. Carol Duncan and Alan Wallach, "The Universal Survey Museum," *Art History* 3, no. 4 (December 1980): 450. There is a long history of the distinction between sacred and secular (or profane) objects in displays. See, for example, regarding the Byzantine empire, Sarah G. Bassett, "'Excellent offerings:' The Lausos Collection in Constantinople," *Art Bulletin* 82, no. 1 (March 2000): 6–25.
10. Irving Howe, *The End of Jewish Secularism* (New York: Hunter College, City University of New York, 1995), 3. Todd M. Endelman, "Jewish Self-Identification and West European Categories of Belonging from the Enlightenment to World War II," in *Religion or Ethnicity? Jewish Ideas in Evolution*, ed. Zvi Gitelman (New Brunswick, NJ: Rutgers University Press, 2009), 105.
11. Ari Joskowicz and Ethan B. Katz, eds., *Secularism in Question: Jews and Judaism in Modern Times* (Philadelphia: University of Pennsylvania Press, 2015), 6–7. Larry Shiner, "The Concept of Secularization in Empirical Research," *Journal for the Scientific Study of Religion* 6 (Autumn 1967): 207, 218. William H. Swatos Jr. and Kevin J. Christiano, "Secularization Theory: The Course of a Concept," *Sociology of Religion* 60, no. 3 (Autumn 1999): 214, 216, 224. See also, Gordon Graham, "Secularity and Modernity," *Philosophy* [Journal of the Royal Institute of Philosophy] 67, no. 260 (April 1992): 185. For the religion-going-quietly quote, "Materialities & Secularization Theory," MAVCOR: The Center for the Study of Material and Visual Cultures of Religion, accessed January 2021, https://mavcor.yale.edu/materialities-secularization-theory.
12. David Biale, *Not in the Heavens: The Tradition of Jewish Secular Thought* (Princeton, NJ: Princeton University Press, 2010), 10–11; Joskowicz and Katz, *Secularism in Question*, 5–10. See also, Endelman, "Jewish Self-Identification," 113.
13. André Desvallées and François Mairesse, "Musealisation," in *Key Concepts in Museology* (Paris: Armand Colin, 2010), 50–52; and the related essay "Object [Museum Object] or Musealia," 61–64. See also, Chang Wan-Chen, "A Cross-Cultural Perspective on Musealization: The Museum's Reception by China and Japan in the Second Half of the Nineteenth Century," *Museum &*

Society 10, no. 1 (2012): 15; and Andre Malraux, "Museum Without Walls," in *The Voices of Silence*, trans. Stuart Gilbert (Princeton, NJ: Princeton University Press, 1978), 14. Andrew McClellan, *Inventing the Louvre: Art, Politics, and the Origins of the Modern Museum in Eighteenth-Century Paris* (Cambridge: Cambridge University Press, 1994), 108–14, 194–96. On aestheticizing objects, see Robert L. Nelson, "Art and Religion: Ships Passing in the Night?" in *Reluctant Partners: Art and Religion in Dialogue*, ed. Ena Giurescu Heller (New York: Gallery at the American Bible Society, 2004), 103. See also, James J. Sheehan, *Museums in the German Art World: From the End of the Old Regime to the Rise of Modernism* (Oxford: Oxford University Press, 2000), 18–42, the "visible history" quote is from p. 40; and Daniel J. Sherman, "Quatremère/Benjamin/Marx: Art Museums, Aura, and Commodity Fetishism," in Sherman and Rogoff, *Museum Culture*, 127–34. The Louvre, as an art museum, is one kind of example, but different types of museums handle religious objects in different ways; Crispin Paine, "Religion in London's Museums," in *Godly Things: Museums, Objects, and Religion*, ed. Crispin Paine (London: Leicester University Press, 2000), 151–70.

14. Judith R. Porter, "Secularization, Differentiation, and the Function of Religious Value Orientations," *Sociological Inquiry* 43, no. 1 (January 1973): 67–69. Ivan Gaskell, "Sacred to Profane and Back Again," in *Art and Its Publics: Museum Studies at the Millenium*, ed. Andrew McClellan (Oxford: Blackwell Publishing, 2003), 149–62; James Clifton, "Truly a Worship Experience? Christian Art in Secular Museums," *RES: Anthropology and Aesthetics* 52 (Autumn 2007): 107–15. See also, regarding visitors' responses, Crispin Paine, *Religious Objects in Museums: Private Lives and Public Duties* (London: Bloomsbury, 2013), 28–30, 32–33.
15. On "aura," the classic text remains Walter Benjamin, "The Work of Art in the Age of Mechanical Reproduction," in *Illuminations*, ed. Hannah Arendt, trans. Harry Zohn (New York: Schocken Books, 1969), 217–51. On the perception of museums as quasi-religious destinations, see Lily Kong, "Re-Presenting the Religious: Nation, Community and Identity in Museums," *Social and Cultural Geography* 6, no. 4 (2005): 495–96. On "museumification," Paine, *Religious Objects in Museums*, 2; see also pp. 13, 37–44, and 71–77. Joan R. Branham, "Sacrality and Aura in the Museum: Mute Objects and Articulate Space," *Journal of the Walters Art Gallery* 52/53 (1994/1995): 33–47; and on "sanctifying spotlights," Susan Vogel, "Always True to the Object, in Our Fashion," in *Exhibiting Cultures: The Poetics and Politics of Museum Display*, ed. Ivan Karp and Steven D. Lavine (Washington, DC: Smithsonian Institution Press, 1991), 197. Ivan Gaskell, "Secularization and Consecration: Museums, Artifacts, and Transformation Through Use" (session response, College Art Association annual conference, Boston, MA, February 2006). Helena Wangefelt Ström, "How Do Museums Affect Sacredness? Three Suggested Models," *ICOFOM Study Series: Museology and the Sacred* 47, no. 1–2 (2019): ¶¶17–30. See, too, the observation concerning a museum's versus source community's values, Mary M. Brooks, "Seeing

the Sacred: Conflicting Priorities in Defining, Interpreting, and Conserving Western Sacred Artifacts," *Material Religion: The Journal of Objects, Art, and Belief* 8, no. 1 (March 2012): 14. On the St. Mungo Museum, see Chris Arthur, "Exhibiting the Sacred," in Paine, *Godly Things*, 1–27; see also, Alison Kelly, "St. Mungo Museum of Religious Life and Art, Glasgow," *Material Religion: The Journal of Objects, Art, and Belief* 1, no. 3 (2005): 435–37. For a taxonomy of religion museums, see Ström, "How Do Museums Affect Sacredness?": ¶6. See also a brief survey that features the Hebrew Union College-Jewish Institute of Religion's museum in New York City (since renamed): "Dr. Bernard Heller Museum," Hebrew Union College-Jewish Institute of Religion, accessed November 2023, https://huc.edu/public-programs-events/museums/dr-bernard-heller-museum-in-new-york/; Ena Giurescu Heller, "Religion on a Pedestal: Exhibiting Sacred Art," in Heller, *Reluctant Partners*, 132–37. Regarding representations of religions' unity of beliefs, see Paine, *Religious Objects in Museums*, 110. On eschewing "concrete representation," see Arthur, "Exhibiting the Sacred," 8. See also, Charles D. Orzech, *Museums of World Religions: Displaying the Divine, Shaping Cultures* (New York: Bloomsbury Academic, 2020).

16. On promoting mutual understanding and community harmony, see Paine, *Religious Objects in Museums*, 93, 99; on education about religion, see Arthur, "Exhibiting the Sacred," 4. See also, Mark O'Neill, "Making Histories of Religion," in *Making Histories in Museums*, ed. Gaynor Kavanagh (London: Leicester University Press, 1996), 188–99; Amanda Millay Hughes and Carolyn H. Wood, *A Place for Meaning: Art, Faith, and Museum Culture* (Chapel Hill: Ackland Art Museum, University of North Carolina at Chapel Hill, 2009); and Bruce M. Sullivan, ed., *Sacred Objects in Secular Spaces: Exhibiting Asian Religions in Museums* (London: Bloomsbury Academic, 2015).

17. Virginia Greene, "'Accessories of Holiness': Defining Jewish Sacred Objects," *Journal of the American Institute for Conservation* 31, no. 1 (Spring 1992): 31–39; Michael Maggen, "The Conservation of Sacred Materials in the Israel Museum," in *Conservation of Living Religious Heritage: Papers from the ICCROM 2003 Forum on Living Religious Heritage, Conserving the Sacred*, ed. H. Stovel, N. Stanley-Price, and R. Killick (Rome: ICCROM, 2005), 102–6; Bernice Morris and Mary M. Brooks, "Jewish Ceremonial Textiles and the Torah: Exploring Conservation Practices in Relation to Ritual Textiles Associated with Holy Texts," in *Textiles and Text: Re-Establishing the Links Between Archival and Object-Based Research*, ed. Maria Hayward and Elizabeth Kramer (London: Archetype Publications, 2006), 244–48. "Sefer Torah" (ספר תורה, usually translated as "scroll of the law") is used by Jews when speaking of a Torah as a physical object. The term "Torah" also has a much broader meaning among Jews and can include, depending on context, rabbinic elucidations and commentaries on the root text; see Skolnik, *Encyclopaedia Judaica*, s.v. "Torah," by Louis Isaac Rabinowitz and Warren Harvey.

18. Skolnik, *Encyclopaedia Judaica*, s.v. "Sefer Torah," by Aaron Rothkoff and Louis Isaac Rabinowitz.
19. The traditional interpretation of Exodus 15:2 comes from the Talmud:

    What is the source for the requirement of: "This is my God and I will glorify Him"? **As it was taught** in a *baraita* regarding the verse: "**This is my God and I will glorify Him [*anveihu*]**, the Lord of my father and I will raise Him up." The Sages interpreted *anveihu* homiletically as linguistically related to *noi*, beauty, and interpreted the verse: **Beautify yourself before Him in *mitzvot*.** Even if one fulfills the mitzva by performing it simply, it is nonetheless proper to perform the mitzva as beautifully as possible. **Make before Him a beautiful *sukka*, a beautiful *lulav*, a beautiful *shofar*, beautiful ritual fringes, beautiful** parchment for a **Torah scroll, and write in it His name in beautiful ink, with a beautiful quill by an expert scribe, and wrap** the scroll **in beautiful silk fabric.** Shabbat 133b.5, Babylonian Talmud, Sefaria, accessed February 2021, https://www.sefaria.org/Shabbat.133a?lang=bi.

    The boldface passages are translations of the Aramaic text (a Hebrew cognate) of the Talmud and the remaining passages are interpolations elucidating it. The treatment of Jewish ritual objects as "art" has a long history. For a brief survey, see Joseph Gutmann, *Jewish Ceremonial Art* (New York: Thomas Yoseloff, 1964). Pioneering treatments of "Jewish art" are in Franz Landsberger, *A History of Jewish Art* (Cincinnati, OH: Union of American Hebrew Congregations, 1946) and, because of the contributing scholars' stature, in Cecil Roth, *Jewish Art: An Illustrated History*, rev. edn. Bezalel Narkiss (Jerusalem: Massada Press, 1971) (an anthology by seventeen scholars). See also, Skolnik, *Encyclopaedia Judaica,* s.v. "Art," by Cecil Roth, Shalom Sabar, Ziva Amishai-Maisals, et al.; and Samantha Baskind and Larry Silver, *Jewish Art: A Modern History* (London: Reaktion Books, 2011). Regarding the historiography of scholarship on Jewish art, see Skolnik, *Encyclopaedia Judaica*, s.v., "Art Historians and Art Critics," particularly the subsection on "Historians of Jewish Art" by Herman S. Gundersheimer and Shalom Sabar. For current research on Jewish art and material culture, see *Images: A Journal of Jewish Art and Visual Culture* and *Ars Judaica: The Bar Ilan Journal of Jewish Art.*
20. For a fairly thorough introduction to the Second Commandment debate, see Joseph Gutmann, "The 'Second Commandment' and the Image in Judaism," in *No Graven Images: Studies in Art and the Hebrew Bible,* ed. Joseph Gutmann (New York: KTAV Publishing House, 1971), 3–16. See also, Gutmann's "Prolegomenon" and essays by other scholars in the same anthology. For a more recent treatment, see Kalman P. Bland, *The Artless Jew: Medieval and Modern Affirmations and Denials of the Visual* (Princeton, NJ: Princeton University Press, 2000). That gradual turn away from Jewish subjects by Jewish artists is evident in the later chapters of Roth, *Jewish Art* and the sections on nineteenth- and twentieth-century art in Skolnik, *Encyclopaedia Judaica*, s.v. "Art," by Roth, Sabar, Amishai-Maisals, et alia; Richard I. Cohen, "The Visual Revolution in Jewish Life—An Overview," in

Visualizing and Exhibiting Jewish Space and History, vol. 26, ed. Richard I. Cohen (Oxford: Oxford University Press, 2012), 3–24.

21. The quote is from the flyleaf of, Baskind and Silver, *Jewish Art*. It echoes Milton W. Brown, "An Explosion of Creativity: Jews and American Art in the Twentieth Century," in *Painting a Place in America: Jewish Artists in New York, 1900–1945*, ed. Norman L. Kleeblatt and Susan Chevlowe (New York: The Jewish Museum, 1991), 27: "The problem of a Jewish art or Jewishness in art remains vexing and possibly insoluble." Exemplifying the difficulty of rendering a coherent account of Jewish art is, Cohen, "The Visual Revolution in Jewish Life," cited above. See also chapter 7 of this book.

Chapter 1

Entering the Contact Zone

An exhibit of Jewish ritual objects, presented by Jews at the 1878 Exposition Universelle in Paris was described by an organizer as "offering fertile ground for observation and study of artistic development in a field that has been so little explored, that of Jewish art of the past." Jewish communities had not heretofore created displays of their ceremonial objects for non-Jews, much less in vast public spectacles like world's fairs. Further, the popularity of international expositions was due in no small part to their often-sensationalistic displays of "Orientals" and the artifacts of Europe's others. Despite the emancipation of French Jews almost a century earlier, they continued to be regarded as more Oriental than Occidental by French scholars, political elites, and ordinary citizens. The exhibit is also noteworthy because it presented Judaica as fine art while simultaneously using it for a quasi-ethnographic introduction to Judaism for non-Jews, an approach that heralded a malleability in future displays of Jewish ritual objects. Understanding the context, aims, and methods of the exhibit's organizers, especially their voluntary secularization of the objects while preserving their sacral meaning, is important because the exhibit informed subsequent exhibitions in London nine years later, the World's Columbian Exposition in 1893, and the origins of the Jewish Museum of New York a decade after that. To investigate the nature and occasion of the exhibit requires untangling a knot of conditions that made it feasible at that point in history. Among them is the Jewish enlightenment and emancipation, especially the widening historical consciousness they engendered; the nature of nineteenth-century world's fairs and the ambitions of the 1878 Paris exposition in particular; and the prehistory of Jewish ritual-objects collecting.[1]

From Ritual Objects to Cultural Artifacts

Throughout the several millennia of their existence, Jews adhered to religious beliefs and practices that materialized in a distinctive array of ritual objects that were never meant to be viewed outside communal worship in synagogues or privately in homes. Nor did Jews possess the kind of historical or ethnic consciousness, a distancing from the materials of their traditions, that would have led them to regard those objects as anything other than the necessary accoutrements of sacred observances. Certainly Jews did not perceive their ritual objects as artifacts to be gathered for the purposes of comparison, classification, and display, whether for each other or for non-Jews. To voluntarily deracinate these objects—that is, to remove them from the contexts of religious rituals and present them in settings where they could be critically regarded for reasons other than their fitness for religious use—required a profound change in Jewish life. Jews had to acquire a type of sociohistorical awareness that distanced them from the objects, a transformation that came with the Enlightenment and Jewish emancipation in late eighteenth-century Europe.

For much of their history, beginning with exile from Judaea following the Babylonian conquest in the 590s BCE, Jews learned to function like an "abstract nation," preserving many vestiges of nationhood bound up with traits of ethnicity: a shared language, code of civil as well as sacerdotal conduct embedded in the Torah, and accompanying sociocultural traditions—everything but a homeland. The diaspora stretched but did not sever the threads weaving Jews into a people that transcended the world's political and cultural boundaries. Their commonality was reinforced by the hostility they encountered as a minority in the societies among which they dwelled, the Jews comprising a locus defined by the "exteriority" of their vicinity. That isolation fostered a measure of autonomy and internal "corporativism" by which Jews organized themselves, sustained the ceremonial observances that defined Judaism, studied and transmitted sacred texts, conducted judicial processes, and provided for their common welfare.[2]

Yet that separateness also limited the Jewish community's contact with cultural developments outside it, among which was the advent of collecting, studying, and classifying objects in sixteenth- and seventeenth-century Europe as a means of building knowledge. Advances in empiricism and epistemology over the course of the eighteenth and nineteenth centuries led to the formation of what would become modern object-based disciplines such as botany, zoology, mineralogy, archaeology, anthropology, and eventually art history, often facilitated by the establishment of museums and the display methods they entailed. Instead of participating in these developments, most learned Jews relied on an ongoing tradition of studying and reinterpreting Judaism's texts as a means of comprehending the world. Collecting and displaying artifacts were eventually pursued by some Jews—but as a byproduct of the "institution" of "court Jews."

They were individuals called to serve monarchs and nobility as viziers and aides starting as early as 900 to 1,000 CE in the Middle East, and by the seventeenth-century, they had become increasingly common in European society. Court Jews typically served sovereigns as traders, commercial and financial advisers, bankers, and occasionally diplomats.[3]

Their employment introduced a new and specific criterion for conferring legal status on Jews, "utility rather than theology," a change that afforded access to the ideas and culture of European elites. Court Jews thereby accumulated sufficient wealth to pursue genteel customs, among them the collecting of precious objects. More broadly transformative, however, was the advent of the Enlightenment and the constellation of ideas regarding rationalism, social integration, and secularism it promulgated. Both "ideationally and institutionally," these ideas arrived from outside the sacred sources of Judaism. They profoundly affected Jewish tradition as did the political and economic benefits of emancipation that began in France in 1791 and spread across Europe in the ensuing decades.[4]

The emancipation of French Jews, which came in the context of the French Revolution and its aspirations for an egalitarian restructuring of society, was limited due to perceived conflicts between Jews' loyalty to France and their adherence to Judaism. After rising to power, Napoleon aimed to clarify the terms of Jewish emancipation in France before extending it to Jewish populations in other European lands he had or was about to conquer. In 1806, he called together and pressured leading representatives of the French Jewish community to affirm that

> the divine Law [in the Torah] . . . contains within itself dispositions which are political and dispositions which are religious: that the religious dispositions are, by their nature, absolute and . . . that this does not hold true of the political dispositions . . . which were taken for the government of the people of Israel . . . when it possessed its own kings, pontiffs and magistrates; that these political dispositions are no longer applicable, since Israel no longer forms a nation. . . . We hereby religiously enjoin on all obedience to the State [of France] in all matters civil and political.

The declaration came at a high price; as one of Napoleon's aides observed, "The Jews ceased to be a people and remained only a religion."[5]

Of this shift, Leora Batnitzky has remarked, "Before Jews received the rights of citizenship, Judaism was not a religion, and Jewishness was not a matter of culture or nationality. Rather Judaism and Jewishness were all of these at once: religion, culture, and nationality" bound together within a "closed world." Following emancipation, that world began fragmenting into separate religious and nonreligious spheres. The privileges of French citizenship were to be enjoyed in public, and religious rituals were to be conducted in private. Yet, the performance of civic duties and participation in the commercial and cultural activities of French society heightened Jews' awareness of the foreignness of their religious observances to gentiles. Also accompanying these changes were fundamental realignments in Jewish thought inspired by the same Enlightenment ideas that impelled emancipation. Those ideas sparked a Jewish enlightenment or *Haskalah* that flowered throughout Europe but particularly in Germany where Enlightenment philosopher Moses Mendelssohn (1729–86) inspired a generation of intellectuals. They drew together in 1819 to form the *Verein für Kultur und Wissenschaft des Judentums* (Association for the Culture and Science of Judaism). If philosophy was the language of progressive thought in eighteenth-century Germany, by the nineteenth century that language was *Wissenschaft* (science). It stood not only for methodological rigor, but also the advent of a heightened historical consciousness within Judaism that comprehended, but separated itself from, the lineage of rabbinic learning that began in antiquity—after the Second Temple's destruction in 70 CE—encompassing the preservation, interpretation, and transmission of religious texts and oral traditions. Although subsequent generations of rabbis possessed a sense of Jewish history, their scholarship retained a style of textual analysis that was inherently "ahistorical." The *Wissenschaft des Judentums* redirected Jewish scholarship from sacral studies "to man and his works," positioning itself outside the rabbinic tradition, which it examined with the "cold eye of the scientist."[6]

That approach, according to Ismar Schorsch, "facilitated the urgent and agonizing effort" of rethinking Judaism and became the primary means of "translating [its] ideas, institutions, and values" into comparable Western terms. Heinrich Graetz (1817–91), an heir of the *Wissenschaft des Judentums* and leading Jewish historian of the nineteenth century, characterized the trajectory of the Jewish people as rising through ever higher levels of historical self-awareness resulting in a "secularization of consciousness" that decoupled the individual from the "authority of religious tradition." Rabbi Hirsch Bär Fassel (1802–83), who studied Jewish civil codes by comparing them with Austrian civil law, declared that the former "became clear to me only by the way of the latter" because the former lacked a nomenclature for "the various nuances, gradations, and differences" necessary to apply it. The study of Judaism engendered for him and many others "a degree of alienation" from rabbinic teaching that nonetheless "increased self knowledge."[7]

For the social integration of emancipation to advance, this heightened reflexivity and the alienation from rabbinic scholarship it involved, had to be transformed into a means of explaining Judaism to non-Jews. Those leading the effort did so in "terms indigenous to the intellectual world of the West" and by shifting their rhetorical methods from apologetics to advocacy. The public exhibition struck some as one means of pursuing these aims. *Wissenschaft* thinker Leopold Zunz (1794–1886), upon visiting a Berlin exhibit on the history of printing, noticed that it lacked Hebrew examples and compared the omission to an antisemitic controversy: "One remembers mendacious accusations but not illustrious achievements. The Jews are self-evidently excluded from the homage lavished on the first printers." In his complaint, Zunz highlighted the pursuit of Jewish advocacy as "an act of justice as well as self-interest," seeing in the forums of public discourse—such as exhibitions—opportunities for introducing non-Jews to Judaism and Jewish accomplishments. Zunz also prefigured the emergence of Jews as their own "anthropological subjects within the larger scope of Europe."[8]

The potential of public exhibitions as vehicles for Jewish education and advocacy was more readily realized in France than Germany, however, revealing their different responses to the Enlightenment's possibilities. Jay Berkowitz found that of the "Jewish intellectuals in the West, [French reformers] evinced the greatest continuity" with its tenets by focusing their efforts on education and public discourse. Whereas the Germans pursued social change through contentious religious reforms inspired by the *Wissenschaft des Judentums*, in France proponents sought more modest changes, hoping to modernize Jewish society without provoking "communal schism and alienation from Judaism." Regardless, Shmuel Feiner found that the secularization flowing from the Jewish enlightenment and emancipation penetrated most of the Jewish community in both countries. Secularization seemed to spread from different levels of Jewish society: the waning of religious commitment appearing first "among the educated elite (secularization 'from above')"; and then the spread of social and economic opportunities altering "behavior among large groups (secularization 'from below')." When French Jews seized the opportunity of the 1878 Paris exposition to display a Judaica collection, they pursued both paths of secularization. To voluntarily present their ritual objects to non-Jews, French Jews readily adopted the exhibitionary tools of desacralization (expressing secularization from above); and they did so in an international exposition, an increasingly popular attraction, where they knew they might reach not only fellow Jews (fostering secularization from below), but also a broad cross section of the French public and other European visitors too.[9]

Expositions, Subalterns, and the Public Sphere

Those steps required adopting taxonomic and display methods that had been developing for several hundred years in the context of Europe's history of collecting. Although evidence indicates that these activities began in classical antiquity, during the Renaissance they become a significant feature of Western culture. The variety and quantity of objects collected, sorted, and displayed grew exponentially, whether for learned inquiry among scholarly sodalities, or amusement among the royalty and aristocracy. The names of the settings where things were gathered and observed—*theatrum naturae*, cabinets of curiosity, *Wunderkammer*—hint at the spellbinding plenitude of marvels they contained. Most collections contained things gathered during contemporary voyages of exploration and conquest, including what, today, might be called ethnographic artifacts, works produced by Europe's others. Early display methods reified taxonomic interests informed by Aristotle's *Organon*; patterns discerned among nature's forms such as seashells or minerals; or the primacy of Christian cosmology over pagan cults. There might be groupings according to *material* that included, for example, all "things made of feathers," such as an Aztec feather shield, a Native American feather headdress, and bird skins. Or there could be groupings based on *form* that contained a variety of "Oriental," African, and ancient European weapons such as daggers, knives, swords, or things that look like them, whether made of bone, flint, or metal. By the nineteenth century, taxonomies were informed by Linnean methods and evolutionary theories. Significantly, most of the artifacts were far from their original contexts and presented in ways alien to the cultures that produced them. That is, whether displayed as natural history or ethnographic specimens, artifacts created by Europe's others were deracinated and—for religious objects—secularized. Intrinsic to this process of cultural dislocation was what Barbara Kirshenblatt-Gimblett calls a "poetics of detachment" that enabled not only the physical separation of objects from their cultural origins, but also a "detached attitude" on the part of the observer conducive to the objects' decontextualization.[10]

The collecting and display of European art during this period were often intended to impress viewers with owners' wealth and prestige but could also serve the interests of art academies and connoisseurs wanting to compare artists' technical and stylistic advances. Here, too, works were removed from their original contexts and redeployed, sometimes in very arbitrary if aesthetically pleasing installations calculated to facilitate their contemplation. Such collections, alongside natural history specimens and ethnographica, were shared with only limited circles of visitors, however. It was not until the late seventeenth century that they began to be opened more widely, eventually in the form of public museums along the lines we think of today, reifying a widely shared interest in using museums to educate and refine citizens. Coupled with building nations or more local civil societies, this step added another dimension to secularization through display.[11]

By the second half of the nineteenth century, these aims and display methods materialized in a new arena that was far more popular and widely attended than any museum: the world's fair, beginning with the 1851 Great Exhibition of the Works of Industry of all Nations outside London. There had been earlier trade fairs in Europe, including important precedents in France, but the Great Exhibition set a far more ambitious standard. Inspired by it, subsequent expositions featured displays of large machinery and small inventions, commercial products and domestic crafts, decorative arts and natural resources, and many other things, typically from the host nation, other participating nations, and their colonies—the latter to highlight the ostensible benefits of imperialism for Europeans and their subalterns alike. Expositions were often organized by national governments with the assistance of tiers of committees, commissions, civic and cultural associations, businesses, and independent entrepreneurs. Their funding came from government treasuries, public lotteries, corporate and individual investors, and exhibition companies; and planners hoped to turn a profit for their sovereign or private investors. Potential income relied on attendance, and leaders did all they could to boost it, partly by expanding each subsequent exposition with more varied and extensive exhibits. In addition to their commercial interests, organizers saw fairs as "encyclopedic educational tools" that would cultivate ideal citizens and consumers. Exposition programs introduced visitors to leading social and cultural debates of the day, and the number of national participants, variety of international tourists, and range of colonial displays comprised something akin to "inter-cultural" festivals. Leaders hoped these great cosmopolitan assemblies not only advanced a widely shared desire for progress, but also promoted "peace among nations," mainly by encouraging friendly competition among former belligerents, and—in France especially—advancing the Enlightenment vision of "universal brotherhood." By the 1870s, world's fairs sprawled over hundreds of acres, comprised thousands of exhibits, and attracted millions of visitors.[12]

Among the fairs' offerings, foreign curiosities were major attractions. Beginning with the Paris exposition of 1867, such exotica came to include foreign peoples as well, usually presented in "tableaux-vivants" and simulated villages. In part, these displays were inspired by an earlier history of urban burlesques, but they were also informed by intertwined developments in Western scholarship. One was the nascence of disciplinary practices such as anthropology's comparative typologies of cultural artifacts; the other was natural history museums' positioning of contemporary Sub-Saharan African, Oceanic, Native American, and other others as raw evidence for social-evolution theories explaining what some caricatured as humanity's deficient branches. Added to this mix of European subalterns were "Orientals," whether from East and South Asia, or the Middle East. As these displays expanded and multiplied at the expositions, however, it is important to note that they were not about the cultures they claimed to illustrate, but rather "Western representations" of them. The international exposition came to enact, as John Burris observes, the era's deepening belief in differences between "civilized" and "primitive" peoples, according to which the latter were defined primarily by ethnicity or race. Deemed "exotic," the latter were also regarded as "either relics of the past or freaks of the present." The differences between the refined accomplishments displayed in European art exhibits and the crude artifacts in exhibits of the continent's others constituted a dialectics of display, together comprising "focal points through which many of the elements of modernization and secularization were introduced to the public."[13]

Contemporary observers also perceived the fairs as offering potent evidence, either of secularism's evils or of the comparative merits of various religious and ethnic groups. Geoffrey Cantor reports objections, voiced by Christian religious leaders in widely circulated "sermons, tracts, newspapers and the religious periodical press," to the 1851 Great Exhibition's valorization as a "Secular Temple." Other Christians, however, regarded the Great Exhibition as a "Monument of Christianity" for demonstrating the supremacy of Christendom over the world's other religions. Jews saw in the Great Exhibition causes for pride and ethnic solidarity. Jewish coverage of the exhibition celebrated Jews' contributions—mainly inventions, manufactured products, and personal possessions loaned for display. In France, international expositions had been presented twice before the 1878 Exposition Universelle, in 1855 and 1867, both of which were reported in Franco-Jewish periodicals. So French Jews were plausibly aware of the opportunities as well as challenges expositions posed for them. Although French Jewry was emancipated nearly a century earlier, it remained alert to the threats and actualities of antisemitism, which had revived in the 1870s, in part due to the accusations of scholars and politicians as well as ordinary citizens. One popular thinker of the time,

Ernest Renan, concluded from his philological-historical studies that, as paraphrased by Edward Said, "the Semites are rabid monotheists who produced no mythology, no art, no commerce, no civilization" and that, in Renan's words, the "Semitic race, compared with the Indo-European," represents "an inferior combination of human nature." Renan's differentiation between Semitic and Indo-European peoples aligned with prevailing distinctions between the Orient and Occident. Jews, as Semites, were considered "Orientals" with all their presumed deficiencies, the opposite of Europe's civilized Occidentals. If "primitive" or "Oriental" peoples comprised the others beyond Europe's shores, Jews were Europe's others within. It did not help that the pace of their integration into European society was too slow for some, leading to accusations of Jewish "tribalism." Comparisons of European achievements with those of its foreign and domestic others were vividly staged in prior expositions in which Oriental artifacts were displayed as inferior to the Occident's fine arts. In America, nearly fifteen years after the 1878 Exposition Universelle, while contemplating the possible participation of Jews in the forthcoming World's Columbian Exposition in Chicago, one Jewish observer remarked, "There is no use denying it, for many . . . non-Jews, we are a curiosity, a freak, an archeological specimen" and Jews would oppose "being paraded as a 'dime museum freak.'"[14]

Placing Judaism on Display

The decision by French Jews to voluntarily show a collection of Judaica at the 1878 exposition was not only courageous, but also novel. It was precedent setting because it was public *and* it featured a Jew's collection. The earliest Judaica collections were those established in eighteenth-century central Europe by Christian theologians, some assisted by apostate Jews. A celebrated "Juden-Cabinet" created in Dresden during the reign of Friedrich August I (or August II the Strong, 1670–1733) included a scale model of the Temple of Solomon and a full-scale replica of a synagogue containing a Torah, a Hebrew Book of Esther scroll, and other ritual objects. Around the same time, at least two other replica synagogues with accompanying Judaica collections were created in Regensburg and Uppsala. Christian patrons studied the objects in pursuit of what Yaacov Deutsch called "polemical ethnographies" of Judaism. Such efforts, which began as early as the Renaissance with investigations of Jewish texts and observances, aimed to buttress Christian doctrine and convert Jews by persuading them of Judaism's failings. Although some visitors saw Juden-Cabinets as curiosities, the more learned—especially Christian scholars—either perused them to reveal "secrets" they thought Jews concealed from gentiles or they used the collections as pedagogical aids for instructing acolytes about the spiritual "poverty" and "superstitions" of Judaism.[15]

Few Jews possessed the income and proclivity to collect objects of any kind at levels comparable to their non-Jewish contemporaries. The exceptions were court Jews or *Hoftjuden*. Some served as intermediaries for their patrons' collecting activities, others presented gifts for their patrons' *Kunstkammern*, and a few developed an appetite for objets d'art—commissioning portraits of themselves and family or becoming collectors, a few pursuing Judaica. One of the earliest, Alexander David (1687–1765), was a courtier and financial agent for a succession of Braunschweigian dukes. Little is known about his collection save that it was kept in a room adjacent to his private synagogue and that he subsequently donated it to the Braunschweig Jewish community. With emancipation and the cultural and economic opportunities it afforded Jews, coupled with the gradual elimination of European monarchies during the nineteenth century, the "institution of Court Jewry" began to dissipate. As Jews entered the mainstream economies of their host nations and acculturated more fully into European society, more began collecting precious things, a handful seeking Jewish ritual objects. It was one among them whose collection furnished the basis for the Judaica exhibit at the 1878 Paris Exposition Universelle.[16]

Scholars who studied the exhibit variously interpreted it as the advent of a process of reinterpreting Jewish ritual objects as art; marking the objects' transition from artifacts of a material culture to commodification as luxury goods; signifying Jewish nostalgia for a vanishing past as the anxieties of assimilation intersected with Romanticism; or repositioning civic discussions about Jews from the Jewish people to Judaism as a means of integrating it into the discourse of civilization and recasting "Jewish particularism in the universalistic terms of art." Each of these assertions is valid to some extent, but in buttressing their arguments the authors bypassed specifics of the display that mark its significance in the history of Jewish participation in the exhibitionary complex.[17]

The exhibit presented the collection of Isaac Strauss (1806–88), an Alsation Jew who descended from a rabbinic lineage and had moved to Paris in the 1820s. He composed and conducted popular music and apparently was something of a bon vivant (Figure 1.1). Strauss attracted the patronage of the monarchy and aristocracy, thereby accumulating the wealth to travel and collect a variety of decorative arts, including

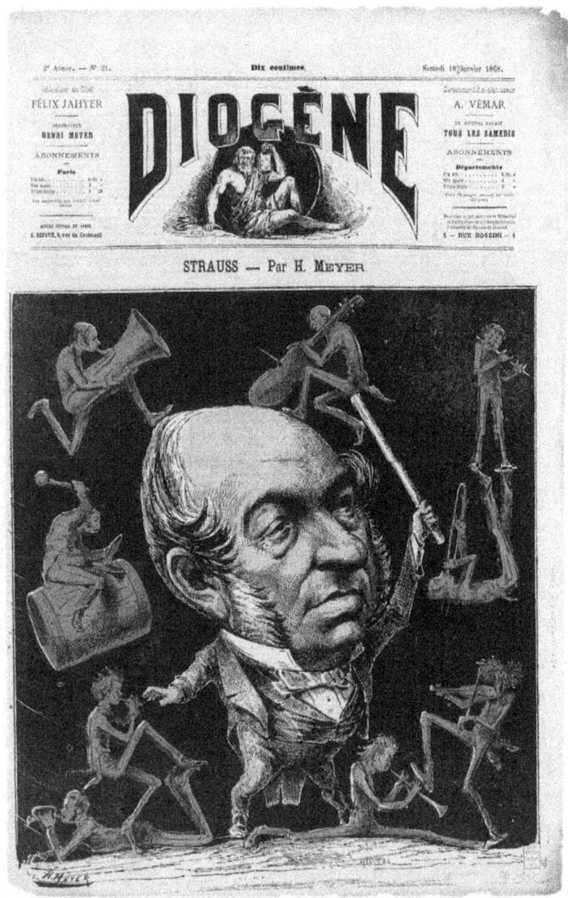

Figure 1.1. Isaac Strauss, from *Diogène*, 18 January 1868. Caricature by Henri Meyer, engraving by Gillot. © Paris Musées / Musée Carnavalet.

Judaica. The display of Strauss's collection was likely arranged by David Schornstein who, under his pen name Georges Stenne, wrote the exhibit's guide. Schornstein (1826–79) was a playwright, fiction writer, and journalist who covered several subjects including Jewish antiquities and works by Jewish artists shown in the annual Parisian salons of the 1860s. Schornstein is remembered for the serialized Jewish historical fictions he published in the French weekly *La Vérité Israélite*, one of the leading platforms of the "Science of Judaism" movement in France. His melodramatic stories, set in a past that sometimes reached back to the Middle Ages, conjure images of violent attacks against Jews and the various ways they overcome such hardships. Through his stories, Schornstein encouraged

Jewish ethnic identification during a period in France when, in the wake of emancipation, Jews were drifting away from religious observance and losing interest in Jewish traditions and history. Schornstein's stories celebrate the promises of emancipation while resisting full integration into French society by "instructing Jews to leave the ghetto, both physically and psychologically," but without abandoning their Jewish identity.[18]

Little is known of the relationship between Strauss and Schornstein save that they both were born and grew up in Alsace. Strauss was on one of the 1878 exposition's organizing committees and no doubt moved among the circles of Parisian cultural leaders engaged in its preparations. Schornstein brought to the collection's interpretation his experience as an author and art critic as well as his views as a founder of the Alliance Israélite Universelle. Established in 1860 and based in Paris, it aimed to assist Jews suffering antisemitism in other countries. Operating in the belief that emancipated Jews should spearhead solidarity with and help for less-fortunate brethren, the Alliance also became a means by which the Jewish community joined in the advancement of France's revolutionary ideals and imperial mission. The motivation for that work was the unfinished business of secularization within French society, especially the elimination of lingering post-revolution church influence over domestic and international policies. By striving to protect and aid their brethren abroad, the Alliance enabled Jews to align themselves with French anti-clerical activists striving for a more secular state. The arena for this collaboration was France's colonies where the nation attempted to spread its conception of civilization by liberating the peoples of Africa and Asia from "tyranny and backwardness," imposing its presumably "superior form of rule," a key element of which was secularization. Alliance leaders thought of their services as supporting France's mission abroad, an opportunity for French Jews to demonstrate their fealty to France's revolutionary ethos, their integration into French society, and their commitment to a "world united under liberal ideals." Schornstein's Alliance activities corresponded with those of other Parisian Jewish intellectuals and community leaders who, in addition to their social welfare and political activities, asserted their presence through the erection and dedication of imposing synagogues. The 1875 public celebration of a prominent new one in Paris trumpeted the community's "sense of belonging" in France's civic sphere. This arrival in the terrain of "symbolic politics" was accomplished by adopting both architectural styles and public ceremonial forms from contemporary French society. Whether assisting brethren abroad or building institutions at home, French Jews like Schornstein skillfully aligned their objectives with the aims of fellow non-Jewish citizens while adhering to their most closely held values. These dual pursuits of fully integrating into French society while preserving Jewish identity and solidarity informed his presentation of the Strauss collection.[19]

The 1878 exposition was sponsored by the French government and resembled its predecessors' aims and structure, but with an additional purpose: demonstrating to other nations and its own citizens the Third Republic's unity and recovery after the devastating losses of the Franco-Prussian War (1870–71). Central to this effort was the exposition planners' emphasis on architecture and the fine and decorative arts. Among the exposition's most prominent features was the newly constructed Palais du Trocadéro, a lavish architectural ode to the French Baroque, an earlier era of national power and accomplishment. It was created in part to exhibit French decorative arts, dating from the distant past to the present, as a visual demonstration that "France reigned supreme in art, that art dominated culture, culture evoked civilization, and hence civilization meant France." The exposition also highlighted France's imperial reach as expressed through extensive displays from its colonies, including an Algerian "native village" (*village indigène*), complete with the first "Oriental" street created at a world's fair and featuring a bazaar with a "liberal number of North Africans." The exposition's 192 acres of displays attracted over sixteen million visitors during its six-and-a-half-month run.[20]

The Strauss collection was displayed in one of the Trocadéro's two wings that, together, contained about forty thousand objects organized to present the progress of civilization from "our primitive ancestors" to modern Europe. The Strauss-collection's wing was reserved for art history and the most precious objects Frenchmen contributed to the exposition; the other wing was designated for "Oriental" and ethnographic objects. The art history wing was divided into fifteen galleries arranged as a chronological tour of artistic development, and the Strauss materials were displayed in the tenth gallery, for late medieval and Renaissance works, in the center of which was a richly carved wood cover for the baptismal font of the Saint-Romain church in Rouen. Strauss's "Judaic curiosities" shared the space with at least one other collection—the latter containing Flemish paintings, statues, carved wooden furniture, tapestries, weapons, and ivory crosses. The Strauss collection did not quite fit its chronological category because many of its contents dated from later periods. Yet the art-history wing displays were nearly all composed of individuals' collections, and the Strauss materials' anachronistic placement was not unique.[21]

No photographs or floor plans of the Strauss exhibit survive, but Schornstein's guide—titled "Collection of M[onsieur] Strauss: Description of Hebrew Religious Art Objects" (*Collection de M. Strauss: Description des*

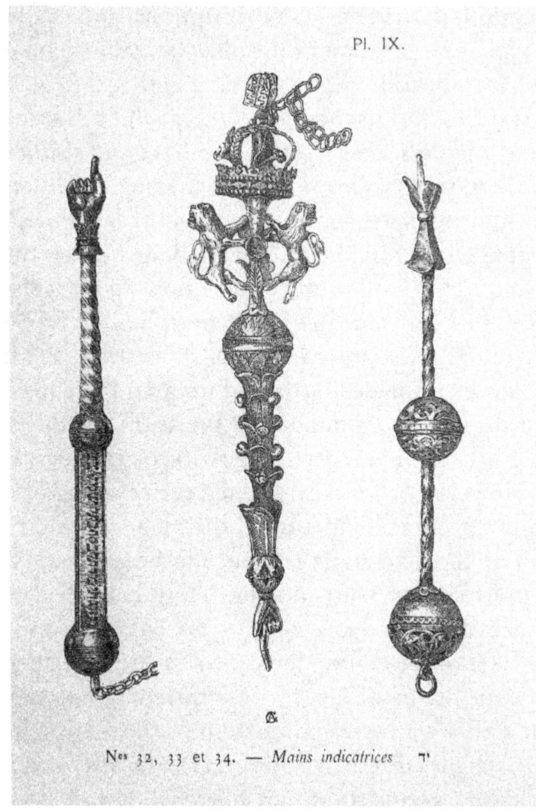

Figure 1.2. Torah pointers, Plate IX from [David Schornstein], *Collection de M. Strauss. Description des objets d'art religieux hébraïques: Exposés dans les galeries du Trocadéro, à l'Exposition Universelle de 1878* (Poissy, France: Typographie de S. Lejay et Cie, 1878). Rendering by Alfred Gérardin.

objets d'art religieux hébraïques)—conveys a sense of the works and their presentation. The display contained eighty-two objects sorted into about twenty categories. There were single items, such as a Torah in a portable ark, and multiple versions of objects in other categories such as ten spice boxes. Among the larger groupings were nine Chanukah lamps, fifteen betrothal rings, and six Torah-reading pointers (Figure 1.2). Most of the pieces were ceremonial objects and eleven were texts—including a Spanish translation of the Torah, six Book of Esther scrolls, two prayer books, a pair of marriage contracts, and a manuscript guide to the Jewish holidays. The objects are individually described in Schornstein's sixty-seven-page guide and twenty-seven are depicted in twelve accompanying plates. The guide also contains a twelve-page introduction. Taken as a whole, the guide's introduction, individual-item descriptions, and illustrations comprise a wide-ranging explanation of the objects' use and import.[22]

Schornstein's introduction begins by highlighting the collection's probable uniqueness because of its focus on Judaica, and he salutes Strauss for his conscientious and persistent research in France and abroad to assemble it. Schornstein then turns to his two main themes, the history of Jewish engagement in the visual arts and the essentials of Jewish religious observances represented by the objects. As Natalia Berger notes, his determination to establish a history of Jewish contributions to art is signaled in the guide's half-title-page epigram, an excerpt from Exodus 35:35 in Hebrew followed by a French translation: "מלא אתם חכמת לב לעשות כל מלאכת חרש וחשב ורקם | L'Éternel a doué ces artistes d'un grand talent pour exécuter toute œuvre de ciseleur, de tisserand et de brodeur (The Eternal One gave these artists a great talent to create any work of carving, weaving, and embroidery)." However, Schornstein altered the meaning of the text with his translation. An accurate rendering of the Hebrew would be closer to: "Them [instead of 'these artists', a reference to Bezalel and Aholiab mentioned in the previous few sentences] has He [God] filled with wisdom of heart, to make all manner of work, of the engraver, and of the cunning workman, and of the embroiderer [or weaver]." By elevating Bezalel and Aholiab to the status of artists, Schornstein seems to be asserting a genealogy of artists tracing back to the very beginning of the Jewish people's Sinai covenant with God. However, Schornstein concedes in the introduction that, in comparison to Christians, Jewish participation in the visual arts was historically very modest, a circumstance he attributes to the Second Commandment prohibition against images and the frequently precarious circumstances of Jewish existence over the centuries. Nonetheless, he argues, the artistic impulse native to all peoples is so powerful that the Jews could not remain complete strangers to the visual arts, especially in Europe. Why Europe? Because, Schornstein continues, the Jews were never wholly separate from Christians there and the milieu stimulated and influenced artistic development among the Jews. As a result of these conditions, although synagogues are typically devoid of large-scale artistic works, Jews were able to create or commission "portable" decorative objects for congregational and personal observances, as exemplified in the Strauss collection. Further, Schornstein added, over time the Jews increasingly evaded and then fully transgressed the Second Commandment.[23]

Tacitly acknowledging that the objects would be unfamiliar to most non-Jews, Schornstein devotes nearly half the introduction to explaining the objects' names and uses in the context of Jewish ritual practices and holidays. Schornstein's task of presenting the Strauss collection as exemplary of Jewish artistry was thus complicated by surmounting the objects' foreignness for exposition visitors. For example, paraphrasing Schornstein, Jews would not think of illuminating a Torah like other Jewish manuscripts because of their veneration of its plain, sacred form, which is prescribed down to the smallest details, including its unusual construction: long strips of parchment, sewn edge to edge, and rolled over two wood rods. His discussions of other classes of ritual objects similarly combine aesthetic concerns with ethnographic explanations. The detachment implicit in Schornstein's approach is nearly always reinforced by his uses of "juif" (Jew) and "israélite" (Israelite). He typically uses the former when referring to Jews in the past—often in the contexts of religious observances and ritual objects; and he usually deploys the latter for Jews in recent circumstances—often in nonreligious contexts. Schornstein's usages reflect a pattern observed by Phyllis Cohen Albert wherein "Juif . . . was the word used by nineteenth-century French Jews to indicate the old national type of unemancipated, ethnic Jew, as opposed to the modern 'Israelite,' the Jew by 'faith' alone." For reasons of consistency and in deference to current English usage, I use "Jews" and "Jewish" for both "israélite" and "juif" when translating or paraphrasing Schornstein's text below.[24]

Toward the end of his introduction, Schornstein returns to the topic of Christian-Jewish relations, asking, "Are these objects the work of Jewish or Christian artists?" ("Ces oeuvres sont elles dues à des artistes Israélites ou Chrétiens?") Although Jewish artists excelled in the jeweler's craft, and as illuminators and embroiderers, he comments, because they were barred from artisans' guilds, there was "no doubt that Christians played a certain role" ("nul doute que les Chrétiens y ont eu une certaine part") in creating Jewish ritual objects. As evidence, Schornstein quotes in full a fifteenth-century contract by which the Jewish community of Arles commissioned a Christian silversmith from Avignon to fashion a Torah crown. The Jews stipulated the design, materials, and ornamentation as well as the silversmith's workplace in Arles; and they prohibited the crown's fabrication on the Sabbath and Jewish holidays. Schornstein also cites examples of Christian artistic influences in the Strauss collection. One is a circa thirteenth-century Chanukah menorah with allusions to Romanesque church design in its pediment shape and piercings suggestive of a colonnade surmounted by a rose window (Figure 1.3). Another is a tass or Torah breastplate that contains depictions of cherubs and more adult

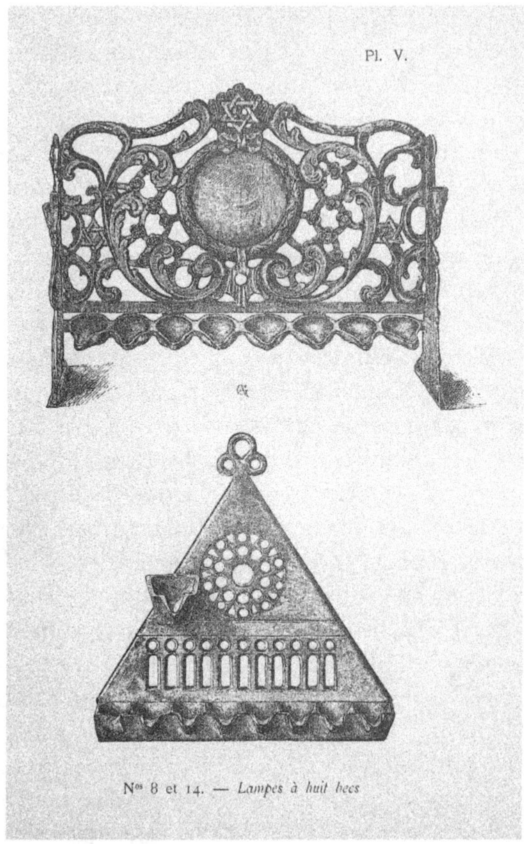

Figure 1.3. Chanukah menorah (bottom), Plate V from [David Schornstein], *Collection de M. Strauss. Description des objets d'art religieux hébraïques: Exposés dans les galeries du Trocadéro, à l'Exposition Universelle de 1878* (Poissy, France: Typographie de S. Lejay et Cie, 1878). Rendering by Alfred Gérardin.

angels, which are not only prohibited by the Second Commandment but appropriated from Christian adoration imagery (Figure 1.4).[25]

Following the introduction are individual item descriptions numbered and arranged in groups by ritual function or object type, rather than art categories of the day such as style, chronology, or geographic origin. In general, the sequence runs from the physically largest to the smallest. An exception is the group of manuscripts that, other than the solitary Torah, comes near the end. Presumably the display was arranged the same way. The individual descriptions appear to be written as though for people walking through the exhibit with guide in hand, using the numbers assigned to each object to relate the text to the work on display. The installation

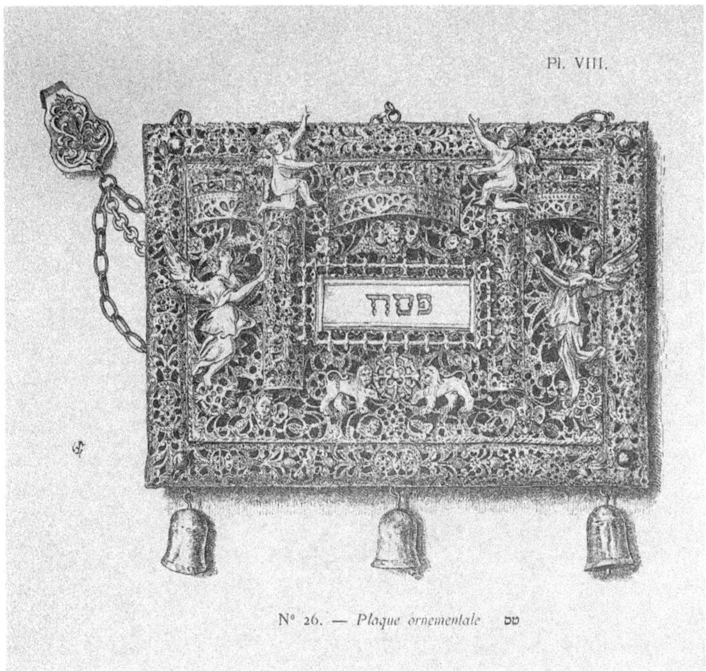

Figure 1.4. Torah breastplate, Plate VIII from [David Schornstein], *Collection de M. Strauss. Description des objets d'art religieux hébraïques: Exposés dans les galeries du Trocadéro, à l'Exposition Universelle de 1878* (Poissy, France: Typographie de S. Lejay et Cie, 1878). Rendering by Alfred Gérardin.

of a London Judaica exhibition mounted just nine years later, in 1887, that included the Strauss collection along with other loans, is suggestive of this method in its use of numbered tags that correspond, in that case, to the London exhibit catalogue (Figure 2.3). The Strauss guide's illustrations support a combination of aesthetic and ethnographic interests. Of the twelve images, six show groups of objects. Of those, one presents four historically unrelated objects arranged in a simulacrum of a synagogue scene: a pulpit with a cloth covering, prayer book, and Chanukah menorah (Figure 1.5). Four other images organize the depicted objects by type (Figures 1.2 and 1.6). The contrast in these presentations is indicative of what Stephen Bann calls the "poetics of the museum," the alternate display methods employed in museums and comparable settings of the era. In this instance, the prayer stand with related objects comprises a synecdoche or mimetic arrangement of artifacts that may never have been joined before, but here are coordinated to suggest a synagogue setting—what Barbara Kirshenblatt-Gimblett calls an "in situ" installation. The groupings of

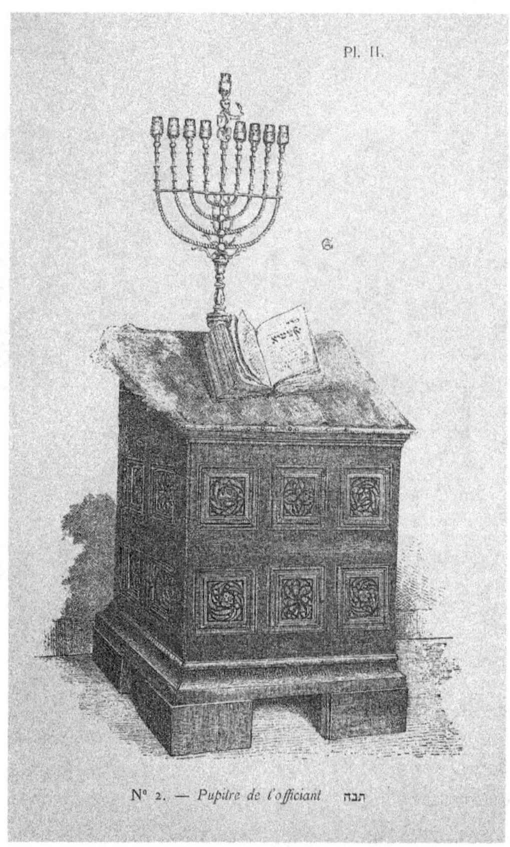

Figure 1.5. Synagogue pulpit with cloth covering, Chanukah menorah, and prayer book; Plate II from [David Schornstein], *Collection de M. Strauss. Description des objets d'art religieux hébraïques: Exposés dans les galeries du Trocadéro, à l'Exposition Universelle de 1878* (Poissy, France: Typographie de S. Lejay et Cie, 1878). Rendering by Alfred Gérardin.

objects by type comprise, in Bann's terms, metonymic displays insofar as each piece "stands for" a different period, region of origin, style, and so forth. Kirshenblatt-Gimblett sees this approach as the opposite of "in-situ," highlighting the arrangement of like objects according to "typologies of form." Contrasts also arise in Schornstein's use of languages. The guide is written in French but includes the Hebrew epigram noted above; and individual object descriptions contain Hebrew quotes and labels. Some are used to highlight and explain inscriptions on the objects, some are the objects' Hebrew names. This also occurs in the illustration captions (see nearly all the figures in this chapter and Figure 2.4). Evidently, Strauss and

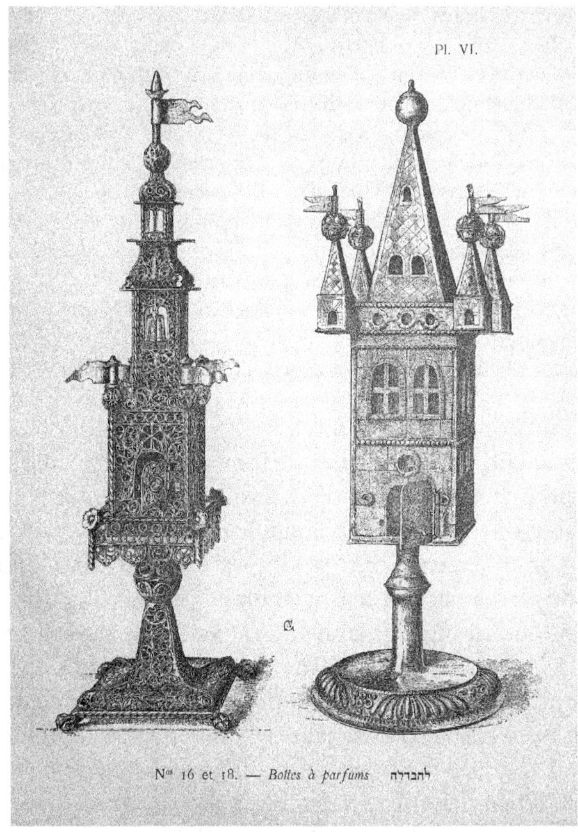

Figure 1.6. Havdalah spice boxes, Plate VI from [David Schornstein], *Collection de M. Strauss. Description des objets d'art religieux hébraïques: Exposés dans les galeries du Trocadéro, à l'Exposition Universelle de 1878* (Poissy, France: Typographie de S. Lejay et Cie, 1878). Rendering by Alfred Gérardin.

Schornstein not only expected Jews to view the exhibit but also anticipated at least some would be sufficiently fluent to read the Hebrew.[26]

When it came to discussing the individual objects, Schornstein faced a formidable set of interpretive goals as he attempted to spotlight the objects' aesthetic significance, relate them to Judaism, and do so in terms meaningful for a mostly non-Jewish, French audience. Nowhere is this more evident than in his discussion of a portable ark (Figure 1.7):

> This ark is made of engraved and embossed silver decorated with silver fleurons whose centers are formed of gemstones of several colors. There are gilded twisted columns at the four corners and the upper entablature bears a crown. On the pinnacle is the figure of a child holding a musical instrument.

> This tabernacle holds the scrolls of the sacred law written on parchment ספר תורה [*Sefer Torah*] and surrounded by the Mappa מפה [*mapah*]. The Mappa is a long strip of white canvas on which the name and birth date of every male child are inscribed and which is held in the temple and used to wrap the sacred texts. It was a kind of birth register, and during the Revolution, when France wanted to establish the exact identity of young Jews who were called to military service for the first time, these strips were used when other documents could not be found.
>
> The scroll itself has one particularly interesting quality. All the columns start with the same letter, the conjunction ו [*vav*], except for six, where tradition indicates the word that should appear first.
>
> This object, which dates to the late 17th century, seems to have been made in Germany. It was used for ceremonies of private worship by the family and was enclosed in a case of embossed leather, which allowed it to be taken when traveling.[27]

In this one caption, Schornstein skillfully integrates information about Jewish material culture, the facture of Torahs, Jewish life and ceremonial practices, aesthetic analysis, and French history. Particularly noteworthy is his discussion of a specific ethnographic feature, the *mapah*. Ivan Karp, commenting on nineteenth-century display alternatives for ethnographic objects, distinguishes between two choices: "exoticizing" or "assimilating." The first option highlights the exotic nature of foreign artifacts and the differences they reify between the viewer's culture and the culture of the viewer's other; the assimilating option minimizes their foreignness, emphasizing instead the commonalities between the viewer's culture and the culture of the viewer's other by teasing out a "sense of the familiar and natural." When Schornstein described the *mapah*'s use in identifying young Jews for French military service, he deftly related it, and the entire ark, to French civic duty and history, thereby minimizing its foreignness. Because the Strauss collection was displayed in a building that contained European decorative arts in one wing and ethnographic objects from non-European cultures in the other, Schornstein seems to have gone extra lengths to explain this unusual object's presence among the more familiar arts of European culture. The particular nature of the portable ark, with its enclosure of a distinctively ethnic artifact in a case covered entirely with Western European ornamentation, called for no less. Schornstein's strategy of integrating the ark and other ethnic objects in the Strauss collection with exemplars of Western decorative arts may also have rendered the collection more accessible for exposition visitors. Schornstein's ability to shift from one interpretive modality to another and then back again also augurs a form of "Jewish primitivism," not as an aesthetic project but an analytical one. By situating his Jewish ethnography in a European present, he "troubled the boundary between observer and observed, . . . subject and object." His was not an "either/or scenario" in which Schornstein

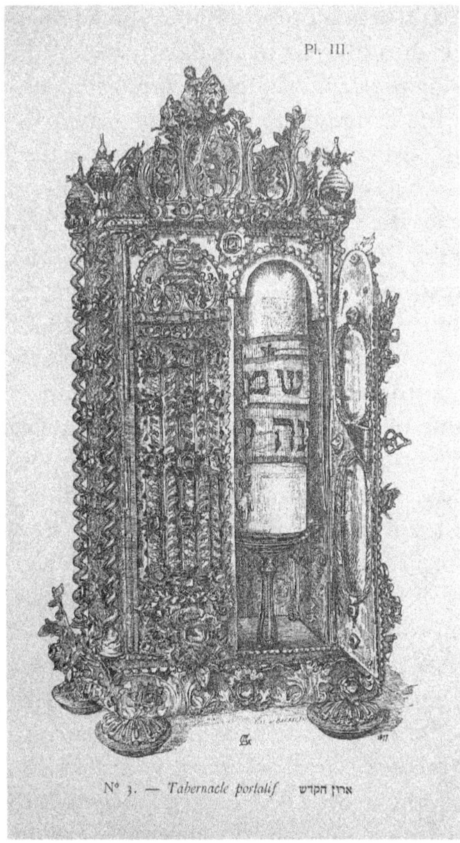

Figure 1.7. Portable ark, Plate III from [David Schornstein], *Collection de M. Strauss. Description des objets d'art religieux hébraïques: Exposés dans les galeries du Trocadéro, à l'Exposition Universelle de 1878* (Poissy, France: Typographie de S. Lejay et Cie, 1878). Rendering by Alfred Gérardin.

was "now on one side and now on the other but one in which the Jew inhabits both positions."[28]

The ark caption is but one example of many in which Schornstein also inserted Strauss collection objects into French aesthetic and historical discourse by relating them to cultural conventions familiar to most exposition visitors. When highlighting the artistic qualities of the objects, Schornstein was using them as proxies for France's Jewish community in helping fulfill one of the Exposition Universelle's primary objectives: demonstrating the supremacy of France's achievements in the decorative arts. By explaining the history of mutually generative relationships between Jewish patrons and Christian artisans, Schornstein showed as well how this Judeo-Christian cooperation augured the promise of Jewish emancipation in France. Visitors to the display heralded its aesthetic qualities as exemplifying the demonstrable accomplishments and possibilities of "Jewish art." The contemporary observer David Kaufmann (1852–99), a prodigious Austrian-born, rabbinically trained scholar, marveled, "Whoever visited the Paris exhibition under the impression that Jews lacked any talent for the visual arts would be in for a pleasant surprise."[29]

The Strauss guide comprised a brave and supple negotiation of the exposition's context, maneuvering as it does among the differences between Judaism and Christianity, Jewish private and public lives, the sacred and secular, ethnography and aesthetics, Hebrew and French. In it, Schornstein confronted a paradox of assimilation—finding for Jews a place at the table of French society without disavowing the religious beliefs and practices that set them apart. No longer possessing a separate way of life, yet asserting a distinctive religious-ethnic identity, Strauss, Schornstein, and their Jewish partners were calling attention to Judaism in a very public forum at a time when emancipation remained still young and unstable. The display and its guide affirm David Sorkin's observation that emancipation was "ambiguous" in that it was neither marked by a particular event nor culminated a linear evolution. Instead, during this period and in subsequent decades, "Jews gained and lost and regained and re-lost rights" and for Jews in France as elsewhere emancipation remained "an interminable project." For that reason, when Strauss and Schornstein mounted their exhibit at the 1878 Exposition Universelle, they entered a "contact zone" of potentially hostile or at minimum uncomprehending attitudes, a setting that compelled the organizers to anticipate the interests and concerns of a predominantly non-Jewish audience. Contact zones, according to Mary Louise Pratt, are "social spaces where disparate cultures meet, clash, and grapple with each other, often in highly asymmetrical relations of domination and subordination." There, as Pratt observes, subalterns offer up an "autoethnography" in which they "undertake to represent themselves in ways that *engage with*" representations others have made of them. Whereas ethnographic texts are those in which Europeans "represent to themselves their . . . others, autoethnographic texts are texts the others construct in response to or in dialogue with" European perceptions. Such texts, as seen here, involve "collaborating with and appropriating the idioms" of the dominant culture. As James Clifford notes, sites like expositions and museums may also be understood as contact zones, places where the notion can be applied to "cultural relations within the same state, region, or city—in the centers rather than the frontiers of nations and empires." In this instance, Schornstein's injection of the Strauss collection into the contact zone of the exposition was aided by the "transculturation" embodied in the objects displayed. A term used by ethnographers, "transculturation" is used to characterize "processes whereby members of subordinated or marginal groups select and invent from materials transmitted by a dominant" culture. Jewish ritual objects fashioned from precious metals in accordance with European decorative-arts styles exemplify one form of transculturation.[30]

By placing their ritual objects in the contact zone of an international exposition, French Jews endeavored to present an autoethnography that aligned Judaism with French values in ways that would, ideally, be appreciated by their non-Jewish viewers. Strauss and Schornstein risked reducing those objects to exotic curiosities in an environment conducive to capitalizing on the foreignness of Europe's others, wagering in effect that instead they might help their community achieve a more equitable place in French society. Word of their display inspired similar efforts over the subsequent two decades in England and the United States, where other Jews embraced the secularizing machinery of display to enter the contact zones of public exhibitions, world's fairs, and museums. There, they created successive autoethnographies tailored to their times and locales as a means of advancing Jewish interests in predominantly non-Jewish societies.

Notes

1. [David Schornstein], *Collection de M. Strauss. Description des objets d'art religieux hébraïques: Exposés dans les galeries du Trocadéro, à l'Exposition Universelle de 1878*, (Poissy, France: Typographie de S. Lejay et Cie, 1878), XII.
2. Regarding "abstract nation," see the discussion of Leo Pinsker's 1882 pamphlet "Autoemanzipation" in, Ahad Ha-Am, "Pinsker and Political Zionism," in *Ahad Ha-Am: Essays, Letters, Memoirs*, trans. and ed. Leon Simon (Oxford: East and West Library, 1956), 185–86. On "exteriority," see Michel Foucault, *The Archaeology of Knowledge and the Discourse on Language*, trans. A. M. Sheridan Smith (New York: Pantheon Books, 1972), 17. On "corporativism," see Howard M. Sachar, *The Course of Modern Jewish History*, rev. edn. (New York: Vintage Books, 1990), 3–6.
3. On the relations between learned communities, collecting, and knowledge formation, see Paula Findlen, *Possessing Nature: Museums, Collecting, and Scientific Culture in Early Modern Italy* (Berkeley: University of California Press, 1994), especially pp. 129–46. See also, Eilean Hooper-Greenhill, *Museums and the Shaping of Knowledge* (London: Routledge, 1992). Selma Stern, *The Court Jew: A Contribution to the History of the Period of Absolutism*

in Europe, trans. Ralph Weiman (Philadelphia: Jewish Publication Society of America, 1950). Some Jews prospered outside the courts and participated in gentile society. Shmuel Feiner, *The Origins of Jewish Secularization in Eighteenth-Century Europe*, trans. Chaya Naor (Philadelphia: University of Pennsylvania Press, 2010), throughout, and especially pp. xiii, 255. Paul Mendes-Flohr and Jehuda Reinharz, eds., *The Jew in the Modern World: A Documentary History*, 2nd edn. (Oxford: Oxford University Press, 1995), 8.

4. Mendes-Flohr and Reinharz, *Jew in the Modern World*, 4–8; regarding court Jews, see also pp. 18–20. There is extensive literature on the uneven impact of the Enlightenment on Judaism and Jewish emancipation; for example, Jonathan Frankel, "Assimilation and the Jews in Nineteenth-Century Europe: Towards a New Historiography?" in *Assimilation and Community: The Jews in Nineteenth-Century Europe*, ed. Jonathan Frankel and Steven J. Zipperstein (Cambridge, UK: Cambridge University Press, 1992), 1–37 and Pierre Birnbaum and Ira Katznelson, "Emancipation and the Liberal Offer," in *Paths of Emancipation: Jews, States, and Citizenship*, ed. Pierre Birnbaum and Ira Katznelson (Princeton, NJ: Princeton University Press, 1995), 3–36.
5. Mendes-Flohr and Reinharz, eds., *Jew in the Modern World*, 135–36; the second quote is from Sachar, *Course of Modern Jewish History*, 51.
6. Leora Batnitzky, *How Judaism Became a Religion: An Introduction to Modern Jewish Thought* (Princeton, NJ: Princeton University Press, 2011), 186. Sachar, *Modern Jewish History*, 6. On the leading figures and founding of the *Wissenschaft des Judentums*, see Michael A. Meyer, *The Origins of the Modern Jew: Jewish Identity and European Culture in Germany, 1749–1824* (Detroit, MI: Wayne State University Press, 1967), especially pp. 144–82; the latter-most quote is from p. 162. See also, Ismar Schorsch, "The Emergence of Historical Consciousness in Modern Judaism," in *Leo Baeck Institute Yearbook*, vol. 28 (1983), the earlier quote is from p. 415. See, too, Shmuel Feiner, *Haskalah and History: The Emergence of a Modern Jewish Historical Consciousness*, trans. Chaya Naor and Sondra Silverston (Oxford: Littman Library of Jewish Civilization, 2002), 341–48; the second to the last quote is from p. 18.
7. Schorsch, "Emergence of Historical Consciousness," 413; the Fassel quote is from p. 428. Ismar Schorsch, *From Text to Context: The Turn to History in Modern Judaism* (Hanover, NH: University Press of New England, 1994), 1, 154–55; the Graetz and following quotes are from Mendes-Flohr and Reinharz, *The Jew in the Modern World*, 3, 54. See also, Batnitzky, *How Judaism Became a Religion*, 43–46 and Feiner, *Haskalah and History*, 18, 341–48. Also relevant is Shmuel Feiner, *The Jewish Enlightenment*, trans. Chaya Naor (Philadelphia: University of Pennsylvania Press, 2004).
8. Schorsch, "Emergence of Historical Consciousness," 428, 431–32; Birnbaum and Katznelson, "Emancipation and the Liberal Offer," 26.
9. Jay R. Berkowitz, *The Shaping of Jewish Identity in Nineteenth-Century France* (Detroit, MI: Wayne State University Press, 1989), 249. On historical consciousness in relation to the Jewish museum in Vienna's creation

in the mid-1890s, see Klaus Hödl, "The Turning to History of Viennese Jews: Jewish Identity and the Jewish Museum," *Journal of Modern Jewish Studies* 3, no. 1 (March 2004): 19–21 and chapter 2. Feiner, *Origins of Jewish Secularization*, xv, 265n1.

10. Oliver Impey and Arthur MacGregor, eds., *The Origins of Museums: The Cabinet of Curiosities in Sixteenth- and Seventeenth-Century Europe* (Oxford: Oxford University Press, 1985). See also, Paula Findlen, "The Museum: Its Classical Etymology and Renaissance Geneology," *Journal of the History of Collections* 1, no. 1 (1989): 59–78; and Findlen, *Possessing Nature*. For a chronologically broader study, see Krzysztof Pomian, *Collectors and Curiosities: Paris and Venice, 1500–1800*, trans. Elizabeth Wiles-Portier (Cambridge, UK: Polity Press, 1990); Elke Bujok, "Ethnographica in Early Modern Kunstkammern and Their Perception," *Journal of the History of Collections* 21, no. 1 (2009): 17–32. Barbara Kirshenblatt-Gimblett, *Destination Culture: Tourism, Museums, and Heritage* (Berkeley: University of California Press, 1998), 18.
11. Thomas DaCosta Kaufmann, "Remarks on the Collections of Rudolf II: The Kunstkammer as a Form of Representatio," *Art Journal* 38, no. 1 (Fall 1978): 22–28; and Colin B. Bailey, "Conventions of the Eighteenth-Century Cabinet de Tableaux: Blondel d'Azincourt's La Première Idée de la Curiosité," *Art Bulletin* 69, no. 3 (September 1987): 431–47. Jeffrey Abt, et al., "Museum," Grove Art Online, Oxford Art Online, Oxford University Press, accessed October 2015, http://www.oxfordartonline.com/subscriber/article/grove/art/T060530; Andrew McClellan, "Collecting, Classification, and Display," in *The Art Museum from Boulée to Bilbao* (Berkeley: University of California Press, 2008), 107–54. Jeffrey Abt, "The Origins of the Public Museum," in *A Companion to Museum Studies*, ed. Sharon Macdonald (Oxford, UK: Blackwell Publishing, 2006), 115–34.
12. For a still-useful survey, Robert W. Rydell, "The Literature of International Expositions," in *The Books of the Fairs: Materials About World's Fairs, 1834–1916, in the Smithsonian Institution Libraries* (Chicago, IL: American Library Association, 1992), 1–42. Paul Greenhalgh, *Ephemeral Vistas: The Expositions Universelles, Great Exhibitions and World's Fairs, 1851–1939* (Manchester, UK: Manchester University Press, 1988); John P. Burris, *Exhibiting Religion: Colonialism and Spectacle at International Expositions, 1851–1893* (Charlottesville: University Press of Virginia, 2001), 20. See also, Peter H. Hoffenberg, *An Empire on Display: English, Indian, and Australian Exhibitions from the Crystal Palace to the Great War* (Berkeley: University of California Press, 2001). Quotes are from Burris, *Exhibiting Religion*, 1–3, 7–13.
13. On the Paris 1867 exposition, see Burris, *Exhibiting Religion*, 82–83; on its English precedents, pp. 46–49. On ethnological typology applied in an exhibit setting, see William Ryan Chapman, "Arranging Ethnology: A. H. L. F. Pitt Rivers and the Typological Tradition," in *Objects and Others: Essays on Museums and Material Culture*, ed. George W. Stocking Jr. (Madison: University of Wisconsin Press, 1985), 15–48. The Pitt Rivers collection was

inspired by the 1851 Great Exhibition, Burris, *Exhibiting Religion*, 69. On the display of subalterns as urban and exposition entertainments, particularly in Britain, see Sadiah Qureshi, *Peoples on Parade: Exhibitions, Empire, and Anthropology in Nineteenth-Century Britain* (Chicago, IL: University of Chicago Press, 2011); Raymond Corbey, "Ethnographic Showcases, 1870–1930," *Cultural Anthropology* 8, no. 3 (August 1993): 338–69. See also, Kirshenblatt-Gimblett, *Destination Culture*, 34–56. Quotes are from, Burris, *Exhibiting Religion*, xiv, xix, 85.

14. Geoffrey Cantor, *Religion and the Great Exhibition of 1851* (Oxford: Oxford University Press, 2011), 151–57, 204; on Jewish participation, pp. 157–65, including loan of a solitary b'somim (spice box), p. 159. Greenhalgh, *Ephemeral Vistas*, 85. On Jewish press coverage of the fairs, see Kirshenblatt-Gimblett, *Destination Culture*, 80, 84; for an example of writing about Jews the fairs stimulated, see Burris, *Exhibiting Religion*, 56. On the revival of French antisemitism, see David S. Landes, "Two Cheers for Emancipation," in *The Jews in Modern France*, ed. Frances Malino and Bernard Wasserstein (Hanover, NH: University Press of New England, 1985), 295–96. "La race sémitique, comparée à la race indo-européenne, représente réellement une combinaison inférieure de la nature humaine," Ernest Renan, *Histoire générale et système comparé langues Sémitiques*, 3rd edn. (Paris: L'imprimerie Impériale, 1863), 4–5; Edward W. Said, *Orientalism* (New York: Vintage Books, 1979), 123–50; the paraphrase is from p. 142 (but Said's citation of the Renan quote is in error). See also, Shlomo Sand, *On the Nation and the "Jewish People,"* trans. David Fernbach (London: Verso, 2010); and Guy G. Stroumsa, *The Idea of Semitic Monotheism: The Rise and Fall of a Scholarly Myth* (Oxford: Oxford University Press, 2021). On French antisemitism and Jews as "orientals," see Paula E. Hyman, *The Jews of Modern France* (Berkeley: University of California Press, 1998), 73, 95–98. On tribalism, see Todd Endelman, "Jewish Self-Identification and West European Categories of Belonging: From the Enlightenment to World War II," in *Religion or Ethnicity? Jewish Identities in Evolution*, ed. Zvi Gitelman (New Brunswick, NJ: Rutgers University Press, 2009), 119–21. On the "othering" of Jews in Europe and how that overlaps with Orientalism and antisemitism, see Jonathan Boyarin, "The Other Within and the Other Without," in *The Other in Jewish Thought and History: Constructions of Jewish Culture and Identity*, ed. Laurence J. Silberstein and Robert L. Cohn (New York: New York University Press, 1994), 424–52. More recent scholarship regards Orientalism as essentially inseparable from secularism and an aspect of "Christian ambivalence toward the Jews." See Joskowicz and Katz, "Introduction"; and Amnon Raz-Krakotzkin, "Secularism, the Christian Ambivalence Toward the Jews, and the Notion of Exile," in Joskowicz and Katz, *Secularism in Question*, 15, 283–87. Two incidents abroad, the latter of which contributed to the founding of the Paris-based Alliance Israélite Universelle, would also have heightened French Jews' concerns about antisemitism, *Encyclopaedia Judaica*, 2nd edn. (2007), s.v. "Damascus Affair"

(1840) and "Mortara Case" (1858) by Grace Cohen Grossman and Avram Biran (Farmington Hills, MI: Macmillan Reference USA, 2007). See also, Phyllis Cohen Albert, "Ethnicity and Jewish Solidarity in Nineteenth-Century France," in *Mystics, Philosophers, and Politicians: Essays in Jewish Intellectual History in Honor of Alexander Altmann*, ed. Jehuda Reinharz and Daniel Swetschinski (Durham, NC: Duke University Press, 1982), 262–65, 267; Pierre Birnbaum, "Between Social and Political Assimilation: Remarks on the History of Jews in France," in Birnbaum and Katznelson, *Paths of Emancipation*, 94–127; and Natalia Berger, *The Jewish Museum: History and Memory, Identity and Art from Vienna to the Bezalel National Museum, Jerusalem* (Leiden, NL: Brill, 2018), 46–49. Jonathan Boyarin, "The Other Within and the Other Without," 424–52. See also, Jonathan Boyarin, *The Unconverted Self: Jews, Indians, and the Identity of Christian Europe* (Chicago, IL: University of Chicago Press, 2009). Jewish self-perceptions as either aligned with or different from the indigenous peoples of the Americas during the early modern period deepen and complicate the history of this question, Limor Mintz-Manor, "Between Neighbors and Strangers: Representations of the Indigenous People of America and Construction of Jewish Identity in Early Modern Western Europe," *Jewish History* 36, no. 3–4 (December 2022): 265–95. For the last quote, see Kirshenblatt-Gimblett, *Destination Culture*, 104. "Dime museums" were proprietary museums that often featured curiosities and freak shows to lure visitors, Andrea Stulman Dennett, *Weird and Wonderful: The Dime Museum in America* (New York: New York University Press, 1997). It would be good to know more about non-Jewish representations of Jews and Judaism in exhibitions or museums not antisemitic in intent. Even with the best of intentions, misunderstandings could happen; see, for example, Lily Kong, "Re-Presenting the Religious: Nation, Community and Identity in Museums," *Social & Cultural Geography* 6, no. 4 (August 2005): 495–513.

15. Michael Korey, "Displaying Judaica in 18th-Century Central Europe: A Non-Jewish Curiosity," in *Visualizing and Exhibiting Jewish Space and History*, vol. 26, ed. Richard I. Cohen, Studies in Contemporary Jewry (Oxford: Oxford University Press, 2012), 25–54. Yaacov Deutsch, "Polemical Ethnographies: Descriptions of Yom Kippur in the Writings of Christian Hebraists and Jewish Converts to Christianity in Early Modern Europe," in *Hebraica Veritas? Christian Hebraists and the Study of Judaism in Early Modern Europe*, ed. Allison P. Coudert and Jeffrey S. Shoulson (Philadelphia: University of Pennsylvania Press, 2004), 202–4. See also, Jerome Friedman, *The Most Ancient Testimony: Sixteenth-Century Christian Hebraica in the Age of Renaissance Nostalgia* (Athens: Ohio University Press, 1983); and Richard I. Cohen, *Jewish Icons: Art and Society in Modern Europe* (Berkeley: University of California Press, 1998), 10–67.
16. Vivian B. Mann and Richard I. Cohen, eds., *From Court Jews to the Rothschilds: Art, Patronage, and Power, 1600–1800* (New York: The Jewish Museum, 1996); Vivian B. Mann, "Forging Judaica: The Case of the Italian

Majolica Seder Plates," in *Art and Its Uses: The Visual Image and Modern Jewish Society,* vol. 6, ed. Richard I. Cohen, Studies in Contemporary Jewry: An Annual (Oxford: Oxford University Press, 1990), 218–19. The Braunschweig community created a Judaica museum in 1865, the holdings of which are the basis of the Braunschweigisches Landesmuseum's Judaica collection, "Judaica," Braunschweigisches Landesmuseum, accessed July 2013, http://www.3landesmuseen.de/Judaica.755.0.html. See also, Rolf Hagen, "Jüdische Altertümer, Handschriften und Kultgeräte Aus dem Ehemaligen Lande Braunschweig," in *Lessings "Nathan" und Jüdische Emanzipation Im Lande Braunschweig* [exhibition catalogue] ed. Rudolf Vierhaus (Wolfenbüttel, Germany: Lessing-Akademie Wolfenbüttel, 1981), 135–50.

17. The interpretations are from, in order, Jeffrey David Feldman, "Exhibiting Judaica or Jewish Exhibitionism: A Comparison of Two Nineteenth-Century Exhibitions" (master's thesis, Oxford University, 1993), 2–4; Cohen, *Jewish Icons*, 154–58; Kirshenblatt-Gimblett, *Destination Culture*, 81–85.
18. Feldman, "Exhibiting Judaica," 4–6, 28, 38–40; Alain Erlande-Brandenburg, "The Isaac Strauss Collection," in Victor A. Klagsbald, *Jewish Treasures from Paris: From the Collections of the Cluny Museum and the Consistoire* (Jerusalem: Israel Museum, 1982), n.p. See also, Berger, *Jewish Museum*, 29, 37, 41–45, 56–65; Cohen, *Jewish Icons*, 155, 159. The collection was subsequently purchased from Strauss's estate for the Musée de Cluny, but now resides in the Musée d'art et d'histoire du Judaïsme (Paris), "History of the Collections," Musée d'art et d'histoire du Judaïsme, accessed October 2015, http://www.mahj.org/en/2_collections/index.php?niv=1&ssniv=0. See also, Berger, *Jewish Museum*, 56–65. Maurice Samuels, "David Schornstein and the Rise of Jewish Historical Fiction in Nineteenth-Century France," *Jewish Social Studies: History, Culture, Society* n.s. 14, no. 3 (Spring/Summer 2008): 39, 42–43, 45, 56n23.
19. Strauss was a member of the "commission d'admission et de classification" for the tenth section: "Instruments anciens de musique," A.-R. de Liesville, *Coup-d'oeil général sur l'Exposition Historique de l'Art Ancien (Palais Du Trocadéro)* (Paris: Honoré Champion, 1879), 137–38. On Schornstein's role in the Alliance, see N. Leven, *Cinquante ans d'histoire L'Alliance Israélite Universelle*, 2 vols. (Paris: Librairie Félix Alcan, 1911), I: 67–68. See also, André Chouraqui, *L'Alliance Israélite Universelle et la renaissance Juivre contemporaine: 1860–1960* (Paris: Presses Universitaires de France, 1965). Interestingly, the Alliance contributed an exhibit to a later international exposition; Alma Rachel Heckman and Frances Malino, "Packed in Twelve Cases: The Alliance Israélite Universelle and the 1893 Chicago World's Fair," *Jewish Social Studies: History, Culture, Society* n.s. 19, no. 1 (Fall 2012): 53–69. See also, Lisa Moses Leff, *Sacred Bonds of Solidarity: The Rise of Jewish Internationalism in Nineteenth-Century France* (Stanford, CA: Stanford University Press, 2006), 3, 11, 232; Albert, "Ethnicity and Jewish Solidarity," 249, 255, 267; and Richard I. Cohen, "Celebrating Integration in the Public

Sphere in Germany and France" [and "Comment" by Jakob Vogel], in *Jewish Emancipation Reconsidered: The French and German Models*, ed. Michael Brenner, Vicki Caron, and Uri R. Kaufmann (Tübingen, Germany: Mohr Siebeck GmbH & Co., 2003), 67–75. Perhaps an additional motivation was word from Germany of "cries to revoke emancipation and circumscribe [Jewish] freedoms (which became widespread from the 1870s)"; Endelman, "Jewish Self-Identification," 122.

20. Greenhalgh, *Ephemeral Vistas*, 65, 102, 116–17, 218; John Allwood, *The Great Exhibitions* (London: Studio Vista, 1977), 58–64, 180. On the arts at the exposition, Greenhalgh, *Ephemeral Vistas*, 203–4; see also, Elizabeth Gilmore Holt, ed., *The Expanding World of Art, 1874–1902: Universal Expositions and State-Sponsored Fine Art Exhibitions* (New Haven, CT: Yale University Press, 1988), 18–51. Regarding the Algerian and other colonial representations, see Corbey, "Ethnographic Showcases," 341; Zeynep Çelik and Leila Kinney, "Ethnography and Exhibitionism at the Expositions Universelles," *Assemblage* 13 (December 1990): 37.

21. de Liesville, *Coup-d'oeil général sur l'Exposition*, x–xi, 27–28; and Hector Gamilly, "L'exposition des arts rétrospectifs, au Trocadéro," *L'Exposition es Paris: Journal Hebdomadaire* 39 (December 1878): 307–8; this description, based in part on the Strauss collection guide is followed by a double-page supplement containing thirteen images and another image, a few pages later, all extracted from illustrations prepared for the guide. "Baptismal Font Cover," Musée des Beaux-Arts, Rouen, http://mbarouen.fr/en/oeuvres/baptismal-font-cover, accessed December 2015. The other collection belonged to a "Mr. Maillet du Boullay" (perhaps the French architect Charles-Félix Maillet du Boullay, 1795–1878?). There may have been a third collection in the gallery. Gamilly describes two collections but, after his Strauss-collection account, continued: "auxquels il faut joindre la collection de manuscrits précieux, Corans, Bibles hébraïques et orientales de M. le grand rabbin Charleville" (to which must be added the collection of precious manuscripts, Korans, Hebrew and Oriental Bibles of Mr. Chief Rabbi Charleville). Either Strauss acquired the materials from Charleville just prior to the exposition and they were not included in the Strauss guide, or the materials were lent by Charleville. Mahir Charleville (1814–88) was born and studied in Metz and served communities in Lyon, Dijon, and Oran (Algeria) before taking a teaching position at Versailles, where he died. Richard Ayoun, *Typologie d'une carrièr rabbinque: L'exemple de Mahir Charleville*, 2 vols. (Nancy, FR: Presses Universitaires de Nancy, 1993). See also, Richard Ayoun, *Un grand rabbin Français au XIXe siècle Mahir Charleville, 1814–1888* (Paris: Les Éditions du Cerf, 1999); Feldman, "Exhibiting Judaica," 39–40, 48–55; Berger, *Jewish Museum*, 50–51; see also, Kirshenblatt-Gimblett, *Destination Culture*, 79–85.

22. [Schornstein], *Collection de M. Strauss*. Other documentation of the Strauss display is scant; see Gamilly, "L'exposition des arts rétrospectifs" and a one-sentence description in, "Section Française," *L'Exposition Universelle*

de 1878 Illustrée, no. 153 (August 1878): 788. Two other descriptions of the Strauss display relied heavily on Schornstein's guide, Wladimir Stassoff, "L'art israélite a l'exposition universelle," *Archives israélites* 41, no. 5 (1878): 5, 14–15, 21, 30–31, 37, 46; and [David Kaufmann], "Aus der Pariser Weltausstellung," *Israelitische Wochen-Schrift* 9, nos. 38–44 (18 September–30 October 1878): 301, 309, 317, 325, 333, 341, 349. A condensed and reworked version of the latter was published as David Kaufmann, "Etwas von Jüdischer Kunst," in *Gesammelte Schriften*, ed. M. Brann, 3 vols. (Frankfurt, Germany: Kommissions-Verlag von J. Kauffmann, 1908–15), 3:150–53. See also, Feldman, "Exhibiting Judaica," 41–48, 92–93, 97–98; Cohen, *Jewish Icons*, 187–92; and Kirshenblatt-Gimblett, *Destination Culture*, 82–84.

23. [Schornstein], *Collection de M. Strauss*, half-title page, 1–3. Berger, *Jewish Museum*, 51–52.
24. [Schornstein], *Collection de M. Strauss*, 3–7. Beginning earlier in the century, particularly in Germany, there was an effort to conduct Jewish ethnography and folkloristics, which continued throughout this period; Barbara Kirshenblatt-Gimblett, "Problems in the Early History of Jewish Folkloristics," in *Proceedings of the Tenth World Congress of Jewish Studies*, 2 vols. (Jerusalem: World Union of Jewish Studies, 1990), 2:21–31; Phyllis Cohen Albert, "Ethnicity and Jewish Solidarity," 261 (emphasis Albert's). Samuels notes that "juif" began to be viewed by some Jews as a pejorative earlier in the nineteenth century and they argued against its use; Samuels, "David Schornstein": 55n18; and Feldman comments that it was a pejorative for Alsatian Ashkenazi Jews, while "israélites" signified "French citizens who practiced the Mosaic religion"; Feldman, "Exhibiting Judaica," 41 (see also p. 126n82). Albert notes, however, that to a certain extent the two terms were used throughout most of the nineteenth century, much as Schornstein did here, Phyllis Cohen Albert, "Israelite and Jew: How Did Nineteenth-Century French Jews Understand Assimilation?" in *Assimilation and Community: The Jews in Nineteenth-Century Europe*, ed. Jonathan Frankel and Steven J. Zipperstein (Cambridge: Cambridge University Press, 1992), 88–109. See also, Hyman, *Jews of Modern France*, 66. Further, Schornstein seems to use "hébraïque" when refering to objects and language only, and in those situations I use "Hebrew" when translating it. On Schornstein's introduction, see also Berger, *Jewish Museum*, 51–56.
25. [Schornstein], *Collection de M. Strauss*, 7–11.
26. The use of a nine-branch menorah in the synagogue-scene arrangement is misleading, however, because synagogues typically have seven-branch versions evoking the ancient Jerusalem temple's furnishings. In addition to the reader's stand and menorah, the other two objects depicted are listed separately in the Schornstein guide: Nos. 70 (p. 39) and 82 (p. 42). Stephen Bann, "Poetics of the Museum: Lenoir and Du Sommerard," in *The Clothing of Clio* (Cambridge: Cambridge University Press, 1984), 77–92; Kirshenblatt-Gimblett, "Objects of Ethnography," 18–23.
27. [Schornstein], *Collection de M. Strauss*, 15–16.

28. Ivan Karp, "Other Cultures in Museum Perspective," in *Exhibiting Cultures: The Poetics and Politics of Museum Display*, ed. Ivan Karp and Steven D. Lavine (Washington, DC: Smithsonian Institution Press, 1991), 374–78. Samuel J. Spinner, *Jewish Primitivism* (Stanford, CA: Stanford University Press, 2021), 20, 180n17.
29. On the interanimations of Jewish patronage and Christian craft, see Feldman, "Exhibiting Judaica," 37, 45. Kaufmann studied in Germany and taught at the rabbinic seminary in Budapest. Inspired by the exhibit to write what is considered the "first significant scholarly article" on Jewish art, Kaufmann continued to study it and advocate its rigorous investigation in terms that aligned with the still-nascent discipline of art history. His work helped consolidate a relocation of Jewish ritual objects from the realm of religion to art in Jewish society and culture. *Encyclopaedia Judaica*, 2nd edn. (2007), s.v. "David Kaufmann," by Moshe Nahum Zobel. [Kaufmann], "Aus der Pariser Weltausstellung," 301, 309, 317, 325, 333, 341, 349; condensed and reworked as Kaufmann, "Etwas von Jüdischer Kunst," 3:150–53. The "significant scholarly" reference is from Joseph Gutmann, "Is There a Jewish Art?" in *The Visual Dimension: Aspects of Jewish Art*, ed. Clair Moore (Boulder, CO: Westview Press, 1993), 1. On Kaufmann's scholarship, see also Margaret Olin, *The Nation Without Art: Examining Modern Discourses on Jewish Art* (Lincoln: University of Nebraska Press, 2001), 73–98. For a somewhat different response, see Vladimir Stasov's, quoted in Cohen, *Jewish Icons*, 187ff. Stasov (1824–1906) was a Russian music and art critic, James R. Miller, ed., *Encyclopedia of Russian History* (2004), s.v. "Vladimir Vasilievich Stasov," by Elizabeth K. Valkenier. See also, Stassoff, "L'art israélite a l'exposition universelle," 5, 14–15; and related observations on pp. 21, 30–31, 37, 46.
30. David Sorkin, *Jewish Emancipation: A History Across Five Centuries* (Princeton, NJ: Princeton University Press, 2019), 4, 356. Mary Louise Pratt, *Imperial Eyes: Travel Writing and Transculturation*, 2nd edn. (New York: Routledge, 2008), 7–9, 36 (emphasis Pratt's). See also, Mary Louise Pratt, "Arts of the Contact Zone," *Profession* (1991): 33–40. James Clifford, "Museums as Contact Zones," in *Routes: Travel and Translation in the Late Twentieth Century* (Cambridge, MA: Harvard University Press, 1997), 192–93, 204.

Chapter 2

Seeding a Seminary Museum

The display potential of Judaica was explored next in London in the 1887 Anglo-Jewish Historical Exhibition, which included works from the Strauss collection, but in a scheme specific to the needs of English Jewry. It was more fully documented and publicized, accelerating the dissemination of information about the exhibition, especially among English-language speakers abroad. Cyrus Adler, a curator at the Smithsonian Institution and rising star among American Jewish scholars and community leaders, was one of them. He was in a unique position to build on the precedents established in Paris and London when he arranged Smithsonian-sponsored Judaica displays for world's fairs in America and guided Judaica collecting and exhibits at the Smithsonian. Adler's expertise and family connections encouraged the donation of a small Judaica collection "as a suggestion for the establishment of a Jewish museum" at the Jewish Theological Seminary in New York that he later headed.[1]

"Jewish Ecclesiastical Art"

The Anglo-Jewish Historical Exhibition presented manuscripts, books, paintings, engravings, coins, and ritual objects to "promote a knowledge of Anglo-Jewish History" by cultivating greater interest in the materials and "relics" documenting it, to help assure their preservation, and to gauge the extent of such records for completing an exhaustive "History of the Jews in England." Because the Enlightenment and emancipation actualized differently in Great Britain than on the continent, however, a project there was felt necessary by exhibit organizers to publicize and secure the "Englishness of Jewish Modernity in England" among British Jews and non-Jews. The exhibit was scheduled to celebrate the jubilee of Queen Victoria's reign, during which most advances in English Jews' lives were obtained. The exhibition's goals were also linked to recent attempts at

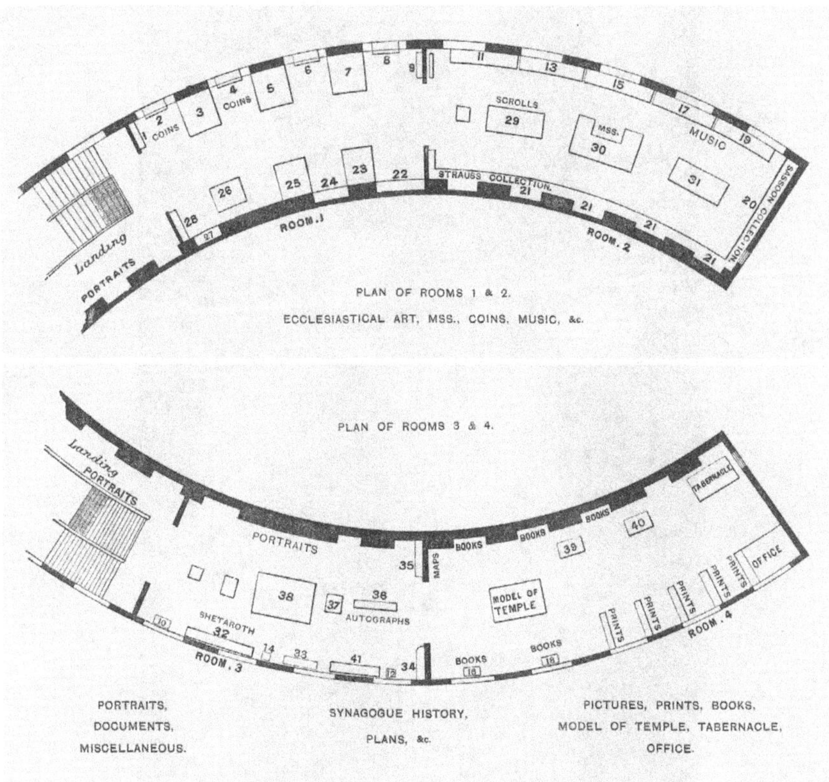

Figure 2.1. Top: "Plan of Rooms 1 & 2"; bottom: "Plan of Rooms 3 & 4," from Joseph Jacobs and Lucien Wolf, eds., *Catalogue of the Anglo-Jewish Historical Exhibition*, Edition de luxe (London: F. Haes, 1888) [unpaginated].

forming an "Anglo-Jewish Historical Society" and a campaign to preserve an early eighteenth-century synagogue—Great Britain's oldest—from demolition. To reach their objectives, the exhibition's organizers assembled over twenty-six hundred works, mostly from private lenders, synagogues, and Jewish organizations. The main site was the Royal Albert Hall, which had been completed just seven years prior. The Public Records Office, the South Kensington Museum (now the Victoria and Albert Museum), and the British Museum complemented the exhibition with displays of more than three hundred pieces of Judaica from their respective collections. The exhibition, which ran from early April through late June 1887, attracted nearly twelve thousand visitors and was accompanied by several activities including organized visits for Jewish school children, a series of scholarly lectures for adults, and a Jewish-music recital.[2]

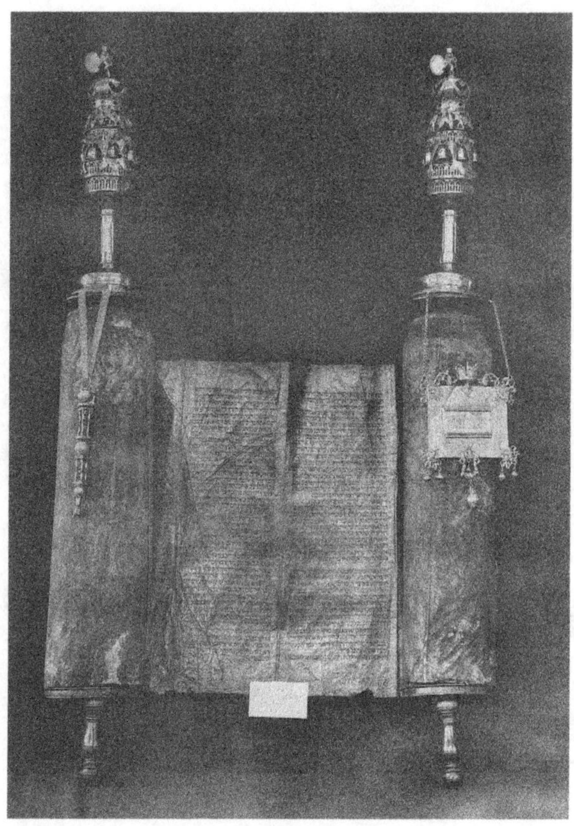

Figure 2.2. "Scroll of Law with Breastplate and Pointer (belonging to Lord Zouch)," from Joseph Jacobs and Lucien Wolf, eds., *Catalogue of the Anglo-Jewish Historical Exhibition*, Edition de luxe (London: F. Haes, 1888), illustration no. 11 (facing catalogue p. 87). Photograph by Frank Haes.

The inclusion of ritual objects, characterized as "Jewish Ecclesiastical Art" by the organizers, was an afterthought. Even so, well over seven hundred were gathered, significantly enhancing the exhibition's visual impact. One of the leaders, Isidore Spielmann (1854–1925), was likely responsible for those and other visual objects' inclusion and the speed with which they were obtained. Though an engineer, he was passionately involved with the visual arts. Spielmann was equally committed to Jewish causes and became the "leading spirit" of the project. His widening art expertise led to his heading subsequent exhibits on Great Britain's behalf at international expositions there, Europe, and America, earning him considerable renown and formal recognition from the crown. While most of the ritual-artifact loans for the Anglo-Jewish exhibition consisted of one

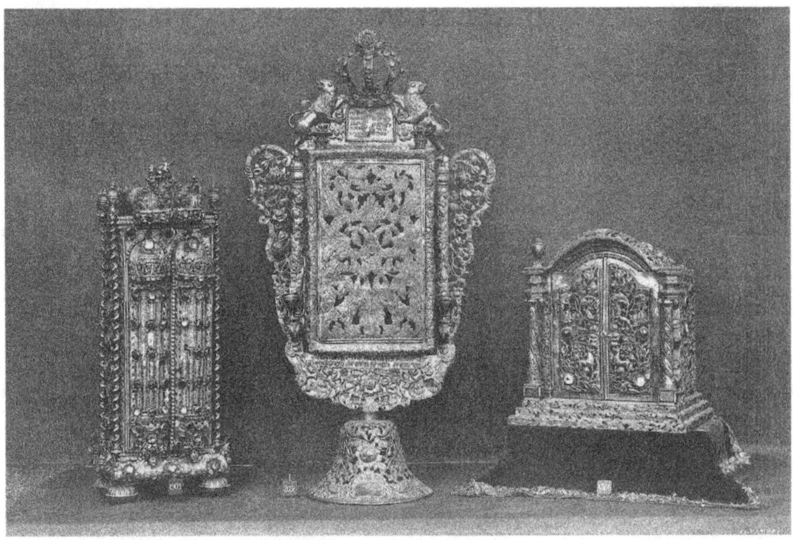

Figure 2.3. "Small Arks for Scrolls of the Law," from Joseph Jacobs and Lucien Wolf, eds., *Catalogue of the Anglo-Jewish Historical Exhibition*, Edition de luxe (London: F. Haes, 1888), illustration no. 9 (facing catalogue p. 85). Photograph by Frank Haes. The Strauss portable ark (see Figure 1.7) is on the left.

or a few objects from individuals, synagogues, and other organizations, they also included about 130 works from Isaac Strauss, his collection apparently enlarged since its Parisian display nine years earlier. The Strauss collection was displayed in "Room 2" of the exhibition (Figure 2.1) while objects from most other lenders were grouped by type (labeled in the floor plans as "Coins," "Scrolls," "Portraits," and "Shetaroth" [Hebrew deeds]) or media (labeled as "Maps," "Books," and "Prints"). Not indicated in the floor plans are three thematic sections set out in the exhibition catalogue: "Synagogue," "Home," and "Personal." Each of those was further subdivided, the synagogue section containing six categories including "Ark and Curtain"; and "Home" with four categories including "Sabbath Requisites."[3]

Installation photographs in the exhibition's "de luxe" catalogue edition convey the scale and complexity of the object displays. Nearly all were presented with numerals corresponding to numbered catalogue entries. Those show that, except for a barely contextualized installation of a Torah scroll, with its accompanying pointer, breastplate, and decorative crowns (Figure 2.2), objects were displayed by type. Accordingly, Strauss's portable ark (Figure 1.7) was presented alongside two from other collections (Figure 2.3); a Strauss breastplate from the Paris exhibit (Figure 1.4) was

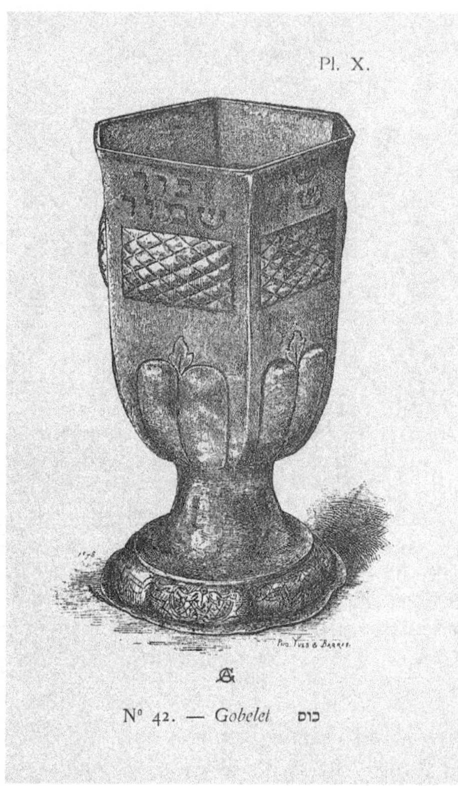

Figure 2.4. Sabbath kiddush cup, Plate X from [David Schornstein], *Collection de M. Strauss. Description des objets d'art religieux hébraïques: Exposés dans les galeries du Trocadéro, à l'Exposition Universelle de 1878* (Poissy, France: Typographie de S. Lejay et Cie, 1878). Rendering by Alfred Gérardin.

displayed with seven others; a Strauss Chanukah menorah (Figure 1.3) was grouped with nine more. In other instances, the stringency of these typological groupings was relaxed, no doubt due to space limitations. Kiddush cups and spice boxes—"Sabbath Requisites"—were intermingled, including a Strauss cup shown in Paris (Figures 2.4 and 2.5). Torah pointers, among which were three Strauss-collection examples (Figure 1.2), were assembled with marriage rings and other smaller objects. The exhibition's overarching typological organization was reinforced in the catalogue section for most of the almost 570 works lent by others than Strauss. In each of its twelve subdivisions, lists of similar objects are prefaced with brief descriptions of the objects' uses in Jewish religious practices. But each item entry emphasizes details about its facture, materials, imagery (when present), provenance (if known), and date. Occasional references

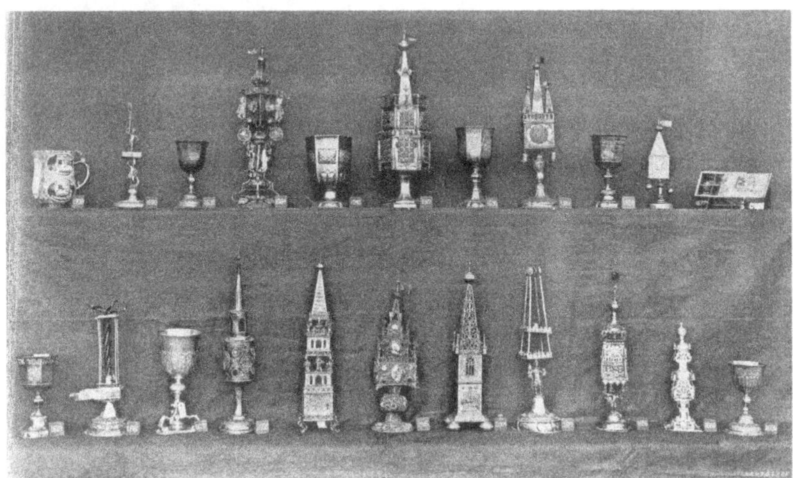

Figure 2.5. "Kiddush Cups, Spice Boxes, &c," from Joseph Jacobs and Lucien Wolf, eds., *Catalogue of the Anglo-Jewish Historical Exhibition*, Edition de luxe (London: F. Haes, 1888), illustration no. 17 (facing catalogue p. 101). Photograph by Frank Haes. The Strauss cup (see Figure 2.4) is on the top row, fifth from left.

to aesthetic concerns such as historical style, decorative genre, or place of origin are also added. Accordingly, the typological presentations of ritual objects invited comparisons based on form, style, workmanship, and material. The secularizing machinery of the display, somewhat reminiscent of natural history or ethnography exhibits that emphasized form over use, is thus evident in the exhibit's installation photographs and item descriptions.[4]

The sheer quantity of the materials abetted an attitude of emotional detachment for Jews and impartiality for non-Jews that resonated with the organizers' goals of advancing research toward and knowledge of Anglo-Jewish history. This stance demanded of Jewish viewers especially a measure of objectivity regarding Judaism, a separation from the fervor of religious practice. For non-Jews the typological exhibits normalized the ritual objects as akin to decorative furnishings one might encounter artfully displayed in London's finer stores. The distancing of historical consciousness is also evident in the exhibition catalogue, where the analytical tone of its narratives is suggestive of ethnologists describing the rituals and artifacts of an exotic tribe. The introduction of the section on ritual objects remarks that not only does each one's origins and use require some explanation, but it is also necessary to elucidate how each one "partake[s] of an artistic character." With guarded language, the authors then offer some blanket observations on "Jewish Ecclesiastical Art," noting, however, that because the subject "has no very distinct existence," it is difficult to detail historically. Instead, it is "more correct to speak of a geography" of Jewish ceremonial art: "For like the jargons of the Hebrew people, their manners and customs, their superstitions and other phenomena of their social life, their art is little more than a composite deposit of the contrastful impressions of a wide geographical dispersion, and of a varied and chequered history." The authors dismissed such considerations as whether the "Hebrew consciousness is normally deficient of artistic sympathies" or has been "dulled" by the Second Commandment injunction against images. Instead, the authors suggested that "the normal artistic capacities" of the Jews "must have been strongly affected, if not altogether transformed" by exile from their biblical homeland and the "perplexing influences of ever-changing surroundings." As a result, Jews were left little time to produce "things of beauty, for the sake of their beauty." The matter-of-fact, detailed explanations of the objects per se align with the authors' larger aim of engendering a historical introduction to Judaism, but one that employs ethnological characterizations, perhaps because most of the objects would have been foreign to non-Jewish viewers and perhaps some Jews as well. On the other hand, the authors include Hebrew words, names, and phrases—much like the Strauss catalogue—in section introductions and occasionally in individual object descriptions, usually but not always with English translations. The use of Hebrew here, as in France, evinces ambiguities about the authors' intentions and sense of their audience. The Hebrew interpolations are reminiscent of methods in scholarly texts wherein textual precision and rigor are prioritized—evident as well in the "Coins and Medals" portion where Latin and Greek words are similarly used.[5]

Though an afterthought, inclusion of Jewish ritual objects was an effective adornment of the exhibition. Pleased by the objects' presence, the organizers—at the conclusion of the catalogue—expanded their list of objectives to include the "advancement of Jewish ecclesiastical art." Enthusiasm over the objects' display also inspired the organizers to suggest their exhibition might elevate beautification of "Jewish domestic worship" in England. Yet, laying the groundwork for a history of English Jews, and assaying the extent of materials for it, remained their highest priority. To that end, they subsequently published three scholarly volumes based on the exhibition's findings. The exhibition's success in generating popular interest and drawing together resources for further study validated the organizers' belief in the potential social, intellectual, and even spiritual value of history for Jews: "To feel oneself a Jew is more nowadays to feel the claims of Jewish history upon our lives," the organizers commented,

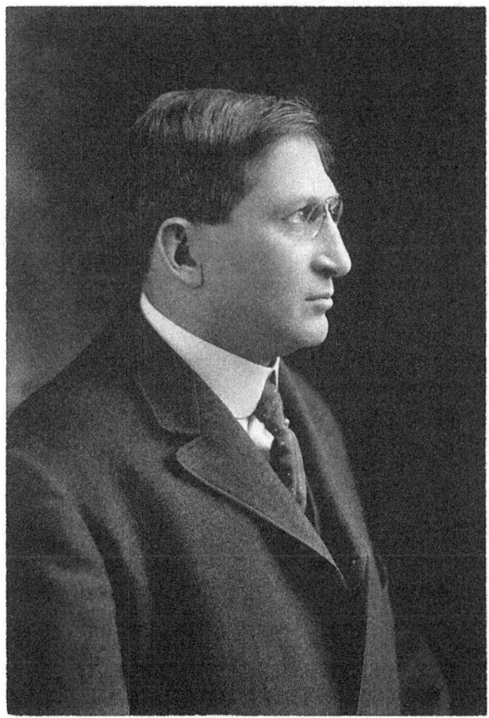

Figure 2.6. Cyrus Adler, ca. 1905. Smithsonian Institution Archives. Image no. SIA_000095_B27_011.

"than to perform the time-honoured Jewish rites." This "hallowing of history" matured with the realization of the organizers' goal of forming the Jewish Historical Society of England. It was envisioned about two decades prior to the exhibition, the success of which encouraged continuation of its work via the society's creation in 1893.[6]

The exhibition also inspired creation of the American Jewish Historical Society. Its origins date to 1886, when Jews began considering ways to mark the quadricentennial of Columbus's landing in North America. One notion was publication of a "memorial history" of American Jews, a project whose underlying aims and means resembled those of the Anglo-Jewish exhibition. Proponents believed the best way to reach their goal was to form an association, and they called upon a rising young talent, Cyrus Adler (Figure 2.6), to organize it. He endorsed their underlying objectives, citing the Anglo-Jewish exhibition's publications, and in 1890 Adler began helping lay the groundwork for its organization, again noting the Anglo-Jewish precedent. The American Jewish Historical Society was launched in 1892, and Adler threw himself into its work, becoming an officer at the founding, later serving as its president, and contributing several articles to its publications, including one on "Americana" at the Anglo-Jewish Exhibition. Adler later allied with one of the London exhibition's organizers, who had since immigrated to New York, to help shepherd an "American Jewish Historical Exhibition" that never materialized.[7]

Judaica for a National Museum

Adler (1863–1940) was not yet thirty at the time, but this and other accomplishments marked him as a "scholar-doer" in American Jewish circles. In subsequent decades, there were few significant cultural projects in Jewish America that did not involve him. It was in the spheres of Jewish research, higher education for rabbis and teachers, and community service that he was most influential, doing "more than anyone before or after . . . to bring Jewish scholarship to America and to make American Jewry culturally independent." An indefatigable and principled impresario among fellow Jews, Adler felt there were few problems that could not be solved by drawing together and organizing people into collective action. A rigorous intellectual, scrupulous administrator, inspiring fundraiser, and religiously observant Jew, he readily earned the trust of many. Yet Adler was also reserved, serious, and intensely private, lending to his correspondence a businesslike coolness that belied his personal warmth. Born in Arkansas and raised in Philadelphia, Adler completed a baccalaureate degree at the University of Pennsylvania while also pursuing private Hebrew-language and Jewish textual studies with Philadelphia rabbis. He continued at Johns Hopkins University, building on previous language training—which included Aramaic and German—with studies in Assyrian, Syriac, Ethiopic, Sanskrit, comparative Indo-European philology, and Arabic. There, Adler became the first person to earn a Semitics doctorate at an American university, specifically in Assyriology. His graduate studies, guided by the prominent German-born Assyriologist Paul Haupt (1858–1926), were essentially philological. At the time, Haupt aspired to conduct archaeological expeditions to support his research and teaching program. Rather than erect the facilities needed to house and perhaps display ancient Near Eastern finds at Johns Hopkins, however—as colleagues at other American universities were doing—Haupt enlisted the Smithsonian Institution in nearby Washington, DC, for a collaborative venture. One result was the Smithsonian's appointment, in 1888, of Haupt and Adler as "honorary curator" and "honorary assistant curator," respectively, to create a Section of Oriental Antiquities at the museum. Although little came of the collaboration, it launched Adler on a career in museum work at the Smithsonian alongside his teaching at Johns Hopkins, where he began lecturing while still a graduate student and joined the full-time faculty in 1888. Adler entered the Smithsonian's ranks in 1889 as an assistant curator of Middle Eastern antiquities. In 1892, he was appointed its librarian while continuing with his curatorial duties and, in 1902, he rose to the Smithsonian's second-ranking position, assistant secretary, retaining it until he left museum work in 1908.[8]

Adler soon mastered the curatorial fundamentals of organizing exhibitions, pursuing acquisitions, and writing scholarly reports. At the time, the Smithsonian was supplying displays for world's fairs in the United States and afterward absorbing objects acquired for them into the museum's permanent collection. Adler cut his teeth on a biblical archaeology exhibit for the 1888 Centennial Exposition of the Ohio Valley, in Cincinnati, and on the Smithsonian's first permanent display of Middle Eastern antiquities the following year. He then organized a dual-faceted contribution to the 1893 World's Columbian Exposition, in Chicago: a display of objects he acquired or borrowed and "foreign villages" he recruited that were staffed by Middle Eastern sponsors. Adler arranged a large display for the 1895 Cotton States International Exhibition in Atlanta and two years later a smaller one for the Tennessee Centennial Exposition in Nashville. In conformance with Smithsonian practices, and drawing on his training in Semitics, Adler used the antiquities he curated to "illustrate ideas" they embodied rather than focusing on materials and craftsmanship. Considering them to be like specimens in the Smithsonian's natural science departments, Adler wanted to present objects as impartially arranged evidence in the field of biblical archaeology—that is, as "object lessons" on the origins of Western religions, but devoid of sectarian bias and theological dogma. He believed knowledge of religious history was one of the last topics to "profit by the awakened impulse" gained from exhibitions and sought effective ways to enlighten viewers with religious artifact displays.

Though similar works were already in many museum collections, they were typically presented as ethnographic specimens or works of art. In creating the Smithsonian's collection, Adler thought the key to "popular education" lay in "imparting the unknown in terms of the known." Successful displays should foster a viewer's understanding of foreign religions by analogizing them with the viewer's own religious beliefs and practices. "Just as the scientific investigator obtains results by the comparison of facts and phenomena," Adler declared, so too the museum visitor

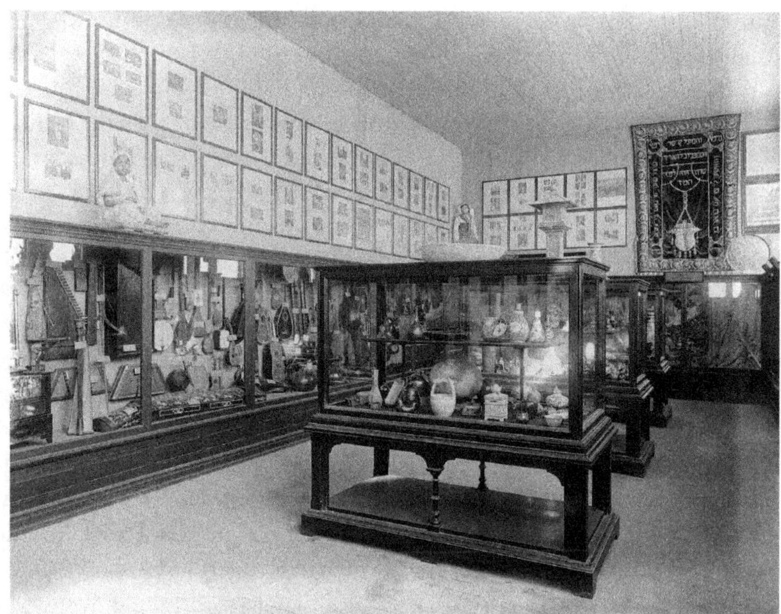

Figure 2.7. Installation view of Smithsonian Institution display on "religious ceremonials" at the World's Columbian Exposition in Chicago, 1893. Smithsonian Institution Archives. Image no. SIA_000095_B64_F08_016. "Ceremonials of the Jewish Religion" are along the far wall. The large Torah ark curtain in the upper right-hand corner is in the National Museum of Natural History, Smithsonian Institution (cat. no. 154758). Several images mounted on the wall above the display cases on the left are from the *Catalogue of the Anglo-Jewish Historical Exhibition*, including ones reproduced earlier in this chapter: Figure 2.5 (top row, second from left); and Figure 2.3 (top row, second from right).

would benefit from "comparing familiar objects with those brought to his knowledge for the first time." That required assembling artifacts representing the history of many religions, ancient and modern, including: "Assyro-Babylonian, Jewish, Oriental Christian, Mohammedan, Greek, and Roman." Adler's methodology was in step with scholarly thinking in European and American universities where the history of religions and comparative religious studies were consolidating as specific disciplinary formations, academic programs, and scholarly associations. His contribution was helping translate those fields of study into exhibition methods.[9]

Adler thought of religion as comprised of beliefs, and rituals associated with those beliefs, which he characterized respectively as "creed" and "cult." For him, creed is made up of concepts, narratives, theologies, and values that cannot easily be presented via exhibits. Cult, on the other hand, consists of communal worship and personal observances employing ritual objects, tangible evidence that *can* be readily displayed. In 1889, Adler assembled a Smithsonian collection illustrating a "comparative history of religion," including Judaism. His approach informed the museum's display at the Chicago exposition in 1893 (Figure 2.7), and Adler subsequently established the Smithsonian's Section of Religious Ceremonial Objects, which evolved into the Division of Historic Religions by 1904. In leading exhibit viewers through "the unknown in the terms of the known," Adler structured his comparative-religion displays by beginning with Judaism, Christianity, and Islam—presented in that order because it was the sequence of "their respective establishments"—followed by presumably less-familiar religions such as Buddhism and Hinduism. Underlying his approach may also have been an unannounced desire to combat antisemitism by persuading fellow citizens that although Jews shared a faith, they did not comprise a race. Placing Judaism alongside Christianity, Islam, and other religions might help assure fellow Americans that Jewish difference was defined only by a not-so-different belief system. Regardless of its basis, Adler's method justified the acquisition of Judaica for the Smithsonian and, by 1908, he could claim its collection of "Jewish ceremonial objects . . . is the largest and most complete, indeed one of the best anywhere." Adler's most significant accomplishment, however, lay in advocating religious tolerance by presenting many religions respectfully and as understood by their adherents. He implicitly assured Judaism's place among the major religious traditions to be studied by highlighting its centrality in the religious foundations of Western civilization.[10]

The Museum of Jewish Ceremonial and Historical Objects

Between 1888 and 1892, while still employed by the Smithsonian, Adler commuted weekly to teach at the Jewish Theological Seminary in New York. The founding head, Sabato Morais (1823–97), a rabbi and Hebrew teacher, was Adler's most valued mentor from his Philadelphia youth. They remained close, and not long after the seminary's opening in 1887 Adler, who participated in its founding and helped assure its curriculum was current, offered gratis a biblical archaeology class. The seminary, a product of the Jewish enlightenment and emancipation, was established to furnish a middle ground between the strict religiosity of recent Eastern European immigrants—which consolidated into modern Orthodox Judaism—and the liberalizing ideology of American Jews eager to assimilate—which seeded the formation of Reform Judaism. The founders believed neither extreme met "the challenge that America—with its separation of church and state, democracy, and modern secularism—offered to Judaism." Adler's contribution, informed by his training as an American-born-and-trained Semitics scholar, fit the seminary's curriculum, which required its students to earn degrees at nearby secular universities, such as Columbia or the City College of New York, alongside their rabbinic studies. Adler's "scientific" approach, embodied in his biblical archaeology course, juxtaposed with other courses on the Old Testament as divine scripture, reinforced the seminary's priority of "marrying western scholarship with Jewish learning."[11]

The seminary foundered, however, and after Morais died Adler helped lead its revitalization, which entailed its reincorporation with a new board of trustees based on "entire secularity" and without rabbis, to avoid the "internecine politics and policies" of congregations. The revivified institution, the Jewish Theological Seminary of America, was launched in 1902 and Adler served as the new board's chair until 1905. It continued its predecessor's underlying principles by avoiding denominational affiliations. The orthodox were still battling reformers, and the seminary's leaders hoped to play an "ecumenical" role by fostering cooperation between the two factions, a stance Adler characterized as "non-partisan Judaism." The faculty was rebuilt with leading scholars headed by Romanian-born Rabbi Solomon Schechter (1847–1915), a towering figure in Talmudic studies renowned for his research on thousands of medieval texts discovered in a Cairo synagogue that vastly expanded knowledge of early Judaism. Schechter had a free hand in assembling the seminary's faculty and he recruited several brilliant scholars, most European who—like him—were adherents of the *Wissenschaft des Judentums*. Collectively, they applied its principles to Judaic studies, transforming the seminary into an intellectual powerhouse and laying the foundations for Jewish scholarship in America. One of them, Alexander Marx (1878–1953), taught Jewish history while heading the seminary's library (Figure 2.8). Born in Germany and having acquired both rabbinic ordination and a doctorate in history, Marx brought to his work a beguiling mix of piety and rigorous learning. His scholarship reflected an interest in sociocultural history intertwined with librarianship, especially Marx's acquisition of primary sources—manuscripts and rare books—building the seminary's holdings into an internationally renowned repository for advanced Judaic research. He published fundamental works, based on those primary sources, in history, historiography, and bibliography while also earning the admiration of generations of students for his geniality, intellectual generosity, and personal warmth; and esteemed by colleagues for his tactfulness, scholarly

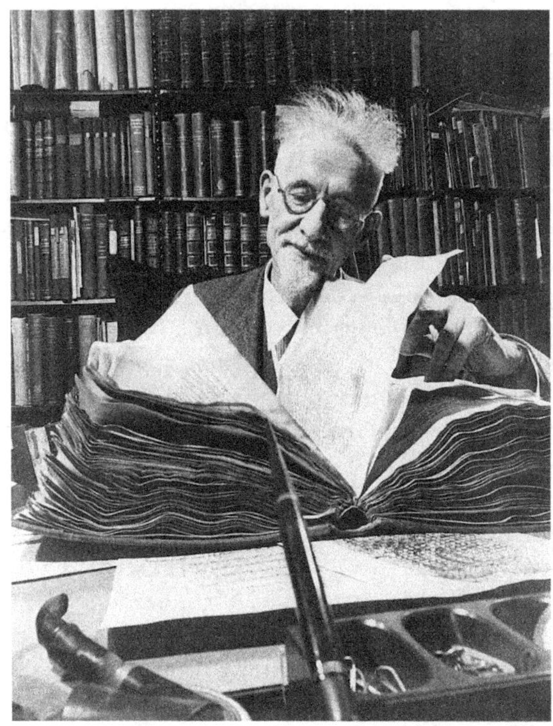

Figure 2.8. Alexander Marx, September 1952. Photograph by Gjon Mili. Gjon Mili/The LIFE Collection/Shutterstock. Courtesy of the Leo Baeck Institute. F 87973.

precision, and tireless service—qualities that led to his being honored with two festschrifts during his lifetime. At the time the seminary had a building in midtown Manhattan, a large and congested five-story brownstone adapted for classrooms, a library, lecture hall, and dormitories. But the new board decided to move with its midtown neighbor, Columbia University, to the upper west side and erect larger accommodations there. The seminary had a modest book collection when Marx arrived, but its new building, dedicated in April 1903 and promptly characterized as "Judaism's Home of Science," allowed for the more extensive library the faculty's scholarly ambitions now demanded.[12]

Mayer Sulzberger (1843–1923), in close collaboration with Marx, accelerated the library's growth with donations of books, manuscripts, and cash, believing that "a great library was indispensable" for the seminary's work. A distinguished jurist and amateur scholar, Sulzberger was a leader of the "Philadelphia Group" of visionary, activist Jews—including Adler—who created or helped form a number of national Jewish institutions that continue to this day: the American Jewish Historical Society, the American Jewish Committee, the Jewish Publication Society, the seminary in both its iterations, and several Philadelphia entities, laying the foundation for an "American Jewish Culture." Sulzberger, along with his father David Sulzberger, also gave Judaica to the Smithsonian Institution during Adler's tenure. Their connections went beyond mutual interests, however. David Sulzberger was Adler's uncle and helped raise him after his father's death. Mayer Sulzberger, as Adler's cousin and one-time housemate, grew into a close collaborator on many projects and became a knowledgeable bibliophile who assembled a formidable library of rare Jewish books and manuscripts. Adler apparently enlisted both Sulzbergers in helping establish the Smithsonian's Judaica collection, and between 1889 and 1900 they donated over twenty objects, several of which remain there to this day.[13]

A year after the seminary dedicated its new building, in 1904, Mayer Sulzberger donated about eight thousand books and manuscripts, to which he added "a number" of ritual objects "to serve as a suggestion for the establishment of a Jewish museum in connection with the Library." His subsequent contributions included more objects, and he periodically corresponded with Marx about mounting displays in the library despite its unsuitability for exhibits and lack of glass cases to protect the objects. Adler rarely advised on the collection's development during its early years beyond cultivating an interest in Judaica collecting among family and friends. Then, too, its small size, want of a dedicated space, and modest uses—in comparison to the Smithsonian—would hardly have benefited from his expertise. Although Adler did not publicly address the collection's formation or display during its nascence, a few years prior to Sulzberger's gift, he commented in another context that a "museum is, above all other agencies, the most valuable ally of the library. It awakens the visitor to a new interest in objects which he would never take up in books, and it serves to vivify the impressions already received from the printed word."[14]

Following Schechter's death in 1915, Adler became the seminary's acting president. By that point, he had left the Smithsonian to, in 1908, become president of the newly created doctoral-only Dropsie College in Philadelphia. It was another Judaic studies institution, yet without the seminary's rabbinic training or theological purposes. Adler remained with the seminary, however, keeping his home in Philadelphia, and traveling to New York as needed, assuming someone else would soon replace him. That arrangement persisted, even after Adler's seminary post eventually became permanent in 1924, and he continued to lead Dropsie, live in Philadelphia, and commute to New York, now twice a week, maintaining

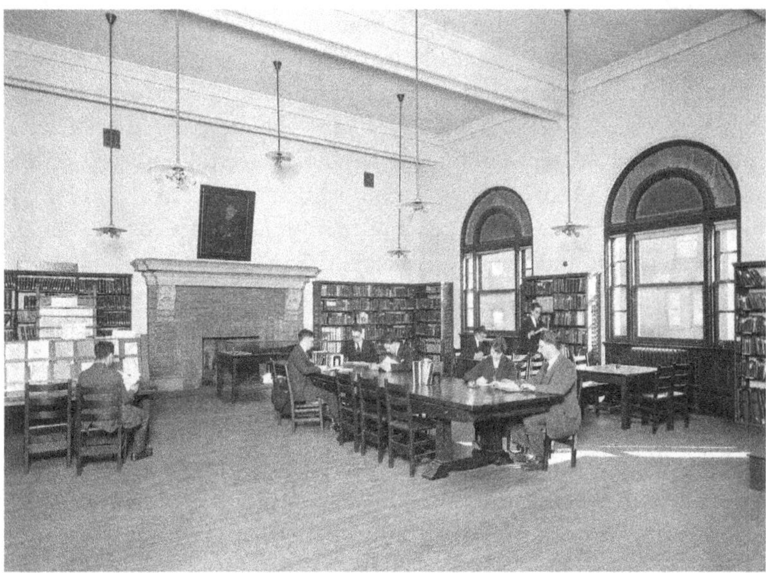

Figure 2.9. Library reading room on the third floor of the Seminary's first building on West 123rd Street, ca. early 1920s. One of the table display cases is by the fireplace. View by Peyser and Patzig Industrial Photographers. Courtesy of the Library of the Jewish Theological Seminary.

that schedule for the rest of his life. The seminary faculty regarded him as a "stepparent," both because of his regular absences and the fact that Adler was neither a rabbi nor an active scholar. Despite that, Adler forged a close working relationship with Marx, possibly because of his experience as Smithsonian librarian; and he adroitly steered the seminary through financial setbacks in the early 1920s and the Depression, eventually growing its endowment, faculty, student body, and campus. Adler prioritized the "Americanization" of Judaism but without compromising his professional and personal devotion to religious observance. He regarded Judaism as "first and foremost" a religion and was offended by the notion of an "ethnic Judaism" devoid of religious practice. Ultimately a pragmatist, however, he was "wary of ideologies and idealogues, whether political or religious" and worked to build and sustain coalitions. Adler cultivated popular support and donations for the seminary from a broad swath of the Jewish community, often by promoting the institution's activities with free lectures, publicity releases, and broadcasts of seminary programs over the new medium of radio.[15]

The seminary's artifacts collection continued to grow during the 1910s and 1920s with donations from a handful of individuals led by Sulzberger.

Some objects were displayed during temporary, usually thematic exhibits Marx arranged in the library's reading and manuscript rooms. The seminary continued to lack appropriate display furnishings, however, and later purchased some glass table and vertical cases (Figure 2.9). These efforts typically involved Adler's gentle nudging and respectful guidance, often against the background of more pressing library concerns. Already by 1906, the library's shelves were "taxed to their full capacity" by the quickening pace of book and manuscript acquisitions—one among many of the seminary's growing pains that included overcrowded classrooms and lack of student amenities. The seminary trustees and Adler considered expansion plans that he aired in a pair of 1923 addresses. In one, priority was given to a much larger library augmented with "a Museum which, though not extensive will . . . be one of distinction." In the other address, after listing "bare necessities," Adler added "the expense of a Museum of which we already have the nucleus."[16]

A year later, Mortimer Schiff (1877–1931) and Felix M. Warburg (1871–1937) pledged $215,000 to erect a new library building that included a museum space. Schiff, like his father, Jacob Schiff, was a New York financier and philanthropist who donated about eleven hundred prints to the seminary in 1921. Warburg, a German-born scion of the Warburg banking dynasty, was a New York investment banker and philanthropic "one-man social welfare agency." Several years earlier, he donated a few of the seminary's display cases, and Warburg followed his building pledge with a gift of some silver ritual objects. His philanthropy was far broader than the Schiffs' in its impact, addressing childrens' health and education across a range of institutions and groups as well as several Jewish interests at home and abroad. Both were among the "Crowd," a constellation of Jewish families in New York linked by marital, social, and business relations that spanned generations. Warburg and Schiff were linked by marriage as well as commerce. The former worked in Jacob Schiff's banking firm, and his wife—Frieda Schiff Warburg—was Schiff's daughter. Jacob Schiff (1847–1920), also German born, was one of the seminary's leading backers in its first iteration, and he worked closely with Adler and others to revivify it. Among the elder Schiff's many philanthropic pursuits was an interest in Semitic studies. He served on a Harvard University advisory committee beginning in 1889, contributed to its Semitics program, and donated the university's Semitic Museum building, which opened in 1903. Although Adler's role in the cultivation of Schiff's Semitics and museum philanthropies is uncertain, the former's participation in the Harvard museum's opening ceremony suggests it became substantial. During that period, Felix Warburg entered the world of art collecting by acquiring masterpieces in the history of Western printmaking, works that were later donated to the Metropolitan Museum of Art and Vassar College; and he followed his father-in-law's museum philanthropy by supporting the Fogg Art Museum at Harvard.[17]

A year after the Schiff-Warburg building gift, Warburg encouraged the purchase of a major Judaica collection for the seminary. Assembled by Hadji Ephraim Benguiat (ca. 1852–1918), a Turkish-born antiquities dealer who immigrated to Boston before the turn of the century, the collection came to Adler's attention in the 1890s while gathering objects for the Smithsonian's Columbian Exposition display. Benguiat loaned more than forty works and, at Adler's behest, subsequently placed the collection on long-term loan with the Smithsonian, adding objects to it until a couple of years before his death. The collection, which had grown to over sixty objects by then, remained there until 1924, when, with Warburg's backing, the seminary purchased it from Benguiat's heirs. Even though the collection was placed in storage until display space was created for it, Adler regarded its acquisition as the actual "origin of our . . . charming little Museum." The museum was later described as Warburg's "brainchild," suggesting his role went beyond funding a dedicated space and worthwhile objects for it. Although, according to A. S. W. Rosenbach, Adler was "enthusiastic over the project," apparently it was Warburg's passion that persuaded Adler to elevate the museum as a seminary priority. Rosenbach (1876–1952), a prominent book dealer who—on behalf of Benguiat's heirs—handled the collection's sale to the seminary, was also president of the American Jewish Historical Society, which enjoyed accommodations at the seminary after the Society's founding.[18]

The seminary expansion, including a new library, opened in 1930. The Jacob H. Schiff Memorial Library, its name designated by Mortimer Schiff and Warburg, contained a gallery on its first floor with a smaller adjoining room for the American Jewish Historical Society. Together, they were called the "Museum of Jewish Ceremonial and Historical Objects," but "and Historical" was soon dropped, a casual abridgment reflecting the museum's origins with ritual artifacts. Its main gallery was a low-ceilinged, oblong room with usable wall space limited by large windows lining the longest sides. The walls were covered with "exhibition cloth" to facilitate temporary as well as permanent exhibits, the coarse fabric designed to camouflage holes in the walls after display changes. Administratively, the museum was a unit within the library and Marx, in his capacity as head librarian, supervised it. With the assistance of a rabbinic "attendant," he arranged the inaugural installation—which drew extensively from the Benguiat collection, prepared individual item labels,

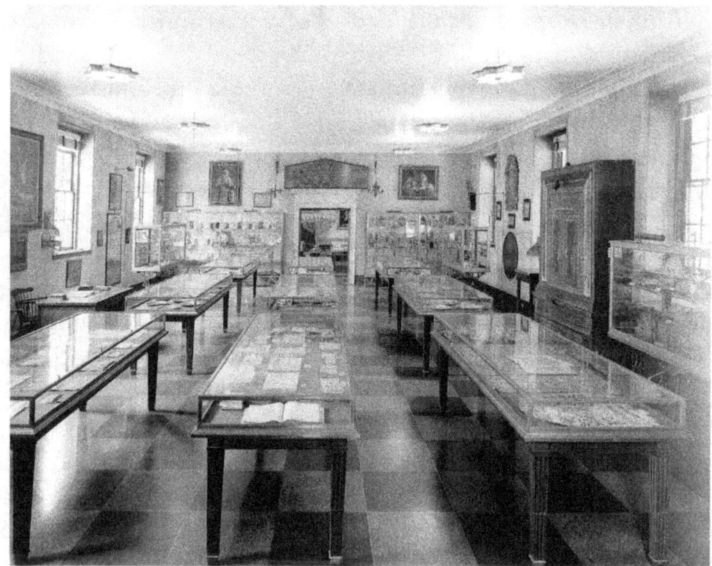

Figure 2.10. Museum of Jewish Ceremonial and Historical Objects, ca. early 1940s. The gallery of the American Jewish Historical Society is visible through the doorway on the far wall. Courtesy of the Library of the Jewish Theological Seminary.

and compiled a checklist of the works added to the Benguiat collection after a Smithsonian catalogue of it was issued in 1899. At the time of its public opening in November 1931, the museum was crowded with 630 objects presented in eighteen glass cases and on adjacent walls (Figure 2.10). A majority, being ritual artifacts, was apportioned among the display cases by function: Torah pointers, Passover plates, Chanukah menorahs, circumcision sets, and so forth. There was also a case of ninety ancient "Palestinian" coins and lamps, and about 140 incunabula, illuminated manuscripts, and decorative book bindings from the library.[19]

The museum was neither the first nor the last devoted to Judaica to be established during this period. Around 1895–1896, one was created in Vienna, another was established in Prague in 1906, and in 1915 one was founded in Budapest and the forerunner of yet another in London. There were others in Berlin, Danzig (Gdańsk), and Warsaw too. Over time, with the exception of the London museum, all the European institutions either dissipated for various reasons or were destroyed by the Nazis—a few partially reconstituted as repositories or memorials after the Second World War. Yet another institution, whose beginnings closely paralleled those of the Museum of Jewish Ceremonial Objects, was established in 1913 at Hebrew Union College—the seminary of Reform Judaism—in

Cincinnati, Ohio, initially as a feature within that seminary's library. Its collections grew and acquired a separate identity and space as the Union Museum, but was relocated to the seminary's West Coast campus and renamed the Skirball Museum. In 1996, it was absorbed into the new, more expansive Skirball Cultural Center. The largest and most extensive Judaica collection began in the early 1900s as an offshoot of the Bezalel Academy of Art and Design, located in Jerusalem. Over time, its collections expanded and found a separate home and identity as the Bezalel National Museum through its association with the Zionist movement. Following the establishment of the State of Israel in 1948, the now even-larger collection was incorporated into the Israel Museum campus of buildings featuring objects from antiquity to contemporary art. It embraced the whole of Jewish material culture that was represented to a greater or lesser extent by the other institutions, including ritual objects, folk arts and crafts, and modern design. The vicissitudes of these museums as a whole reflect Jewish history in Europe, America, and the land of Israel over the course of the twentieth century. As with its peer institutions, the future of the Museum of Jewish Ceremonial Objects depended on a host of circumstances, some of which were comparable to those of the other museums and some unique to its institutional parent, the sociocultural setting of New York, and the nature of the city's Jewish community.[20]

After its inaugural exhibition, the museum drifted into a pattern of using vertical cases for ritual objects, undoubtedly because they readily accommodated the shapes and sizes of varied three-dimensional works; and reserving horizontal cases for books, manuscripts, and other forms of written material because such texts efficiently resided—and were more easily read—in the shallow confines of table-like vitrines. Under Marx's leadership, the preponderance of works presented in temporary exhibits, often to mark holidays and other special occasions, were texts from the library's increasingly vast holdings. As a result, the horizontal cases became the museum's main venue for temporary exhibits while the vertical cases along the gallery walls became by default the seldom-changed province of mostly ritual objects and other three-dimensional artifacts. The theme of objects displayed in the vertical cases and adjacent walls was "the continuity of Jewish history," meaning the survival of religious traditions over nearly two millennia. It was illustrated with ancient clay lamps from the era of the Old Testament Book of Judges, proceeded through the Middle Ages with manuscript fragments, letters, and a mid-thirteenth century ark; continued into the Renaissance and the beginning of printing with incunabula; detoured to East Asia via inscription rubbings and a nineteenth-century ark fashioned in Japan; and culminated with a variety of objects and texts—as well as paintings, drawings, and prints depicting Jewish figures and subjects—from the 1700s to the present day. Rosenbach believed anyone curious about "Jewish Antiquities, in the Arts and Crafts, in the things that touch on Jewish life generally" would be rewarded by visiting the seminary's "small and gracious Museum." The museum's visibility and public access was hindered, however, by its being just a room tucked away in a large building on a seminary campus. It was unlike independent and university-based museums in America that by then were erected as separate buildings that captured the attention of passersby with imposing, purpose-built, richly ornamented structures. As a new entity in New York's cultural landscape, enclosed within a seminary's walls, the Museum of Jewish Ceremonial Objects was ill-positioned to be noticed by city residents.[21]

Rosenbach later recalled that several seminary officials and trustees, particularly Adler, Schiff, and Warburg, thought of the museum as "one of the pillars of popular education." A "teaching Museum," they agreed, should be "based on the well known dictum that 'A good educational Museum consists of a series of carefully prepared labels with well selected specimens attached.'" The dictum originated with Adler's Smithsonian colleague George Brown Goode (1851–96), who directed the National Museum and worked with Adler on several Smithsonian projects. Goode's pronouncement was indeed familiar among museum professionals at the time, and Rosenbach probably learned it from Adler who quoted it in his own writings. "Popular education" embraced the public, and from the moment of the museum's inception its founders thought of it as a service to the population outside the seminary's walls, non-Jews and Jews alike. The museum's other ostensible purpose, serving the research and teaching of seminary faculty, did not figure in its collection development or exhibit programming. Dedicated to training rabbis and others headed for careers in congregational service, the faculty had little need for the types of university-based, research-and-pedagogy museums Schiff and Warburg supported at Harvard. Then, too, Judaic studies as a scholarly discipline outside the ambit of rabbinic training was just coalescing in European and American universities. Scholarly studies of Jewish ritual objects and historical artifacts had barely advanced beyond cataloging.[22]

Finding an Audience

About a month after the museum's opening, Marx appointed Paul Romanoff to be its curator on Adler's recommendation. Romanoff (1898–1943) was born in Russia and studied surveying in Vilna, architecture at the

University of Moscow, topography at the University of Berlin, and geology at the Sorbonne in Paris. In 1920, he moved to Palestine, where he worked in Jerusalem's public works department for nearly a decade rendering maps and plans. During the 1920s, Romanoff also pursued Jewish religious studies at Hebrew University and privately, earning rabbinic ordination, and he served as the Jewish Archaeological Society's architectural consultant. He immigrated to America in 1928 for a two-year Dropsie College fellowship and, after completing a doctorate there in 1930, obtained a year-long Yale University fellowship in semitics. Romanoff's formal studies, though broad, did not prepare him to curate a collection of Judaica. Nor was he conversant with museum education, outreach, and public relations—all areas of increasing professionalization in American museums. But Adler wanted to help a Dropsie alum in an era of desperate financial need because the Depression in America and rising tensions in Palestine left Romanoff with few good alternatives. Adler told Romanoff, however, that the appointment was to be of very short duration due to the seminary's Depression-ravaged finances. He thought the arrangement would be mutually agreeable because it supported Romanoff as he transitioned into an archaeology career without obligating him or the seminary to a commitment neither wished to sustain. But Adler was also guarded about Romanoff, perceiving the latter as capricious, hopping from one educational pursuit or vocation to another without building toward a durable career. Romanoff, for his part, was an eager learner, anxious to please, and privately hopeful his labors would earn him a secure job at the museum. There was a misalignment of expectations among all involved and, as a result, because Adler and Marx assumed Romanoff would soon find a better position, he entered the museum curatorship with no prospects and little mentoring.[23]

Romanoff's appointment was split, with about one-third in the library cataloging books and the balance in the museum looking after visitors and helping cultivate the interest of outside educational institutions and the public. He zealously applied himself to these tasks—though he could hardly escape them at the outset because, single at the time, he was living and dining in a seminary dorm, paying two-thirds of his salary for the accommodations. Marx assisted with public relations by example and by arranging external contacts. Romanoff caught on quickly, but he wanted to perform curatorial tasks too, including acquisitions, organizing temporary exhibitions, and lecturing about the collections. He sought, for example, Marx's permission to solicit inherited "objects of Jewish interest," arguing they "must and could be saved" lest the heirs, lacking other alternatives, discard such treasures. On his initiative and apparently without institutional backing, Romanoff coupled a vacation in Palestine with a side trip through Poland to scout "Ancient Ceremonial Treasures" for the museum. These initiatives were gently rebuffed by Marx who preferred to handle them personally, especially if objects in question were to be displayed in the museum as part of a donor-cultivation process.[24]

At the beginning of his tenure, Romanoff unsuccessfully proposed temporary exhibits, but those initiatives tapered off and Marx did not invite more. The outcome of one Romanoff proposal is telling. During fall 1932, in anticipation of a forthcoming Chanukah holiday, he recommended an exhibit of menorahs. The project took five years to materialize, however, and only then with the assistance of an outside consultant. For this and many other exhibits, Romanoff's role amounted to little more than record-keeping after the fact (Figure 2.11). Exhibit organization, label writing, and installation, as well the production of checklists and catalogues, were often handled by others—usually Marx's secretary, Anna Kleban (1899–1990)—and occasionally outside specialists under Marx's supervision. Despite this cumbersome arrangement, between 1932 and 1945, the museum presented forty-five exhibits, about three a year. Because of Marx's expertise, most of the exhibits addressed topics best illustrated with manuscripts and printed books: "Purim"—consisting of illuminated Book of Esther scrolls from the seventeenth to the nineteenth centuries; "Ketubot"—illuminated marriage contracts from the eighteenth and nineteenth centuries; or "Jewish Music"—from early medieval manuscript fragments to contemporary scores. Just a handful of exhibits contained ritual objects, including the Chanukah project, or works of art such as "Prints of Jewish Types and Prominent Personalities."[25]

Although Adler's Smithsonian experiences informed the museum's development, that knowledge was infrequently offered and filtered through Marx. When, for example, photographs of some Jewish ceremonial objects were sent to Adler for purchase consideration, after declining the offer he forwarded the photographs to Marx, not Romanoff, for retention as research materials. When the New Jersey chapter of the National Council of Jewish Women requested a selection of ritual objects to show at the New Jersey State Museum, Adler asked Marx to handle it. Instead of involving Romanoff, however, Marx asked for Adler's recommendations on theme and presentation. Occasionally Adler would encourage Marx to have Romanoff assist with these tasks, but Marx thought Romanoff was incapable of handling them. Meanwhile, Adler was far too busy, his attention and residences divided between Philadelphia and New York, to spend much time on the museum. For Marx, it was a low-priority distraction in the face of the library's needs and those of the faculty and students it served.[26]

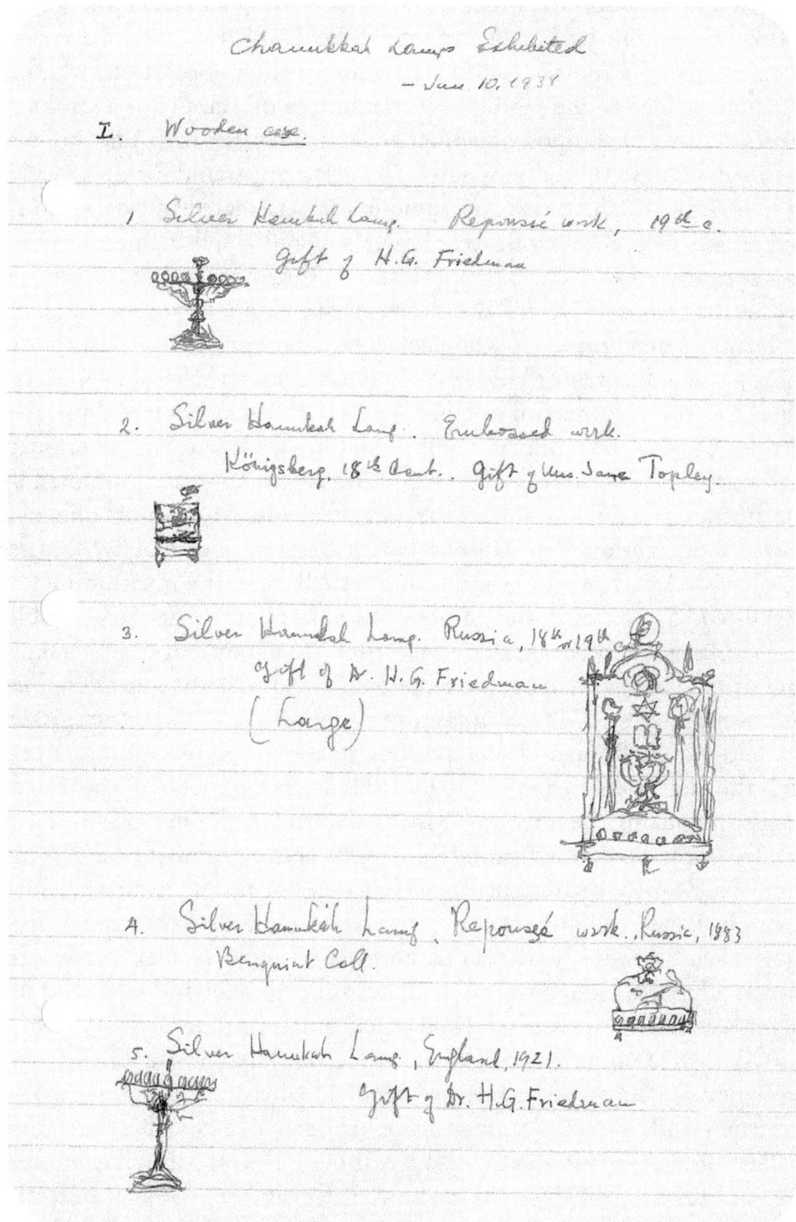

Chanukkah Lamps Exhibited
— Jan. 10, 1938

I. Wooden case.

1. Silver Hanukah Lamp. Repoussé work, 19th c.
Gift of H.G. Friedman

2. Silver Hanukah Lamp. Embossed work.
Königsberg. 18th Cent.. Gift of Mrs. Jane Topley

3. Silver Hanukah Lamp. Russia, 18th or 19th c.
Gift of Dr. H.G. Friedman
(Large)

4. Silver Hanukkah Lamp. Repoussé work. Russia, 1883
Benguiat Coll.

5. Silver Hanukah Lamp, England, 1921.
Gift of Dr. H.G. Friedman

Figure 2.11. First page of notes, Paul Romanoff, "Chanukkah Lamps Exhibited," 10 January 1938. Paul Romanoff Papers, Ms. 16. Courtesy of the Library at the Herbert D. Katz Center for Advanced Judaic Studies, Kislak Center for Special Collections, Rare Books and Manuscripts, University of Pennsylvania.

Romanoff was, on the other hand, an effective popularizer and public speaker. Early on, he hoped to leverage his familiarity with the collections by giving seminary lectures for additional compensation, whether in courses added to the seminary curriculum or off campus as a seminary representative. He proposed seminary talks and courses that Adler politely declined because of the seminary's financial constraints or an already-full curriculum. There was also some uneasiness shared by Marx, Adler, and others over Romanoff's scholarly rigor and English fluency. On a few occasions, Marx checked the texts of Romanoff's museum lectures before they were delivered. But Marx et alia were less concerned about Romanoff's off-campus appearances and radio interviews, particularly those given in Hebrew or Yiddish on local radio stations. Sensing opportunities elsewhere, Romanoff assembled a slide collection to give illustrated lectures outside the seminary's ambit, and he signed on with a commercial venture, the New York City–based Art Lecture Bureau. Promoted by the Bureau as a "Scholar, Lecturer, Archaeologist," Romanoff offered a selection of eight different talks on Jewish art and a course of five lectures on "Jewish Art Throughout the Centuries." Back at the museum he was permitted to give tours and impromptu talks about temporary exhibits and works from the permanent collection. Romanoff's duties of "taking care of the visitors" and "getting the public, particularly educational institutions, interested" in the museum's exhibits became his strong suit. By the mid-1930s, Romanoff was speaking to about 150 tour groups a year with the total rising to about 230 by 1939. Marx later saluted Romanoff's success in making the museum "a living part of Jewish life" with his tours and less-formal talks for visitors. Romanoff's accomplishment was all-the-more noteworthy because of the wide variety of people he served: Jews and non-Jews, religious school classes from many denominations, synagogue adult groups, and college students brought by their professors. Romanoff's popular appeal was evident in the number and variety of his tributes. Children's classes gathered "small amounts of money . . . for the purchase of some new item [for the collection] as a token of their appreciation." A substantial number of individual visitors and groups were Christian, and once the "Sunday School children of a New Jersey Church made a similar contribution." A "12-year old girl wrote after having seen the . . . Museum, she does not see how Hitler can hate the Jews." Thanks to Romanoff, Marx concluded, a "considerable number of non-Jewish visitors carry away a better understanding of Jewish life and . . . customs."[27]

Some visits were from a seminary neighbor, the parish school of Corpus Christi Church located about a block away. Like the seminary and other institutions on New York's upper west side, the church and school traced their origins to the turn of the century; and they too had recently expanded. In 1936, a new priest replaced the school's teachers, the Sisters of Charity of New York, with the Dominican Sisters of Sinsinawa, Wisconsin, "to bring the best of progressive education" to the parish's children. The seminary had been heckled by Catholic children in the neighborhood who threw "pebbles at the windows, sometimes breaking panes of glass, or while visiting the Museum" mutilating or taking display labels. Romanoff attributed the problems to the kids' ignorance of the seminary and to "social conditions"; that is, prejudices that had been exacerbated by "Coughlin meetings . . . constantly being held on the street corners near the Seminary." Father Charles Coughlin (1891–1979) was a Canadian born, Detroit-area priest who began weekly radio broadcasts in the 1920s that by the mid-1930s attracted an audience numbering in the millions. The broadcasts, augmented with a weekly paper, became a platform for Coughlin's increasingly provocative economic and political views that evolved from anti-socialist and anti-communist to pro-fascist as Hitler and Mussolini rose to power. Though once a supporter of Franklin Roosevelt's Depression-era recovery programs, Coughlin turned against what he perceived as Roosevelt's pro-capitalist policies, privileging the wealthy at the expense of average laborers, and by the late 1930s, Coughlin began weaving antisemitic claims into his messages. A resulting outcry led radio stations to cancel his broadcasts, arousing Coughlin followers to demonstrate against what they viewed as censorship—and prompting counter protests. New York witnessed much of the turmoil, possibly because of an event there in February 1939: a pro-Nazi rally at one of the city's largest indoor arenas, Madison Square Garden, organized by the German American Bund and attracting about twenty-thousand supporters. When two Dominican sisters from Corpus Christi Church visited the museum in September 1939, Romanoff suggested they return with their "teacher-Sisters" for a tour. He introduced the group to Jewish "objects, customs, and the origin of many of their [Christian] ceremonies . . . in [Jewish] ritual," and how the Bible "could be visually illustrated" with the museum's collection. The sisters were impressed and subsequently brought several groups of children who became engaged "as never before." The antisemitic incidents all but disappeared and, Romanoff believed, the tours succeeded in "establishing good feeling and understanding in our immediate neighborhood."[28]

If for non-Jews Romanoff's tours helped bridge divides, for Jewish groups his tours cultivated a greater sense of solidarity and pride. The sisterhood leader of the Hebrew Tabernacle in New York wrote, "We well can be proud of our history and I feel the future ever holds glorious things for us Jews." A tour for the Temple Israel of New York sisterhood "opened [members'] eyes to the antiquity and beauty of the [museum's] collections, and that we have an art to be proud of." The National Council of Jewish Women from Passaic, New Jersey, noted that its members "did not realize our heritage was so replete with such wonderful works of art," while the president of Keren Hatarbut of New York reported that Romanoff had awakened "a desire to possess these contributions of art and beauty." The rabbi of Temple Emanuel of Providence, Rhode Island, felt Romanoff had "a gift for lecturing . . . in a very entertaining and amusing manner," especially with children, a skill the rabbi of Brooklyn's Congregation Shaari Israel attributed to Romanoff's understanding of "the psychology of children" and his "pleasant demeanor" toward them.[29]

When Romanoff was not giving tours and answering "innumerable questions" about Jewish artifacts and their uses, he was lobbying Marx and Adler to raise the museum's public profile and improve its educational effectiveness. He recommended instructional programs for area schools, museum-hosted teas for local print and radio journalists, listings in regional museum directories, and outreach to area and national Jewish organizations. Romanoff also wanted a supply of collection photographs for print-media use; and souvenir catalogues, guidebooks, and postcards for purchase. Inspired by questions about unfamiliar display-label nomenclature, Romanoff compiled a "Glossary to be mimeographed and . . . given to visitors." While Marx endorsed most of Romanoff's ideas in principle, he often declined them if they entailed expenditures. The growing size and significance of the museum, and its rising popularity—its annual attendance rose from the low ten thousands after its opening to the low twenty thousands by the early 1940s—did little to elevate it on the seminary's list of priorities. The Depression's lingering effects continued to undercut the seminary's finances and fiscal constraints were repeatedly cited in responses to Romanoff's appeals for more outreach support. So, too, fiscal austerity held his salary down in spite of his repeated requests for increases to alleviate his financial struggles. Because Adler and Marx could not substantially boost Romanoff's pay or offer more job security, their deflection of his ideas also signaled their aversion to giving him false hope that his position and salary might improve. Romanoff's ambitions for the museum, his financial need, and the seminary's limits came to a head following yet another appeal in 1938. Suggesting Romanoff's training better "fitted [him] for archaeological work in Palestine," Adler encouraged Romanoff to plan his future elsewhere. Nothing changed in the following year and then, in 1940, Adler fell ill and died. Romanoff's health began deteriorating a couple of years later, and he passed in 1943.[30]

Marx's responsibility for the museum over this period was never formally acknowledged. That changed after Adler's death and the onset of Romanoff's illness when, on the recommendation of Adler's successor, seminary trustees recognized Marx's role with the title of "Director." But that was all. When Marx suggested museum stationery be printed to avoid the "awkwardness" of his conducting museum business on library letterhead, he was turned down, signifying that despite his personal recognition, the museum's standing at the seminary had not changed. That Marx's role was not formally acknowledged until after Adler's death suggests that the latter either assumed ultimate responsibility for it or that he wanted to avoid assigning the museum a higher level of institutional status, which the "Director" title would have implied. Apparently, Marx was not offended by that arrangement and, to the contrary, after Adler's death, Marx saluted the former's support of the museum. Further, Marx had no reason to elevate the museum's needs in comparison to the library's, indicative of latter's far greater proximity to and role in the seminary's research and teaching programs.[31]

Even though the museum was not a high priority for the seminary during the Depression, and later during the Second World War, it was growing into a significant collection that was beginning to attract the interest of Jews outside the seminary's campus and the non-Jewish citizens of New York. At the same time, Romanoff's success in making the museum meaningful for Jews and non-Jews modeled a role for it in bolstering Jewish pride while also advocating Judaism's contributions to American society. How then might the seminary make better use of the museum?

Notes

1. Mayer Sulzberger, "January 20, 1904. To Doctor Cyrus Adler. . . ," in *Biennial Report, The Jewish Theological Seminary of America* (New York: Jewish Theological Seminary of America, 1906), 49–50.
2. Joseph Jacobs and Lucien Wolf, *Catalogue of the Anglo-Jewish Historical Exhibition*, Edition de luxe (London: F. Haes, 1888), v–vii; 210–12; Kathrin Pieren, "Migration and Identity Constructions in the Metropolis: The Representations of Jewish Heritage in London Between 1887 and 1956" (PhD diss., University of London, 2011), 79–100; and Jeffrey David Feldman, "Exhibiting Judaica or Jewish Exhibitionism: A Comparison of Two Nineteenth-Century Exhibitions" (master's thesis, St. Cross College, Oxford University, 1993), 57–78. See also, Barbara Kirshenblatt-Gimblett, *Destination Culture: Tourism, Museums, and Heritage* (Berkeley: University of California Press, 1998), 85–86; Richard I. Cohen, *Jewish Icons: Art and*

Society in Modern Europe (Berkeley: University of California Press, 1998), 192–97; and Natalia Berger, *The Jewish Museum: History and Memory, Identity and Art from Vienna to the Bezalel National Museum, Jerusalem* (Leiden, NL: Brill, 2018), 66–91. Todd M. Endelman, "The Englishness of Jewish Modernity in England," in *Toward Modernity: The European Jewish Model*, ed. Jacob Katz (New Brunswick, NJ: Transaction Books, 1987), 225–46. Lucien Wolf, "Origin of the Jewish Historical Society of England," *Transactions, Jewish Historical Society of England* VII, Sessions 1911–1914 (Edinburgh & London: Ballantyne, Hanson & Co., 1915): 206–21.

3. Jacobs and Wolf, *Catalogue of the Anglo-Jewish Historical Exhibition*, xiii–xxv, 83–131, 181–82, 207. *Jewish Encyclopedia* (1907), s.v. "Sir Isidore Spielmann," by Joseph Jacobs; Olga Somech Phillips, "Sir Isidore Spielmann (1854–1925)," *Jewish Quarterly* 3, no. 2 (Autumn 1955): 30; Wolf, "Origin": 212–13. The Strauss collection contained 149 objects by 1888; Alain Erlande-Brandenburg, "The Isaac Strauss Collection," in *Jewish Treasures from Paris: From the Collections of the Cluny Museum and the Consistoire*, compiled by Victor A. Klagsbald (Jerusalem: Israel Museum, 1982), n.p.
4. Other works from the Strauss collection shown in London are (the Anglo-Jewish ["AJ"] catalogue number with illustration and facing-page numbers, followed by the Strauss ["S"] catalogue and plate numbers): AJ 1901 (no. 22, p. 120), S 1 (pl. I); AJ 1905 (no. 18, p. 107), S 5 (pl. IV); AJ 1948 (no. 21, p. 115), S 48 (pl. XII); AJ 1993 (no. 20, p. 112), S 47 (pl. XI); AJ 1949, 1952–63, 1995–96 (no. 21, p. 115), S 49–53 (pl. XII); AJ 1974 (no. 23, p. 125), S 74. Objects listed but not depicted in the Strauss catalogue that are included in the Anglo-Jewish catalogue are no. 17, p. 101: AJ 1915, 1917, 1919–20, 2004; no. 20, p. 112: AJ 1979; and no. 21, p. 115: AJ 1934, 1936, 1991, 2001, 2003, 2008.
5. Jacobs and Wolf, *Catalogue of the Anglo-Jewish Historical Exhibition*, 83–84; for descriptions containing Hebrew transcriptions with or without translations, see p. 123 (item no. 1943) and p. 115 (item no. 1828); "Coins and Medals," pp. 151–74.
6. Jacobs and Wolf, *Catalogue of the Anglo-Jewish Historical Exhibition*, vii, xxv, 213. *Papers Read at the Anglo-Jewish Historical Exhibition*, Publications of the Anglo-Jewish Historical Exhibition, no. 1 (London: Office of the Jewish Chronicle, 1888); M[yer] D[avid] Davis, ed., שטרות *Shetarot: Hebrew Deeds of English Jews before 1290*, Publications of the Anglo-Jewish Historical Exhibition, no. 2 (London: Office of the Jewish Chronicle, 1888); Joseph Jacobs and Lucien Wolf, comps., *Bibliotheca Anglo-Judaica: A Bibliographical Guide to Anglo-Jewish History*, Publications of the Anglo-Jewish Historical Exhibition, no. 3 (London: Office of the Jewish Chronicle, 1888). The quote is from Pieren, "Migration and Identity Constructions," 103; on the "hallowing of history," see Feldman, "Exhibiting Judaica or Jewish Exhibitionism," 72–73. On the exhibition's link with the English historical society, see Wolf, "Origin," 206–21.
7. For a comparison of the two societies during their early years, see Robert Liberles, "Postemancipation Historiography and the Jewish Historical

Societies of America and England," in *Reshaping the Past: Jewish History and the Historians*, ed. Jonathan Frankel (Oxford: Oxford University Press, 1994), 45–65. The American Jewish history call was from [Abram S. Isaacs,] "America's Discovery," in *The Jewish Messenger*, 12 November 1886. CA, "[Open Letter] Sources of American Jewish History," *The Menorah* V (July–December 1888): 191–93; and Ira Robinson, ed., *Cyrus Adler, Selected Letters*, 2 vols. (Philadelphia, PA: Jewish Publication Society of America, 1985), I:12–20. On CA's role in the society's founding, see Gayle Meyer Coolick, "The Public Career of Cyrus Adler" (PhD diss., Georgia State University, 1981), 104–10; Abraham A. Neuman, *Cyrus Adler, a Biographical Sketch* (Philadelphia, PA: Jewish Publication Society of America, 1942), 48–55; and CA, *I Have Considered the Days* (Philadelphia, PA: The Jewish Publication Society of America, 1941), 266–67. CA, "American Jewish Historical Society" [ca. February–March 1892], CAP 2:5, AJHS; "Jewish Historical Society," *New York Times*, 7 June 1892; Nathan M. Kaganoff, "AJHS at 90: Reflections on the History of the Oldest Ethnic Historical Society in America," *American Jewish History* 71, no. 4 (June 1982): 466–85. CA, "Americana at the Anglo-Jewish Exhibition," *Publications of the American Jewish Historical Society* 1 (1893): 109–10; Joseph Jacobs, "A Plea for an American Jewish Historical Exhibition," *Publications of the American Jewish Historical Society* 9 (1901): 13–17; [CA], "A Proposed American Jewish Historical Exhibition" (1901), in *The American Jewish Year Book 5662*, ed. David Singer and Ruth R. Seldin (New York: American Jewish Committee and Jewish Publication Society, 1993), 104–8; see also, Grace Cohen Grossman with Richard Eighme Ahlborn, *Judaica at the Smithsonian: Cultural Politics as Cultural Model*, Smithsonian Studies in History and Technology, vol. 52 (Washington, DC: Smithsonian Institution Press, 1997), 49, 61n59, 92–93. The London exhibit's organizer was Joseph Jacobs; Pieren, "Migration and Identity Constructions," 304.

8. Jonathan D. Sarna, "Cyrus Adler and the Development of American Jewish Culture: The 'Scholar-Doer' as a Jewish Communal Leader," *American Jewish History* 78, no. 3 (March 1989): 382–94; the quotes are from pp. 386, 394. See also, Coolick, "The Public Career of Cyrus Adler," 19–22, 41–43, 241–42. CA, "The Annals of Sardanapalus [Ashurbanipal]: A Double Transliteration, Translation, Commentary, and Concordance of the Cuneiform Text" (PhD diss., Johns Hopkins University, 1887). On Haupt, see "Dr. Cyrus Adler's Address" and W[illiam] F. Albright, "Professor Haupt as Scholar and Teacher," in *Oriental Studies Published in Commemoration of the Fortieth Anniversary of Paul Haupt*, ed. CA and Aaron Ember (Baltimore, MD: Johns Hopkins University Press, 1926), xviii–xix, xxi–xxxii; *Dictionary of American Biography* (1936), s.v. "Paul Haupt"; and CA, *I Have Considered the Days*, 48–64. See also, Neuman, *Cyrus Adler*, 20–24; and CA, "The Semitic Seminary of Johns Hopkins University," in *Lectures, Selected Papers, Addresses* (Philadelphia, PA: Privately printed, 1933), 162–71. On university museums, see Jeffrey Abt, *American Egyptologist: The Life of James Henry Breasted and the Creation of His Oriental Institute* (Chicago, IL: University of Chicago Press, 2011), 62–71, 345–58; Percy C. Madeira Jr., *Men in*

Search of Man: The First Seventy-Five Years of the University Museum of the University of Pennsylvania (Philadelphia: University of Pennsylvania Press, 1964); Christopher Ratté, "Kelsey Museum of Archaeology: 1928–2017," in *Object Lessons & the Formation of Knowledge: The University of Michigan Museums, Libraries, & Collections, 1817–2017*, ed. Kerstin Barndt and Carla M. Sinopoli (Ann Arbor: University of Michigan Press, 2017), 252–58. On Haupt's and CA's SI appointments, see S. P. Langley to CA, 2 February 1888, CAP 1:27, AJHS; CA, 30 June 1888, "Report of the Section of Oriental Antiquities," Record Unit 158, 5:2, SIA. See also, Bruce Kuklick, *Puritans in Babylon: The Ancient Near East and American Intellectual Life, 1880–1930* (Princeton, NJ: Princeton University Press, 1996), 34, 104–5.

9. Grossman with Ahlborn, *Judaica at the Smithsonian*, 23, 36, 38, 42–56; CA, "Museum Collections to Illustrate Religious History and Ceremonials," *Report of the U. S. National Museum, Annual Report of the Board of Regents of the Smithsonian Institution . . . for the Year Ending June 30, 1893*, House of Representatives, 53d Congress, 2d Session, Mis. Doc. 184, Part 2 (1895): 758–59. See also, Kirshenblatt-Gimblett, *Destination Culture*, 88–105; and Steven W. Holloway, "The Smithsonian Institution's Religious Ceremonial Objects and Biblical Antiquities at the World's Columbian Exposition (Chicago, 1893) and the Cotton States and International Exposition (Atlanta, 1895)," in *Orientalism, Assyriology and the Bible*, ed. Steven W. Holloway (Sheffield, UK: Sheffield Phoenix Press, 2006), 95–138.

   For the context of CA's World's Columbian Exposition work, see John P. Burris, *Exhibiting Religion: Colonialism and Spectacle at International Expositions, 1851–1893* (Charlottesville, VA: University Press of Virginia, 2001), 123–66. Eric J. Sharpe, *Comparative Religion: A History*, 2nd edn. (La Salle, IL: Open Court, 1986); Joseph M. Kitagawa, "The History of Religions in America," in *The History of Religions: Essays in Methodology*, ed. Mircea Eliade and Joseph M. Kitagawa (Chicago, IL: University of Chicago Press, 1959), 1–30. See also, Guy G. Stroumsa, *A New Science: The Discovery of Religion in the Age of Reason* (Cambridge, MA: Harvard University Press, 2010).

10. Grossman with Ahlborn, *Judaica at the Smithsonian*, 23, 33, 36–39, 50, 63. CA, "Museum Collections to Illustrate Religious History and Ceremonials," 759, 761. CA and I. M. Casanowicz, *The Collection of Jewish Ceremonial Objects in the United States National Museum* (Washington, DC: US Government Printing Office, 1908), 701–3. Kirshenblatt-Gimblett, *Destination Culture*, 5–6, 92–94. See also, Burris, *Exhibiting Religion*, 132–33, 142–43. On faith and race, see Eric L. Goldstein, *The Price of Whiteness: Jews, Race, and American Identity* (Princeton, NJ: Princeton University Press, 2006), 86–89.

11. CA, *I Have Considered the Days*, 14, 16, 41, 66; Neuman, *Cyrus Adler*, 10–12, 49; Hasia Diner, "Like the Antelope and the Badger: The Founding and Early Years of the Jewish Theological Seminary, 1886–1902," in *Tradition Renewed: A History of the Jewish Theological Seminary*, ed. Jack Wertheimer,

2 vols. (New York: Jewish Theological Seminary of America, 1997), I:6–7, 23, 26, 36; Robert E. Fierstien, "Sabato Morais and the Founding of the Jewish Theological Seminary," in *When Philadelphia Was the Capital of Jewish America*, ed. Murray Friedman (Philadelphia, PA: Balch Institute Press, 1993), 75–91. For context, see Naomi W. Cohen, *Encounter with Emancipation: The German Jews in the United States, 1830–1914* (Philadelphia, PA: Jewish Publication Society, 1984).

12. Mel Scult, "Schechter's Seminary," in Wertheimer, *Tradition Renewed*, I:46–48, 59, 61–65, 68–71, 75–76. On "non-partisan Judaism," see Coolick, "Public Career of Cyrus Adler," 223. *Encyclopaedia Judaica*, 2nd. edn. (2007), s.v. "Solomon Schechter"; and Shuly Rubin Schwartz, "The Schechter Faculty: The Seminary and 'Wissenschaft Des Judentums' in America," in Wertheimer, *Tradition Renewed*, I:295–325. See also, Herbert Rosenblum, "The Shaping of an Institution: The 1902 Reorganization of the Seminary," *Conservative Judaism* XXVII, no. 2 (Winter 1972): 35–48. Joshua Bloch, "Alexander Marx ז"ל (1878–1953)," *Publications of the American Jewish Historical Society* 43, no. 4 (June 1954): 241–52; and *American National Biography* (1999), s.v. "Alexander Marx," by Menahem Schmelzer. Jenna Weissman Joselit, "By Design: Building the Campus of the Jewish Theological Seminary," in Wertheimer, *Tradition Renewed*, I:271–74; Joseph B. Abrahams, "The Buildings of the Seminary," in *The Jewish Theological Seminary of America: Semi-Centennial Volume*, ed. CA (New York: Jewish Theological Seminary of America, 1939), 65–67. Diner, "Like the Antelope and the Badger," I:18.

13. AM, "Mayer Sulzberger," in *Essays in Jewish Biography*, reprint of 1948 edn. (Lanham, MD: University Press of America, 1986), 227; David G. Dalin, "The Patriarch: The Life and Legacy of Mayer Sulzberger," in Friedman, *When Philadelphia Was the Capital*, 62–63; Herman Dicker, *Of Learning and Libraries: The Seminary Library at One Hundred* (New York: Jewish Theological Seminary of America, 1988), 17–18; Mayer Sulzberger, "The Seminary Library," in *Biennial Report, The Jewish Theological Seminary of America* (New York: [Jewish Theological Seminary of America], 1906), 116–18. Dianne Ashton, *The Philadelphia Group and Philadelphia Jewish History: A Guide to Archival and Bibliographic Collections* (Philadelphia, PA: Center for American Jewish History, Temple University, 1993), 5–8; Jonathan D. Sarna, "The Making of an American Jewish Culture," in Friedman, *When Philadelphia Was the Capital*, 145–55. See also, Herman Dicker, ed., *The Mayer Sulzberger-Alexander Marx Correspondence, 1904–1923* (New York: Sepher-Hermon Press, 1990); and Julie Miller and Richard I. Cohen, "A Collision of Cultures: The Jewish Museum and the Jewish Theological Seminary, 1904–1971," in Wertheimer, *Tradition Renewed*, II:312–323; E[phraim] Deinard, *Or Mayer, Catalogue of the Old Hebrew Manuscripts and Printed Books of the Library of Hon. M[ayer] Sulzberger of Philadelphia, Pa.* (New York: J. Aronson, 1896) [in Hebrew]. The Sulzberger Smithsonian gifts are documented in Grossman with Ahlborn, *Judaica at the Smithsonian*, 239–41; illustrations of some are

on pp. 104–5, 110, 114–15, 126–27. The object detailed on pp. 126–27, an Esther scroll, was borrowed for the World's Columbian Exposition and later retained for the SI's permanent collection, CA to David Sulzberger, 22 March 1893, ARC MS 26--120:26, LKCAJS.

14. Mayer Sulzberger, "January 20, 1904. To Doctor Cyrus Adler. . . ," in *Biennial Report, The Jewish Theological Seminary of America* (New York: [Jewish Theological Seminary of America], 1906), 49–50; Bilski, "Seeing the Future Through the Light of the Past," 9. CA, "Museums of Art, History, and Science," *Library Journal* 23 (August 1898): 95.
15. Frank J. Rubenstein, *The Early Years, 1908–1919: The Dropsie College of Hebrew and Cognate Learning* (Philadelphia, PA: Dropsie University, 1977). Dropsie College no longer exists. It ceased granting degrees in 1986, when it became the Annenberg Research Institute, hosting just a postdoctoral fellowship program. It was absorbed by the University of Pennsylvania in 1993 and renamed the Annenberg Research Center; and after being endowed in 2008, it was renamed the Katz Center for Advanced Judaic Studies. "About the Katz Center: An Illustrious History," accessed May 2017, http://katz.sas.upenn.edu/about. Ira Robinson, "Cyrus Adler: President of the Jewish Theological Seminary, 1915–1940," in Wertheimer, *Tradition Renewed,* I:107, 111–12, 114–17, 132–33, 145. See also, CA, "The Standpoint of the Seminary," in *Lectures, Selected Papers, Addresses by Cyrus Adler*, 251–63.
16. On Sulzberger's additional Judaica contributions and exhibit interests, see *Mayer Sulzberger-Alexander Marx Correspondence*, 38, 52, 92–95, 100; AM to CA, 7 November 1923, ARC 1–4–42 and AM to CA, 11 December 1924, ARC 80–15–Correspondence, Adler, Cyrus, 1924, LJTS. On borrowing and later purchasing exhibit cases, and installing exhibits, CA to AM, 15 April 1920, 10 October 1922, and 9 January 1923, ARC 1–4–42, LJTS; J. M. Casanowicz to CA, 19 May 1922, ARC 80–100–"Museum," LJTS. Joselit, "By Design," I:275–76. CA, "Address . . . at the Commencement of the Jewish Theological Seminary of America," 3 June 1923, ARC MS26--55:10 and CA, "Remarks . . . at the Jewish Theological Seminary of America Commencement Exercises," 10 June 1923, ARC MS 26–55:7, LKCAJS.
17. Joselit, "By Design," I:279. $215,000 = $7.32 million in 2020 (CPI), Samuel H. Williamson, "Seven Ways to Compute the Relative Value of a U.S. Dollar Amount, 1790 to present," MeasuringWorth, accessed 2022, www.measuringworth.com/uscompare/. "Schiff Gave Freely to Social Service," *New York Times*, 5 June 1931. "F. M. Warburg Dies at 66 in Home Here," *New York Times*, 21 October 1931; and *Dictionary of American Biography*, suppl. 1–2: to 1940, s.v. "Felix Moritz Warburg"; Stephen Birmingham, *"Our Crowd": The Great Jewish Families of New York* (New York: Harper and Row, 1967); Ron Chernow, *The Warburgs: The Twentieth-Century Odyssey of a Remarkable Jewish Family* (New York: Random House, 1993); regarding Felix's philanthropy, see p. 97. On Warburg's Judaica donation, AM to CA, ARC 1–4–42, 6 April 1923, LJTS. On Jacob Schiff's JTS support, see Diner, "Like the Antelope and the Badger," I:15, 19; Scult, "Schechter's Seminary,"

I:47–57; CA, *Jacob Henry Schiff: A Biographical Sketch* (New York: American Jewish Committee, 1921), 22–26, 35–36; and CA, *Jacob H. Schiff: His Life and Letters*, 2 vols. (New York: Doubleday, Doran and Company, 1928), I:18–33, 52–59. *Encyclopaedia Judaica*, 2nd edn. (2007), s.v. "Jacob H. Schiff"; *Jewish Encyclopedia* (1901–1906 edn.), s.v. "Semitic Museum, Harvard University," by CA; CA, *The Semitic Museum of Harvard University* (Cambridge, MA: Harvard University, 1903), 14–18, 21–24; and CA, "The Living Past," in *Lectures, Selected Papers, Addresses by Cyrus Adler*, 159–61. On the context of Schiff's Harvard donations, see Rachel Hallote, "Jacob H. Schiff and the Beginning of Biblical Archaeology in the United States," *American Jewish History* 95, no. 3 (September 2009): 225–47; Dorothy Limouze, "Introduction: The History of the Warburg Gift," in *The Felix M. Warburg Collection: A Legacy of Discernment* (Poughkeepsie, NY: Loeb Art Center, Vassar College, 1995), 9–22; Kathryn Brush, *Vastly More Than Brick & Mortar: Reinventing the Fogg Art Museum in the 1920s* (Cambridge, MA: Harvard University Art Museums, 2003), 27–28, 45, 59, 62, passim.

18. On Adler's cultivation of Benguiat, Grossman with Ahlborn, *Judaica at the Smithsonian*, 54–55. See also, Mordecai Benguiat, "A Jewish Museum in America," in *Jewish Texts on the Visual Arts*, ed. Vivian B. Mann (Cambridge: Cambridge University Press, 2000), 158–60; CA and Immanuel M. Casanowicz, *Descriptive Catalogue of a Collection of Objects of Jewish Ceremonial Art Deposited in the U.S. National Museum by Hadji Ephraim Benguiat*, reprinted from Report of the US National Museum [Smithsonian Institution] for 1899 (Washington, DC: US Government Printing Office, 1901); and CA and I. M. Casanowicz, *The Collection of Jewish Ceremonial Objects*. "Brain-child" quote is from, LF to FSW, 6 January 1944, RG 1–41–37, LJTS. CA, "Semi-Centennial Address" and A. S. W. Rosenbach, "The Seminary Museum," in *The Jewish Theological Seminary of America: Semi-Centennial Volume*, 14, 144; CA, "Felix M. Warburg in Memorium," *Bulletin of the American Schools of Oriental Research* 68 (December 1937): 2; *Encyclopaedia Judaica*, 2nd edn. (2007), s.v. "Abraham Simon Wolf Rosenbach." On Rosenbach and the museum's beginnings, see AM, "Address on the Tenth Anniversary of the Opening of the Museum," 12 January 1941, ARC 60–2–4, LJTS, 3; AM, "Address Delivered . . . at the Preview of the Jewish Museum," 6 May 1947, ARC 60–1–6; and AM to Dexter Teed, 29 February 1944, ARC 60–1–4, LJTS. On subsequent Warburg donations, see AM to FSW, 6 November 1933 and AM to Felix M. Warburg, 8 November 1933, RG 1–16–62, LJTS.
19. Joselit, "By Design," I:279–85; Abrahams, "Buildings of the Seminary," 68–70. Rosenbach, "Seminary Museum," 147. CA and Casanowicz, *Descriptive Catalogue*. [PR], Display cases inventory, Museum of Jewish Ceremonial Objects, JTS, June 1932, ARC 80–100–Museum, LJTS; "Museum of Jewish Ceremonial Objects" (publicity release), 27 June 1932 and Placard, Museum of Jewish Ceremonial and Historical Objects, ca. March 1932, ARC 60–1–9, LJTS.

20. For a survey, see *Encyclopaedia Judaica*, 2nd edn. (2007), s.v. "Museums," by Avraham Biran and Grace Cohen Grossman. On the museums of Vienna, Prague, Budapest, and Palestine/Israel, Berger, *The Jewish Museum*, 95–546. See also, for Vienna, Felicitas Heimann-Jelinek and Wiebke Krohn, eds., *The First Jewish Museum* (Vienna, Austria: Jüdisches Museum der Stadt Wien, 2005); Klaus Hödl, "The Turning to History of Viennese Jews: Jewish Identity and the Jewish Museum," *Journal of Modern Jewish Studies* 3, no. 1 (March 2004): 17–32; and Leon Kolb, "The Vienna Jewish Museum," in *The Jews of Austria: Essays on Their Life, History, and Destruction*, ed. Josef Fraenkel (London: Vallentine Mitchell and Company, 1967), 147–59. Also relevant are Joseph Gutmann, "The Kirschstein Museum of Berlin," *Jewish Art* 16/17 (1990/1991): 172–76; Tobias Metzler, "Collecting Community: The Berlin Jewish Museum as Narrator Between Past and Present, 1906–1939," in *Visualizing and Exhibiting Jewish Space and History*, ed. Richard I. Cohen (Oxford: Oxford University Press, 2012), 55–79; Heinrich Frauberger, "The Need to Collect Images of Jewish Art," in Mann, *Jewish Texts on the Visual Arts*, 156–58; François Guesnet, "Mathias Bersohn," in *The Yivo Encyclopedia of Jews in Eastern Europe*, ed. Gersohn David Hundert, 2 vols. (New Haven, CT: Yale University Press, 2008), I:169–70; Cecil Roth, introduction to *Catalogue of the Permanent and Loan Collections of the Jewish Museum, London*, ed. R[ichard] D. Barnett (London: Harvey Miller, 1974), xiii; Adolph S. Oko, *A History of the Hebrew Union College Library and Museum* (Cincinnati, OH: Hebrew Union College Press, 1944), 9–12; and Nancy M. Berman, "Visions, Revisions, and Reverberations: The Evolving Hebrew Union College Skirball Museum," in *New Beginnings: The Skirball Museum Collections and Inaugural Exhibition*, ed. Grace Cohen Grossman (Los Angeles: Skirball Cultural Center, 1996), 17–25.
21. On the displays, see AM, "Address on the Tenth Anniversary of the Opening of the Museum," 12 January 1941, ARC 60–2–4, LJTS, 12; Rosenbach, "Seminary Museum," 149–53. On museum architecture, see Ingrid A. Steffensen-Bruce, *Marble Palaces, Temples of Art: Art Museums, Architecture, and American Culture, 1890–1930* (Lewisburg, PA: Bucknell University Press, 1998).
22. Rosenbach, "Seminary Museum," 147–48. G. Brown Goode, *The Museums of the Future* (Washington, DC: [United States National Museum, Smithsonian Institution] Government Printing Office, 1891), 433; *Dictionary of American Biography*, s.v. "George Brown Goode." See also, Grossman with Ahlborn, *Judaica at the Smithsonian*, 18–21, 36, 50–52. On CA quoting Goode, see CA, "Museums of Art, History, and Science," 95. On university research-and-teaching museums, see nn. 8 and 17, above. *Encyclopedia of Religion*, 2nd edn., s.v. "Jewish Studies: Jewish Studies Since 1919"; and *Encyclopaedia Judaica*, 2nd edn. (2007), s.v. "Jewish Studies." On Jewish material-culture studies, see Vivian B. Mann and Gordon Tucker, eds., *The Seminar on Jewish Art, January–September 1984: Proceedings* (New York: JTS and JM, 1985); and Joseph Gutmann, "Jewish Art and Jewish Studies," in *The State of*

Jewish Studies, ed. Shaye J. D. Cohen and Edward L. Greenstein (Detroit, MI: Wayne State University Press for JTS, 1990), 193–211.

23. AM to PR, 16 December 1931, ARC 60–2–3; and PR to CA, 22 December 1931, RG 1–22–39, LJTS; see also, AM to PR, 3 May 1932, ARC 60–2–3, PR to CA, 19 May 1932; and CA, File memo, 26 May 1932, RG 1–22–39, LJTS. Isaac Rivkind, "The Odyssey of a Scholar and Saint: A Tribute to Dr. Paul Romanoff (1898–1943)," *Jewish Advocate*, 28 December 1944; see also, N. B. Minkoff, "Authority on Jewish Art," *B'Nai B'Rith Messenger* 52, no. 7 (1 October 1948): 31–32; and "Dr. Paul Romanoff, A Museum Curator," *New York Times*, 13 December 1943. On PR's Palestine work, see PR to LF, 2 April 1936, RG 1–22–39, LJTS; PR, *Onomasticon of Palestine: A New Method in Post-Biblical Topography*, reprint from *Proceedings of the American Academy for Jewish Research*, vol. 7 (New York: Jewish Publication Society, 1937). On rising museum-professional standards at the time, see Laurence Vail Coleman, *The Museum in America: A Critical Study*, 3 vols. (Washington, DC: American Association of Museums, 1939), II:297–366.
24. AM to PR, 16 December 1931, ARC 60–2–3, LJTS. On PR's JTS room and board, see PR to CA, 19 May 1932, RG 1–22–39, LJTS. AM [to Jewish journalists], 21 January 1932, ARC 60–1–9; AM to Dr. A. Mukdoni [of the *Morning Journal*], 25 February 1932, ARC 60–1–2; and AM to David Joseph [of the *New York Times*], 25 February 1932, ARC 60–1–9, LJTS. On soliciting donations, see PR to AM, 31 October 1932, ARC 60–2–3, LJTS; Gdynia America Line Information Department, "Jewish Museum Curator to Search Poland for Ancient Ceremonial Treasures," publicity release, 1 July [1936], ARC MS 26--93: 5, LKCAJS. Regarding exhibit loans to cultivate Judaica gifts, see AM to CA, 28 December 1938 and 17 March 1939, RG 1–16–65, and PR to AM, 18 May 1939, ARC 60–2–3, LJTS.
25. PR to AM, 31 October 1932, ARC 60–2–3, LJTS. On the consultant, see AM to "Miss Avery," 2 December 1937, ARC 60–1–2, LJTS; "Chanukkah Exhibit Opens," *New York Times*, 29 November 1937; PR, "Chanukkah Lamps Exhibited," 10 January 1938, ARC MS 16--[Box 1--unprocessed file], LKCAJS; *American Jewish Year Book*, vol. 92 (1992), s.v. "Anna Kleban." Regarding Kleban's role, see AM, "Address on the Tenth Anniversary of the Opening of the Museum," 12 January 1941, ARC 60–2–4, 12–13; AM to LF, 17 May 1945, ARC 80–30–Correspondence-LF, 1945; [AM], "Exhibitions, Loans, Accessioning, Photography," [ca. 13 May 1947], ARC 60–1–6, LJTS. For exhibit figures, see AM to SG, 13 May 1947, and [AM], "Exhibitions, Loans, Accessioning, Photography" [ca. 13 May 1947], ARC 60–1–6, LJTS. On exhibit subjects, see Rosenbach, "Seminary Museum," 152–53; see also, "Museum of Jewish Ceremonial Objects" sections of the annual *Jewish Theological Seminary of America, Register* (New York: Jewish Theological Seminary, 1931–1945).
26. On the photos, see CA to AM, 13 October 1932, ARC 60–1–2, LJTS. On the loan exhibit, see CA to AM, 1 December 1933, RG 1–16–62; and "For the Outlook," publicity release, 1 February 1934, ARC 60–2–1, LJTS.

Museum loans rose from a single object in 1933 to thirty-seven in 1946; AM to SG, 13 May 1947 and [AM], "Exhibitions, Loans, Accessioning, Photography," [ca. 13 May 1947,] ARC 60–1–6, LJTS. On AM's perception of the museum as a library department, see *Jewish Theological Seminary of America, Register, 1931–1932* (New York: Jewish Theological Seminary, 1931), 154.

27. On PR's JTS lecture and course proposals, see PR to CA, 1 January 1931 and CA to PR, 4 and 19 January 1932, PR to CA, 13 December and CA to PR, 16 December 1937, LF to PR, 13 April 1939, RG 1–22–39, LJTS; see also, PR to LF, 2 April 1936, RG 1–22–39, LJTS. On AM's review of PR's texts, see PR to CA, 18 February 1935, RG 1–22–39, LJTS. Berl Cohen, "Pinkhes Romanov (Paul Romanoff)," *Yiddish Leksikon* (blog), 26 May 2019, http://yleksikon.blogspot.com/2019/05/pinkhes-romanov-paul-romanoff.html. *Paul Romanoff, Ph.D.: Scholar, Lecturer, Archaeologist*, promotional brochure (New York City: Art Lecture Bureau, [1936]); copy seen in ARC 60–2–3, LJTS. One of PR's few lectures at JTS (perhaps in the museum) was "Jewish Culture as Seen Through Art and Ceremonial Objects," see "Events Today," *New York Times*, 27 April 1941. On the quantity and quality of PR's tour talks, see PR to AM, 13 May 1938 and 18 May 1939, ARC 60–2–3, and PR to CA, 10 May 1939, RG 1–22–39, LJTS. See also, PR, "Museum, Comments on Dr. Romanoff's Lectures" [ca. December 1939]; and PR to AM, 2 December 1932, ARC 60–2–3, LJTS. For PR's colorful style, PR, see "The Tale of a Letter by Rambam," *Jewish Exponent*, 19 April 1935. On PR's approach to children's tours, see PR, exhibit tour notes, ca. December 1939–March 1940, ARC MS 16–[unprocessed file], LKCAJS. The tour was of an exhibit marking the nine hundredth anniversary of Rashi's birth that ran from 24 December 1939 to 8 April 1940; see *Jewish Theological Seminary of America, Register, 1940–1941* (New York: Jewish Theological Seminary, 1940), 80. On AM's remarks, see AM, "Address on the Tenth Anniversary of the Opening of the Museum," 12 January 1941, ARC 60–2–4, LJTS.

28. "History, Corpus Christi Church," Corpus Christi Church (New York City), accessed August 2017, http://www.corpus-christi-nyc.org/history. "American Nazis Rally in New York City," United States Memorial Holocaust Museum, accessed March 2019, https://newspapers.ushmm.org/events/american-nazis-rally-in-new-york-city#. Donald I. Warren, *Radio Priest: Charles Coughlin, The Father of Hate Radio* (New York: Free Press, 1996). "WMCA Contradicts Coughlin on Jews," 21 November 1938, "'Patriotic' Rally Has Anti-Semitic Tinge," 25 May 1939 and "8 Held in Coughlin Rows," *New York Times*, 29 May 1939; PR to LF, 24 November 1939; and Sister Mary Oswin to PR, 28 October 1939, RG 1–22–39, LJTS. See also, Laura Schiavo, "What to Do with Heritage: The Museum of Jewish Ceremonial Objects, 1931–43," in *Radical Roots: Public History and a Tradition of Social Justice Activism*, ed. Denise D. Meringolo (Amherst, MA: Amherst College Press, 2021), 395–426.

29. PR, "Museum, Comments on Dr. Romanoff's Lectures" [ca. December 1939], ARC 60–2–3, LJTS. On Jewish sisterhoods, museums' (including the JM's) roles in the "Jewish Home Beautiful" movement, and cultivating pride in Jewish material culture, see Jenna Weissman Joselit, *The Wonders of America: Reinventing Jewish Culture, 1880–1950* (New York: Hill and Wang, 1994), 163–69.
30. On "innumerable questions," see AM, "Report on the Library and Museum," 31 May 1939, RG 25–1–27, LJTS. On outreach, see PR to AM, 17 January 1932; and AM to PR, 5 February 1932, ARC 60–2–3, LJTS. See also, Israel S. Chipkin to Principal, 10 February 1932, ARC 60–1–9, LJTS. On stock photographs, see PR to AM, 31 October 1932, ARC 60–2–3, LJTS; on catalogues, guidebooks, and postcards, see PR to AM, 2 December 1932, 13 August 1934, 18 May 1939, ARC 60–2–3, LJTS. PR to CA, 2 November 1937; and PR, "Glossary of Jewish Ceremonial Objects in the Synagogue and Home," ca. 2 November 1937, RG 1–22–39, LJTS. See also, PR to AM, 18 May 1939, ARC 60–2–3, LJTS. For attendance figures, see PR to AM, 18 May 1939 and "Statistics – Museum, June 1, 1940 – December 31, 1941," n.d., ARC 60–2–3, LJTS; see also, "Museum, Jewish Theological Seminary: Monthly and Yearly attendance, 1931–1940," [ca. June 1940,] ARC 60–1–12, LJTS (the total from November 1931 through December 1940 was 157,035). Concerning PR's financial needs and additional work to supplement it, PR to CA, 11 February 1932, ARC MS 26--93:5, LKCAJS and PR to CA, 16 July 1937 and PR to AM, 13 May 1938, ARC 60–2–3, LJTS. See also, Bertha Romanoff to CA, 16 August 1938 and PR to CA, 10 May 1939, RG 1–22–39, LJTS. On PR's salary appeals, see PR to CA, 1 July 1938, CA to PR, 6 July 1938, PR to CA, 17 July 1938, RG 1–22–39, LJTS. They continued after CA's death; see PR to LF, 29 May 1941, LF to PR, 3 June 1941, RG 1–22–39, LJTS. On PR's illness, see AM, "Report on the Library and Museum," 22 June 1942, RG 1–16–62, LJTS; see also, Bertha Romanoff to LF, 29 December 1943, RG 1–39–14, LJTS. "Dr. Paul Romanoff, a Museum Curator," *New York Times*, 13 December 1943.
31. On AM's director designation, see LF to AM, 27 May 1942, ARC 80–30–Correspondence-LF, Jan-July, 1942, LJTS. On stationery, see AM to LF, 15 June 1942, RG 1–16–65, LJTS. AM, "Report on the Library and Museum," 1 May 1940, RG 25–1–27, LJTS.

Chapter 3

A New Venue, a New Purpose

A 1944 gift allowing the Museum of Jewish Ceremonial Objects to move from the seminary's campus on New York's upper west side to a far more prominent location along Fifth Avenue presented unique opportunities and unforeseen outcomes. The relocation coincided with a change in the seminary's administration from Cyrus Adler's cautious institution building to his successor's daring vision of a leadership role for Judaism in American social thought and culture. The prospect of greater visibility and far more space for the museum magnified the part it might play in that vision. To guide that potential transition, advice was sought from museum professionals and scholars who seized the occasion to reimagine the museum. The ensuing discussions redirected the museum from its original function of prioritizing ritual objects and treating them as religious and historical artifacts. Added to those founding purposes was the exhibition of modern art created by Jews. After the appointment of a new museum head with a background in art history, an appetite for work by living Jewish artists, and the encouragement of an adviser immersed in New York's contemporary art world, the museum opened itself to the possibilities of the avant-garde, including works by non-Jews. The changes altered both the museum's mission and its identity among Jews and non-Jews alike. Before long, an artist observed "You don't have to be Jewish to show at the Jewish Museum."[1]

Reimagining the Museum: Interfaith Dialogue

Sometime after 1938, Frieda Schiff Warburg (1876–1958) began contemplating the disposition of her large six-story neo-French Gothic mansion (Figure 3.1). It was designed to accommodate a family with five children, spacious "etching rooms" to house the Warburgs' collection of old master works (Figure 3.2), an upstairs music parlor with a grand piano

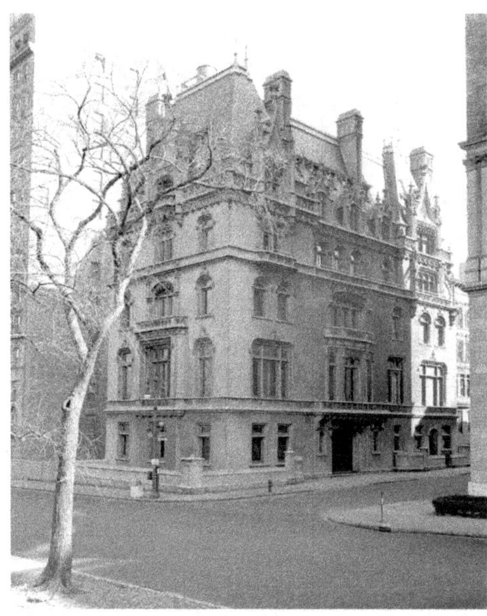

Figure 3.1. Warburg family mansion, ca. 1944, designed by Charles Pierrepont Henry Gilbert (1861–1952) and completed in 1908. Courtesy of the Library of the Jewish Theological Seminary.

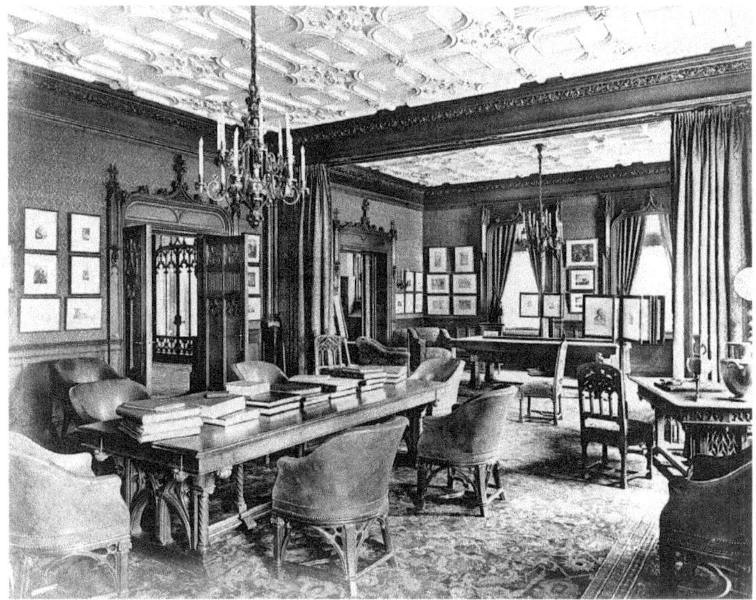

Figure 3.2. Etching rooms, Warburg family mansion, ca. 1930s. The Jewish Museum, New York/Art Resource, NY.

and Aeolian player pipe organ, and a spacious dining room that doubled as a "small civic center" for the many organizational and philanthropic meetings convened by her husband, Felix Warburg. With imposing exterior and ornate interiors, the mansion offered a nearly ideal setting for a museum. With its history as a locus of art collecting, music, and discourse among Jewish-community leaders, it was also an auspicious site for the kinds of programs a Jewish museum might offer. When completed in 1908, the mansion's location—at the corner of Fifth Avenue and 92nd Street—was considered by fashionable New Yorkers as the "remote northern wilderness." By the 1930s, however, the mansion's setting near cultural amenities, including the Metropolitan Museum of Art to the south and other museums across Central Park, had become far more desirable. Yet it became a burden for Warburg after the children, now adults, had moved out and Felix passed away. Proper, insightful, and firm, Frieda Warburg was a full partner in Felix's numerous charitable activities; and, after his death in 1937, she succeeded him on the boards of several organizations they had backed. Among them was that of the seminary, becoming its first female trustee. Another trustee, Alan M. Stroock (1908–85), who was the Warburg family lawyer and conversant with the couple's past contributions for the seminary's museum, suggested she donate the mansion to serve as its new home even though the mansion was some distance from the seminary. The idea was appealing for other family reasons. Warburg's father and brother, Jacob H. Schiff and Mortimer Schiff, respectively, were seminary benefactors, a philanthropic legacy she honored with the commission of ornamental iron gates for the seminary's main entrance by metalworks artist Samuel Yellin.[2]

Warburg and Stroock were also aware that the museum's collection had outgrown its space. Between its opening in 1931 and a decade later, the collection grew from about four hundred objects to nearly twenty-three hundred. Almost all the additions came from two sources: the Jewish community of Danzig (Gdańsk, Poland) and a New York collector. In July 1939, Danzig's Jews, fearing a Nazi takeover, sent the museum over 520 ceremonial objects, many rare and precious, with the stipulation that they be held for fifteen years, and if the community remained free and safe, the objects should be returned. If not, they were to remain with the museum in perpetuity. A month after the objects arrived in New York, the Nazis occupied Danzig and the community was obliterated. The other collection of about 1,250 objects was donated in the early 1940s by Harry G. Friedman (1882–1965). It also included rare ritual works—many acquired as they entered the market from Jews fleeing the Nazis—as well as "specimens of Jewish folk-art." The Danzig artifacts were not exhibited in the museum for want of space. Instead, they were shown in a congested "five room suite" on the sixth floor of the seminary's dormitory, where they could only be viewed by a few persons at a time because most of the objects were "on open display, not in cases" necessitating close supervision. Other works, including those from the Friedman collection, were haphazardly crammed into closets and rooms throughout the seminary. By 1943, Marx, who continued to supervise the museum, was urging further donations be declined for want of space.[3]

Just as Warburg was contemplating her mansion's future, Rabbi Louis Finkelstein succeeded Cyrus Adler as the seminary's president. Finkelstein (1895–1991) was born in Cincinnati, the son of an Orthodox rabbi, and earned undergraduate and doctoral degrees at the College of the City of New York and Columbia University while concurrently studying at the seminary, where he was ordained in 1919. He was soon recognized by his teachers and peers as a brilliant scholar with a gift for elucidating the history of Judaism from antiquity through the Middle Ages with penetrating, socially contextualized studies of fundamental texts. After receiving his doctorate, he was invited to teach Talmud and later theology part-time at the seminary, all the while serving as a congregational rabbi in New York. Adler saw in Finkelstein the leadership abilities of a possible successor, arranged Finkelstein's full-time appointment as associate professor in 1931—enabling him to resign his pulpit, and Adler started handing Finkelstein ever larger administrative responsibilities. Before long, Finkelstein became assistant to the president and subsequently assumed the newly created position of provost. Highly regarded by colleagues and governing board members alike, he was promptly appointed seminary president after Adler's death in 1940. Finkelstein brought to the task a reputation as a "charismatic personality, forceful leader, and passionate advocate." He was a prodigious scholar who published nearly four hundred books and articles over his career, thanks to a work ethic that had him rising daily about 4:00 a.m. to study, write, and attend morning prayers before attending to his seminary duties. Learned and exacting in his adherence to religious strictures, Finkelstein was also a generous teacher, patient colleague, and kind friend to many, including those less religiously observant than him. Those who knew him regarded Finkelstein as an "amalgam of biblical prophet, rabbinic sage, 19th-century *rav* [rabbi], and 20th-century executive."[4]

While still provost, Finkelstein envisioned a larger role for Judaism, and thereby the seminary, in American public affairs. The year after his appointment, he articulated a plan to increase "understanding among various faiths, and also among the various intellectual disciplines," to strengthen "the moral and spiritual fiber of the American people." Finkelstein was motivated by several concerns: that the rise of Nazism resulted from a moral collapse in Germany symptomatic of a deeper and infectious malaise in Western society; that American Jews' survival depended on the understanding of other religious groups; and that the younger generation was disaffiliating and undercutting the future of all American religions. He was also alarmed by misperceptions of Judaism among educated Jews and non-Jews who, he felt, should know better. Without exaggeration, Finkelstein claimed, Judaism could be called "the unknown religion of our time." By reaching out to non-Jewish intellectuals, clerics, and opinion leaders particularly, he hoped to introduce them to Judaism *and* secure a leadership role for it in elevating the place of religious ideals as a driving force in American public policy that, in turn, would reengage disaffected Jews. Underlying Finkelstein's vision was his conviction that Judaism's teachings were indispensable to American democracy, that the nation's moral tenets were endangered, and that Jews were uniquely positioned to unify the major religions in addressing America's challenges.

His first project, begun in the late 1930s, was called the "Institute for Interdenominational Studies" (later reconstituted as the "Institute for Religious and Social Studies"), an ongoing program of meetings and publications facilitating "intergroup" conversations among prominent religious scholars and leaders from different faiths. To it, Finkelstein added an annual "Conference on Science, Philosophy, and Religion," a think tank organized around meetings for which prominent scholars and intellectuals provided papers to be read in advance, debated when participants gathered, and subsequently published. To overcome the fragmentation of modern research, it drew together scholars and scientists from an array of disciplines addressing topics of common interest. Ideally, the juxtaposition of diverse arrays of learning would result in an "integration of knowledge" conducive to democratic values and moral progress. Where the Institute for Religious and Social Studies concentrated on promoting interreligious understanding, the Conference on Science, Philosophy, and Religion focused on pure research, functioning, in the words of one participant, as the "organized conscience" of American civilization. Over subsequent decades, attendance at these and related intergroup programs numbered over seventy-five thousand and their publications reached many more.[5]

The most prominent and far-reaching of Finkelstein's outreach efforts, however, were his media broadcasts. In the 1930s, the seminary experimented with occasional programs, but in 1944, Finkelstein launched continuing radio and later television series. The radio broadcasts were

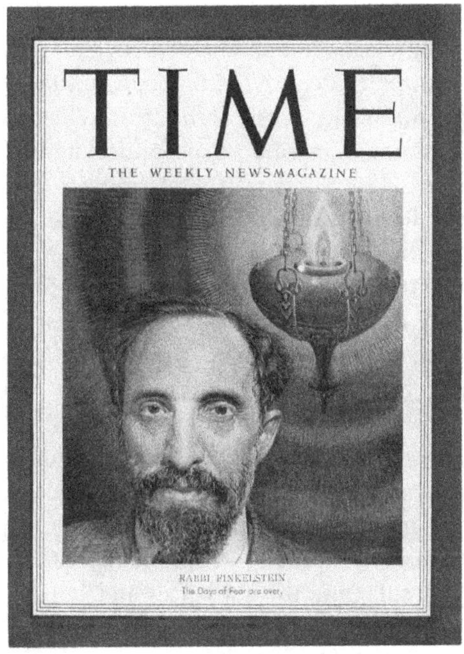

Figure 3.3. Louis Finkelstein, cover of *Time* 58, no. 16 (15 October 1951). Artwork by Giro (Guy Rowe). From TIME.

initially dramatizations featuring the experiences of Jews during and after the Second World War, the lives of prominent Jews, stories of Jewish contributions to American society and culture, and adaptations based on Jewish folklore and literature. The longest running was *The Eternal Light*, which, over its nearly forty-five-year duration, produced almost nineteen hundred broadcasts. It was usually aired Sunday mornings by some thirty National Broadcasting Company stations, a number that rose to over one hundred by the 1950s, and was subsequently carried by the US Armed Forces Radio Service and the nation's overseas outlet, Voice of America. *The Eternal Light* reached a national audience of between five and six million per show and earned several industry and critics' awards. The seminary also contributed segments for previously established ecumenical television series such as *Lamp Unto My Feet* and *Frontiers of Faith*. As with his other initiatives, Finkelstein sought to explain Judaism to Americans, present it as "a moral force" helping confront major challenges of the day, and offer non-affiliated Jews a fuller "appreciation of their heritage." His media programs helped transform Sundays from a time when American

Christians converged around interests "marked not only by doctrinal but also by ethnic, class, racial and regional divides, into a day for exploring and celebrating common interests." Finkelstein's outreach efforts vaulted him into national prominence as one of the most influential Jewish leaders of the era. He communicated with major political figures as well, including past and current US presidents, one of whom—John F. Kennedy—appointed Finkelstein to represent the nation at the coronation of Pope Paul VI in 1963. The leading newsweekly magazine of the day, *Time*, heralded him as "A Trumpet for All Israel" (Figure 3.3).[6]

During this period, New York became the "Jewish Capital City" of America, whether measured by population, national Jewish-organization headquarters, array of cultural and educational institutions, or philanthropic infrastructure. The seminary occupied a leading place in this constellation. The opportunities that status afforded Finkelstein's institute, conference, and broadcast initiatives, and the objectives they represented were much on his mind when he learned Warburg might donate her home to the seminary. By virtue of its location, it offered an even more visible platform for enlarging the audiences and impact of Finkelstein's programs. When, in January 1944, he reached out to her to formally invite the donation, he sketched out the mansion's use as both a museum and a site for his institute—which Warburg began supporting a year earlier—and conference programs. Finkelstein argued that having them in proximity would be advantageous because the exhibits could complement his intergroup activities. Noting the Warburg and Schiff families' previous contributions to the museum and its resulting success, including a current attendance of nearly three thousand visitors per month, "about half of them Christians," Finkelstein reasoned that public interest would only grow when all these efforts were under one roof in a more central location. He assumed the museum would retain its present mission and play a subsidiary role, much as it had on the seminary's campus (Figure 3.4), captured in his proposed name for the soon-to-be-transformed mansion: "Felix M. Warburg Center."[7]

Warburg happily donated the mansion, and Finkelstein began organizing its adaptation and staffing. Renovations were necessary for its museum functions, and an administrative realignment was needed because the new setting would be too distant for Marx, whose library responsibilities required his presence on the seminary campus. Finkelstein organized a planning committee of Jewish and non-Jewish museum professionals and scholars to advise him on the changes. This was emblematic of Finkelstein's leadership style, which was consultative and deferential. When problems arose outside his areas of expertise, he sought specialists and relied—sometimes naively—on their suggestions. He perceived his

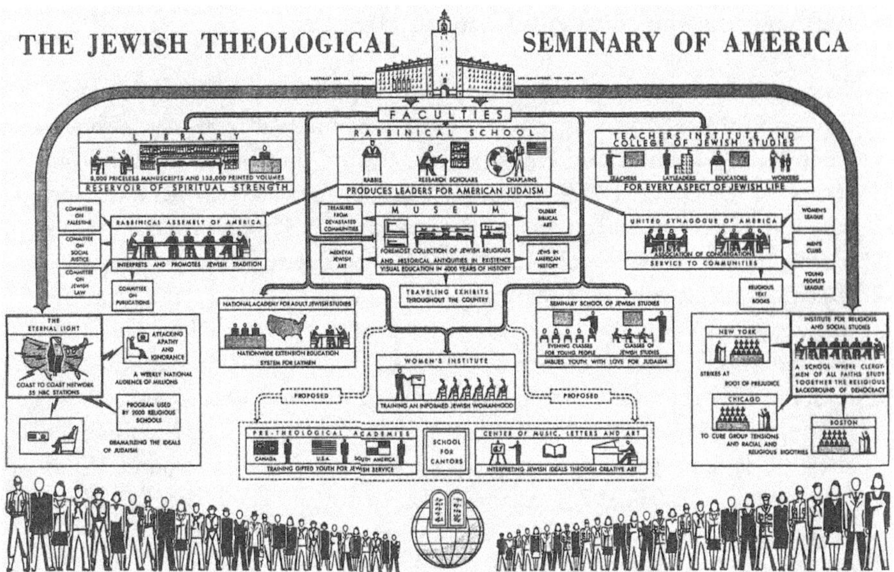

Figure 3.4. Poster, Jewish Theological Seminary, ca. 1945. Note blocks for the museum (center near top), Eternal Light (lower left), and Institute for Religious and Social Studies (lower right). Courtesy of the Library of the Jewish Theological Seminary.

role as setting high standards and ambitious objectives, both by example and occasional admonitions. Regarding the museum, Finkelstein declared it should be more than "just another," and although its scope would be limited, he intended it to compare favorably with the "finest institutions of its type." By that, he may have meant higher education-based museums of which there were a fair number in the United States—the only other Jewish one being Hebrew Union College's Union Museum. He also asked the planners to assure that the museum introduced Jews and non-Jews to the "significance of Judaism as a force in civilization." The planning committee, led by members from the Metropolitan Museum of Art and Brooklyn Museum, recommended the mansion be renovated and staffed in accordance with the museum profession's standards. While the committee acknowledged that the museum's mission should be aligned with the seminary's and not exist "merely as a collection," it nonetheless focused on matters specific to museums such as hiring an architect expert on them, a curator knowledgeable about art history and Judaism, and trained guards. Finkelstein, having envisioned the building as primarily "an academic center" for his intergroup programs, was taken aback. But the planning emphasis, now driven by the committee, was solely on the museum.[8]

Reimagining the Museum: Cultural History

The planning committee included three art historians: Richard Krautheimer, Guido Schoenberger, and Meyer Schapiro. All were of Jewish descent but their contributions to scholarship on Judaism's visual culture varied. Krautheimer (1897–1994), who was born, earned his doctorate, and taught in Germany, had emigrated to America in 1935. His dissertation was on medieval synagogue architecture, but he never returned to Jewish topics afterward, specializing instead in early Christian architecture, Baroque architecture, Roman urbanism, and Renaissance sculpture. Krautheimer's research situated his subjects within the immediate cultural, social, and physical contexts in which they took form and looked at the iconographic traditions and theological preferences that informed them. Finkelstein met Krautheimer after the latter began teaching at Vassar College, probably around 1940. Schoenberger (1891–1974), also from Germany, earned a doctorate in art history at Freiburg University in 1917 where he began teaching and serving in various administrative capacities there and in Frankfurt. In 1928, he added curatorial responsibilities at the Stadtgeschichtliches (City History) Museum in Frankfurt. He lost both posts when the Nazis came to power, however, and found work instead at the Museum jüdischer Altertümer (Jewish Antiquities Museum) in Frankfurt before emigrating to America in 1939. Schoenberger initially specialized in medieval and Renaissance decorative arts but began studying Jewish ceremonial objects when he joined the Museum jüdischer. He was one of just a few art historians researching Jewish ritual objects at the time and was known for contextualizing them within broader non-Jewish artistic traditions and cultural history. After arriving in New York, he found work at the Institute of Fine Arts, New York University, as a lecturer and researcher, rising to head its visual-resources department by 1944. Starting in 1940, Schoenberger also assisted the seminary on a part-time, short-term basis cataloging and preparing the Friedman collection for exhibition. Despite Schoenberger's qualifications, Finkelstein offered Krautheimer the museum directorship, but he declined. As a result of their conversations, however, Finkelstein invited Krautheimer to head an envisioned research program at the museum on a part-time basis so he could continue teaching at Vassar. Krautheimer accepted, hoping to reshape the museum into "a center of Jewish scholarly and cultural life." Shortly thereafter, Schoenberger was asked to assist with curatorial research and museum planning, still on a part-time basis. Meanwhile, Finkelstein urged the planning committee to proceed while he searched for a director. Its ensuing discussions surveyed alternatives that, in part, reflected the art historical and museological trends of the era.[9]

Schoenberger inaugurated the conversation with his "General Plan for a Museum of Jewish Culture." Although he thought of the collection as comprised of aesthetic objects, he resisted organizing the museum based solely on the collection's artistic value. Instead, he argued objects should be interpreted in the context of their "importance to Jewish cultural life." Displays should feature documents alongside objects because "'historical quality' is a category of importance, just as [is] 'artistic quality.'" The museum must be "popular and approachable" both for Jews and non-Jews, he added, but ought to maintain high scholarly standards with content-rich exhibits and effective labels. Its overarching aim would be to guide visitors through the history of Jewish cultural life up to the present. Schoenberger conceived of "cultural life" as an amalgam of Jews' religious beliefs, practices, and "historical mission." Aware his historical emphasis could result in displays that were "boring, tiring or graveyards," he wanted the visitor experience to be "a living one." The antidote to historical deadening was modernity or, in his terms, "actuality," which could be achieved, for example, by exhibiting depictions of contemporary synagogues and ritual objects created in "modern form." To illustrate his plan, Schoenberger outlined a permanent collection display arranged chronologically, beginning with "The Jews Before the Diaspora" and concluding with "The Jews of the Diaspora in the Western World" ("The Americas" and "New Palestine"). He envisioned an array of topics to be pursued within each period and region including: "worship" (the ancient temple and synagogue architecture), ritual objects, and festivals; learning (sacred texts and commentaries); "the family" (religious observances at home); "administration" (institutions for common welfare other than synagogues); and relations with "gentile authorities." Knowing the museum's collections were insufficient to support these ambitions, Schoenberger proposed using photographic reproductions, maps, plans, and models to flesh out the narrative. Altering the collection's interpretation, however, demanded a different name to signal this new approach. In place of "Museum of Jewish Ceremonial Objects," Schoenberger proposed three options: "Jewish Museum," "Museum of Jewish Culture," or "Museum of Jewish Cultural History."[10]

Krautheimer agreed with most of Schoenberger's suggestions and focused only on their differences. Regarding the institution's name, he mentioned two others: "Judaic Museum" and "Museum of Jewish Art," though he preferred "Jewish Museum" for its simplicity, modesty, and flexibility. The potential meanings of "Jewish" gave him pause, however. If it were construed as "something like a Jewish race," the museum would be limited to showing only objects by Jews even if the works in question lacked any "specific Jewish implications," a French landscape by impressionist Camille Pissarro or a manuscript by Karl Marx being examples. If the term referred to religion, only ritual objects would be featured while works created for Jews' secular uses might be excluded. Krautheimer urged that "Jewish" be understood as a "collective unit, whether religious or secular or both." After all, he remarked, secular and religious experiences were often intertwined in Jewish history, and an accurate representation of Judaism must accommodate each. While Krautheimer welcomed the cultural-history approach, he fretted that without a sharper definition of its scope, the museum would be deluged with "family heirlooms." He was equally skeptical of the other extreme: reshaping the institution as a "Museum of Jewish Art." Krautheimer perceived the number of available works as too limited, and further believed "the quality of Jewish art is rarely so outstanding . . . as to make it an object of purely aesthetic interest." He considered it largely a "folk art" and compared its place in Jewish history to the function of art in "colonial America: rarely outstanding and never on a pedestal, yet part of the community's religious and daily life." Krautheimer proposed a middle course, emphasizing "the visual"; that is, representing "Jewish life in visual form" by featuring aesthetically interesting objects, even if they did not rise to the level of "high" art. To be avoided was the "tiresome repetitiousness" of shelves of typological groupings of Sabbath wine cups or spice boxes. He also simplified Schoenberger's historical categories, limiting them to "great periods in Judaism," presented as period-room displays, his examples including medieval Europe (the Jewish community of Prague), the Dutch Golden Age (Rembrandt's depictions of Jews and Jewish subjects), and colonial America (the Jewish community and synagogues of Newport, Rhode Island). Krautheimer's approach is reminiscent of the uses of *Kulturgeschichte* (cultural history) as a display ideology in German museums that influenced the creation of period rooms in American art museums from the late 1800s through the 1930s. Yet, Krautheimer was uneasy about an overly rigid chronology and wondered if a reverse sequence would be more stimulating, reasoning that "prehistoric objects mean little to the layman. On the other hand, modern Judaism means a great deal." Though he acknowledged the difficulties of arranging displays "backward all the time," even if the museum's displays were mostly chronological, they should begin with twentieth-century Judaism.[11]

A consensus formed around foregrounding the modern Jewish experience, featuring visual expressions of Judaism, even if the new institution was not to be a "museum of art," and adopting visual aids to enliven displays. The planners agreed that the museum must offer permanent displays on "worship in the community" (centered on the synagogue and its accoutrements) and "life in the family" (organized around home-based religious observances and objects). Meanwhile, Krautheimer made plans for a study collection, scholarly library, research agenda, related publications, and academic programs separate from but complementing those of the museum and Institute for Religious Studies. Committee members continued tinkering with the museum's name, adding to earlier ideas "The American Jewish Museum," "Jewish Museum of America," and "Museum of Jewish Religion and Culture"—evidence of lingering irresolution over the institution's ultimate aims.[12]

Reimagining the Museum: Modern Jewish Art

The planners hoped the renovations would be complete by the first anniversary of Warburg's gift, January 1945. The project was slowed, however, by delays in organizing a governing committee, staff hiring, and architect selection. Krautheimer supervised architect interviews and recommended Percival Goodman, likely because he was sympathetic to Finkelstein's vision and unusually qualified to realize it. Goodman (1904–89) rose to prominence with dozens of bold synagogue designs exemplifying his conviction that the simplicity, truth to materials, and scale of modern architecture were ideal for creating spaces conducive to spiritual inspiration. He was also known for his contributions to social thought, urban planning, and architectural preservation, and was ahead of his time in criticizing urban-renewal schemes that swept away established neighborhoods, arguing that most buildings could be adapted for new uses. Goodman's renovation plan, which met Finkelstein's goals and the museum professionals' standards, was approved and sent out for bids in February 1945. Finkelstein was stunned by the responses. They were several times higher than the seminary could afford, and the planners began contemplating alternatives, including selling the Warburg mansion and using the proceeds to erect a new building adjacent to the seminary. High construction costs due to wartime shortages and the difficulty of fundraising raised the possibility of putting the project on hold until after the war. The idea of constructing a new building, however, led Finkelstein to imagine an enlarged "Extension Program" including art, dance, music, and theater activities alongside the museum functions. Word of the scheme reached Krautheimer, who opposed abandoning the Warburg mansion's prominent location and subordinating the museum and his research center to extension activities. Citing these factors along with increased duties at

Vassar, Krautheimer resigned. After Krautheimer's departure, Finkelstein asked Marx to oversee the project, but he resisted, and Finkelstein asked Meyer Schapiro (Figure 3.5)—who replaced Krautheimer as Finkelstein's lead museum adviser—to head the museum for a year. Finkelstein knew Schapiro from their childhoods together in Brooklyn.[13]

Meyer Schapiro (1904–96) was born in Lithuania and brought to America at the age of three by his parents. His father, a descendant of Talmudic scholars, abandoned Jewish orthodoxy under the influence of the *Haskalah* and the Jewish Socialist Bund, views Schapiro imbibed and translated into a lifelong commitment to Enlightenment values of rationalism over religion, egalitarianism, and social activism. He entered Columbia University at sixteen, earned his bachelor's degree in art history and philosophy before he was twenty, and completed his doctorate at Columbia—also in art history—by twenty-five. Schapiro acquired Latin while an undergraduate, taught himself German via Yiddish, and became fluent in other modern languages. He possessed a remarkable visual memory and total recall, sometimes remembering not only published sources, but chapter headings and page citations as well. Multidisciplinary in approach, Schapiro's scholarship ranged from Romanesque sculpture to nineteenth- and twentieth-century painting including Impressionism, Abstract Expressionism, and the avant-garde—the most challenging artistic explorations of his time. Despite his relatively small number of major scholarly publications, Schapiro had an outsized impact as an art historian, critic, and public intellectual. His entire teaching career was at Columbia, where he inspired generations of future scholars, but he also lectured at the New School for Social Research in lower Manhattan between 1936 and 1952, galvanizing numerous artists and writers there, and attracting many to his uptown classes at Columbia. Concerning his scholarship, David Rosand observes that the "larger aim of Schapiro's project might be termed the reclamation of the artist in and from history." Whether studying Romanesque stone carvers or contemporary painters, Schapiro sought out the humanity of his subjects and the relationship between their work and their social circumstances. That search led him into the studios of contemporary painters and sculptors where he became a "passionate friend" of over three generations of artists and earned a reputation as "the conscience of the art world."[14]

Throughout his life, Schapiro was an unapologetic atheist, ardent socialist, and self-described radical. He began staking out his views on the interrelationships of art and society in the 1930s, often in the context of Marxist thought, and he never ceased engaging in social activism via scholarly writings, occasional papers, public statements, and service. When

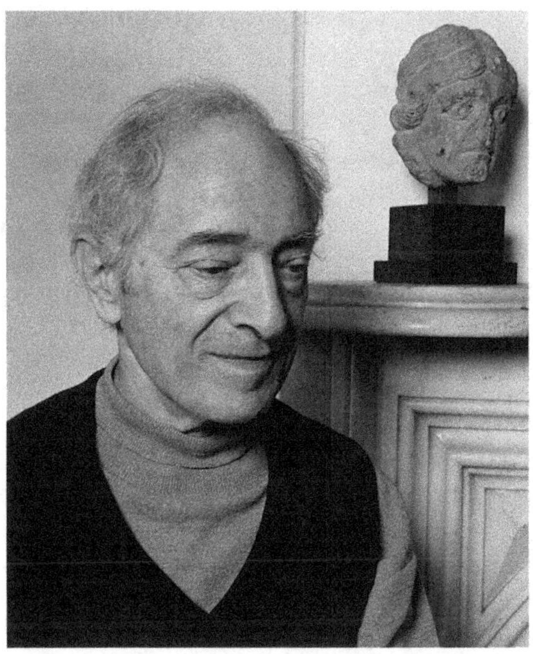

Figure 3.5. Meyer Schapiro, 1980. Photograph by Arthur Mones. Courtesy of the Rare Book and Manuscript Library, Columbia University Libraries.

leftist contemporaries began drifting to the right during the Cold War, Schapiro remained steadfast in his beliefs. He opposed America's pursuit of the Vietnam War by lending his name to anti-war petitions and advertisements and by speaking at Columbia University's largest anti-war protest. Less visibly, Schapiro was a founding editor of the *Marxist Quarterly* and served on the steering committee of the Democratic Socialists of America and the editorial board of the socialist journal *Dissent*. His was an "undogmatic Marxism," as evident from Schapiro's earliest applications of Marxist theory. He parted ways with socialist art theorists who, enamored of Social Realist art, were "hostile" to abstract art—which he championed starting in the 1930s—or who, unlike Schapiro, insisted on socioeconomic conditions as the *only* valid framework for studying art. While he certainly embraced socialist theory and helped advance it as a methodological tool in art history, Schapiro was equally attuned to the role of the artist as a free-thinking, creative individual, one capable of deviating from and even subverting sociocultural norms.[15]

The most significant of Schapiro's scholarly contributions along these lines, relevant to his work with the seminary museum, grew out of the nature of two interests: Romanesque art and contemporary art. From the outset, Schapiro wrote about both, attracted to both eras for what Rosand identifies as the "tense dialectic between the individual and the social." In Schapiro's research on Romanesque sculptural works, chiefly in the abbeys of Moissac and Souillac (France) and Silos (Spain), the tension was between the monasteries' religious purposes and the artists' secular interests. Though the wall reliefs, columns, and marginal stone carvings Schapiro studied were created to serve the religious needs of monastic orders, he discerned in them indications of the individual sculptors' pleasure in craft, invention, and whimsy, suggestive of decidedly nonspiritual enthusiasms and every-day life experiences. On the other hand, when studying the works of modern artists, created in a secular society and time, Schapiro found traces of spiritual longing and fervor. The contradictions arose, Donald Kuspit notes, "between religious institutions and secular individuals (in the case of significant medieval art) and spiritual individuals and secular institutions (in the case of significant modern art)." As an atheist, Schapiro sought to rescue the Romanesque artist from scholarly submersion within the far-reaching influence of religion; and as a Marxist, he strove to rescue the modern artist from critical submersion within the all-pervasive influence of capitalism. In both cases, Schapiro perceived elements of a yet deeper and persistent tension—between individual freedom and oppressive societal structures, whether organized religion or capitalist economies. By the time Schapiro started advising Finkelstein, these ideas had largely coalesced into two configurations "framing his analysis of art: the relationship between the religious and the secular, and between institutional authority and individual autonomy." They also informed his approach to the seminary museum, the Jewish community, and contemporary artists.[16]

Schapiro declined Finkelstein's museum-directorship offer, suggesting instead Stephen S. Kayser (1900–88). Born into an orthodox Jewish home in Germany where he learned Hebrew before German, Kayser (Figure 3.6) went on to earn a doctorate at the University of Heidelberg, studying aesthetic philosophy, art, and music history. He taught at the universities of Karlsruhe, Mannheim, Berlin, and Brno, Czechoslovakia, before fleeing to America in 1938. Kayser became fascinated with Jewish ritual objects and art along the way, starting a personal slide collection of noteworthy works while still in Europe. He expanded his expertise during brief stints at Hebrew Union College in Cincinnati, and the libraries of Columbia University and the University of California, Berkeley. Although Kayser's adherence to Orthodox Judaism waned over time, his interest in the spiritual as well as historical meanings of its ritual objects grew. He

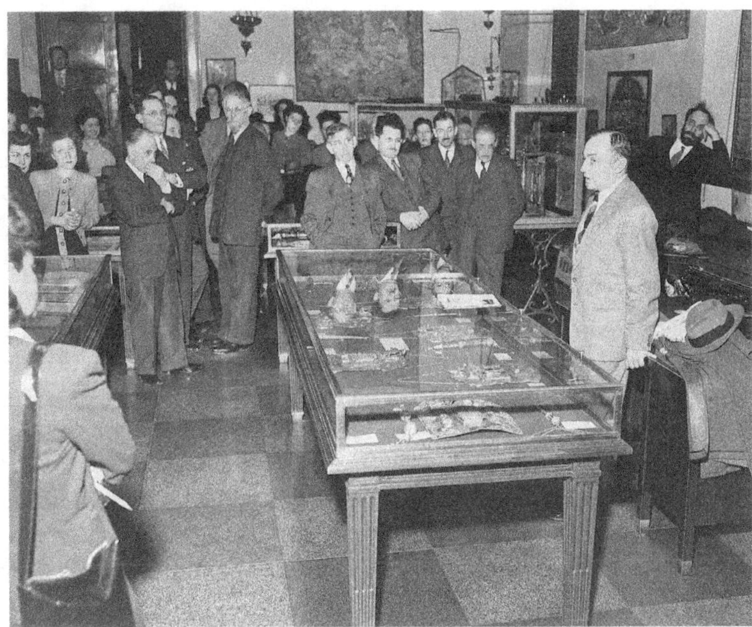

Figure 3.6. Stephen S. Kayser (second from right), ca. February 1947. Closing ceremony for Museum of Jewish Ceremonial and Historical Objects (with Louis Finkelstein, far right, and Alexander Marx, center left with beard and facing camera). Courtesy of the Library of the Jewish Theological Seminary.

had settled into a faculty position at San Jose State College in California, starting in 1944, when the museum job came up. Kayser and Schapiro met while the former was at Columbia; they remained in touch, and when Schapiro mentioned the seminary's museum job, Kayser promptly applied, indicating his interest in organizing exhibits of modern Jewish art as well. Finkelstein offered the post, and Kayser accepted in September 1946. Each side was plunging into the unknown. From Finkelstein's perspective, Kayser was inexperienced as a curator or administrator; and unbeknownst to the former, Kayser was inept at handling finances. While he brought a wealth of knowledge about and passion for Jewish art broadly conceived, and he was a compelling teacher and storyteller, Kayser could also be prickly and tactless with some, even as he charmed others with his personal warmth and enthusiasm. For his part, Kayser saw great potential in the museum, but had no assurances Finkelstein would provide the resources to make that vision a reality.[17]

By then, Finkelstein had settled on the mansion as the museum's best location, found money for a limited renovation, and work was underway.

The conversion created galleries on the first through third floors, the fourth and sixth floors were left relatively untouched (the Institute for Religious and Social Studies was to be on the fourth floor), and the fifth floor was transformed into an apartment for Kayser and his wife, Louise Darmstaedter Kayser. She was an artist, and their accommodations included a studio for her that doubled as a museum workspace so she could help install the museum's exhibits and design and illustrate its publications, much "like a rabbi's wife who does a lot of work in the synagogue but gets no pay." When he announced the renovations, Finkelstein endorsed the museum's turn toward modernity, highlighting plans for exhibits of "Jewish art and life up to the present day." Ideally, he declared, the museum would also become "a center for creative artists." Because Kayser had yet to arrive, it was up to Schapiro to flesh out these goals.[18]

He prepared a fresh plan summarizing the principles formulated by Krautheimer and Schoenberger and mapped them onto the renovated mansion's spaces, adjusting the temporary-display components of earlier plans firmly in favor of modern art. Schapiro relegated permanent collection displays of antiquities, ritual objects, and other works to the second floor as a study collection alongside a gallery for seasonal exhibits related to the Jewish holiday cycle. First floor galleries were designated for changing exhibitions, primarily of modern art. The inaugural exhibit was to consist of thirty to forty paintings, sculptures, and prints by contemporary Jewish artists ranging from Social Realists to Abstract Expressionists. Ideally, the works would represent "Jewish themes or . . . marked Jewish sentiment," but that was not a rigid requirement. In the future, there were to be four or five shows a year of which all but one should be modern; and among them, there ought to be at least one solo exhibition for an established artist and a group exhibit of work by Jewish artists under the age of thirty-five.[19]

The museum's name remained undecided when Kayser arrived in January 1947, now just five months before its opening. Frieda Warburg, who closely monitored the mansion's renovation, endorsed "Judaic Museum." The seminary's board of directors, however, preferred "The American Jewish Museum." She countered that for reasons of appropriateness and simplicity they should drop "American." Kayser disliked the name's vagueness and proposed "Museum of Arts," "Museum of Arts and Antiquities," or "Art Museum"—all "of the Jewish Theological Seminary." The seminary's executive committee declined his suggestions and offered "The Jewish Museum, Jewish Theological Seminary of America." Warburg intervened again, this time striking the first "Jewish" as redundant, but Finkelstein believed both "Jewish"s were necessary, and they settled on "The Jewish Museum" with the tag "under the auspices of The Jewish

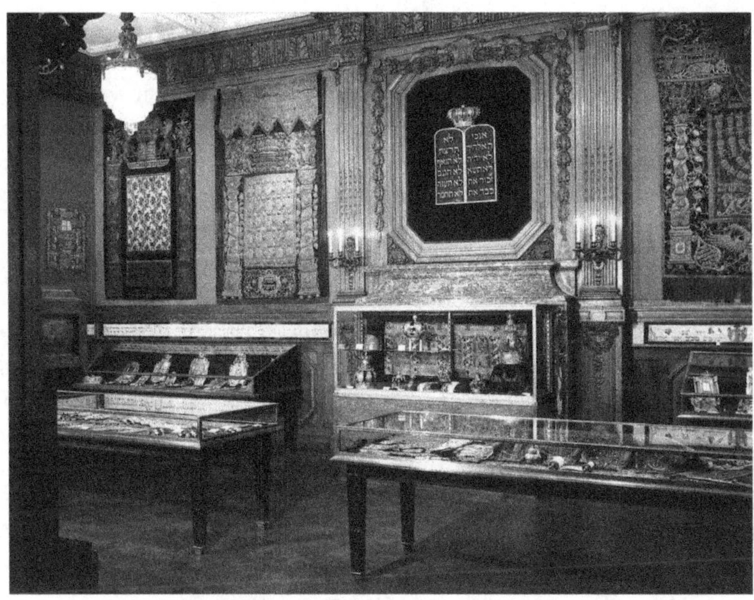

Figure 3.7. Gallery of Torah-related ceremonial objects, ca. 1947. Courtesy of the Library of the Jewish Theological Seminary.

Theological Seminary of America," the name it retains to this day. Despite the consensus, the name nonetheless obscured the museum's increasing emphasis on art.[20]

Kayser closed the old museum, packed up and moved the collections, and started the new installations, including a loan exhibit of contemporary Jewish art. He followed Schapiro's scheme, but as he and a newly formed advisory committee dug into the details, content questions arose. To complement the permanent collection display, they thought of borrowing notable works from other museums including "early Christian representations" of subjects from Jewish scripture. Despite apprehensions about exhibiting works by non-Jews, the committee approved, provided the works did not violate the Second Commandment. At the same time, when word circulated that Kayser was featuring the works of living Jewish artists in the inaugural exhibit, an observer suggested that doing so would expose them to "public criticism" because they would no longer be considered "as American but as Jewish artists only." Kayser asked Finkelstein for advice, but the latter replied that he felt "quite useless" when it came to art and declined to offer guidance. The indirection notwithstanding, Kayser plunged ahead and opened the inaugural exhibition in May 1947. Its theme, *The Giving of the Law and The Ten Commandments*, was presented in three parts: "Jewish Art of Late Antiquity," "Works of Contemporary Artists," and "The Torah in Synagogue Art." The first floor featured a gallery of full-size photomurals of the ancient synagogue at Dura-Europos and related objects (art of antiquity) and a gallery of contemporary paintings and sculptures by Jewish artists. The Torah-related objects were installed on the second floor (Figure 3.7) because Kayser wanted to reserve the first floor for a bold visual impact on visitors as they entered the museum. Kayser anticipated questions about the artists' fidelity to Jewish subjects, because those pursuing abstraction would "not 'please' everybody." He hoped visitors would empathize with the artists who, due to the nature of their work, "feel rather separated from the Jewish community." That separation, he thought, was a fate shared with pioneering artists of every generation. But, he added, works produced by Jewish artists that are devoid of identifiable Jewish subject matter—such as bearded rabbis or biblical figures—may also reflect the frailty of faith among contemporary Jews: "The security of olden days is gone, and if the artist cannot restore it, he should not be blamed for the inner tension of our age." The plight of Jewish artists came up during the museum's dedication ceremony as the speakers worked through the occasion's meaning from an array of public perspectives.[21]

The May 1947 program included brief addresses by the kinds of leaders, non-Jewish and Jewish, Finkelstein had been engaging through his intergroup activities: Nelson A. Rockefeller (1908–79), Assistant Secretary of State for American Republic Affairs; Lewis L. Strauss (1896–1974), a member of the just-established Atomic Energy Commission; and Sam A. Lewisohn (1884–1951), an industrialist, financier, and philanthropist devoted to several causes including penal reform, unemployment insurance, and the creation of the Social Security Act. Rockefeller used the exhibition's Ten Commandments theme to advocate the "way to peace" through education and the role of institutions such as the museum and seminary in advancing the "supremacy of moral law." Strauss observed that there are several museums in New York featuring "the Hellenic concept of the Holiness of *Beauty*." Here, he asserted, is one devoted to "the Hebraic concept of the Beauty in *Holiness*." Lewisohn, also a modern-art collector and advocate of the arts in public policy, argued against pigeonholing Jewish art as an expression of ethnicity because to do so is to deny art as "an international language." Jewish artists eluded that narrowness via "a deeper spirituality and increased earnestness." "Through the arts," Lewisohn added, the Jewish artist had shown that "no walls, be they prisons or concentration camps, can prevent his spiritual escape." The issue of spirituality would come up again.[22]

Art's Usefulness for Jews

Once the opening festivities concluded, Kayser turned to completing installations on the third and fourth floors that were for ritual objects and installations illustrating their use. He wanted to stress their "art historical aspect" without diminishing their "devotional content." He did so by juxtaposing similar objects in different ways. Kayser "systematically arranged" objects in display cases by typology—such as Torah pointers—to invite comparisons of their stylistic differences, while in the same gallery he presented a pointer contextualized in a sixteenth-century Italian ark "with the interior brightly illumined and showing the [Torah] scrolls in their ornate covers, . . . for dramatic effect" and, ideally, spiritual inspiration. Kayser installed a few scenes including one suggestive of a synagogue interior with an ark and facing prayer stand (Figure 3.8). One reviewer endorsed this approach, observing that "a museum of religious . . . art" ought not be confined to displays of objects in "strictly chronological and typological sequence." Far more desirable is "a synthesized presentation" by which one can learn how the ritual objects are used. The galleries also included temporary displays illustrating Jewish holidays, such as a table setting for Passover, and a "Sabbath Room" installation of a presumably representative dining room on a Friday evening (Figure 3.9).[23]

The new museum attracted over one hundred thousand visitors during its first seven months, women comprising about two-thirds, alone, with children or friends, or as members of Jewish women's groups—most, Kayser surmised, "interested in 'Judaizing' their homes with beautiful ceremonial objects." Other visitors included "aged, bearded Jews with peoths [earlocks], young boys (obviously of yeshivoths [Jewish schools]) speaking only Yiddush, Hebrew School youngsters, children of Temple Sunday Schools (one bus-load in from Philadelphia)—all reacting similarly: acquiring a greater sense of dignity, self-respect, knowledge and feeling. . . . This WAS Jewish Education in the highest sense." Another constituency was "our Christian friends" who carefully read exhibit labels and were repeat visitors. Most Jewish viewers came away with a "profound feeling of pride" in Judaism's past. But there were also complaints. Some non-Jews were mystified by exhibits of "breastplates, crowns and such." One, likening them to a museum display of Native American artifacts that was "understandable only to the Indians themselves," said she had no "idea what the 'torah' was," an experience reminiscent of the first time she saw an "Indian ceremonial 'kiva.'" Kayser's modern art program was also a concern, some complaints coming from Frieda Warburg. Although Finkelstein soothed her, he was less accommodating with others.

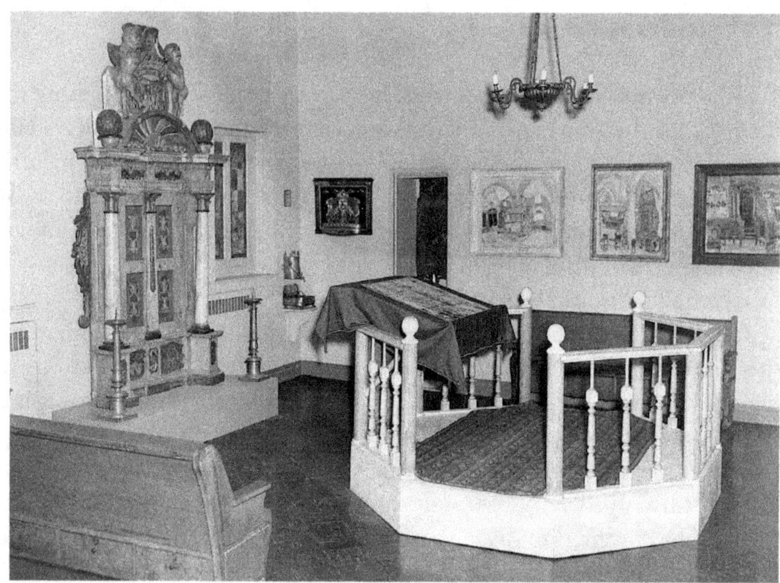

Figure 3.8. Synagogue-like installation with depictions of synagogue interiors on far wall (to the right), ca. 1947. The Jewish Museum, New York/Art Resource, NY.

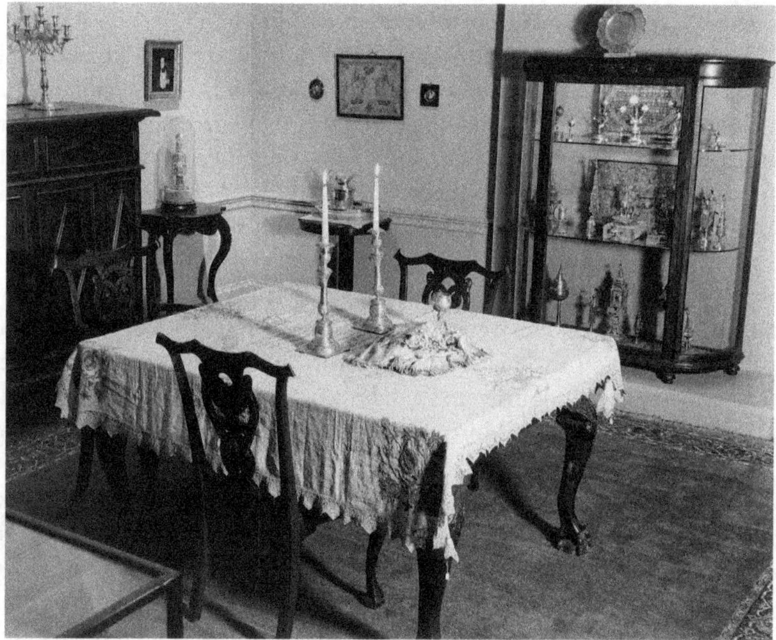

Figure 3.9. "Sabbath Room," ca. 1947. The Jewish Museum, New York/Art Resource, NY.

Responding to one grievance, he said that contemporary art exhibits "are always controversial," he trusted the museum's expert art advisers, and that Christians as well as Jews commended the exhibits, some finding the museum "from a visual point of view what the Eternal Light is to its listening audience." On the museum's first anniversary in its new location, the seminary board applauded the modern art shows, and its museum subcommittee endorsed "a freer policy" to encourage more Jewish artists to associate with the museum. Another committee backed Kayser's art emphasis over "explaining Jewish ritual or custom" and Kayser reported that "more art-conscious visitors" wished the museum would expand its modern art offerings.[24]

Despite support for his modern art exhibits, Kayser's approach to the shows remained cautious. Though he was "not fond of old b'somim [spice] boxes, but very much in favor of the fertile trends in contemporary art," in practice, his exhibition philosophy was more nuanced. While he emphasized the "visual values" of ritual objects in his displays to avoid the appearance of "ethnological exhibit[s]," Kayser did not want the museum to be "purely" aesthetic and its modern art exhibits only "l'art pour l'art." In a move evocative of the "taste culture," Sally M. Promey found liberal Protestants cultivating at the time, Kayser was guiding Jews trying to create "beautiful Jewish surrounding[s]." When he argued to congregational leaders that nineteenth-century-style portraits of venerable rabbis were incompatible with the interiors of the modern synagogues they were erecting, he learned that, for them, "Jewish art was unthinkable without a substantial display of beards." He responded by establishing a museum-based workshop for the design, creation, and sale of modern ritual objects as well as classes to disseminate these skills to others. Yet he struggled to balance shows of Jewish ritual objects and modern art. Kayser did want to show contemporary work, which often included "l'art pour l'art," even when it was not as "Jewish" as were designs for contemporary ritual objects. Yet he also believed "Jewish art is art applied to Judaism," the applications being instances in which "art is essential as a means to an end." Kayser characterized his definition as "functional" because it did not accept just anything as "Jewish in art" unless it served Judaism as a "way of life." Kayser's utilitarian outlook was an outgrowth of his interpretation of art's place in Jewish history. He understood that, after emancipation, Jews were free to follow their muses, and some became prominent artists. But, he argued, after the advent of modern art, theirs was "a contribution by Jews, not a Jewish contribution." As a result, "Today we have an overproduction of [these] 'fine' arts while the interiors of our synagogues, community houses, schools and social halls are empty." Nonetheless, he acknowledged the "themes of universal interest" pursued by Jewish artists' and their contributions to "general culture," even if the results did not look Jewish. Ideally, his exhibitions of such work would somehow close the gap between what artists were making and what their potential patrons in the Jewish community needed—whether they realized it or not.[25]

As Kayser developed his program, he began falling out of step with Schapiro, who saw a different role for contemporary art in Judaism's future. In a 1949 lecture marking the museum's second anniversary, Schapiro remarked "the ideal is not to create an official Jewish religious art," such as modern ritual objects, but to provide a hospitable setting for modern art in the Jewish community. He set the matter in the context of larger considerations he believed were important to Jews "because of our place in world culture." Schapiro argued that ceremonial objects and depictions of Jewish subjects did not rise to the level of pure artistic expression, meaning contemporary abstraction. He pointed out that although this new art was "based on the individual" rather than the community from which the artist emerged, it nonetheless "creates a confraternity of values rooted in the basic humanity of cultural work." For that reason, Jews ought to embrace the work of these artists because it reifies Jewish "values of individuality as free, mutual, creative." He was aware, however, that those contemporary Jewish artists who had achieved wide renown as part of the avant-garde did so in an era when "modern art is completely secular," by which he meant that it is independent of "any specific religious approach or ideas." In contrast to artists of the past who were patronized by religious institutions that dictated the subjects of their creations, the modern artist created out of personal experiences "not bound by a given set of doctrines." Nonetheless, there has been in recent years a "spontaneous production" of works by artists who "are not 'believers'" but whose work possesses "religious insight" and expresses "religious ideas and feelings." Works by artists outside the ambit of organized religion that inspire religious thoughts or emotions are more subtle and less accessible, Schapiro said, than modern paintings on religious subjects, such as images based on Old Testament stories. He did not believe the latter type of work possessed the "religious depth" of the contemporary art he had in mind because it was based on "illustrating ideas." He likened the "highly religious quality" of modern art, on the other hand, to the intellectual challenges of rigorous scholarship. "If a religious thinker or philosopher," Schapiro held, were to address this subject, one would have to grapple with those ideas and "take a stand" over them, recognizing them as comprising a "fresh approach to religious problems." Paintings merely depicting religious themes may be skillfully done, but they do not add anything new to "our awareness of the religious world." For these reasons, Schapiro cautioned, the prevalence of so many Jewish artists should not encourage Jews to expect the appearance of more overtly Jewish subject matter. To the contrary, for contemporary artists and critics alike, mere illustrations of Jewish themes—such as illustrations of Old Testament stories—are retrograde.[26]

Schapiro began considering modern art's relationship to society over a decade earlier in two essays, "The Social Bases of Art" in 1936 and "Nature of Abstract Art" a year later. Both related abstraction to the history of art by resisting formal interpretations of abstract art that disassociated it from the trials of contemporary life. In the first essay, Schapiro argued against a common misconception of modern artists as isolated from society and their work as "unaffected by social and economic changes." To the contrary, its "social aspect" was obscured by the "personal and aesthetic contexts of secular life . . . just as religious beliefs and practices in the past conditioned the formal character of religious art." In the second essay, Schapiro proposed that abstract art, despite its "exclusion of natural forms" and "unhistorical universalizing," not be interpreted as a mere reaction against representational traditions in past art. Instead, it must be understood as reifying "the changing material and psychological conditions surrounding modern culture," especially economic and political conflicts. Those conditions, captured in abstract forms rendered with highly expressive uses of paint, embody the artist's "mood" or state of mind as accurately as earlier depictions of landscapes represented the scenes upon which they were based. The "most responsive" of the artist's viewers is the one who is "similarly concerned" and "finds in such pictures not only the counterpart of his own tension, but a final discharge of obsessing feelings" captured in the explosive gestures of abstract expressionism.[27]

Schapiro initially pursued these ideas independently and later in dialogue with Clement Greenberg (1909–94). A near contemporary of Schapiro, and also of Jewish descent, Greenberg too was born in New York and studied art, but he followed a different trajectory, earning an undergraduate degree in literature at Syracuse University and afterward working in New York-based federal-government posts. Starting in the 1930s, Greenberg published literary and cultural criticism for the *Nation* and the *Partisan Review*, subsequently assuming editorial responsibilities at the latter and then for the periodical that became *Commentary*. By the early 1940s, he turned increasingly to art criticism, becoming a leading proponent of the "New York School" and what he termed "painterly abstraction," the work of abstract expressionist artists including Willem de Kooning, Robert Motherwell, and Jackson Pollock, and postpainterly abstraction—or color field painting—by such artists as Morris Louis, Kenneth Noland, and Jules Olitski. Greenberg's essays established him as a leading interpreter of modernist painting and sculpture, a reputation he consolidated by organizing exhibitions and teaching at several elite universities. He remains arguably the most influential and controversial critic of twentieth-century American art. Subsequent developments—especially postmodern theory and criticism—reflect the lingering force of his ideas and efforts to counter if not supplant them.[28]

Schapiro and Greenberg were close at one time and collaborated on a significant exhibition of avant-garde painting in 1950 before they began moving in separate directions. When Greenberg started writing more frequently about abstract art in the late 1930s, his emulation of Schapiro's thought, combined with the "combative verbal style of 'the Lionels' Abel and Trilling"—two prominent New York intellectuals—earned Greenberg the nickname "Lionel Schapiro." Schapiro's influence is evident in two of Greenberg's most important essays which, in turn, informed Schapiro's thinking in the late 1940s and 1950s as he was advising the Jewish Museum. The essays, "Avant-Garde and Kitsch" (1939) and "Towards a Newer Laocoon" (1940) mark a particular shift in emphasis, however. Where Schapiro saw in abstraction a new art form that was intimately related to and a product of the society from which it emerged, Greenberg perceived an art form that broke with the past in its rejection of the uses of painting for pictorial depiction to, instead, explore the very nature of paint and the methods of its application. "'Art for art's sake' and 'pure poetry' appear" in this work, he claimed, "and subject matter or content becomes something to be avoided like a plague." Greenberg drew distinctions between avant-garde art and other types of contemporary work based on the differences between a purity of form, that emerged from the artist's concentration on the plasticity of paint per se, and the uses of paint to depict subjects. Contemporary representational art—including modern Jewish artists' depictions of Judaic subjects that Schapiro regarded as retrograde—was characterized by Greenberg as "ersatz culture, kitsch." Greenberg believed the problem with representational art lay not with "realistic imitation in itself," but rather in the use of "realistic illusion in the service of sentimental and declamatory" work. Modern depictions of bearded rabbis and comparable Jewish subject matter would have struck Greenberg as "ersatz" Jewish culture in their sentimentality and overt uses of Judaic images to beguile Jewish viewers. While Kayser disliked "substantial display[s] of beards," he would have disagreed with Greenberg that other forms of Jewish art were kitsch. Schapiro, on the other hand, not only agreed with Greenberg but also identified qualities of modern art, even works devoid of Jewish content or those by non-Jews, that he thought Jews would nonetheless find spiritually meaningful.[29]

When Schapiro opposed depictions of Jewish subjects, however, it was not only because they were backward or ersatz, but also because of their particularism. He believed avant-garde art transcended sectarian interests by being "fundamentally democratic, universal, innocent of prejudice." He felt that Jews willing to grapple with the challenges posed by the avant-garde would appreciate its "universally human" values and, in the process, form a "fresh relation to [Jewish] tradition" in the present. Schapiro acknowledged the paradox that modern art, as a manifestation of a secular age, might nonetheless nurture a deeper spirituality, albeit one that was nonsectarian. Modern art might not "win Jews for the synagogue," he conceded, but it might "win art for the Jews" because they will learn that "art is the spiritual element in secular life." Schapiro was convinced that if one approached modern art with a "disinterested love of spiritual excellence," that attitude would be rewarded with "more religious insight."[30]

Behind these discussions was a sense of precariousness in the wake of the Second World War and the Holocaust addressed by Heinz (Heinrich) Politzer. An Austrian-born Jew who immigrated to America in 1947, Politzer (1910–78) earned a doctorate in German language and literature from Bryn Mawr College, entered the professorate, and was known for his work on Kafka. He likened the Jewish Museum's ritual-object displays to those of a "*Volkskundemuseum*" (folklore museum) and argued that for modern Jews the pieces represented barely more than memories of their ancestors' "strange customs" and the old country, "best cast off" to thrive in contemporary America. This was because current religious thinking stressed "the direct personal *confrontation*" of each "modern believer with the divine." While Politzer sympathized with Jews' nostalgia for ritual objects after the Holocaust, he argued it was "a fundamental contradiction—even a sacrilege" for Kayser to prioritize displaying them and encouraging the creation of new ones. Politzer, like Kayser, saw Jewish avant-garde artists as detached from the Jewish community. Yet, he argued, the artists *did* confront the modern Jewish condition insofar as their work reflected the perilous "social, intellectual, and even religious contexts from which the modern Jew has fallen, or fears to fall." For Jewish artists, the "safeguards of tradition" were all but gone. This uncertainty was shared by non-Jewish artists as well, indicative of the universal condition noted by Schapiro. For Politzer, the Jewish artist had "become the prototype of the modern artist, or one might say, the modern artist has become a Jew." Other contemporaries had also "suffered the fate of the Jew in foreboding and anxiety" resulting from the "collapse of authority" and "lost years" of the Second

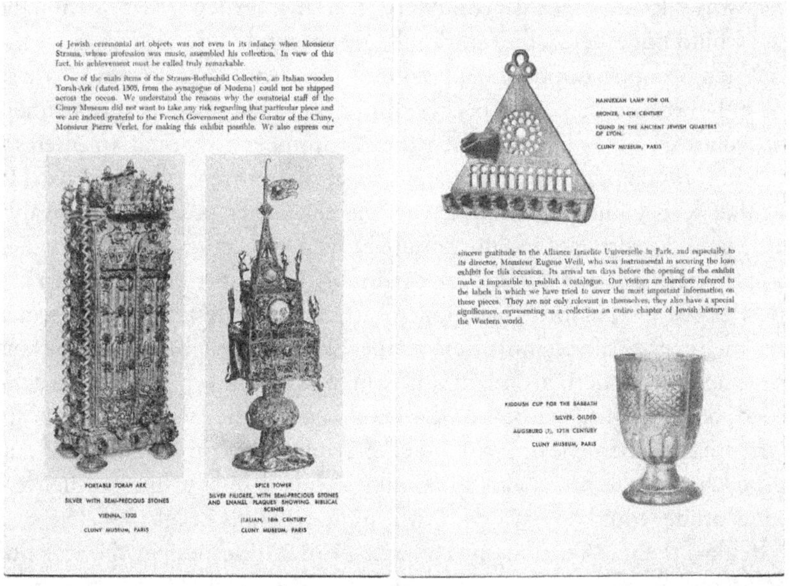
of Jewish ceremonial art objects was not even in its infancy when Monsieur Strauss, whose profession was music, assembled his collection. In view of this fact, his achievement must be called truly remarkable.

One of the main items of the Strauss-Rothschild Collection, an Italian wooden Torah-Ark (dated 1505, from the synagogue of Modena) could not be shipped across the ocean. We understand the reasons why the curatorial staff of the Cluny Museum did not want to take any risk regarding that particular piece and we are indeed grateful to the French Government and the Curator of the Cluny, Monsieur Pierre Verlet, for making this exhibit possible. We also express our

PORTABLE TORAH ARK
SILVER WITH SEMI-PRECIOUS STONES
VIENNA, 1720
CLUNY MUSEUM, PARIS

SPICE TOWER
SILVER FILIGREE, WITH SEMI-PRECIOUS STONES AND ENAMEL PLAQUES SHOWING BIBLICAL SCENES
ITALIAN, 16th CENTURY
CLUNY MUSEUM, PARIS

HANUKKAH LAMP FOR OIL
BRONZE, 14TH CENTURY
FOUND IN THE ANCIENT JEWISH QUARTERS OF LYON
CLUNY MUSEUM, PARIS

sincere gratitude to the Alliance Israelite Universelle in Paris, and especially to its director, Monsieur Eugene Weill, who was instrumental in securing the loan exhibit for this occasion. Its arrival ten days before the opening of the exhibit made it impossible to publish a catalogue. Our visitors are therefore referred to the labels in which we have tried to cover the most important information on these pieces. They are not only relevant in themselves, they also have a special significance, representing as a collection an entire chapter of Jewish history in the Western world.

KIDDUSH CUP FOR THE SABBATH
SILVER, GILDED
AUGSBURG (?), 17TH CENTURY
CLUNY MUSEUM, PARIS

Figure 3.10. Facing pages from [Stephen S. Kayser], *The Jewish Museum: 1947, 1957* ([New York]: [Jewish Museum, Jewish Theological Seminary], 1957) [unpaginated]. Courtesy of the Library of the Jewish Theological Seminary. Regarding the portable Torah ark on the left, see also Figures 1.7 and 2.3; for the spice box (second from left), see also Figure 2.5 (bottom row, center); for the Hanukkah lamp (third from left), see also Figure 1.3; for the Kiddush cup (far right), see also Figures 2.4 and 2.5.

World War era. As a result, "Everyman has become a Jew, the Jew has become Everyman." If there were to be a meaningful role for the Jewish museum, Politzer suggested, it was not via tokens of Judaism, but rather by emphasizing the nature of Jewish thought as expressed in modern art: the questioning of human existence. Because the very existence of "the thinking man" had become an urgent and widely shared concern, many people might visit the museum "to seek the counsel of their fellow-sufferers and the sustenance of beauty." The audience Politzer envisioned consisted of those who shared with Jews a precarity "as individuals amid mass forces, the knowledge of this precarious position and the desire to overcome it."[31]

Abstraction, Renunciation, Faith

Between the museum's inauguration in its new quarters and its tenth anniversary there in 1957, Kayser mounted nearly forty exhibitions. Of them, not quite thirty featured contemporary Jewish artists—most of

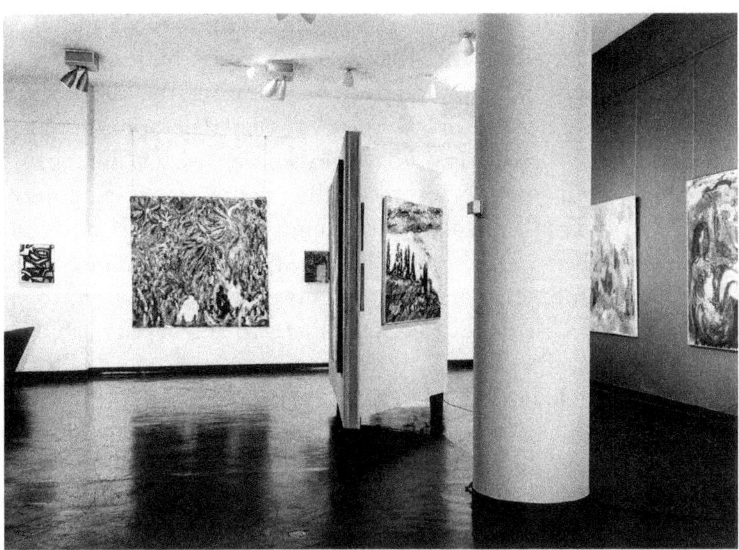

Figure 3.11. Installation view, *The New York School, Second Generation*, ca. March 1957. Photograph by Frank J. Darmstaedter. The Jewish Museum, New York/Art Resource, NY.

whom addressed Jewish subjects, three exhibits were of modern ceremonial objects, and fewer than ten were of older Jewish art or on topics from Jewish history. The museum marked its tenth anniversary with three exhibitions, two of which were arranged by Kayser: a selection of over ninety ceremonial objects loaned by the Cluny Museum, Paris, all from the Strauss collection and including several displayed in the 1878 Exposition Universelle and London's Anglo-Jewish Historical Exhibition (Figure 3.10); the other containing over fifty major works, mostly paintings borrowed from New York–area collectors, including a Rembrandt self-portrait as a biblical high priest, paintings from subsequent eras, and recent museum acquisitions such as a richly ornamented Torah breastplate. A reviewer noted that these two treasure exhibits were selected purely "for their beauty, without historical or associative criteria" and did not communicate a larger theme.[32]

The third celebratory exhibit was *The New York School, Second Generation*, which consisted of over forty paintings and mixed-media pieces selected by Schapiro (Figure 3.11). Most of the work, by twenty-three Jewish and non-Jewish artists, lacked any visible Jewish content and represented the most challenging avant-garde work of the time. The exhibit took a step the museum's leadership acknowledged was an experiment and "radical" departure from past practices. The title signaled that the artists, as a group, succeeded a generation of abstract expressionists and like the latter were based in New York. That next generation built on the earlier movement's immersion in gestural paint handling and the medium's plasticity by embracing a much broader range of materials, applications, and conceptual approaches. Several of the artists were virtual unknowns at the time but would go on to become leading figures in contemporary art including Helen Frankenthaler, Jasper Johns, Joan Mitchell, and Robert Rauschenberg. Their works, especially those of Johns and Rauschenberg, had little in common except "certain points of departure" from the previous generation. Where the museum's other two anniversary exhibits returned to the past, this one looked to the future.[33]

The exhibit catalogue was introduced by Leo Steinberg (1920–2011), an art historian and critic who was born in Russia to Jewish parents, sojourned in Germany and Britain—where he studied sculpture and drawing at London's Slade School of Fine Art, and after the Second World War immigrated to America. Upon arriving in New York, Steinberg turned increasingly to criticism and scholarship completing a doctorate at the Institute of Fine Arts, New York University. His teaching career began at Hunter College, and he later moved to the University of Pennsylvania. Though still a relative newcomer when he wrote the introduction, Steinberg was establishing himself as a fresh critical voice. He did so by widening the topics of contemporary criticism from the materials and techniques of art to other considerations, including the metaphorical nature of artists' practices and the mechanisms of viewer response—what would become reception theory in art, in effect helping lay the foundations of postmodern art criticism.

"No sense pretending," Steinberg began his catalogue essay, "that the work of these . . . painters is easily understood. It is not. With few exceptions it is deliberately recondite, uncompromising." Interpreting the artists as a group was complicated because they, unlike those of the first New York School generation, were not in revolt against earlier traditions and the artists' intentions could not be discerned by what they were resisting. Steinberg acknowledged the exhibition was a deviation from the museum's usual Jewish programming, but even so, this "conjunction of the modern in art and the Jewish" had "certain aptnesses. Both Jewry and modern art are masters of renunciation, having at one time renounced all the props on which existence as nation, or art, once seemed to depend. Jewry survived as an abstract nation, proving, as did modern art, how much is dispensable." Steinberg's use of "abstract" in this context echoed ideas then circulating. Clement Greenberg observed in 1944 that there "is a Jewish bias toward the abstract, the tendency to conceptualize as much

Figure 3.12. Jasper Johns, *Green Target*, 60" x 60", encaustic on newspaper and cloth over canvas, 1955. Richard S. Zeisler Fund, Museum of Modern Art no. 9.1958. © 2023 Jasper Johns / Licensed by VAGA at Artists Rights Society (ARS), NY. © The Museum of Modern Art/Licensed by SCALA / Art Resource, NY.

as possible"; and two years later, French existentialist philosopher Jean-Paul Sartre (1905–80) wrote in *Anti-Semite and Jew* of Jews as comprising "an abstract historical community." They all characterized modern, post-emancipation Judaism as a culture that had been compelled to eschew traditional practices and marks of religious difference that set Jews apart. The result, these thinkers believed, was a paring back of Judaism to essential truths, just as the best in modern art had stripped away superficialities to achieve pure expression.[34]

Steinberg's assertion concerning renunciation mirrored his developing ideas about avant-garde art and its audiences, especially his belief that viewers had to cast off their preconceptions to understand the artists' dispensing with theirs. He sympathized with the "shock of discomfort, or the bewilderment, or the anger" which many experienced when confronted by modern art by disclosing an experience of his own. Steinberg aimed to show why the struggle was worthwhile by discussing his first encounters with the work of Jasper Johns, including a painting in the *New York School* exhibit (Figure 3.12), which prompted "a state of anxious uncertainty [caused] by the painting, about painting, about myself." Modern art, he counseled, "always projects itself into a twilight zone where no values are fixed. It is always born in anxiety" and the art's function is "to transmit this anxiety to the spectator." Like existentialist philosopher "Kierkegaard's God, the picture seems arbitrary, cruel, irrational, demanding your faith, while it makes no promise of future rewards."[35]

No doubt Steinberg was invited to write the catalogue essay because his views so closely paralleled Schapiro's. The extent to which the exhibit was a team project is evident in the latter's address at the exhibit opening and an article published a few months later. Schapiro spoke to the "confrontation" with modern art that requires of the viewer an "effort of attention, understanding, sympathy, doubt, and recovery from doubt." Unlike Steinberg, he approached the artworks in the context of the artists' lives as a way of connecting their humanity to that of the viewers. In contrast with Steinberg's moment of anxiety and the faith required to overcome it, Schapiro believed that encountering modern art should not be disturbing, even if absorbing its meaning required a kind of monastic effort. Doing so would "induce an attitude of communion and contemplation," leading the viewer to "an equivalent of what is regarded as part of religious life: a sincere and humble submission to a spiritual object." Significant here is the phenomenon of two secular Jews employing the language of faith and spirituality to interpret avant-garde art.[36]

The year *The New York School, Second Generation* appeared, Nathan Glazer (b. 1923), a leading sociologist specializing in ethnicity and race in the nation's urban centers, published *American Judaism*. In it he captured the contours of the museum's modern art experiment when he wrote that the "insistence" of "Jews on remaining Jews . . . has a potentially religious meaning" in that modern Judaism was finding expression outside traditional worship. Jews attempting to find a "relatedness to tradition" in "religiously indifferent forms"—such as sentimental depictions of Jewish subjects—were performing a mere "act of piety," acting as little more than "the custodians of a museum." Glazer's hypothetical museum was a Judaism that had ceased to evolve and, like the Jewish Museum's religious artifacts collection, only worthy of preservation and study as though a relic of another age. When Schapiro and Steinberg advocated engaging with avant-garde art as akin to an act of faith and a "part of religious life," they were positing a source of religious meaning outside the Jewish tradition that might nonetheless be meaningful for contemporary Jews. In contrast, the modern art featuring Jewish subjects preferred by Kayser was regarded by critics like Politzer and Schapiro as "religiously indifferent" because they saw it as at best dutiful but spiritually empty recitals of the past. Kayser's approach led to just the kind of museum the others wanted to avoid, a graveyard of Judaism.[37]

By all accounts, *The New York School, Second Generation* was a triumph. It garnered favorable reviews and a large enthusiastic crowd for the opening including artists, apparently identifiable by their dress—"not to mention the variety of beards (artistic rather than religious)" as well as art critics and collectors. In the weeks following the opening, the museum was crowded by "arty young people" who would "sit for hours in front of one picture discussing its significance." A seminary staff member thought the exhibit was "a real artistic success and the sort of thing that should be done . . . at intervals." Another, a rabbi and senior member of the seminary administration, appreciated the "sincere effort" and "honest expression" of the exhibit and noticed an ancillary benefit of its success: "new interest" in the museum's permanent collection. He added hopefully that the "older objects take on new meaning" and that the visitor "is challenged to see them in a light other than merely as relics of a by-gone day." With their exhibit, Schapiro and Steinberg seemed to have modeled a path for the museum to acquire new audiences while retaining its present constituency. But the most intense interest was aroused among Jews and non-Jews active in New York's contemporary art world, especially artists, collectors, and dealers. Leo Castelli (1907–99), an increasingly prominent dealer of contemporary art, was "thunderstruck" by the Jasper Johns painting, learning of the artist's work for the first time. "Oddly enough," Castelli recalled, the Jewish Museum might now play "an important part in my career, in my life." Perhaps, the exhibition's most enthusiastic art-world respondents—especially Jews—hoped, *The New York School* might herald a new form of community service the museum might continue offering. Jews celebrating the work of non-Jews were hungry for more and encouraged the museum to alter its aims. Kayser understood the exhibit as precedent setting because of its non-Jewish content and was willing to pursue the experiment, admitting that until then he was known less for "the things I've shown but the things I've kept out of the museum!"[38]

Notes

1. Adolph Frederick Reinhardt, *Art-as-Art: The Selected Writings of Ad Reinhardt*, ed. Barbara Rose (New York: Viking Press, 1975), 190. Reinhardt (1913–1967) was a non-Jewish abstract expressionist painter; Michael Corris, *Ad Reinhardt* (London: Reaktion, 2008).
2. Julie Miller, "Planning the Jewish Museum, 1944–1947," *Conservative Judaism* 47, no. 1 (Fall 1994): 60–73; Julie Miller and Richard I. Cohen, "A Collision of Cultures," in *Tradition Renewed: A History of the Jewish Theological Seminary*, ed. Jack Wertheimer (New York: Jewish Theological Seminary of America, 1997), II:324–61; Edward M. M. Warburg, *'1109': The Warburg House*, 2nd rev. edn. (New York: Jewish Museum, 2008). See also, Ron Chernow, *The Warburgs: The Twentieth-Century Odyssey of a Remarkable Jewish Family* (New York: Random House, 1993), 93–94; "Warburg Mansion," New York Preservation Archive Project, accessed November 2019, http://www.nypap.org/preservation-history/warburg-mansion/. The mansion, at the time of its construction, could be likened to Jewish country houses in the UK; "Jewish Country Houses," University of Oxford, accessed January 2023, https://jch.history.ox.ac.uk/. FSW, *Reminiscences of a Long Life* (New York: Privately printed at the Thistle Press, 1956), 130–33, 146, 184–85, 191; FSW, "The Saga of This House," *Hadassah Newsletter* (June–July 1947): 9; "Mrs. Warburg, 82, Arts Patron, Dies," *New York Times*, 14 September 1958; Julie Miller, "Frieda Schiff Warburg," *Jewish Women: A Comprehensive Historical Encyclopedia* 27 (February 2009), Jewish Women's Archive, accessed June 2019, https://jwa.org/encyclopedia/article/warburg-frieda-schiff; "Alan M. Stroock, 77, Lawyer and Jewish Leader, Is Dead," *New York Times*, 30 March 1985. On Schiff and Warburg JTS contributions, see chapter 2. Regarding the gates, see Jenna Weissman Joselit, "By Design: Building the Campus of the Jewish Theological Seminary," in Wertheimer, *Tradition Renewed*, I:285–86; Publicity release, 5 October 1934, CAP 1:24, AJHS; CA, "Address . . . at the Dedication of the Gates of the Jewish Theological Seminary," 26 September 1934, ARC MS 26--55:15, LKCAJS. The mansion donation may also have been inspired by sale of FSW's brother-in-law's mansion to New York University for conversion into its new Institute of Fine Arts, Miller and Cohen, "A Collision of Cultures," II:324. There are parallels and relevant family friendships, but neither FSW nor anyone else mentioned them at the time. "P. M. Warburg Home to Be Art Institute," *New York Times*, 21 December 1937; Dumas Malone, ed., *Dictionary of American Biography*, s.v. "Paul Moritz Warburg" (New York: Charles Scribner's Sons, 1936); FSW, *Reminiscences*, 141.
3. AM, "Address on the Tenth Anniversary of the Opening of the Museum," 12 January 1941, ARC 60–2–4, LJTS, 5–10; Sheila Schwartz, ed., *Danzig 1939, Treasures of a Destroyed Community* (Detroit, MI: Wayne State University Press for the Jewish Museum, New York, 1980), 9. AM, "Report on the Library and Museum," 22 June 1942, RG 1–16–62, LJTS, 15–17. See also, H. G. Friedman, "Letter to Dr. Alexander Marx Concerning the H. G.

Friedman Collection of Judaica, 24 December 1941," in *Jewish Texts on the Visual Arts*, ed. Vivian B. Mann (Cambridge: Cambridge University Press, 2000),163–66. Friedman continued to donate works in subsequent decades; "Harry Friedman, Financier, Dies; Leader in Jewish Philanthropies," *New York Times*, 23 November 1965; see also, Grace Cohen Grossman, "Dr. Stephen S. Kayser: A Personal Testimony," in *A Crown for a King: Studies in Jewish Art, History and Archaeology in Memory of Stephen S. Kayser*, ed. Shalom Sabar, Steven Fine, and William M. Kramer (New York, NY: Gefen Publishing House, 2000), 6. On museum storage, see AM to LF, 18 May 1943, ARC 80–3–Correspondence-LF, Jan–July, 1943 and 26 November 1943, ARC 80–30–Correspondence-LF, Aug–Dec, 1943, LJTS.

4. Ira Robinson, "Cyrus Adler," in Wertheimer, *Tradition Renewed*, I:140–44. Ari L. Goldman, "Louis Finkelstein, 96, Leader of Conservative Jews," *New York Times*, 30 November 1991; and Abraham J. Karp, "Louis Finkelstein (1895–1991)," in *American Jewish Year Book*, ed. David Singer and Ruth R. Seldin (New York: American Jewish Committee and Jewish Publication Society, 1993), 528, 534. See also, *Encyclopaedia Judaica*, 2nd edn., s.v. "Louis Finkelstein."
5. Michael B. Greenbaum, "The Finkelstein Era," in Wertheimer, *Tradition Renewed*, I:167–69, 191–94; Fred Beuttler, "For the World at Large: Intergroup Activities at the Jewish Theological Seminary," in Wertheimer, *Tradition Renewed*, II:669–735; the attendance figures are on p. II:674, the "organized conscience" quote is from Harold Laswell, p. II:696; Finkelstein preferred the term "intergroup" over such expressions as "interreligious" or "interfaith" because, according Beuttler, there is "only one faith . . . and that was faith in God," II:731n4. For the "unknown religion" quote, see LF, "Foreword," in *The Jews: Their History, Culture, Religion*, 4 vols., ed. LF (Philadelphia, PA: Jewish Publication Society of America, 1949), I:xxvi.
6. Jeffrey Shandler and Elihu Katz, "Broadcasting American Judaism: The Radio and Television Department of the Jewish Theological Seminary," in Wertheimer, *Tradition Renewed*, II:364–401. See also, Lila Corwin Berman, *Speaking of Jews: Rabbis, Intellectuals, and the Creation of an American Public Identity* (Berkeley: University of California Press, 2009), 76–84; and Greenbaum, "The Finkelstein Era," I:188. "A Trumpet for All Israel," *Time* 58, no. 16 (15 October 1951): 52–59.
7. Eli Lederhendler, *New York Jews and the Decline of Urban Ethnicity, 1950–1970* (Syracuse, NY: Syracuse University Press, 2001), 24–31. Greenbaum, "The Finkelstein Era," I:190. On FSW and the Institute for Religious and Social Studies, see FSW to LF, 6 January 1943, RG 1–41–37, LJTS. LF to FSW, 6 January 1944; on Warburg Center, see LF to FSW, 14 January 1944, RG 1–41–37, LJTS. On academic center, see LF to FSW, 6 April 1944, RG 25–1–28, LJTS.
8. On the formal gift, see FSW to LF, 13 January 1944, RG 1–41–37, LJTS. Announcement of Warburg mansion gift, [ca. 30 January 1944], RG 25–1–29, LJTS; "Warburg Mansion Goes to Seminary," *New York Times*, 25

January 1944. LF to FSW, 10 September 1944, RG 1–41–38, LJTS. On the advisory committee, see LF to FSW, 31 January; on the museum's governance, see LF to FSW, 2 March 1944, RG 1–41–38, LJTS. For a survey of seminary-affiliated museums at the time, see Laurence Vail Coleman, *The Museum in America: A Critical Study*, 3 vols. (Washington, DC: American Association of Museums, 1939), III: "Appendix K, College and University Museums." On the Union Museum, see chapter 2. For planning committee members, see *The Jewish Museum* (New York: Jewish Museum, [1947]), [unpaginated]. On committee recommendations, see LF to FSW, 6 April 1944, RG 1–41–38, LJTS. On professionalization of museum work, see Paul J. DiMaggio, "Constructing an Organizational Field: U.S. Art Museums, 1920–1940," in *The New Institutionalism in Organizational Analysis*, ed. Paul J. DiMaggio and Walter W. Powell (Chicago, IL: University of Chicago Press, 1991), 267–92.

9. Nicholas Adams, James S. Ackerman, Pamela Askew, et alia, "In Memoriam: Richard Krautheimer (1897–1994)," *Journal of the Society of Architectural Historians* 54, no. 1 (March 1995), 4–7, 115–21. Richard Krautheimer, *Mittelalterliche synagogen* (Berlin: Frankfurter Verlags-Anstalt, 1927). LF to MS, 18 December 1940, MSC 127: 2, CUL. On Krautheimer, Schoenberger, and SSK, see Karen Michels, "Art History, German Jewish Identity, and the Emigration of Iconology," in *Jewish Identity in Modern Art History*, ed. Catherine M. Soussloff (Berkeley: University of California Press, 1999), 167–79. Rachel Wischnitzer, "Guido Schoenberger (1891–1974)," *Journal of Jewish Art* 3–4 (1977): 132; see also, GS, "Academic Record" (attached to), Walter W. S. Cook to FSW, 17 January 1944, RG 1–39–66 and Publicity release, [ca. 22 August 1974], RG 11–44–21, LJTS; "Dr. Guido Schoenberger, Art Historian, 83, Dies," *New York Times*, 23 August 1974; and Anna-Carolin Augustin, "Dealing with Germany and Reclaiming Jewish Ceremonial Objects: Guido Schönberger's Postwar JCR Mission Reconsidered," *Dubnow Institute Yearbook*, vol. 19, ed. Yfaat Weiss (Göttingen: Vandenhoeck & Ruprecht, 2023), 159–88. On GS's Friedman-collection work, see AM, "Address on the Tenth Anniversary," 12. On Krautheimer's JM roles, see LF to Richard Krautheimer, 11 May 1944, RG 1–36–12; LF to FSW, 1 June and 13 July 1944, RG 1–41–38; LF to Richard Krautheimer, 19 July 1944, RG 1–49–64; Richard Krautheimer to LF, 25 July 1944, RG 1–36–12, LJTS. For GS's appointment, see LF to GS, 19 July 1944, RG 1–39–66, LJTS. See also, LF to FSW, 21 September 1944, RG 1–41–38, LJTS.

10. GS to LF, 15 September 1944, RG 1–39–66; GS to AM, 15 September 1944; and attachment [GS], "General Plan for a Museum of Jewish Culture in New York," [15 September 1944], RG 25–1–27a, LJTS.

11. Richard Krautheimer to GS, 29 September 1944, and enclosure [Richard Krautheimer], "Comments on the Memorandum, 'General Plan for a Museum of Jewish Culture in New York'" [29 September 1944], RG 25–1–27a, LJTS; see also, Richard Krautheimer, "On Collecting for the New

Jewish Museum, New York," in Mann, *Jewish Texts on the Visual Arts*, 166–69. Kathleen Curran, *The Invention of the American Art Museum: From Craft to Kulturgeschichte, 1870–1930* (Los Angeles, CA: Getty Research Institute, Getty Publications, 2016). An unsolicited proposal was also received; Paul Goodman and Benjamin N. Nelson, "Notes for a Museum of the Jewish Faith" [ca. December 1944], RG 25–1–29, LJTS; published as Paul Goodman and Benjamin Nelson, "Project for a Modern Jewish Museum," *Commentary* 1, no. 4 (February 1946): 15–20. Goodman was the brother of architect Percival Goodman. The proposal was regarded by Krauthheimer as "a spirited theory best realized in a book. . . . But a museum is not a book." Krautheimer to LF, 29 December 1944, RG 25–1–29, LJTS.

12. SG to LF, 26 October 1944, RG 25–1–28, LJTS; "Jewish Museum" [meeting minutes] and "A Short Outline Regarding the Name, Classification, Purpose and General Scheme of Display of the New Museum in the Warburg House," 31 October 1944, RG 25–1–27a, LJTS. Richard Krautheimer to LF, 20 September 1944, RG 1–36–12; Richard Krautheimer, "Budget for Research Center on Jewish Art," 20 December 1944, RG 25–1–28, LJTS.
13. On Goodman's selection, see Percival Goodman to Richard Krautheimer, 2 August 1944, RG 1–33–61; LF to Richard Krautheimer, 11 August 1944, RG 1–36–12, and LF to FSW, 11 August 1944, RG 1–41–38, LJTS. "Percival Goodman," in *The Scribner Encyclopedia of American Lives*, ed. Kenneth T. Jackson, Karen Markoe, and Arnold Markoe, vol. 2: 1986–1990 (New York: Charles Scribner's Sons, 1999), 340–41; Paul Goldberger, "Percival Goodman, 85, Synagogue Designer, Dies," *New York Times*, 12 October 1989. On the bids, see LF to GS, 26 January 1945, RG 1–53–38; and "Architect's Report," 8 February 1945, RG 25–1–2, LJTS. The "best bid" was $200,000 or about $3.12 million in 2022, "How much is a dollar from the past worth today?" *MeasuringWorth*, accessed February 2022, www.measuringworth.com/dollarvaluetoday/. Minutes, Joint meeting of Building Committee and Executive Museums Committee, 7 March 1945, RG 25–1–2, LJTS. On delays and alternatives, see LF to FSW, 10 April, FSW to LF, 14 April, LF to FSW, 1 May 1945, RG 1–55–15, LJTS. Richard Krautheimer to LF, 1 May 1945, and [Richard Krautheimer], "Memorandum Concerning Changes in Plan for the Jewish Museum" [1 May 1945], RG 25–1–27a, LJTS. See also, Krautheimer, "On Collecting," 168–69. LF to Richard Krautheimer, 2 May 1945, RG 1–49–64, LJTS. AM to LF, 17 May, LF to AM, 28 May, and AM to LF, 5 June 1945, ARC 80–30–Correspondence-LF, 1945, LJTS. See also, LF to FSW, 27 June 1945, 30 October, 28 November, 3 and 28 December 1945, RG 1–55–15, LJTS. LF to MS, 13 December 1945, MSC 127: 2, CUL. Concerning the acquaintance of LF and MS, see DF, oral history interview by Nicki Tanner, 13 February 1993, transcript, UJA-FNYC, I-433, AJHS, 11; see also, DF, *The Way Forward: My First Fifty Years at Ruder-Finn* (New York: Millwood Publishing, 1998), 81. On prior contacts between LF and MS, see MS to LF, 17 April, and LF to AM, 19 April 1937, ARC 60–1–2, AM to MS, 16

October 1944, LF to MS, 10 March and MS to LF, 13 March 1944, RG 1–39–56, LJTS. On MS's ascent to lead advisor, see LF to FSW, 8 March 1946, RG 1–55–15, LJTS and LF to MS, 20 April 1946, MSC, 127: 2, CUL.

14. John Russell, "Meyer Schapiro, 91, Is Dead; His Work Wove Art and Life," *New York Times*, 4 March 1996; *Encyclopedia of Aesthetics*, 2nd edn., s.v. "Meyer Schapiro" by David Rosand (Oxford: Oxford University Press, 1998); for the reclamation quote, see David Rosand, "Meyer Schapiro (1904–1996)," *Journal of the History of Ideas* 57, no. 3 (July 1996): 547–49; for the passion quote, see Thomas B. Hess, "Sketch for a Portrait of the Art Historian Among Artists," *Social Research* 45, no. 1 (Spring 1978): 14. See also, Helen Epstein, "Meyer Schapiro: 'A Passion to Know and Make Known,'" *Art News* [part 1] 82, no. 5 (May 1983): 60–85; and [part 2] 82, no. 6 (Summer 1983): 84–95; and C. Oliver O'Donnell, *Meyer Schapiro's Critical Debates: Art Through a Modern American Mind* (University Park: Penn State University Press, 2019). On MS's publications, see *Meyer Schapiro: The Bibliography*, comp. by Lillian Milgram Schapiro (New York: George Braziller, 1995). For conscience quote, see Epstein, "Meyer Schapiro," 82, no. 6: 89. Arthur Danto, "The Artworld," *The Journal of Philosophy* 61, no. 19 (15 October 1964): 571–84; and Howard Becker, *Art Worlds* (Berkeley: University of California Press, 1982), 34–39, 93–130.
15. MS, "The Social Bases of Art," in *First American Artists' Congress Against War and Fascism* (New York, 1936), 31–37. On the conservative turn of MS's contemporaries, see Alan M. Wald, *The New York Intellectuals: The Rise and Decline of the Anti-Stalinist Left from the 1930s to the 1980s*, 30th anniversary edn. (Chapel Hill: The University of North Carolina Press, 2017). On MS's differences with the left, see MS, "On David Siqueiros—A Dilemma for Artists," *Dissent* X, no. 2 (Spring 1963): 106, 197; and Francis Frascina, "Meyer Schapiro's Choice: My Lai, *Guernica*, MoMA and the Art Left, 1969–70," *Journal of Contemporary History* 30, nos. 3 and 4 (July and October 1995): 481–511, 705–28. On MS's undogmatic Marxism, see Alan Wallach, "Marxist Art Historian: Meyer Schapiro, 1904–1996," *Against the Current* 62 (May–June 1996): 52; Gerardo Mosquera, "Meyer Schapiro, Marxist Aesthetics, and Abstract Art," *Oxford Art Journal* 17, no. 1 (Meyer Schapiro special issue 1994): 76–80; MS, "The Nature of Abstract Art," *Marxist Quarterly* 1, no. 1 (January–March 1937): 78–97 [reprinted as MS, "Nature of Abstract Art (1937)," in *Modern Art: 19th & 20th Centuries, Selected Papers* (New York: George Braziller, 1978), 185–211]; Wayne Andersen, "Schapiro, Marx, and the Reacting Sensibility of Artists," *Social Research* 45, no. 1 (Spring 1978): 67–92. MS's efforts on behalf of the JM and living artists, as an expression both of his social activism and Jewish identity—reflected in this and subsequent chapters—is addressed more fully in Jeffrey Abt, "Meyer Schapiro, the Jewish Museum, and Living Artists: A Scholar's Overlooked Activism," *Modern Judaism: A Journal of Jewish Ideas and Experience* 43, no. 2 (May 2023): 127–47.

16. On tense dialectic, see *Encyclopedia of Aesthetics*, 2nd edn., s.v. "Meyer Schapiro," by David Rosand. MS, "On the Aesthetic Attitude in Romanesque Art (1947)," in *Romanesque Art: Selected Papers* (New York: George Braziller, 1977), 1–27. Relevant to that article is Michael Camille, "'How New York Stole the Idea of Romanesque Art': Medieval, Modern, and Postmodern in Meyer Schapiro," *Oxford Art Journal* 17, no. 1 (Meyer Schapiro special issue 1994): 65–75. Donald B. Kuspit, "Meyer Schapiro's Marxism," *Arts Magazine* 53, no. 3 (November 1978): 143. For the lattermost quote, see Donald B. Kuspit, "Dialectical Reasoning in Meyer Schapiro," *Social Research* 45, no. 1 (Spring 1978): 115.
17. Grossman, "Dr. Stephen S. Kayser," 1–4; SSK, "After Displacements I Find Coherence Again," in *The Hour of Insight: A Sequel to Moments of Personal Discovery*, ed. R. M. MacIver (New York: Institute for Religious and Social Studies [JTS], 1954), 42–49. SSK to MS, 28 January 1944, 16 December 1945, and 21 January 1946, MSC 140:6, CUL. See also, SSK, "The Shapes of Time," oral history interview by Sybil D. Hast, 24 March–9 May 1987, transcript, Oral History Program, University of California, Los Angeles, 293–98, 308–12, 320–23, 330–34; LF to SSK, 11 March, SSK to LF, 28 March, LF to SSK, 2 May, LF to SSK, 27 August, SSK to LF, 5 September 1946, RG 1–49–45, FSW to LF, 11 September 1946, RG 1–55–15, and SSK to LF, 29 September 1946, RG 25–1–3, LJTS. William M. Kramer, "Stephen S. Kayser in Los Angeles: A Personal Memoir," in Sabar et alia, *A Crown for a King*, 23–28. SSK's title was "Curator" not "Director" because LF, doubting SSK's administrative skills, appointed a senior seminary official to supervise him; LF to FSW, 8 March and 26 April 1946, RG 1–55–15, LF to SSK, 28 October 1946, Shirley R. Levitton to SSK, 23 September 1946, RG 1–49–45, LJTS.
18. LF to FSW, 28 November and 3 December 1945, RG 1–55–15, LJTS. Publicity release, "Seminary Begins Museum Renovation -- Mrs. Warburg's Former Home to be Opened as Museum October 1, 1946," 26 December 1945, RG 25–1–2, LJTS. Percival Goodman to LF, 18 February 1946, RG 25–1–18, LJTS. On the Institute, see Richard Krautheimer to LF, 20 September 1944, RG 1–36–12, LJTS. On the Kaysers' apartment, see Cissy Grossman, "Recollections of the Stephen and Louise Kayser Era at the Jewish Museum," in Sabar et alia, *A Crown for a King*, xv; SSK, "After Displacements," 41; Grossman, "Dr. Stephen S. Kayser," 4. On the rabbi's wife, see Abram Kanof (JTS and JM board member, late 1940s–late 1960s), oral history interview by Judy Tenney, 19 November 1990 and 26 May 1992, transcript, UJA-FNYC, I-433, AJHS, 20.
19. MS, "Memo for J[ewish] M[useum]," 25 June 1946, RG 25–1–3, LJTS. MS also advised on the renovation; LF to SSK, 13 November 1946, RG 1–49–45, LJTS.
20. FSW, JM dedication plaque text, [4 April,] LF to FSW, 8 April, and FSW to LF, 12 April 1946, RG 1–55–15, LJTS; Minutes, Inner Museum Committee, 9 January 1947, RG 25–1–21, Minutes, Inner Museum Committee meeting,

20 January 1947, RG 25–1–3, LJTS; LF to FSW, 4, 11, and 24 February 1947, RG 1–63–16, LJTS; LF to Percival Goodman, 2 March 1947, RG 25–1–14, LJTS. For an earlier take, in Germany, on problems with a similar name, see Richard I. Cohen, "The Visual Revolution in Jewish Life—An Overview," in *Visualizing and Exhibiting Jewish Space and History*, ed. Cohen (Oxford: Oxford University Press, 2012), 10. "The Jewish Museum," Jewish Theological Seminary of America, accessed March 2016, http://www.jtsa.edu/Academics/Registrar/Academic_Bulletin/AB_Jewish_Museum.xml.

21. On closing the old museum, see SSK to Simon Greenberg et alia, 31 January 1947, RG 25–1–19, LF, open letter, 7 February 1947, RG 25–1–5, "The Jewish Museum, Jewish Theological Seminary of America," press release, 11 February 1947, RG 25–1–31, and Minutes, Inner Museum Committee, 19 February 1947, RG 25–1–21, LJTS. On installing the new museum, see SSK to Moshe Davis, 16 October 1946, RG 1–49–45, LJTS. See also, Grossman, "Dr. Stephen S. Kayser," 4. On Christian works, see Minutes, Inner Museum Committee meeting, 4 March 1947, RG 25–1–5; on modern art, see SSK to LF, 31 March 1947 and LF to SSK, 1 April 1947, RG 25–1–16, LJTS; [SSK], "Memorandum on the Jewish Museum" [museum handout?] 28 April 1947, RG 25–1–5, LJTS; SSK, "Our Opening Exhibit," in *The Jewish Museum* [New York: Jewish Museum, Jewish Theological Seminary, 1947], unpaginated.

22. "A New Museum," *New York Times*, 9 May 1947; "Program of Dedication Ceremonies," 6 May–15 June 1947, RG 25–1–3, LJTS; and AM, "Address Delivered... at the Preview of the Jewish Museum," 6 May 1947, ARC 60–1–6, LJTS; FSW, "The Saga of This House": 8–9, 12. Richard Norton Smith, *On His Own Terms: A Life of Nelson Rockefeller* (New York: Random House, 2014); Richard Pfau, *No Sacrifice Too Great: The Life of Lewis L. Strauss* (Charlottesville: University Press of Virginia, 1984). *Nelson A. Rockefeller, Lewis L. Strauss: Remarks at the Dedication of the Jewish Museum* . . . (New York: Jewish Theological Seminary of America, 1947) (emphasis Strauss's); John Garraty, ed., *Dictionary of American Biography*, s.v. "Sam Adolph Lewisohn" (New York: Charles Scribner's Sons, 1977); "Sam A. Lewisohn, Financier, Is Dead," *New York Times*, 15 March 1951; "Will of Sam A. Lewisohn Leaves Paintings Valued at $1,000,000 to Six Institutions," *New York Times*, 21 March 1951; Sam A. Lewisohn, *Painters and Personality: A Collector's View of Modern Art*, rev. edn. (New York: Harper, 1948). Quotes are from Sam A. Lewisohn, "The Jew in Art," in *The Jewish Museum* [New York: Jewish Museum, Jewish Theological Seminary, 1947], unpaginated; see also Sam A. Lewishohn, "The Jew in Art," [6 May] 1947, RG 25–1–7, LJTS.

23. "A Live Museum," *Reconstructionist* 13, no. 6 (2 May 1947): 6. Grossman, "Dr. Stephen S. Kayser," 1. For an illustrated description of the galleries about this time, see Jacob S. Golub, *The Jewish Museum* (New York: Jewish Education Committee of New York, [ca. 1949]); and Hannah L. Goldberg, "The Jewish Museum -- An Interview with Its Curator, Stephen S. Kayser,"

The Reconstructionist 16, no. 8 (2 June 1950): 10–16. The "Sabbath Room" installation was not the first of its kind; Bernhard Purin, "Isidor Kaufmann's Little World: The 'Sabbath Room' in the Jewish Museum of Vienna" and Felicitas Heimann-Jelinek, "Inventory of the Sabbath Room," in *Rabbiner – Bocher – Talmudschüler: Bilder Des Weiner Malers Isidor Kaufmann, 1853–1921* (Vienna: Jüdisches Museum der Stadt Wien, 1995), 129–45, 147–63; see also, "The Parlour" in Heimann-Jelinek and Wiebke Krohn, eds., *The First Jewish Museum* (Vienna: Jüdisches Museum der Stadt Wien, 2005), 14–17.

24. On attendance, see [SSK], "Report to the Museum Committee of the Board of Overseers," 15 December 1948, RG 21–1–31, LJTS; Goldberg, "Jewish Museum," 12; William B. Furie, "The Jewish Museum," *Jewish Advocate*, 22 May 1947 (emphasis Furie's). On Jewish home beautification, particularly via the JM, see Jenna Weissman Joselit, *The Wonders of America, Reinventing Jewish Culture, 1880–1950* (New York: Hill and Wang, 1994), 163–69. On explanations and Native American references, see Frances Hawkins to Edward M. M. Warburg, 24 March 1949 (see also, Edward M. M. Warburg to LF, 28 March 1949), RG 1–80–42, LJTS. FSW was not "fond of very modern things"; Jessica Feingold to FSW, 5 October 1956, RG 1–151–34, LJTS; see also, Meeting minutes, Building Committee, 28 December 1945, RG 25–1–20, LJTS. LF to Irving Bennett, 21 May 1947, RG 25–1–16, LJTS. Minutes, Inner Museum Committee, 29 March 1948, RG 25–1–21, [JTS Board of Overseers], "Draft resolution, Museum" [ca. May 1948], RG 21–1–31, Minutes, Board of Overseers, Museum Committee meeting, 4 November 1948, RG 21–1–32, LJTS. Edward M. M. Warburg, "A Report . . . on the Possible Reorientation of the Jewish Museum" [ca. 13 May 1949], RG 25–5–4, LJTS. After the JM's opening, SSK: accessioned Judaica uprooted by Nazis; mounted an ongoing display at JTS's University of Judaism, its Los Angeles-based extension program; prepared loan exhibits for Jewish and other groups; hosted television broadcasts; lectured outside the museum; and provided design advice on synagogue ornamentation and ritual accouterments. Judaica acquired after the Second World War include the Mintz Collection, Minutes, Inner Museum Committee, 23 April, RG 25–1–21 and SG to Rose Mintz, 12 May 1947, RG 25–1–3, LJTS; and Judaica looted by the Nazis and redistributed by Jewish Cultural Reconstruction, see Herman Dicker, *Of Learning and Libraries: The Seminary Library at One Hundred* (New York: Jewish Theological Seminary of America, 1988), 54–57, 109–12; and Grossman, "Dr. Stephen S. Kayser," 7–8. [SSK], "Report to the Board of Overseers, Committee on Museum," 14 March 1949, RG 21–1–49, LJTS. On the University of Judaism, see Deborah Dash Moore, "Another Glowing Chapter: The University of Judaism," in Wertheimer, *Tradition Renewed*, I:794–815; LF to FSW, 14 May 1947, RG 1–63–15 and LF to FSW, 9 October 1947, RG 1–63–17, LJTS.

25. On "b'somim-boxes," SSK to MS, 21 August 1946, MSC 140:6, CUL. SSK, "Report," 8 April 1949, RG 25–5–4; and [SSK], Report on JM Planning

[February–March 1950], RG 21–1–58, LJTS. See also, Grossman, "Dr. Stephen S. Kayser": 16n11. On acquiring contemporary art, see [SSK,] "Jewish Museum Report to the Board of Overseers" [ca. June 1947,] RG 25–1–5, LF to FSW, 14 July 1947, RG 1–63–17, LJTS; Sally M. Promey, "Taste Cultures: The Visual Practice of Liberal Protestantism, 1940–1965," in *Practicing Protestants: Histories of Christian Life in America, 1630–1965*, ed. Laurie F. Maffly-Kipp, Leigh E. Schmidt, and Mark Valeri (Baltimore, MD: Johns Hopkins University Press, 2006), 250–93. On encouraging creation of modern ritual objects, see SSK, "A Live Museum," 6 and [SSK?], *Designing of Modern Jewish Ceremonial Art* ([New York]: Jewish Museum, 1953); a copy is in RG 25–2–25, LJTS. On the workshop, see chapter 4. SSK, "Defining Jewish Art," in *Mordecai M. Kaplan Jubilee Volume*, 2 vols. (New York: Jewish Theological Seminary of America, 1953), English section: 457–58, 462, 466; SSK, introduction to *Jewish Ceremonial Art*, ed. SSK (Philadelphia, PA: Jewish Publication Society of America, 1955), 9–10. SSK, "Visual Arts in American Jewish Life," *Judaism: A Quarterly Journal* 3, no. 4 (Fall 1954): 443–45. SSK, "The Jewish Museum After Ten Years," *Adult Jewish Education: A Quarterly Journal*, (Spring 1957): 8; republished as, [SSK], *The Jewish Museum: 1947, 1957* ([New York]: [Jewish Museum, Jewish Theological Seminary], 1957), [unpaginated].

26. MS, "JTS talk," 16 May [1949], MSC 198:22, CUL and "Anniversary of Museum," *New York Times*, 15 May 1949; MS, "Religion and Modern Art," 24 January 1950, MSC 198:21, CUL (delivered at one of LF's intergroup conferences).
27. MS, "The Social Bases of Art," in *First American Artists' Congress Against War and Fascism* (New York: [Privately published], 1936), 33–34; MS, "Nature of Abstract Art (1937)," in *Modern Art: 19th & 20th Centuries, Selected Papers* (New York: George Braziller, 1978), 186–88, 198, 202. On the context of MS's ideas, see Serge Guilbaut, *How New York Stole the Idea of Modern Art: Abstract Expressionism, Freedom, and the Cold War*, trans. Arthur Goldhammer (Chicago, IL: University of Chicago Press, 1983), 20–21, 24–26, 208n20.
28. *Encyclopedia of World Biography*, s.v. "Clement Greenberg"; *Encyclopedia of Aesthetics*, 2nd edn., s.v. "Clement Greenberg"; and Florence Rubenfeld, *Clement Greenberg: A Life* (New York: Scribner, 1997). On his critical writings, see Donald B. Kuspit, *Clement Greenberg, Art Critic* (Madison: University of Wisconsin Press, 1979); and Caroline A. Jones, *Eyesight Alone: Clement Greenberg's Modernism and the Bureaucratization of the Senses* (Chicago, IL: University of Chicago Press, 2005). On Greenberg's art training, see John O'Brian, introduction to *Clement Greenberg: The Collected Essays and Criticism*, ed. John O'Brian, 4 vols. (Chicago, IL: University of Chicago Press, 1986–93), I:xx–xxi. "New York School" appears to have been coined by one of its leading artists; Robert Motherwell, *The School of New York* (Beverly Hills, CA: Frank Perls Gallery, 1951). See also, Maurice Tuchman, ed., *New York School, The First Generation: Paintings of the 1940s*

and 1950s, rev. edn. (Greenwich, CT: New York Graphic Society Ltd., 1971), 7–8.

29. On MS and Greenberg collaborations, see Howard Devree, "American Roundup," *New York Times*, 30 April 1950; and Grace Glueck, "Kootz is Closing Art Gallery; Will Write About His Career," *New York Times*, 8 April 1966; Jones, *Eyesight Alone*, 132–35. Contemporary Authors Online (Detroit: Gale, 2001), *Biography in Context*, s.v. "Lionel Abel," accessed June 2016, doi: GALE|H1000000118; *Contemporary Authors Online* (Detroit, MI: Gale, 2002), *Biography in Context*, s.v. "Lionel Trilling," accessed June 2016, doi: GALE|H1000099871. Also on the MS and Greenberg dialogue, see Philip Fisher, *Making and Effacing Art: Modern American Art in a Culture of Museums* (Oxford: Oxford University Press), 167–72; Clement Greenberg, "Avant-Garde and Kitsch" and "Towards a Newer Laocoon" in *Clement Greenberg: Collected Essays and Criticism*, I:5–38 (the quotes at the end are from pp. I:8–9). My use of "avant-garde" is guided by the American, as opposed to European, experience even though its origins are European, and of its social as well as aesthetic ramifications, much as is articulated in Harold Rosenberg, "Collective, Ideological, Combative," in *Art News Annual* XXXIV, ed. Thomas B. Hess and John Ashbery (New York: Macmillan Company, 1968), 74–79. See also, Harold Rosenberg, "The Avant-Garde," *Discovering the Present: Three Decades in Art, Culture, and Politics* (Chicago, IL: University of Chicago Press, 1973), 74–87. See also, David Cottington, *The Avant-Garde: A Very Short Introduction* (Oxford: Oxford University Press, 2013), especially on "the growth of a network of wealthy collectors of modernist art" in New York accelerating the transition from European origins to an American "home-grown culture," pp. 19–20. See also, Renato Poggioli, *The Theory of the Avant-Garde*, trans. Gerald Fitzgerald (Cambridge, MA: Harvard University Press, 1968). *Clement Greenberg: Collected Essays and Criticism*, I:12, 27 and "Modernist Painting," in *Clement Greenberg: Collected Essays and Criticism*, IV:85–94.
30. MS, "JTS talk," 16 May [1949], MSC 198:22, CUL; MS, "Religion and Modern Art," 24 January 1950, MSC 198:21, CUL.
31. Heinz Politzer, "The Opportunity of the Jewish Museum: How Best to Encourage Art?" *Commentary* 7, no. 6 (June 1949): 589–90, 592–93 (emphasis Politzer's). *Biography in Context* (2001), s.v. "Heinrich Politzer." On the Jew as "everyman" and "everyman a Jew," see also, Alexander Bloom, *Prodigal Sons: The New York Intellectuals & Their World* (Oxford: Oxford University Press, 1986), 150–53. Greenberg and another critic of Jewish descent, Harold Rosenberg (see chapter 7), shared "the same conception of the Abstract Expressionist artist" as "the tragic Jew of American art, . . . suffering the same problems of identity and adaptation as the Jew, who is always regarded as an outsider. . . . The American artist is always in a Jewish situation, trapped between autonomy and assimilation"; Donald Kuspit, "Critics, Primary and Secondary," in *American Art in the 20th Century: Painting and Sculpture, 1913–1993*, ed. Christos M. Joachimides and Norman Rosenthal

(Munich: Prestel, 1993), 145. On the applicability of the Jewish experience to "contemporary man generally in his peculiar dilemmas," see Elliot E. Cohen, "The Intellectual and the Jewish Community: The Hope for Our Heritage in America," *Commentary* 8 (1 January 1949): 25.

32. On JM's exhibits between 1947 and 1957, see [JM,] "Jewish Museum Exhibitions: 1947–Present," 2 September 2009, an unpublished spreadsheet maintained by JM staff for internal purposes. [SSK], "Loan Exhibit from the Cluny Museum, Paris" and "Collectors' Exhibit," in *The Jewish Museum: 1947, 1957,* [unpaginated]; Dore Ashton, "Art: The Jewish Museum Celebrates," *New York Times*, 16 May 1957. Regarding the Strauss Collection and the 1878 Paris and 1887 London exhibits, see chapters 1 and 2. J. S., "Tenth Anniversary," *ARTNews* 56 (June 1957): 20.
33. Foreword in SSK, ed., *The New York School, Second Generation* (New York: Jewish Theological Seminary of America, 1957), 3. SSK conceived the exhibit's title, SSK, "The Shapes of Time," oral history interview by Sybil D. Hast, 24 March–9 May 1987, transcript, Oral History Program, University of California, Los Angeles, 322–23. Artists included in the exhibit characterized themselves as "followers" of MS, "Jewish Museum . . . Report to the Board of Overseers," 8 January 1958, RG 21–3–12, LJTS. See also, Annie Cohen-Solal, *Leo and His Circle: The Life of Leo Castelli*, trans. Mark Polizzotti (New York: Alfred A. Knopf, 2010), 241–43.
34. Ken Johnson, "Leo Steinberg, Art Historian, Dies at 90," *New York Times*, 14 March 2011; *Encyclopedia of Aesthetics*, 2nd edn. (2014), s.v. "Leo Steinberg"; Leo Steinberg, introduction to *The New York School*, 4, 7–8; Clement Greenberg, "Under Forty: A Symposium on American Literature and the Younger Generation of American Jews," in *Clement Greenberg: Collected Essays and Criticism*, I:177; Jean-Paul Sartre, *Anti-Semite and Jew*, trans. George J. Becker (New York: Schocken Books, 1976), 66; originally published as Jean-Paul Sartre, *Réflexions sur la question juive* (Paris: Paul Morihien, 1946). See also, Jonathan Judaken, *Jean-Paul Sartre and the Jewish Question: Anti-Antisemitism and the Politics of the French Intellectual* (Lincoln: University of Nebraska Press, 2006). On "abstract nation," see also chapter 1.
35. Leo Steinberg, "Contemporary Art and the Plight of Its Public," *Harper's Magazine* 224, no. 1342 (March 1962): 32, 39.
36. MS, "Address" [edited transcription], 7 March 1957, MSC 199:14, CUL; for another copy, see RG 1–160–18, LJTS. MS, "The Liberating Quality of Avant-Garde Art," *Art News* 56, no. 4 (Summer 1957): 41. For parallels in a Catholic context, see Pamela G. Smart, *Sacred Modern: Faith, Activism, and Aesthetics in the Menil Collection* (Austin: University of Texas Press, 2010), 1–45.
37. Nathan Glazer, *American Judaism* (Chicago, IL: University of Chicago Press, 1957), 142. *Encyclopaedia Judaica*, 2nd edn., s.v. "Nathan Glazer"; Leonard Dinnerstein and Gene Koppel, introduction to *Nathan Glazer: A Different Kind of Liberal*, ed. Leonard Dinnerstein and Gene Koppel

(Tucson: University of Arizona, 1973), v–vii, 53–55. Harvard historian Oscar Handlin said the same year, "The danger is not so much that the Jewish community will disappear, but that its culture will become a museum piece, preserved out of curiosity and ancestral piety, but devoid of meaning," in "Big Changes Seen for Jews in U.S.," *New York Times*, 13 May 1957.

38. For reviews of the exhibit, see E. P., "Young Americans," *Arts Magazine* 31 (April 1957): 57. JTS staff comments are in Jessica Feingold to FSW, 12 and 14 March 1957, RG 1–161–28, LJTS; SG to MS, 21 March 1957, MSC 137: 15, CUL. Castelli, of Italian and Austro-Hungarian Jewish descent, immigrated to America in the early 1940s; Cohen-Solal, *Leo and His Circle*. The Castelli quotes are from, respectively, Calvin Tomkins, *Off the Wall: A Portrait of Robert Rauschenberg*, rev. edn. (New York: Picador, 2005), 129; and Leo Castelli, oral history interview by Paul Cummings, 14 May 1969 and 8 June 1973, transcript, AAA, SI [unpaginated]. [SSK], "After Ten Years," in *The Jewish Museum: 1947, 1957* [unpaginated]. For the closing SSK quote, see D[ore] A[ashton], "Vivid Exhibition by Younger Painters Marks 10th Anniversary of Museum," *New York Times*, 14 March 1957; for the other quote, see Reinhardt, *Art-as-Art*, 190.

Chapter 4

Creating a Way and Space for Avant-Garde Art

The New York School, Second Generation appeared toward the end of the 1950s when the city was consolidating its reputation internationally for having stolen "the idea of modern art" from Paris. The institutions that helped foster that shift, however, especially the Museum of Modern Art, the Whitney Museum of American Art, and the Guggenheim Museum, were now perceived as mired in the past and inattentive to newer developments. The art-world success of *The New York School* reflected an unmet demand for exhibits of the latest in contemporary art, suggesting the Jewish Museum's potential for addressing it. Doing so meant further altering the museum's mission and persuading seminary officials to endorse the change. The ensuing discussion invoked comparisons not with other museums, but with other Jewish cultural institutions in New York successfully coping with the challenges of universalism versus parochialism and secularism versus religion. That discussion also coincided with a surge of Jewish philanthropic contributions to a variety of cultural institutions within and outside the community. A participant in the Jewish Museum's discussions donated a building addition to expand its temporary-exhibit galleries for modern, large-scale art. The aim was to "reflect the life of the Jew" in contemporary culture by showing avant-garde works validated by Jewish collectors "as giving expression to the central . . . ideals of Judaism."[1]

The Premise of Universality

The New York School, Second Generation might have seemed to mark a sharp change in the museum's exhibits, but Kayser believed it was no more than an extension into the avant-garde of views he had always held. After all, it was presented on the museum's first floor, which he used for works by modern Jewish artists "known and unknown." Another of Kayser's goals was displaying "the impact of Biblical and Jewish tradition upon the arts in general," "the arts in general" referring to non-Jewish artists' works. Regarding *The New York School* show per se, he believed the creations by young Jewish artists and those by non-Jews "exposed to the same experiences" were best understood when viewed together. Kayser included in his definition of "Jewish artists" those who emerged after emancipation and thus do not "necessarily produce Jewish art." For these reasons, Kayser explained, his first-floor exhibits "often deal with themes of universal interest rather than of an exclusively Jewish nature." The use of "universal" and its cognates recurred with increasing frequency in conversations about the museum's aims during this period. They were manifestations of a multifaceted discourse among Jews about their place in American society, such as drives for anti-discrimination legislation or enforcement of the separation of church and state in public education. Arguing that these steps would benefit many Americans, not just Jews, invoked "a rhetoric of universalism, obscuring the distinctively Jewish interests at stake." The nomenclature of universalism among Jewish Americans started to gain currency earlier, however, during the 1930s and 1940s among a circle of intellectuals, including art critics such as Meyer Schapiro and Clement Greenberg.[2]

Sharing ideals rooted in Marxist theory, they and fellow thinkers envisioned a socialist utopia of international economic, political, racial, and ethnic equality. For Jews, the appeal of socialism's transnational ethos was grounded in cosmopolitan centers—and in art, those were Paris and New York. There, radical philosophies promised "a world where being Jewish" made no difference and antisemitism ceased to be a concern. Those asserting the benefits of Marxism, especially for Jews, often thought of themselves as "non-Jewish Jews," individuals who would have been considered heretics by religiously observant Jews. Jewish socialists were, after all, secularists and their pursuit of political universalism was emphatically nonsectarian and anti-nationalist as they strove to universalize "the best of Judaism by freeing its ethical kernel from the husk of the Law." But the affinity of so many Jews with socialism is striking. Perhaps, as David Biale observed, "Secular universalism for these heretics paradoxically became a kind of Jewish identity." But the utopian appeal of Marxism began withering in the face of international conflicts in the late 1930s and 1940s, compelling thinkers to choose sides. The attitudes of "Cosmopolitan radicals, interested more in Continental culture than in American society," were changed by the Second World War causing them to turn away from "universal radicalism and toward America." Similarly, Jewish thinkers' passion for universalism before the war bypassed Jewish interests and dampened concerns about the Nazis. That changed as the full extent of Nazi atrocities became known. Stunned by the Holocaust, Jewish intellectuals pivoted, sometimes awkwardly, to matters of identity in which nationality, ethnicity, religion, and social activism became deeply entangled. As the universalist utopianism of Marxist ideology waned, however, an inchoate longing for another kind of universalism emerged.

For some it was found in art, especially new forms of expression that transcended social, religious, and ethnic barriers in postwar America. Schapiro spoke to these issues in a 1949 talk prepared for the Jewish Museum's second anniversary. Addressing the contradictions of a Jewish seminary's museum exhibiting "essentially secular" modern art, he acknowledged that the "creativeness of Jews in modern art" presented a problem. If, as he held, "the values of modern art are universally human and individual, and make possible a fresh relation to [Jewish] tradition," why should a Jewish museum limit itself just to works with Jewish subject matter? Only a few years prior, another critic noted that "'International,' like 'national,' has . . . a kind of political connotation. It refers to politically separated groups rather than humanity; whereas 'universal' [is rooted in] individual experience and for that reason may have a profound appeal for individuals everywhere."[3]

Kayser began incorporating these views, reporting that the museum's function was gradually evolving to "present the particular as to strip it of parochialism: so to illumine Jewish art that it reflects universal light." He continued to believe there had to be a clear connection between the art exhibited by the museum and Judaism, even if the works were by non-Jews, so long as the works were influenced by Jewish thinkers, owned by Jewish collectors, or treated Jewish topics. But arranging an agreeable balance of Jewish and non-Jewish exhibits after *The New York School, Second Generation* became more challenging. Although he welcomed the avant-garde in subsequent years, mounting daring shows by abstract expressionist painters Adolf Gottlieb (1903–74) in 1957–58 (Figure 4.1) and Helen Frankenthaler (1928–2011) in 1960, both artists were of Jewish descent. But Kayser resisted presenting solo exhibits of non-Jewish art by non-Jews. His struggle between particularism and universalism was hardly unique. It "weighed heavily on many modern Jews," observed Biale, who noted that tension had become "a central feature of modern Jewish culture." At the museum, it moved to the fore as Jewish collectors—inspired by the avant-garde, sharing Schapiro's interpretation of the "values of modern art" as "universally human," and excited by *The New York School*—pressed for change.[4]

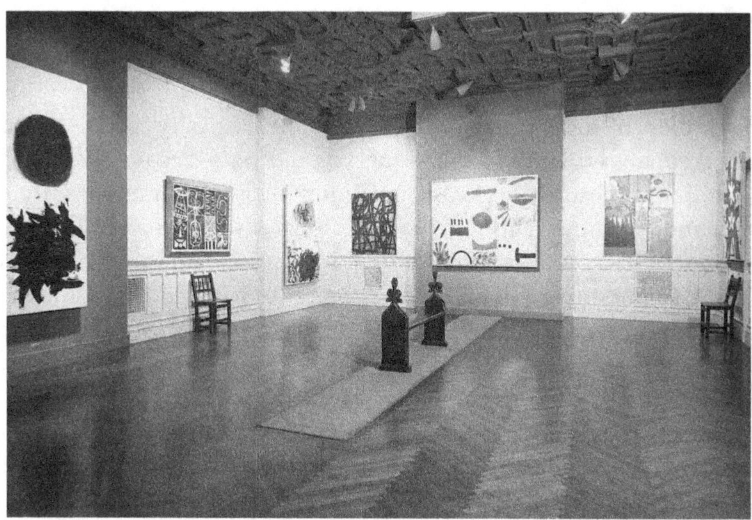

Figure 4.1. Installation view, *An Exhibition of Oil Paintings by Adolf Gottlieb*, ca. November 1957. Photograph by Frank J. Darmstaedter. The Jewish Museum, New York/Art Resource, NY.

Reshaping the Museum

The participation of Jews in modern-art collecting, especially of works by non-Jewish artists or without Jewish content, occurred with ever greater frequency in late nineteenth-century Europe and early twentieth-century America. The topic and its relation to the development of modern-art institutions on both sides of the Atlantic led to "difficult issues that Jewish identity raises" concerning the roles of Jewish scholars, collectors, museum professionals, and dealers in the history of modern art. One example is the not-uncommon notion that pursuing "innovative art" was a way for Jews "to resolve the paradox of not quite belonging" to a segment of society they aspired to join: the community of non-Jewish collectors and tradition-bound museums and commercial galleries of their time. The collectors, museum leaders, and dealers most closely associated with the Jewish Museum during the late 1950s and 1960s could be seen as complicating that story as they engaged with issues of ethnic particularism inherent to the museum's mission as a Jewish institution. If there was a feeling of "not quite belonging" for Jewish advocates of the avant-garde in New York during that period, some nonetheless came to own or lead as much as "a third of the city's [commercial] art galleries." Of the collectors and museum professionals, because of their interests they were as likely to be regarded more skeptically by fellow Jews who disliked avant-garde art than by the non-Jews of New York's art world who enthusiastically welcomed it.[5]

Regardless of these crosscurrents, "So enthusiastically [had] American Jews taken to the cultural explosion" of the post–Second World War period, Jewish leaders began complaining that arts interests were diverting money and attention from traditional Jewish causes. When Jews began serving on the boards of cultural institutions such as symphonies, operas, and museums, Jewish welfare federations ceased to be "the main channel for upward social mobility and high communal visibility." By the mid-1960s, Jews constituted a proportionately higher segment of the culture-consuming public, becoming a significant presence in America's art world as critics, collectors, philanthropists, museum heads, dealers, and artists. The phenomenon was a byproduct of other social trends including assimilation, rising wealth, and an increasing measure of security that enabled Jews not only to participate in but also begin leading American cultural institutions outside the Jewish community. Exemplary of this trend was Vera G. List (Figure 4.2), who was appointed to the Jewish Museum's advisory "Museum Committee" in 1957. List (1908–2002) was a contemporary-art enthusiast and cultural activist who threw herself into several volunteer activities and leadership positions. Her husband, Albert A. List (1901–87), was an industrialist and financier who built a fortune allowing them to join the "large-scale [art] collectors, whose numbers jumped in the affluent" 1960s. The two also poured their wealth into a family foundation in 1952 through which they began making ever-larger gifts to a variety of institutions such as the Lincoln Center for the Performing Arts, The New School for Social Research, M.I.T., the Jewish Theological Seminary, and she later helped establish the New Museum for Contemporary Art. She began collecting art early in their marriage and as he built the family's wealth, her art purchases and their philanthropy also grew. They were a team, and while he accumulated the money for their many charitable activities, "the ideas were hers." In recognition of Vera List's cultural initiatives and service, US president Bill Clinton awarded her a National Medal of Arts in 1996. The Lists' relationship with the seminary began with a scholarship they endowed in 1955. That, along with subsequent support, prompted Finkelstein to court Albert for the seminary's board of trustees, an effort to which Albert succumbed in 1960. Among the Lists' donations was a sculpture Vera presented to the Jewish Museum in memory of her father. The arrangements for the sculpture's installation brought her to the attention of seminary and museum staff, resulting in her appointment to the museum's advisory

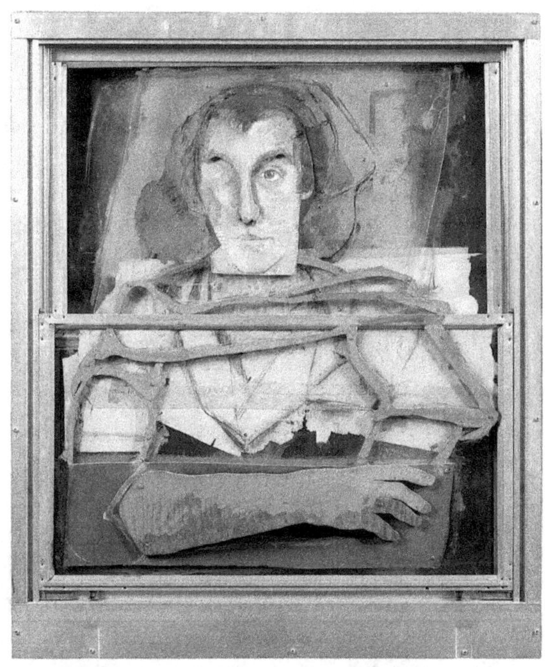

Figure 4.2. *Portrait of Vera List*, ca. 1965. Assemblage by Larry Rivers, 32" x 27" x 4", charcoal, wood, tape, plexiglass, and aluminum window frame. © 2023 Estate of Larry Rivers / Licensed by VAGA at Artists Rights Society (ARS), NY. The Jewish Museum, New York/Art Resource, NY.

committee. No doubt she was recruited because of the Lists' past and potential contributions. But Vera was "not a boastful person—very much the opposite" who could still be counted on to express "her opinions frankly and firmly"; and she was "a pillar of strength." List also possessed a "sense of adventure" and curiosity about new art as well as courage in airing unconventional ideas, qualities that suggested she could be a thoughtful participant in the museum's governance as it opened itself to the avant-garde.[6]

After serving on the advisory committee for a couple of years, she began, in early 1960, urging change. She marshaled an ad hoc subcommittee to establish "a degree of excellence" in the museum's administration by studying its governance structure, relationship with the seminary, and by-laws. List also wanted the museum to "make more of an impact on the art scene . . . generally and as a Jewish museum." In addition to exhibitions on "Jewish Life and/or customs," "Jewish artists," and "Jewish interest," the museum should henceforth address the art interests of "the whole community," meaning non-Jews as well. List's aims were driven partly by her observations of the museum and how it fit into New York's art world, but also by her personal appetites. She acknowledged that "the Judaica—everything that pertained to Jewish interest and Judaism particularly—played a necessary role in the museum." Yet, "as a Jew living today," List was also "interested in contemporary art—whoever did it—Catholic, Protestant, Jew. It was the aesthetic value" that she held paramount and how she "reacted to it as a human being. After all, Jews are human and non-Jews are also human," and what counted most was "man's urge to express," a trait that "is universal and has meaning." Although she knew the museum had successfully "reflected the life of the Jews, say in seventeenth-century Italy," she felt that "the Jewish Museum in 1950–1960–1970 should reflect the life of the Jew" in the present.[7]

The administrative and governance recommendations of List's ad hoc committee were adopted, but the question of future mission remained. She continued to push conversations about it, now sweetened with the Lists' promise of lead funding for a building addition. It was initially for a larger special exhibition space, to accommodate modern-art shows, and to shift the museum's entrance from 92nd Street to Fifth Avenue facing Central Park—steps aimed at boosting the museum's visibility and public access. As the Lists became more deeply immersed in the planning, they decided to fully underwrite what by then had grown into a three-story addition. One or both of the upper floors would accommodate a hoped-for gift of a major Judaica collection from another donor and the first floor was for "contemporary shows." Questions remained, however, about the contemporary-art exhibit opportunities the space could accommodate, how the exhibits would be determined, and their costs—which the seminary could ill afford.[8]

Also at issue were doubts over Kayser's stewardship in general and now, with the Lists' donation, his ability to administer an expanded museum and the exhibits it enabled. He was perceived as lacking "vision" and running the museum "like a mom-and-pop store," its functions "confused and disorganized"; and there was concern about his "scattered, themeless, minor exhibitions" on the museum's first floor and "musty Jewish exhibits" upstairs. Though he was valued for his Judaica expertise and eagerness to share that knowledge, the seminary leadership and his advisory committee also found him to be testy and undiplomatic. The problems came to a head when he took off the previous summer, delegating responsibilities to an inexperienced administrator and failing to plan the museum's fall schedule. Shortly after List's study commenced, Kayser, perhaps responding to the intensifying scrutiny, announced plans to leave,

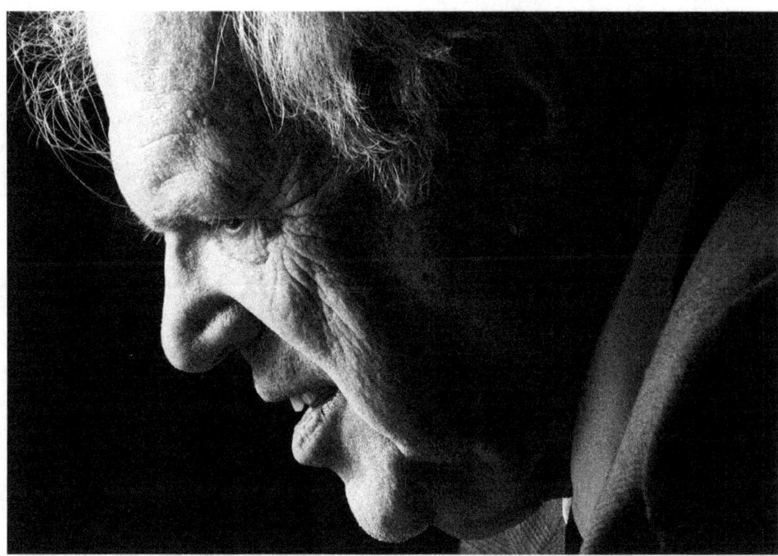

Figure 4.3. David Finn, ca. 1980. Photograph by Chester Higgins Jr. © Chester Higgins Jr. All Rights Reserved.

rendering himself a lame duck in the ensuing discussions. Soon seminary and museum leaders began looking to others for guidance on his replacement. Among them was David Finn (1921–2021), cofounder of a large, industry-leading public relations firm, Ruder & Finn, and nephew of Louis Finkelstein. Regarded as a "dominant figure" in his field's creation, Finn (Figure 4.3) was also an aspiring painter and sculptor on the side, and an accomplished photographer, citing Meyer Schapiro as one of his "early guides." He and his partner launched their firm in 1948 as Art in Industry with the aim of having clients use the fine arts to promote their products. Although it changed, Ruder & Finn continued to urge clients to support the arts as a feature of their community relations. "Rumpled and soft spoken," Finn did not fit the stereotype of the cunning publicist. To the contrary, he was known to admonish clients who rejected criticism instead of addressing its causes, or those who prioritized profits above all else, including giving back to their communities. Finn admitted that he was no "hard-headed businessman," high returns were not a driving concern, and his agency was sometimes knocked for "sloppy business practices." Even so, Finkelstein invited Finn to the seminary board in 1960 and subsequently, because of his art knowledge and prior business acquaintance with the Lists, he began helping at the museum. Finn brought to the museum's deliberations a professional's ability to patiently assist

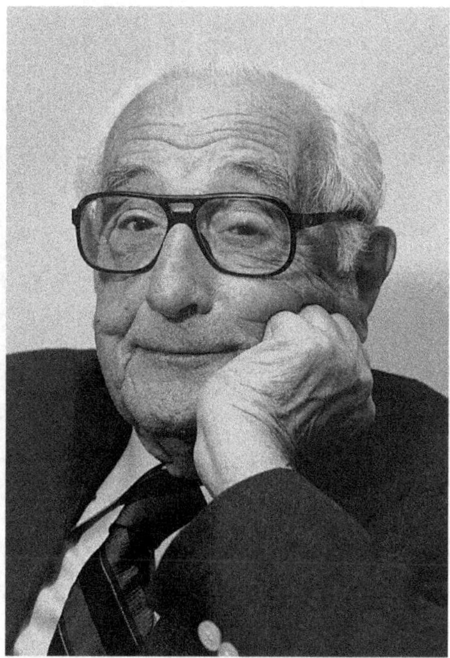

Figure 4.4. Abram Kanof, ca. late 1970s–early 1980s. Courtesy of Elizabeth Kanof Levine.

others in articulating the institution's unique characteristics while also mediating opposing views of what that might mean.[9]

With Kayser's departure announcement, discussions of the museum's mission were now accompanied by a search for his successor. Finkelstein also reached out to Schapiro for nominees noting that some museum advisers "are much more interested in the work of modern Jewish artists" than in its Judaica collections. While Finkelstein and his aides contacted candidates suggested by Schapiro and others, advisory committee members considered the museum's future. Discussions were led by the committee's chair at the time, Abram Kanof (Figure 4.4), and Vera List. Kanof (1903–99) was born in Russia and brought to America at the age of two. He was raised in a religiously observant home, earned a bachelor's degree at Columbia University, served in the US Navy during the Second World War, and trained to be a pediatrician at the State of New York Medical School. In the 1940s, Kanof and his wife began collecting paintings by early twentieth-century American artists and, later, Yiddish theater and film posters dating from the late nineteenth to mid-twentieth century. As his interest in Jewish culture grew, Kanof became active in the American Jewish Historical Society and, through its one-time close relationship with the seminary's museum, aware of its transformation into the Jewish Museum. His background as a collector, measured demeanor, humor, and practicality made Kanof a welcome addition to the museum's lay advisers. He was appointed to a seminary trustees subcommittee on the museum in the late 1940s, chaired a museum committee following an administrative reorganization in 1957, and headed the advisory committee after it was formed. During this period, with the benefit of Kayser's advice, Kanof developed a reverence for and began collecting Jewish ritual objects. Kanof and his wife donated funds to establish the Tobe Pascher Workshop—named after her mother—where, in the museum's basement, the crafting of modern Jewish ritual objects was supported and taught; and they later contributed an acquisition fund to acquire for the museum's permanent collection the best of the workshop's output. As the museum-planning discussions proceeded, Kanof represented "the traditional view of Jewish ceremonial objects as an art" and List, "very much involved with [the Museum of Modern Art] and new trends in the art world," advocated contemporary art.[10]

The group's findings opened with Kayser's observation that the "problem of defining Jewish art" had "long distressed those . . . professionally concerned with this field." But the issue was dismissed because participants thought "'Jewish art' is a sterile term"—meaning they were uninterested in limiting its definition—and, in any case, "the display of Jewish art, no matter how . . . defined" was obviously the museum's purpose. Casting a wide net, the group committed the museum to "significant examples of fine and applied arts, both of the past and contemporary, having significant relation to Jewish life, traditions, literature and spiritual values." That broad scope anticipated "the new formulation," which the List addition made "inevitable." While the museum would continue its Judaica program, it would also display artworks "which shed light . . . on the Jewish contribution to art," that is, not only "works by Jewish artists which reflect the artists' heritage," but also those by others "which relate to Judaism by virtue of their subject or point of view." Significantly, in a nod to another way by which art might acquire Jewish meaning, they included "works which have appealed to a *Jewish collector* as giving aesthetic expression to the central . . . ideals of Judaism."[11]

There were other Jews to be considered as well. Although discussions of the museum's future proceeded without Finkelstein's active participation, Marjorie Wyler (1915–2002), the seminary's publicist at the time, represented its interests. Having handled the seminary's media relations starting in the late 1930s, and the museum's beginning in the 1950s, she thought of the museum as an educational "arm" of the seminary and likened it to Finkelstein's *Eternal Light*. Wyler noticed that when the museum began mounting exhibits like *The New York School, Second Generation*, "Jews who had no other connection with Judaism" started coming to its openings. Among them, she recognized fundraising-dinner attendees at major philanthropies—such as the Jewish Federation, United Jewish Appeal, and American Jewish Joint Distribution Committee—none of whom came "any place near the seminary." Seeing an opportunity to cultivate them via future avant-garde exhibits, Wyler in effect endorsed them as a way of reaching these "'marginally affiliated' Jews."[12]

As preparations for the List addition continued into 1962, it became clear that the building expansion entailed increased operating costs. Recognizing the museum was unable to quickly increase its annual income, and the seminary was incapable of boosting its support, an ambitious fundraising campaign was proposed. Vera and Albert List observed these discussions from their respective perches on the museum's and seminary's governing bodies. Confident about the future promise of the museum's turn toward contemporary art, they pledged a three-year grant to carry the museum through this fiscal transition. Along the way, the advisory committee recommended—and the seminary approved—its reconstitution as a "Board of Governors" with a greater degree of independence from the seminary but more fiscal responsibility. All the while, preparations for the addition proceeded. The cornerstone was laid in May 1962 and the new wing's opening slated for the following December. The search for the museum's new director was widened with a job posting that subtly reflected the changes underway, including the museum's increased independence—the seminary was not mentioned. The successful candidate would be responsible for developing a "program in Historical and Traditional Art, Contemporary Art, and General Art Appreciation, as illumination of Jewish tradition through an understanding of historical and contemporary life." To attract applicants, the posting highlighted the newly expanded exhibition space and the desirability of a "broadly trained art museum administrator," adding "scholarship in historical Judaica not required." Behind the scenes, Alan R. Solomon (Figure 4.5) emerged as the leading candidate.[13]

The Art World's 92nd Street Y, New School, and *Commentary*

Solomon (1920–70), who was of Jewish descent, earned his undergraduate and doctoral degrees at Harvard, was in the last class of its renowned "Museum Course" taught by Paul J. Sachs, and wrote his dissertation

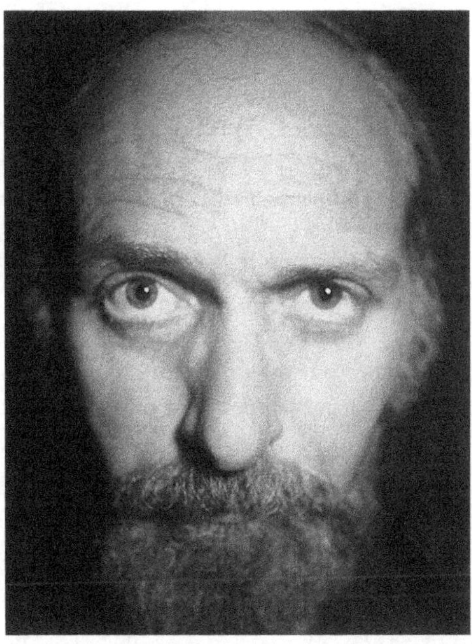

Figure 4.5. Alan Solomon, ca. 1960s. Alan R. Solomon Papers, 1907–1970, Archives of American Art, Smithsonian Institution.

on the iconography of Picasso's synthetic-cubist still lifes. In 1952, while still completing his doctorate, Solomon began teaching at Cornell University and the following year spearheaded establishment of the university's Andrew Dickson White Art Museum. He became its inaugural director, serving until 1960, assembled works from across the campus to seed its permanent collection, and organized over two hundred exhibits. For his modern-art courses and exhibit work, Solomon regularly visited New York to familiarize himself with its contemporary art scene. During that time, he formed a keen interest in contemporary art and applied to its interpretation a "probing, analytical mind, disciplined by the methodology of scholarship." These qualities were amplified by an aura of erudition that lent to his exhibitions and discussions of them equal measures of passion and intellectual authority. Also charismatic, intense, and inspiring, Solomon had entered the field at a moment when museum directors and curators were regarded as "a little more mythic and larger than life." For Vera List, Solomon was "the most brilliant" museum professional she knew, and she found her encounters with his piercing sensibility and driven nature "a fantastic experience." Leo Castelli, with whom Solomon began forging a professional and personal relationship in 1958, said the latter never dwelled on "the previous movement" and was always searching out the new, immediately grasping the next significant trends in contemporary art. Restless and ready to move from bucolic upstate New York, Solomon sought the Jewish Museum's directorship.[14]

During his interviews, however, Solomon was appalled by the museum's "untidy" galleries and behind-the-scenes operations. Further, the demands of implementing the building addition, upgrading the original building, establishing professional standards, and fundraising were staggering. Equally disturbing was the ongoing debate about the museum's mission into which Solomon was immediately immersed. Solomon confided to a seminary official that the governing board was far from settling "basic issues," leaving him with at best "a clear picture of the most extreme positions at either end." Kanof and his allies continued to prioritize Judaica programming while List and her cohort prioritized the avant-garde. Solomon tried to help, observing to List, Kanof, and the others that the "modern emancipated Jew is a heterogeneous figure, unlike his predecessor in the Ghetto" whose limited experiences would have resulted in a more "precise cultural definition" of the museum's ambit. The board's conflicting views reflected the heterogeneity of modern Jewry and for that reason there was not a "right [or wrong] position" for it to take. Rather, he advised, the members should determine "arbitrarily . . . whatever policy decisions suited them as the principals concerned" without attempting to rationalize them. Being modern Jews, their beliefs were sufficient justification, ipso facto, and the resulting exhibitions would thereby be legitimate expressions of modern Judaism. Solomon validated the positions of both factions, but without taking sides.[15]

Solomon's characterization of the difference between emancipated Jews and those of the ghetto echo a schism at the time between Jewish intellectuals and rabbinic stewards of congregational Judaism. That divide was addressed by art and culture critic Harold Rosenberg. He noted that he and his fellow intellectuals freely acknowledged their Jewish identity, differed among themselves and others on various topics of Jewish interest, and distanced themselves from Judaism as "an organized group." Perhaps for that reason, if they criticized Jewish institutions, they would be attacked by rabbinic leaders as negative and incapable of providing "constructive criticism" because the intellectuals were "detached," "rootless," and insufficiently committed to "the Jewish enterprise." Rosenberg countered that their position outside organized Judaism was "not brought about by them but by the historical situation" in which all Jews of the era lived, both observant and non-observant. Due to this circumstance, he argued, fidelity to Jewish values should not "be delineated by any static concept of Judaism nor represented monopolistically by any 'organized group.'" Like Rosenberg, Solomon witnessed divisions in the Jewish community and accepted how, on the museum's board, opposing views played out.[16]

The search committee welcomed Solomon's professionalism, dynamism, and candor, and they, along with seminary officials who were equally impressed, recommended Solomon for the directorship. Finkelstein offered the position in June 1962 and Solomon accepted despite the administrative and policy challenges that lay ahead. In the appointment letter and subsequent announcements, Finkelstein remarked that with the List addition, the museum would "expand its function in the area of contemporary art," but added that the museum's commitment to its Judaica collection would not change. Finkelstein's formulation belied, however, continuing indecision among the others about the comparative emphasis to be placed on contemporary art versus Judaica and, moreover, what was meant by "contemporary art."[17]

Solomon shared Schapiro's insights concerning representation and abstraction in works by Jews, applying them more fully to the museum. Although it had committed itself to modern art since relocating to the Warburg mansion, Solomon believed it had not fully realized that goal because the museum concentrated too much on exhibiting works by Jewish artists who "illustrate specific iconographical ideas (like scenes from the Bible, genre episodes, etc.)." As a result, the museum overlooked artists in "the main stream of contemporary art" since the 1930s who, instead, pursued "purely formal ideas on the one hand, or more abstract, metaphysical or subjective iconographical ideas on the other." Solomon argued that Jewish subjects were not treated in post-1930s abstraction because the methods of abstract art cannot readily be adapted to "parochial interpretation." Even though many "philosophical or psychological concepts" of modern painting may come from the "Hebraic tradition," he continued, it is rarely possible "on an iconographic basis and never on a stylistic basis" to recognize such work as Jewish, even when the artist is Jewish. The Hebraic "philosophical or psychological concepts" to which Solomon referred were "certain ethical values, spiritual ideas, or cultural attitudes." Yet, he argued, even if observers could agree those qualities were necessarily Judaic, it would be "absurd . . . to lay exclusive claim" to them. Solomon hoped to resolve the dilemma of finding an essential Jewishness in art useful for the museum without resorting to "negative," that is, exclusionary, definitions. His solution lay in "defining the Museum positively, as an institution with a dual commitment—to universal aesthetic values, on the one hand, and to certain particular values of Judaism on the other." Solomon found a model in an institutional neighbor just three blocks away: the 92nd Street Young Men's Hebrew Association—today's "92nd Street Y."[18]

Established by German Jews in lower Manhattan in 1874, it moved to successive locations farther north, settling into its current location in 1898 when Jacob Schiff, Frieda Warburg's father, acquired it for the Y. Created to foster the vocational and social advancement of young Jewish men, the Y's programming and facilities expanded in subsequent decades to support physical recreation, cultural opportunities, and continuing education for its core constituency and the neighboring community. Religious training and observances increased at the Y as it served ever-larger numbers of non-affiliated Jews. It formed an Educational Department to oversee "classes of a 'general' nature" while "those with 'Jewish' content" were handled by a Religious Department. That distinction between "general" and "Jewish" seeded a perception of the Y as lacking a "commitment to Jewish life," prompting a debate between religious leaders and community-center advocates over the Y's mission. But that demarcation, rendered for institutional purposes, was misleading. In actuality, it enabled the Y's lay and professional leaders "to express their Jewish identity . . . from the less to the more consciously sectarian." Significantly, the leaders' pursuit of Jewishness "through association and patronage, and . . . participation in nonparochial American culture" was, Naomi Jackson found, "itself a distinguishing aspect of their identities as modern New York Jews." It included contemporary dance, theater, and music—an initiative that began in the 1930s and fully flowered in the post-Second World War era. At the Y, the "word *contemporary*" described ideas and artworks of the time welcomed as "new and exciting by the intellectual New York community."[19]

Another outpost of that community Solomon would have known was The New School for Social Research, a progressive undergraduate and graduate training institution established in lower Manhattan in 1919. Early on, it offered visual arts courses led by several eminent artists and scholars, including Meyer Schapiro who, in addition to his Columbia duties, taught there from the 1930s to 1950s. Contemporary art figured prominently in The New School's curriculum as a means of introducing students to "the arts as a living entity related to modern life" while also reflecting "the interests of New York Jewry." Vera List took evening sculpture classes there and she along with Albert became major funders of The New School starting in the mid-1950s. For Jews at the Y and The New School, "expressing one's Jewishness through the general, contemporary arts became the acceptable and preferred way of being Jewish in America." In the Y and The New School, and the multiple constituencies they served, Solomon had models for nonsectarian programming that might appeal to the large portion of New York's Jewish community thriving outside the synagogue.[20]

He also envisioned the museum becoming analogous to *Commentary* magazine, which by then was a significant platform for critical debates on contemporary American society. *Commentary* was created by the American Jewish Committee in 1945 to replace an in-house journal focused on the organization's affairs and priorities. From the outset, it featured leading New York intellectuals, including Meyer Schapiro, Clement Greenberg, and Leo Steinberg, to establish itself as a respected and timely outlet addressing the most urgent political and cultural issues of the day, especially as they affected American Jews. *Commentary* aspired to be "both Jewish and non-parochial" and thus to treat matters of general interest while remaining "identifiably Jewish" in content. One of the more contentious topics of the day turned on the boundaries of that discourse, especially the Jewish community's tolerance for "decent self-criticism." It was subsumed in a "Jewish Cold War" over the differences between "Jewish self-hatred" and constructive critique that devolved into a bitter debate over questions of "Jewish group loyalty, Jewish group 'survival,' and Jewish nationalism." This battle—related to the one characterized by Rosenberg above—which pitched exponents of "Jewish particularism and nationalism" against those of "liberal universalism and cosmopolitanism," touched as well on the place of Jews in a non-Jewish society. Across the pages of *Commentary* during the 1940s and 1950s, the universalists were compelled to defend their Jewishness against allegations of disloyalty to the Jewish community while combating the idea that it was even necessary to "choose between an unambiguous partisanship with . . . Jewishness and its abandonment." As a result, the magazine was seen as endorsing "fluid concepts of Jewish identity" that encompassed fresh and sometimes unsettling notions of secularity as well as explorations of the ways Jewishness itself might be understood as both intrinsic and American. Especially relevant for Solomon, the magazine had become "a vehicle for exploring new forms of Jewishness." Finn saw Solomon's likening of a future Jewish Museum to *Commentary* to mean that just as "Jews have always been at the vanguard of thinking . . . they should be that in the arts." The museum "should do cutting edge stuff, the newest ideas" and become "the *Commentary* of the museum world."[21]

By following these models, Solomon felt the museum could successfully feature contemporary art even if it lacked visible Jewish content or was by non-Jews. Showing the newest art would, in fact, enable the museum to more fully honor the unique "values of Judaism" by representing "universal esthetic values" meaningful both for Jews and non-Jews.

He, like others, compared the "universal aspects" of the program he envisioned with the *Eternal Light*, the Institute for Religious and Social Studies, and Finkelstein's other initiatives. As with those, Solomon believed contemporary art exhibits would call attention to "the influences of Judaism upon our culture." In prioritizing new art, however, he did not think the museum would be competing with the Museum of Modern Art, the Whitney Museum of American Art, or the Guggenheim Museum. To the contrary, because the Jewish Museum was much smaller and less operationally cumbersome, it could respond to the latest developments far more nimbly than its lumbering neighbors. The museum's most likely competitors in displaying the avant-garde were commercial galleries and they offered only handfuls of artists' works in group shows or, in solo shows, very small selections of an artist's output. Accordingly, Solomon argued, that left a gap the Jewish Museum was perfectly situated to fill: three- to ten-year retrospectives for emerging or early-career artists culled from works still in their studios or from their dealers and collectors.[22]

Solomon distilled his ideas for seminary approval prior to the List addition opening, now scheduled for February 1963. Aware of the discomfort his policy might cause, Solomon added that it was "frankly . . . an experiment, without any definitive commitment beyond . . . several years to test its validity." He also reassured proponents of specific Jewish programming by promising appointment of a Judaica specialist to mount exhibits on that subject. To secure the plan's endorsement, Finn aligned it with seminary policy by arguing that the contemporary-art program echoed the seminary's priority of "relating traditional values to a modern world" and the museum's Judaic programming elevated "aesthetic expression and religious experience" by supporting "the practices of contemporary Jewish living."[23]

Solomon then added that the contemporary art initiative was also an expression of "the traditional Jewish attachment to . . . intellectual freedom and the spiritual importance of the creative process." The identification of his program with intellectual freedom echoed a public policy rationale for the diplomatic uses of contemporary art then underway. During the late 1940s and 1950s, America began confronting the Soviet Union's rise as an international rival. In what became the Cold War, art, literature, and music were deployed in a widening propaganda battle between the two powers as the merits of American democracy, capitalism, and religious freedom were pitted against Soviet communism. In America's search for cultural advantage, "Abstract expressionism constituted the . . . perfect contrast to 'the regimented, traditional, and narrow' nature of 'socialist realism'" by demonstrating "the virtues of 'freedom

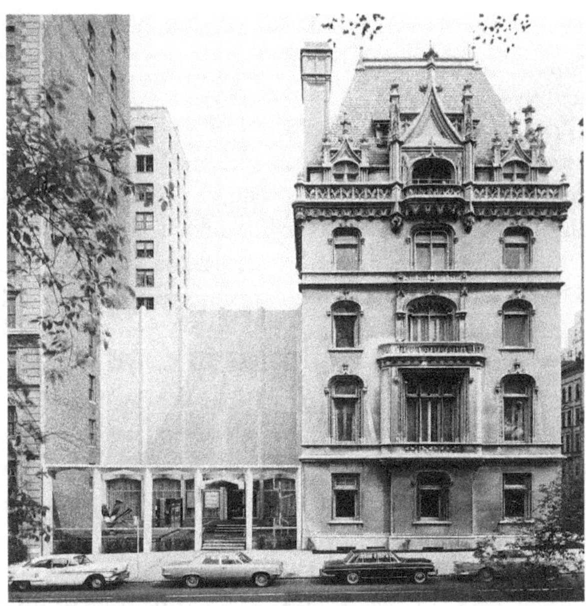

Figure 4.6. Albert A. List Building (to the left, compare with Figure 3.1), mid-1960s, designed by Samuel Glaser (1902–83) and completed in 1962. The Jewish Museum, New York/Art Resource, NY.

of expression' in an 'open and free society.'" Unwittingly, for most of the artists—and over the objections of others—their work was packaged into exhibits circulated by American and European entities with covert Central Intelligence Agency (CIA) funding. Crucially, the "CIA sought to influence the foreign intellectual community" by demonstrating the fruits of American freedom of expression in contrast to the Soviet Union's repression of political dissent and creative works perceived as counter revolutionary. Solomon's reference to the spiritual in this context points to Soviet anti-religious campaigns and promotion of atheism starting in the first decades of Soviet communism—state policies that were reinvigorated during the late 1950s.[24]

Inaugurating the List Addition

The seminary approved Solomon's plan but, citing "questions of a specific nature," said its approval was for public relations purposes only and not to be "construed as official policy." With that tepid endorsement, Solomon turned to opening the museum's addition in February 1963. The museum had been closed since the previous June for the addition's construction and its joining with the original building's first three floors and basement. The severely modernist structure (Figure 4.6) was designed by Vera List's brother, Boston architect Samuel Glaser (1902–83). He used the opportunity to explore current design trends and materials, especially concrete aggregate, to create what one architectural critic called "the last word in contemporary facade clichés." Glaser's juxtaposition of old and new was characterized as "a kind of shotgun . . . marriage" of architectural styles. Where the French Gothic style of the Warburg mansion "had what is inelegantly called 'class,'" the Glaser addition's "class quotient lies somewhere between resort modern and [Fifth] avenue's jazzier apartment house entrances." The addition filled most of what had been a small yard at the back of the Warburg mansion along Fifth Avenue. Glaser retained just enough space to form a small courtyard with an entryway canopy and patio for the sculpture group List had donated a few years earlier. His design relocated the museum's entrance to the Fifth Avenue side and provided an entrance lobby, large gallery, and gift shop on the first floor. The second floor was another large gallery—at the time "one of the largest . . . in New York"—and the third floor contained three smaller gallery spaces and storage. The basement housed an expanded Tobe Pascher Workshop. The walls and ceilings of the adjoining Warburg-mansion rooms, including decorative moldings and reliefs, were painted, respectively, white and black, some matching the severe interior treatment of the addition's galleries. Even so, transitions between the two structures' interiors were as abrupt as their exterior. The three years of operating funds donated by the Lists paid for a much-expanded exhibition program and an accompanying lecture series. These and prior List gifts starting in the late 1950s came to just over $1 million. In recognition of their generosity, the addition was named the Albert A. List Building.[25]

The dedication for the List addition and museum's reopening highlighted its forthcoming contemporary art program. Despite that emphasis, the two exhibits inaugurating the addition looked to the past: *The Silver and Judaica Collection of Mr. and Mrs. Michael M. Zagayski* and *The Hebrew Bible in Christian, Jewish and Muslim Art.* Featuring them reflected the exigencies of donor cultivation, bought time for Solomon to organize his first avant-garde exhibit, and softened the transition to his plan. The Zagayski exhibit (Figure 4.7), loaned by prominent collectors and museum friends, contained 252 objects selected from their Judaica holdings of more than four hundred works dating from the sixteenth to the nineteenth centuries, most ritual objects. The exhibit was the second in over a decade of efforts to coax the collection's donation to the

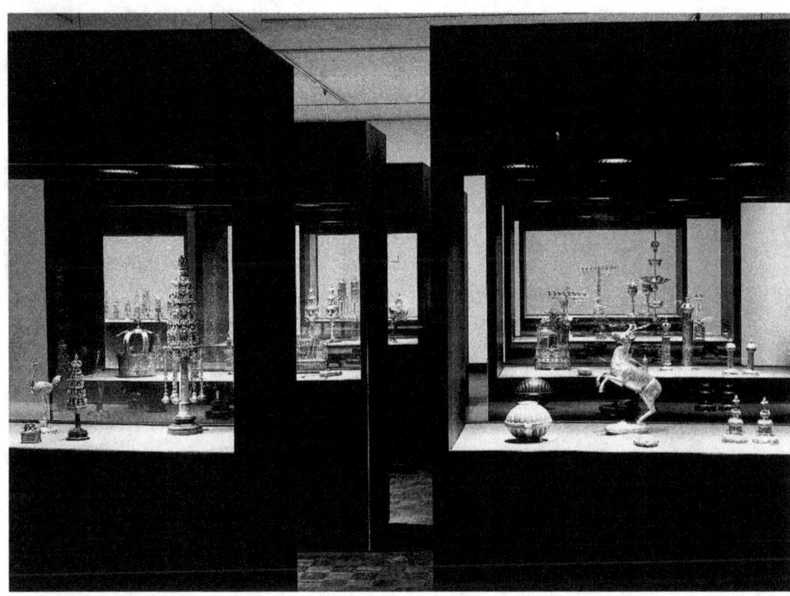

Figure 4.7. Installation view, *The Silver and Judaica Collection of Mr. and Mrs. Michael M. Zagayski*, ca. February 1963. The Jewish Museum, New York/Art Resource, NY.

museum, the first being in 1951. As part of the Zagayski cultivation plan this time, the Lists' building gift allotted dedicated space for it. The collection was strenuously sought because its representation of seventeenth- and eighteenth-century ceremonial objects was particularly strong and its acquisition would fill gaps in the museum's holdings. While the List addition was still under construction, however, the Zagayskis chose to sell the collection, the museum could not afford it, and most of the objects were auctioned. The exhibit did serve one purpose, however, affirming the museum's ongoing commitment to collecting and displaying Judaica.[26]

The Hebrew Bible in Christian, Jewish and Muslim Art (Figure 4.8) was organized by the prolific and influential Jewish editor, theologian, and novelist Arthur A. Cohen (1928–86). Thematically ambitious, Cohen's project explored the "Hebrew Bible" as a source for the "creative imagination of the Christian, Jewish, and Muslim worlds." Cohen's interpretation included the Apocrypha along with the Old Testament, and for evidence he relied on depictions of biblical figures and stories to survey "the styles, media, attitudes, and cultures" they represented. The exhibit contained 120 works—borrowed from over fifty museums, other repositories, commercial galleries, and individual collectors—arranged by figure or topic sequenced according to biblical chronology. The oldest object was a Roman

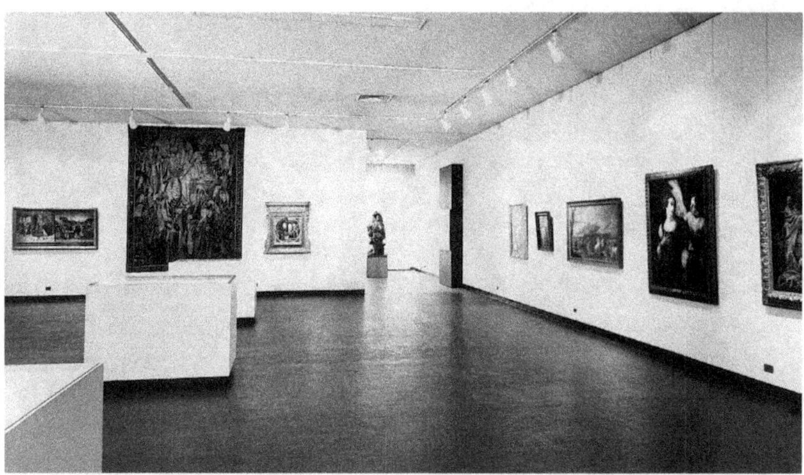

Figure 4.8. Installation view, *The Hebrew Bible in Christian, Jewish and Muslim Art*, ca. February 1963. The Jewish Museum, New York/Art Resource, NY.

bowl and the most recent ones were works by notable twentieth-century artists including Picasso, Chagall, Brancusi, Dubuffet, and Redon. There were illuminated manuscripts; ritual objects; Renaissance engravings and paintings by Durer, van Leyden, Breughel the Elder, and Cranach the Elder; Dutch Golden Age prints and paintings by Rembrandt and Steen; Persian miniatures and images from Armenia, Afghanistan, and Egypt; folk art; and toys.

Cohen denied having a "theological intention" but did admit a "theological orientation." He hoped the exhibit might help reduce "the hopeless and irremediable alienation of religion and art" in the modern day. He believed there were modern artists who never addressed biblical subjects but who nonetheless might be expressing their "understanding of God." That such works might be overlooked could be evidence "that something has happened to the artist *and* to religious institutions" whereby the works are misunderstood as "disjunct and alien" from religious traditions. In ruminating about the troubled relationship between contemporary artists and organized religion, Cohen found justification for a theologian to organize an art exhibition. The artist and the theologian walk along parallel paths, Cohen posited, and he offered his exhibition not "to instruct the artist about his history," but to exchange ideas "as human beings together in search of significant meaning."[27]

With his essay, Cohen echoed Schapiro's ideas concerning the museum's potential as a bridge between modern society and its artists, and as a site where viewers may discover art as nurturing spiritual renewal in a secular culture. Unlike Schapiro, however, Cohen probed the "alienation of religion and art" without addressing the secular ethos of the era as its context. Yet he did share Schapiro's vision of how the museum might confront its dilemma as a seminary-owned institution about to plunge into the avant-garde. The seminary was, after all, a citadel of organized Jewish religion in America. Its stake in the particulars of Judaism as a motive force in modern society was not easily translated into such notions as Schapiro's belief that "art is the spiritual element in secular life." Nonetheless, if the museum could serve as a forum in which contemporary artists and the religiously inclined could find common ground, that might be enough. For those doubting a contemporary art program's value in the seminary's mission, the arguments advanced by Schapiro, List, Solomon, Cohen, and their allies may not have been persuasive for religious traditionalists. Even so, Solomon and the others forged ahead, convinced that the latest in contemporary art could elevate and render more impactful the "traditions" taught by the seminary. Inspired by that bright vision, the museum's leaders and their seminary backers mutually committed themselves to the "significant meaning" they believed would be found in the avant-garde.[28]

Notes

1. Serge Guilbaut, *How New York Stole the Idea of Modern Art: Abstract Expressionism, Freedom, and the Cold War*, trans. Arthur Goldhammer (Chicago, IL: University of Chicago Press, 1983). On modern art museums, see Calvin Tomkins, *Off the Wall*, rev. edn. (New York: Picador, 2005), 187–88; Emily Genauer, "Crowds See Jewish Museum's Exhibit on East Side Life," *World Journal Tribune*, 22 September 1966; AK, "The Jewish Museum: An Institution Adrift," *Judaism* 17, no. 3 (Summer 1968): 292; Arthur C. Danto, "Postmodern Art & Concrete Selves: The Model of the Jewish Museum," in *From the Inside Out: Eight Contemporary Artists*, ed. Susan Tumarkin Goodman (New York: Jewish Museum, 1993), 13.
2. [SSK], *The Jewish Museum: 1947, 1957* ([New York]: [Jewish Museum, Jewish Theological Seminary], 1957), unpaginated. On universalism, see Hasia R. Diner, *The Jews of the United States, 1654–2000* (Berkeley: University of California Press, 2004), 281–82.
3. Alexander Bloom, *Prodigal Sons: The New York Intellectuals & Their World* (Oxford: Oxford University Press, 1986), 46–51, 80–81, 105–6, 112, 131, 138, 140–42. David Biale, *Not in the Heavens: The Tradition of Jewish Secular Thought* (Princeton, NJ: Princeton University Press, 2010), 1. On kernel, see Ruth R. Wisse, "The New York (Jewish) Intellectuals," *Commentary* 84,

no. 5 (November 1987): 34. For the second-to-last quote, see MS, "JTS talk," 16 May [1949], MSC 198:22, CUL. Edward Alden Jewell, "When is Art American?" *New York Times*, 1 September 1946; Jewell (1888–1947) was the *Times* art critic, "Edward A. Jewell, Art Critic, is Dead," *New York Times*, 12 October 1947. On modern art and universality, see Kathrin Pieren, "Negotiating Jewish Identity Through the Display of Art," *Jewish Culture and History* 12, nos. 1 and 2 (Summer/Autumn 2010): 289. Guilbaut, *How New York Stole the Idea*, 44, 174. See also, Chelsea Haines and Gemma Sharpe, "Art, Institutions, and Internationalism, 1945–73" and Nikolas Drosos, "Modernism and World Art, 1950–72," *ARTMargins* 8, no. 2 (June 2019): 3–14, 55–76.

4. SSK, "Jewish Museum . . . , Report to the Board of Overseers," 8 January 1958, RG 21–3–12, LJTS. *An Exhibition of Oil Paintings by Adolf Gottlieb*, intro. Clement Greenberg (New York: Jewish Museum, Jewish Theological Seminary of America, 1957). Lawrence Alloway et alia, *Adolph Gottlieb, A Retrospective* (New York: Arts Publisher in association with the Adolph and Esther Gottlieb Foundation, 1981). *An Exhibition of Oil Paintings by Frankenthaler*, intro. Frank O'Hara (New York: Jewish Museum, Jewish Theological Seminary of America, 1960); John Elderfield, *Frankenthaler* (New York: Abrams, 1989). Biale, *Not in the Heavens*, 137.
5. Catherine M. Soussloff, "Introducing Jewish Identity to Art History" and Robin Reisenfeld, "Collecting and Collective Memory: German Expressionist Art and Modern Jewish Identity," in Catherine M. Soussloff, ed. *Jewish Identity in Modern Art History* (Berkeley: University of California Press, 1999), 4–5, 116. See also, Annette Weber, ed., *Jüdische Sammler und Ihr Beitrag Zur Kultur der Moderne* (Heidelberg, Germany: Universitätsverlag Winter, 2011); and Charles Dellheim, *Belonging and Betrayal: How the Jews Made the Art World Modern* (Waltham, MA: Brandeis University Press, 2021). On New York's art galleries, see Jeffrey S. Gurock, *Jews in Gotham: New York Jews in a Changing City, 1920–2010* (New York: New York University Press, 2012), 116.
6. On Jews and the arts, see Alvin Toffler, *The Culture Consumers: A Study of Art and Affluence in America* (New York: St. Martin's Press, 1964), 34–35; and Zvi Gitelman, "Conclusion: The Nature and Viability of Jewish Religious and Secular Identities," in *Religion or Ethnicity? Jewish Identities in Evolution*, ed. Zvi Gitelman (New Brunswick: Rutgers University Press, 2009), 314. Roberta Smith, "Vera G. List, 94, Is Dead; Philanthropist and Collector," *New York Times*, 13 October 2002. See also, "Deaths," *New York Times*, 12 October 2002. Elizabeth Neuffer, "Albert A. List, 86, Industrialist Who Supported Many Causes," *New York Times*, 12 September 1987; and "Biography of Albert A. List" and "Vignette of Albert A. List," 3 December 1959, RG 1–188–3, LJTS. On Lists' collecting, Irving Sandler, *American Art of the 1960s* (New York: Harper and Row, 1988), 113, 125–26n35; Leo Castelli, oral history interview by Paul Cummings, 14 May 1969 and 8 June 1973, transcript, AAA, SI, 105–6; and Sotheby's (firm), *Property from the Estate of Vera G. List* (New York: Sotheby's, 2003); *Sourcewatch*, The

Center for Media and Democracy, s.v. "Albert A. List Foundation," accessed July 2019, https://www.sourcewatch.org/index.php?title=Albert_A._List_Foundation. On Lists' JTS gifts, see LF to Albert A. List, 27 April 1955, RG 1–139–22, Albert A. List to Max Arzt, 7 January 1957, RG 1–157–44, Jessica Feingold to Albert A. List, 12 May 1958 and SG to Albert A. List, 8 October 1958, RG 1–167–25, LJTS. On Albert List's election to JTS board, see Simon H. Rifkind to Albert A. List, 19 October 1955, RG 1–139–22, LF to Albert A. List, 3 May 1957, RG 1–157–44 and LF to Albert A. List, 27 July 1959, RG 1–177–5, LJTS; "Prominent Industrialist Elected to Board of the Jewish Theological Seminary, 2 December [1960], RG 1–188–3, LJTS. On sculpture gift, see VL to SG, 5 April 1957, RG 1–157–44 and SG to VL, 9 June 1958, RG 1–167–25, LJTS; "Jewish Museum to Open Garden," *New York Times*, 8 May 1959; VL, oral history interview by Nicki Tanner, 27 March 1990, transcript, UJA-FNYC, I-433, AJHS, 8–9; and VL, oral history interview by Paul Cummings, 9 January 1973, AAA, SI (unpaginated). Abram Kanof, oral history interview by Judy Tenney, 19 November 1990 and 26 May 1992, transcript, UJA-FNYC, I-433, AJHS, 37. On VL's JM board invitation, see SG to VL, 13 September 1957 and VL to SG, 18 September 1957, RG 1–157–44, LJTS. VL also backed a JM program, 1969–2000, commissioning artists to create limited-edition prints each Jewish new year; Ruth Erickson, *30 Years of New Year Graphics from the Jewish Museum: The Albert and Vera G. List Graphics Commissions*, essay by Jane Kent (Burlington, VT: Burlington City Arts, 2006).

7. Abram Kanof to VL, 2 February 1960, RG 1–188–3, LJTS. [VL,] "A Draft of By-Laws for the Jewish Museum Committee," [ca. April 1960], RG 25–5–4, LJTS. On "degree of excellence," see VL, oral history interview by Paul Cummings, 9 January 1973, transcript, AAA, SI (unpaginated); on the "Jew living today," see VL, oral history interview by Nicki Tanner, 27 March 1990, transcript, UJA-FNYC, I-433, AJHS, 18–19.
8. "Annual Report of the Jewish Museum," September 1960–June 1961, RG 11–44–11, LJTS. VL to SG, 8 April 1960 and SG to VL, 21 April 1960 [two letters], RG 1–188–3, LJTS. On budget worries, see SG to Joseph F. Kauffman, 29 August 1960, RG 25–4–36, LJTS. On the building donation, see Albert A. List to LF, 7 September 1960, RG 1–188–3, Joseph F. Kauffman to Alan Stroock, 30 September 1960, RG 25–4–36, and Publicity release, 10 February [1961,] RG 25–8–3, LJTS; see also, Philip Benjamin, "$2,600,000 in Gifts Aids Groups Here," *New York Times*, 9 March 1961. On the prospective Judaica collection donation, see below. On the study, Publicity release, "Jewish Museum to define objectives," 21 December [1961], RG 25–8–3, LJTS.
9. On unprofessional conduct, see VL to Abram Kanof, 23 October 1961, and SG to VL, 26 October 1961, RG 1–197–55, VL to Abram Kanof, 29 November 1961, RG 25–4–24, LJTS. On SSK's performance, see Janet Solinger (JM Administrator, 1961–1965), oral history interview by Nicki Tanner, 10 May 1993, transcript, UJA-FNYC, I-433, AJHS, 7–8; DF, oral history interview by Nicki Tanner, 13 February 1990, transcript, UJA-FNYC,

I-433, AJHS, 13–14; Abram Kanof (JTS and JM board member, late 1940s–late 1960s), oral history interview by Judy Tenney, 19 November 1990 and 26 May 1992, transcript, UJA-FNYC, I-433, AJHS, 16–17. On SSK's absence, JM exhibits, and the JM's board at the time, see Janet Solinger, oral history interview, 6–9; on musty exhibits, see Marjorie Wyler (JTS publicist, 1938–1993), oral history interview by Dorothy Bamberger, 11 January and 11 May 1995, transcript, UJA-FNYC, I-433, AJHS, 28. SSK was complimented by LF and SG in prior years; LF to SSK, 21 December 1960, RG 1–187–4 and SG to SSK, 7 March 1961, RG 1–197–9, LJTS. On SSK's departure, see Minutes, Administrative Council, JM, 10 January 1962, RG 25–7–6, LJTS and Grace Cohen Grossman, "Dr. Stephen S. Kayser: A Personal Testimony" and William M. Kramer, "Stephen S. Kayser in Los Angeles: A Personal Memoir," in *A Crown for a King: Studies in Jewish Art, History and Archaeology in Memory of Stephen S. Kayser*, ed. Shalom Sabar, Steven Fine, William M. Kramer (Jerusalem and New York: Gefen Publishing House, 2000), 12–13, 25–27. See also, Publicity release, 31 May 1962, RG 1–206–12, LJTS. SSK felt he was treated shabbily in subsequent months; SSK to SG, 7 May 1962, RG 1–206–12, AKatz to SSK, 20 December 1962 and AKatz to SG, 21 December 1962, RG 25–4–24, LJTS. *Contemporary Authors Online* (Detroit, MI: Gale, 2003) *Biography in Context*, s.v. "David Finn," accessed July 2019, doi: GALE|H1000031814; Joanne Lipman, "Family Affair, Ruder Finn P.R. Firm is Roiled by Defections Amid Nepotism Issue," *Wall Street Journal*, 2 July 1986; James R. Hagerty, "David Finn, an Aspiring Artist, Prospered in Public Relations," *Wall Street Journal*, 28 October 2021; and Glenn Rifkin, "David Finn, Co-Founder of a Public Relations Power, Dies at 100," *New York Times*, 19 October 2021. DF donated his photographs, many of which were part of, or the basis for, over one hundred books; "David Finn Archive, Collection Summary," National Gallery of Art Library, accessed February 2023, https://library.nga.gov/permalink/01NGA_INST/puoc5q/alma991738973804896 (see also, link to pdf of "Published sources for photographs in the David Finn Archive" on the same page). His family's original name was Finkelstein; DF, *Way Forward*, 3. See also, *Presenting David Finn*, exhibit announcement (New York: Harrison Blum Gallery, 1960); and DF, *How to Visit a Museum* (New York: Harry N. Abrams, Inc., 1985). On Ruder & Finn, see *International Directory of Company Histories* (Farmington Hills, MI: St. James Press, 2014); and *Business Insights: Essentials*, s.v. "Ruder Finn Group, Inc.," accessed July 2020, doi: GALE|I2501318432. On Ruder & Finn's encouragement of corporate art patronage, see also, Toffler, *Culture Consumers*, 97. "Ruder · Finn," Ruder · Finn, accessed July 2020, http://www.ruderfinn.com/ (the ampersand between the two names was replaced with the dot in the 1970s). On DF's involvement with LF and JTS affairs, and DF's work with Albert List and the Lists' philanthropies, see DF, *Way Forward*, 79–81, 98–99. On DF's JTS board appointments, see LF to DF, 22 June and Alan M. Stroock to DF, 5 October 1960, RG 1–184–61, LJTS. DF, oral history interview by Nicki Tanner, 13 February 1993, transcript, UJA-FNYC, I-433, AJHS, 3, 9–10.

10. On job search, see LF to MS, 11 January 1962, MSC 127: 2, CUL; LF to SG, 24 January 1962, RG 1–209–19, SH to Horace Richter, 7 February 1962, and AKatz to SH, 16 March 1962, RG 25–4–27, LJTS. Margaret Kanof Norden, "Dr. Abram Kanof, 1903–1999," *American Jewish History* 87, no. 1 (March 1999): 95–96; Chuck Twardy, "Saluting a Patron of Judaic Art in His Adopted State," *News and Observer* (Raleigh, North Carolina), 11 January 1998; and Geoff Edgers, "Art Museum Patron Kanof Dies at Age 95," *News and Observer* (Raleigh, North Carolina), 20 March 1999. On Kanof's association with JTS and the JM, see Board of Overseers, Committee on the Museum, [ca. May] 1948, RG 21–1–31, "Recommendations of the Museum Subcommittee to the Museum Committee of the Board of Overseers, [1950], RG 21–2–14, and Abram Kanof to LF, 27 May 1957, RG 1–156–50, LJTS. On the workshop, see Abram Kanof to "Miss Warburg," 11 May 1955, RG 1–138–39, Abram Kanof to LF, 27 May 1957, RG 1–156–50, "Abram and Frances Kanof Collection of Ceremonial Objects, Schedule of Collections and Expenditures" [ca. January] 1962, RG 25–6–7, and Abram Kanof to SG, 31 January 1962, RG 25–6–7, LJTS. See also, Kanof, "The Tobe Pascher Workshop," in Nancy M. Berman, *Moshe Zabari: A Twenty-Five Year Retrospective* (New York: Jewish Museum, 1986), 6, and Abram Kanof, oral history interview by Judy Tenney, 19 November 1990 and 26 May 1992, transcript, UJA-FNYC, I-433, AJHS, 29–31. On the acquisition fund, see "Abram and Frances Kanof Collection of Ceremonial Objects" [ca. January] 1962, RG 25–6–7, LJTS and Abram Kanof, "The Tobe Pascher Workshop, 1956–1986," in Berman, *Moshe Zabari*, 6. On the Kanofs' poster collection, see "Theater and Film Poster Collection of Abram Kanof," Center for Jewish History, accessed February 2023, https://archives.cjh.org/repositories/3/resources/6736. Kanof served as AJHS president 1961–1964. After retiring, the Kanofs moved to Raleigh, North Carolina, where he established a Judaica collection at the local art museum and served as a trustee 1979–1986, "Judaic," North Carolina Museum of Art, accessed February 2023, https://ncartmuseum.org/collection/museum-collection/judaic/. On planning discussions, Marjorie Wyler, oral history interview by Dorothy Bamberger, 11 January and 11 May 1995, transcript, 30–31, 64–65; and Janet Solinger, oral history interview by Nicki Tanner, 10 May 1993, transcript, UJA-FNYC, I-433, AJHS, 9–11.
11. "Memorandum on the Jewish Museum," [ca. February–March?] 1962, RG 25–7–6, LJTS (emphasis added). See also, SSK, "Defining Jewish Art," 457–67; Minutes, Administrative Council, JM, 14 February 1962, RG 25–7–6 and "The Jewish Museum, Its philosophy, objectives and function," 2 March 1962, RG 25–1–43, LJTS.
12. [Marjorie Wyler,] "A Word of History," 12 March 1962, RG 25–1–43, LJTS. Edna S. Friedberg, "Marjorie Wyler," *Jewish Women: A Comprehensive Historical Encyclopedia*, Jewish Women's Archive, accessed July 2009, https://jwa.org/encyclopedia/article/wyler-marjorie; Marjorie Wyler, oral history interview by Dorothy Bamberger, 11 January and 11 May 1995, transcript, UJA-FNYC, I-433, AJHS, 25–26, 28, 30–31, 60–61.

13. Herbert Unterberger, "Survey – The Jewish Museum, Financial Policy of the Jewish Museum," 10 April 1962, RG 25–6–5, LJTS. AKatz, "Survey – The Jewish Museum: Administrative Section, Draft," 10 April 1962, AF, Box 1, JMA. On Lists' pledge, Unterberger report and AK, "Jewish Museum," 291. "Resolution of Nominating Committee to the Administrative Council of the Jewish Museum" [ca. May 1962], RG 25–5–11, "Revised Draft, Administrative Organization (Short Form)" [ca. May 1962], RG 25–1–43, and "Changes to Revised Draft, Administrative Organization (Short Form)," 11 May 1962, RG 25–1–43, LJTS. "Administrative Organization (Short Form), Jewish Museum, Revised Draft," 11 May 1962, AF, Box 1, JMA. On "Board of Governors" policy, see "Report of the Nominating Committee to the Administrative Council [JM]," 4 June 1962, RG 25–5–11 and Minutes, Administrative Council, JM, 4 June 1962, RG 25–7–6, LJTS. Marjorie Wyler and Beatrice Ellenoff to Members, Public Relations Committee, Jewish Museum Advisory Council, 15 May 1962 [accompanied by "Outline: Opening of the New Wing of the Jewish Museum," 14 May 1962,] RG 25–8–3, LJTS. "Fact Sheet: The Albert A. List Building" [ca. mid-May 1962,] RG 25–8–3, LJTS; "Cornerstone to Be Laid for Wing at Jewish Museum," *New York Times*, 20 May 1962; Publicity release, 23 May [1962], RG 25–8–3, LJTS. "Within the Profession . . . , New York, N.Y., Jewish Museum: Director," *Museum News* 40, no. 9 (May 1962): 46. Correspondence with AS began earlier; AKatz to SH, 16 March 1962, RG 25–4–27, AKatz to AS, 19 March 1962, RG 1–209–56, LJTS; AKatz to AS, 5 April 1962, Alan R. Solomon Papers, 1907–1970, box 1, folder 24, AAA, SI.
14. AS to AKatz, 21 March 1962 [accompanied by AS, "Curriculum Vitae," 5 February 1962,] RG 1–209–56, LJTS. Sam Hunter, "Alan R. Solomon, 1920–1970," *New York Times*, 1 March 1970; Norman L. Kleeblatt, "Alan Solomon," *Brooklyn Rail*, November 2016. See also, "Dr. Alan Solomon Dies at 49; Ex-Director of Jewish Museum," *New York Times*, 19 February 1970. Sally Anne Duncan and Andrew McClellan, *The Art of Curating: Paul J. Sachs and the Museum Course at Harvard* (Los Angeles: Getty Research Institute), 23, 247. AS, "Pablo Picasso: Symbolism in the Synthetic Cubist Still Life: A Study of His Iconography From 1911–1927" (PhD diss., Harvard University, 1962). The White Museum became the Herbert F. Johnson Museum of Art. "Jamuse: The Johnson Museum Turns 40," accessed July 2019, https://museum.cornell.edu/exhibitions/jamuse-johnson-museum-turns-40. AK to AS, 27 April 1962, Alan R. Solomon Papers, 1907–1970, box 1, folder 24, AAA, SI. VL, oral history interview by Paul Cummings, 9 January 1973, transcript, AAA, SI [unpaginated]. Leo Castelli, oral history interview by Paul Cummings, 14 May 1969 and 8 June 1973, transcript, AAA, SI, 141–42. On the AS/Castelli relationship, see Annie Cohen-Solal, *Leo and His Circle: The Life of Leo Castelli*, trans. Mark Polizzoti (New York: Alfred A. Knopf, 2010), 271–75, 287–303, 355.

15. AS to AKatz, 8 and 27 May 1962, RG 1–209–56, LJTS. See also, DF, oral history interview by Nicki Tanner, 13 February 1993, transcript, UJA-FNYC, I-433, AJHS, 14–15.
16. Harold Rosenberg, "Jewish Identity in a Free Society," in *Discovering the Present: Three Decades in Art, Culture, and Politics* (Chicago, IL: University of Chicago Press, 1973), 259–69. On Rosenberg, see chapter 7.
17. LF to AS, 4 June and LF to Members of the JM Administrative Council, 18 June 1962, RG 1–209–56, LJTS. See also, Publicity release [draft], [ca. July 1962], RG 1–209–56, LJTS and "Jewish Museum Names Director of Operations," *New York Times*, 8 July 1962.
18. [AS], "Confidential --- Not for Publication," 1 August 1962, AF, Box 1, JMA; see also, [AS,] Untitled proposal, [ca. July 1962], RG 25–1–43, LJTS. On the 92nd Street Y analogy, see also, Janet Solinger (JM Administrator, 1961–1965), oral history interview by Nicki Tanner, 10 May 1993, transcript, UJA-FNYC, I-433, AJHS, 12–13.
19. Naomi M. Jackson, *Converging Movements: Modern Dance and Jewish Culture at the 92nd Street Y* (Middletown, CT: Wesleyan University Press, 2000), 5, 22–26, 32–34, 51–53 (emphasis Jackson's). The 1898 building was replaced with a larger facility at the same location in 1928, pp. 30–32.
20. Peter M. Rutkoff and William B. Scott, *New School: A History of the New School for Social Research* (New York: The Free Press, 1986), 60–62, 221, 233–34.
21. Nathan Abrams, "'America is Home': *Commentary* Magazine and the Refocusing of the Community of Memory, 1945–1960"; and Nathan Glazer, "*Commentary*: The Early Years" in *Commentary in American Life*, ed. Murray Friedman (Philadelphia, PA: Temple University Press, 2005), quotes are from p. 66. On self-criticism, see Elliot E. Cohen, "The Intellectuals and the Jewish Community: The Hope for Our Heritage in America," *Commentary* 8 (1 January 1949): 28. On Jewish Cold War, see Susan A. Glenn, "The Vogue of Jewish Self-Hatred in Post-World War II America," *Jewish Social Studies* n.s. 12, no. 3 (Spring/Summer 2006): 100, 109–10; on fluidity, see Steven J. Zipperstein, "*Commentary* and American Jewish Culture in the 1940s and 1950s," *Jewish Social Studies* n.s. 3, no. 2 (Winter 1997): 18–19. On *Commentary* as vehicle, see Marcus Krah, *American Jewry and the Re-Invention of the East European Jewish Past* (Berlin, Germany: De Gruyter Oldenbourg, 2018), 75. DF, oral history interview by Nicki Tanner, 13 February 1993, transcript, UJA-FNYC, I-433, AJHS, 15.
22. [AS], "Confidential --- Not for Publication," 1 August 1962, AF, Box 1, JMA. Regarding commercial galleries and the avant-garde, see Mary Lublin, "American Galleries in the Twentieth Century: From Stieglitz to Castelli," in *American Art in the 20th Century: Painting and Sculpture, 1913–1993*, ed. Christos M. Joachimides and Norman Rosenthal (Munich, Germany: Prestel, 1993), 163. On AS and the JM in the 1960s avant-garde, see Sandler, *American Art of the 1960s*, 105, 110, 120–23, 130, 135–37.

23. Meeting notes, "Confidential: Points in discussion," 24 August 1962, RG 25–4–33, LJTS; "Statement on the Jewish Museum. . . ," 6 September 1962, AF, Box 1, JMA. [AS], Policy statement, 26 September 1962, RG 25–4–25 and [AKatz,] "The Jewish Museum," 4 October 1962, RG 25–4–34, LJTS. On experiment, see [AS,] "Memorandum Concerning Jewish Museum Policy," 5 October 1962, AF, Box 1, JMA. A Judaica curator was hired, AKatz to Tom Freudenheim, 25 June and 31 August 1962, RG 25–4–21, LJTS; see also, chapter 5 below. [AS], "The Jewish Museum" [working draft], 8 January 1963, Alan R. Solomon Papers, 1907–1970, box 4, folder 2, AAA, SI; [AS], "Policy Draft: The Jewish Museum" [ca. January 1963] and [AS], "Draft – Policy Statement: The Jewish Museum, 15 January 1963, DF to AS, 15 January 1963, AF, Box 1, JMA.
24. Eva Cockcroft, "Abstract Expressionism, Weapon of the Cold War," in *Pollock and After: The Critical Debate*, 2nd edn., ed. Francis Frascina (London: Routledge, 2000), 150–52. See also, Jane de Hart Mathews, "Art and Politics in Cold War America," *American Historical Review* 81, no. 4 (October 1976): 762–87; and Manfred J. Holler and Barbara Klose-Ullmann, "Abstract Expressionism as a Weapon of the Cold War," in *Culture and External Relations: Europe and Beyond*, ed. Jozef Bátora and Mokre Monika (Farnham, UK: Routledge, 2016), 119–35. Dimitry V. Pospielovsky, *Soviet Anti-Religious Campaigns and Persecutions* (London: Macmillan, 1988). Yuriy Kogan, "The Museum on the Frontlines of the War on Religion" [1932, trans. Bela Shayevich], in *Avant-Garde Museology*, ed. Arseny Zhilyaev (Minneapolis, MN: E-flux Classics [distributed by University of Minnesota Press], 2015), 569–80. On spiritual, see chapter 3.
25. AKatz to AS, 5 February 1963, AF, Box 1, JMA. "The Jewish Museum to Reopen . . . New Albert A. List Building" [publicity release], 7 February 1963, Alan R. Solomon Papers, 1907–1970, Box 4, Folder 2, AAA, SI. Ada Louise Huxtable, "Architecture: Designs for American Synagogues," *New York Times*, 5 October 1963. On the second-floor gallery size, see Kynaston McShine, oral history interview by Carolyn Lanchner (compiled by David Frankel), 1 April 2010–13 January 2011, transcript, Oral History Program, Museum of Modern Art, 19, 22. Also on the interiors, see Silvia Tennenbaum, "Jewish Home for the Graven Image," *Midstream: A Monthly Jewish Review* 12, no. 6 (June–July 1966): 17–18. Martin H. Grabois to AKatz, 13 February 1963 and "Albert A. List Commitment and Receipts," 31 January 1963, RG 25–7–23, LJTS. $1 million = $9.3 million in 2022, "How much is a dollar from the past worth today?" MeasuringWorth, accessed March 2022, www.measuringworth.com/dollarvaluetoday/. Kanof contributed additional money for the Tobe Pascher Workshop and a "Contemporary Ceremonial Crafts Fund"; AKatz to Abram Kanof, 24 December 1962, RG 1–206–7, LJTS; see also, "Museum Workshop to Offer New Courses," 7 February 1963, RG 25–7–23, LJTS.
26. "The Dedication of the Albert A. List Building of the Jewish Museum," 17 February 1963, RG 25–7–23, LJTS; "The Jewish Museum Opening

Exhibitions" [publicity release], 7 February 1963, and "The Jewish Museum . . . presents previews of Two Exhibitions" [17 February 1963], Alan R. Solomon Papers, 1907–1970, box 4, folder 2, AAA, SI; "The New Program of the Jewish Museum" [publicity release], 7 February 1963, RG 25–7–23, LJTS. Stuart Preston, "Jewish Museum Opens an Annex," *New York Times*, 28 February 1963. AS, introduction to *The Silver and Judaica Collection of Mr. and Mrs. Michael M. Zagayski*, ed. GS and Tom L. Freudenheim (New York: Jewish Museum, 1963). "Michael M. Zagayski, 74, Dies; A Leading Collector of Judaica" and "Major Sale in 1964," *New York Times*, 19 February 1967; "Michael Zagayski, Collector of Judaica, Dead in Florida, Aged 74," *Daily News Bulletin, Jewish Telegraphic Agency* XXXIV, no. 35 (20 February 1967): 4. *Loan Exhibit of Antique Ceremonial Objects and Paintings from the Collection of M. Zagayski* (New York: Jewish Museum, 1951); and [Harry G. Friedman], Untitled manuscript [Remarks at opening of Zagayski Collection exhibit], 7 May 1951, RG 25–4–17, LJTS. On the List building vis-à-vis Zagayski cultivation, see Albert A. List to LF, 7 September 1960, RG 1–188–3, Joseph F. Kauffman to Alan Stroock, 30 September 1960, RG 25–4–36, SSK to LF, 17 November 1961, RG 1–197–9, LJTS; on the effort's failure, see AS to LF, 14 January 1963, LF to AS, 17 January 1963, RG 1–219–9, LJTS. On the auction, see *Important Judaica: Silver, Gold, Pewter, Brass and Other Objects of Historic Interest . . . Collection of Michael M. Zagayski . . . March 18 and 19, 1964* (New York: Parke-Bernet Galleries, 1964). The JM acquired some items; "Zagayski Collection of Rare Jewish Ritual Objects Sold in New York," *Daily News Bulletin, Jewish Telegraphic Agency* XXXI, no. 58 (23 March 1964): 4; and "Jewish Museum Buys Ritual Objects," *New York Times*, 20 March 1964. See also, Harry G. Friedman to Janet Solinger, 22 January 1964, Alan M. Stroock to Harry G. Friedman, 27 March 1964, RG 25–4–22, Harry G. Friedman to Janet Solinger, 12 May 1964, and LF to Hans van Weeren-Griek, 9 June 1964, RG 1–227–83, LJTS.

27. Edwin McDowell, "Arthur A. Cohen, Author, Dies at 58," *New York Times*, 1 November 1986; and David Stern, "Arthur A. Cohen," in *Encyclopedia of Religion*, 2nd edn., ed. Lindsay Jones (Detroit, MI: Macmillan Reference USA, 2005), 1848–50. "The Jewish Museum Opening Exhibitions" [publicity release], 7 February 1963, Alan R. Solomon Papers, 1907–1970, Box 4, Folder 2, AAA, SI. Arthur A. Cohen, introduction to *The Hebrew Bible in Christian, Jewish and Muslim Art* (New York: Jewish Museum, 1963), [unpaginated], emphasis Cohen's. For an exhibit review, see Alfred Werner, "The Living Arts: Art," *American Judaism* 14, no. 1 (Fall 1964): 19, 62.
28. On spiritual element, see MS, "JTS talk," 16 May [1949], MSC 198:22, CUL and chapter 3.

Chapter 5

The Avant-Garde or Judaica?

Explaining the first of Solomon's avant-garde exhibitions to a fellow rabbi, a seminary official observed that Jews were often "in the forefront of many new and exciting developments in all fields." The 1962 List addition and accompanying three-year grant propelled the museum into the vanguard of New York's art world. Solomon stewarded these resources into daring explorations of the newest of new art, usually featuring works devoid of Jewish content created by non-Jews. The addition facilitated that change by doubling the museum's size with spacious galleries that readily accommodated the ever-larger works artists were creating in the early 1960s. The museum continued to alternate Judaica or Jewish-themed exhibitions with the avant-garde shows, but the latter attracted far more attention. From the beginning, they were applauded by New York's art-world denizens and questioned within the Jewish community. Despite these differing responses, the avant-garde program continued, sparking debates among the seminary's closest friends over its relevance to the Jewish community. Counterintuitive views were articulated by the museum's backers and critics alike as they witnessed the phenomenon of a Jewish museum allotting resources to wholly secular exhibits and reaping rewards in the form of critical acclaim and high attendance. The challenges posed by the avant-garde stimulated telling conversations about its meaning and uses within the Jewish community while also posing questions about making the Judaica collection's displays equally compelling.[1]

The Nature of a Real Explosion

As planned, Solomon followed the Zagayski and Hebrew bible exhibits with a solo show of fifty-five works by Robert Rauschenberg (1925–2008), a thirty-seven-year-old, non-Jewish artist living in New York. The

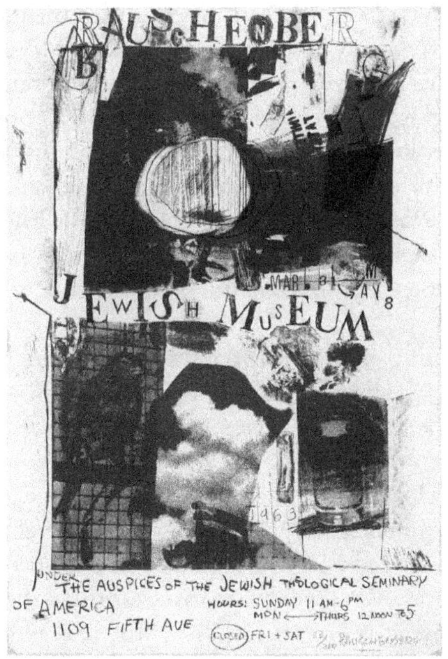

Figure 5.1. Robert Rauschenberg, Jewish Museum exhibition poster, 31 7/8" × 22", lithograph printed by Universal Limited Art Editions in black ink on wove paper, 1963. Gift of Lydia Winston Malbin, accession no. 71.273, Detroit Institute of Arts. © 2023 Robert Rauschenberg Foundation / Licensed by VAGA at Artists Rights Society (ARS), NY. Detroit Institute of Arts/Bridgeman Images.

exhibit, Solomon declared, inaugurated the museum's new contemporary-art program and he considered it an especially fitting start (Figure 5.1). Though Rauschenberg was considered among the "precursors of the newest tendencies in modern art," his work had heretofore received comparatively little exposure. It had been in a few small solo shows in commercial galleries, some contemporary-art group exhibits, and acquired for a handful of collections. The exhibition, a "midcareer" retrospective of Rauschenberg's work, constituted both the first extensive survey of Rauschenberg's work and the first to be presented in a museum setting. Museum-based midcareer retrospectives were "a rarity" until Rauschenberg's show, so it was precedent-setting as well. The artist's daring and career potential exemplified the qualities Solomon wanted to feature in the museum's contemporary-art series. This was not the first time the museum showed Rauschenberg's work, however. Four small pieces were included in the *New York School, Second Generation* exhibit six years earlier. In the intervening years, he expanded the media, techniques, and scale of his work and Solomon's selection of fifty-five works represented Rauschenberg's development across the full range of the artist's interests. The largest of the pieces, *Barge* (1963) was over six feet high and thirty-two feet long and it, most of the wall works, and all the sculptures employed a variety of found objects including, famously, a preserved eagle in *Canyon* (1959) and a stuffed Angora goat with a car tire around its middle in *Monogram* (1955–59). Just as Solomon hoped, the exhibit attracted wide critical praise, cementing Rauschenberg's reputation as a rising star.[2]

The show's opening, in March 1963, was also memorable. One observer characterized it as "the first of the wide-open, see-and-be-seen, roaring art world galas that became such a part of the sixties scene." Many young artists came to the opening and "the still somewhat unfamiliar, sweetish scent of marijuana" hung in the air as the museum's regulars "gazed with amazement and apprehension at the mass of disheveled art lovers . . . some of whom looked almost as outlandish as the art on display." Most responded to the ways Rauschenberg's work captured the temper of a new era. "Youth had taken over contemporary art, just as it had taken over American politics. The high spirits, the wit, the energy, the lightness of touch" in the artist's work, "seemed to echo . . . [then-president] John F. Kennedy's televised press conferences—and underlying both was a heady sense of power linked to imagination, of new approaches to old problems, of optimism without sentimentality." The exhibition was "in the nature of a real explosion," not only boosting Rauschenberg's renown, but also attracting far more attention to the Jewish Museum than it had ever known before. The added scrutiny, however, raised unwelcome questions.[3]

Before the exhibit even opened, word of its audacity and what that implied about the museum began worrying its Jewish outsiders. In fielding queries, Ben Heller (1925–2019), an art collector and dealer who loaned work for the show, reached out to another lender, the prominent art book publisher and collector Harry N. Abrams (1904–79). Both served on the List addition opening-dedication committee and were subsequently invited to its governing board. Responding to this "vague unrest," Heller suggested appending "of Art" to the museum's name. Adding those words, he thought, identifies it "as an art museum taking the stress . . . off the word Jewish." Thereby, if someone questions why the museum is hosting an exhibit like the Rauschenberg show, "the answer is simply, it's a Jewish Museum of *Art*." To a disgruntled patron wondering if the museum had abandoned Judaica in favor of "incomprehensible" art, Vera List replied that the museum continued featuring ritual objects and pointed to the

Zagayski exhibit and permanent collection galleries. As for the avant-garde, she said new art often offended observers in the past. List did not mean to suggest that "fifty years from today Rauschenberg will be considered the Cezanne or Matisse . . . of the '60's." But, she added, "Should we not try to withhold judgement—have an open mind—try to *see* and *understand*?" The exhibit was similarly defended by a seminary official, Arthur Katz, the recently appointed liaison between the museum and the seminary who was in effect Solomon's supervisor. Responding to criticism from a congregational rabbi, Katz also mentioned the museum's Judaica exhibits. The Rauschenberg exhibit merely reflected an "additional function" of the museum, a "contribution to the field of contemporary art appreciation." Katz tried to assuage the rabbi's concerns by acknowledging that as "with all new art forms, . . . there is a great difference of opinion regarding its validity." Nonetheless, he felt, since "Jews in our country have generally been in the forefront of many new and exciting developments in all fields of endeavor," the seminary believed this "innovation in art would be understood for its experimental purposes."[4]

Another, more wide-ranging critique came from seminary trustee Alan M. Stroock, the one who—about two decades prior—suggested the Warburg mansion's donation for the museum. Stroock, representing fellow trustees, complained about Solomon's fiscal management, neglect of the Judaica collection, and alignment of visiting hours with the Sabbath. These concerns led to an accelerated performance review schedule for Solomon, creation of a museum finance committee, and formal appointment of Meyer Schapiro to advise Solomon and the museum board on exhibition policy. While issues with Solomon's leadership were being aired, he also began revitalizing the museum's Judaic programming in accordance with his modernist sensibilities. Atop his initiatives was the exhibition *Recent American Synagogue Architecture* for which Solomon hired as guest curator Richard Meier (b. 1934), a still-young architect of Jewish descent and an emerging star. Meier, who also designed the exhibit installation, selected seventeen building projects by fifteen individuals or firms, including several of the most prominent non-Jewish architects of the day: Philip Johnson, Frank Lloyd Wright, and Minoru Yamasaki. Meier's selection concentrated on the previous decade and featured examples selected for the character of the designs rather than the designers' Jewish identity, though several others were of Jewish descent. The exemplars, along with brief statements from the architects, were accompanied by essays on the synagogue as an architectural form, "The Synagogue in Jewish Law," and statements by prominent Orthodox, Conservative, and Reform rabbis on synagogue architecture from their

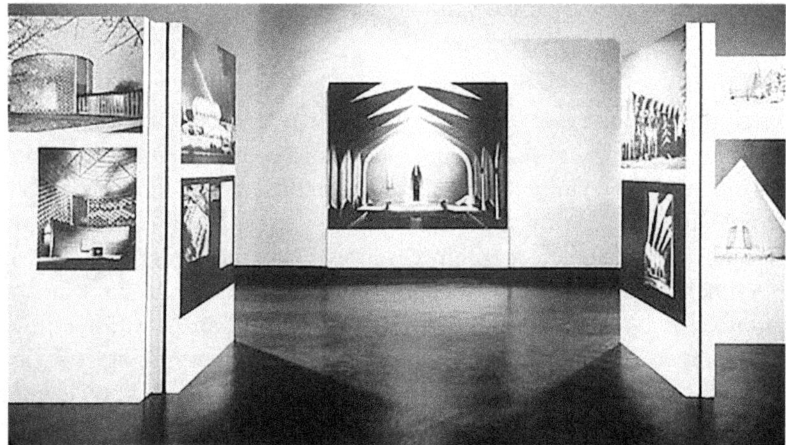

Figure 5.2. Installation view, *Recent American Synagogue Architecture*, ca. October 1963. The Jewish Museum, New York/Art Resource, NY.

denominations' perspectives. The projects shown were either completed, under construction, or still in the design stages; and one, by Abstract Expressionist painter Barnett Newman—of Jewish descent, consisted of drawings for an imagined sanctuary. The projects were represented with models, photographs, and architectural elevations and floor plans (Figure 5.2), all accompanied by labels applauded by a critic as written "with commendable clarity."[5]

The exhibit's purpose, Solomon said, was to inform the public—especially Jews—about the challenges of and solutions to "reconciling the traditional values" of synagogue history "with modern social, economic and architectural needs." Its catalogue was thus intended to serve as a "kind of handbook" for planners wrestling with those difficulties. Meier added that because, historically, synagogues were constructed in the prevalent styles of the localities and times in which Jews lived, he highlighted designs that accommodated traditional synagogue requirements while incorporating "contemporary means and attitudes." In detailing his criteria, Meier echoed ideas advanced by Kayser (discussed in chapter three). Kayser wanted to modernize the works ornamenting synagogues by supplanting "Jewish art . . . unthinkable without a substantial display of beards" with contemporary works that in their interpretation of Jewish themes "will be judged only on the basis of artistic truth." Meier approached this task by excluding truth's opposite, the falsification of architectural form. He cited synagogues that "depend on symbolism" for their designs, for example, one that employed the six-pointed Star of David to shape its floor plan.

That approach "falsifies the form" because the interior space's function is "compromised" to achieve that shape. Moreover, it is lost on congregants because, Meier notes, they are inside the building and its symbolic form "can only be 'read' from above the structure" or in its blueprint. Likening true architects to creatively free artists, Meier argued, the "difference between an expert synagogue maker and an architect" is "similar to the distinction between a portrait painter and an artist." The former is "producing a commercial product" and the latter is "manifesting an idea."

In surveying recent trends in synagogue design, the exhibit also revealed the "willingness of congregations to turn freely" to designers offering "the most imaginative and inventive solutions." As was the case in past generations when Jews commissioned designs for synagogues or the creation of ritual objects, it mattered little whether the creators were Jewish. Although Jewish architects were available during the period of the exhibit's examples—no doubt including many "expert synagogue makers"—many non-Jewish ones were hired instead. Clearly the most important criteria for those congregations choosing them were that the results be both religiously proper *and* spiritually meaningful, no matter whether the architect was Jewish or not. *Recent American Synagogue Architecture* exemplified a modern take on the museum's Judaic mission by setting Jews' spiritual aspirations in the context of contemporary architecture. It was a fitting complement to the avant-garde art Solomon, List, and their allies were pursuing.[6]

The next in Solomon's avant-garde program, *Black and White* (Figure 5.3), was a collaborative effort led by Ben Heller. The exhibit featured thirty-nine works, by twenty artists, dating from 1939 to 1963—the year of the exhibit. Solomon characterized the exhibit as continuing the museum's shows featuring younger, under-recognized artists, but also revealing the "continuity between new artists and the traditions of contemporary painting." This was visible in "a major area of exploration" in American painting starting with the Abstract Expressionists and continuing into the present—a "reduction of means" from color to just black and white. Heller disclosed, however, that his exhibit plan had "no thesis" beyond showing black-and-white paintings of the past two decades. Brian O'Doherty (1928–2022), then–art critic for the *New York Times*, said the exhibit raised "provocative" questions without offering "any intelligent answer." Further, he thought the selection of works was "done remarkably badly," problems that could not "be excused by disavowing any thesis." Another reviewer, Donald Judd (1928–94)—better known today as a leading sculptor—believed "black and white as the purpose of a show" was uninteresting. Yet he found it to be "handsome" and possessing "some

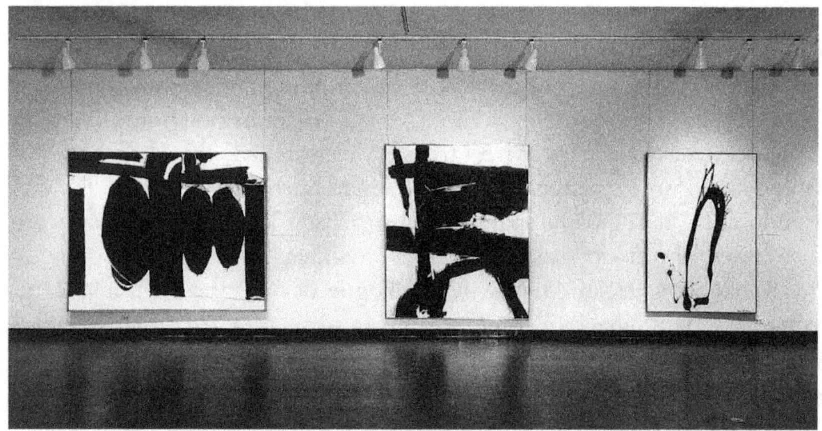

Figure 5.3. Installation view, *Black and White*, ca. December 1963. The Jewish Museum, New York/Art Resource, NY.

relevance" by virtue of the paintings' other qualities. Perhaps Heller's inspiration for the show echoed a trend in American fashion design vividly captured by a *Look* magazine photo shoot in the exhibition (Figure 5.4).[7]

Pursuing a Greater Balance

Although Solomon was attracting new audiences, there was mounting disquiet among Jews who either disliked the avant-garde program or objected to what they perceived as its prioritization over Judaica. Responding to one complaint, Katz—as the museum's seminary liaison—conceded that emphasizing contemporary art "lends itself very easily to overshadowing" the museum's ritual objects. Replying to another, he gamely defended the "experimental program," but reported that seminary officials were evaluating the museum's past year "with very serious concern." Hopefully, Katz wrote, the museum would find "a greater balance" between the avant-garde and Judaic programming. In the meantime, he pleaded for "all our friends" to allow time for the experiment to continue so that, with additional experience, the museum's policies could be brought "into more mature development." Behind the scenes, Solomon's leadership was also a rising concern. Already in spring 1963, near the Rauschenberg show's conclusion, board members and seminary officials began discussing Solomon's possible replacement. Katz started feeling out prospective candidates, as well, in anticipation of Solomon's dismissal by midsummer. Among them was Karl Katz (no relation), then a curator at

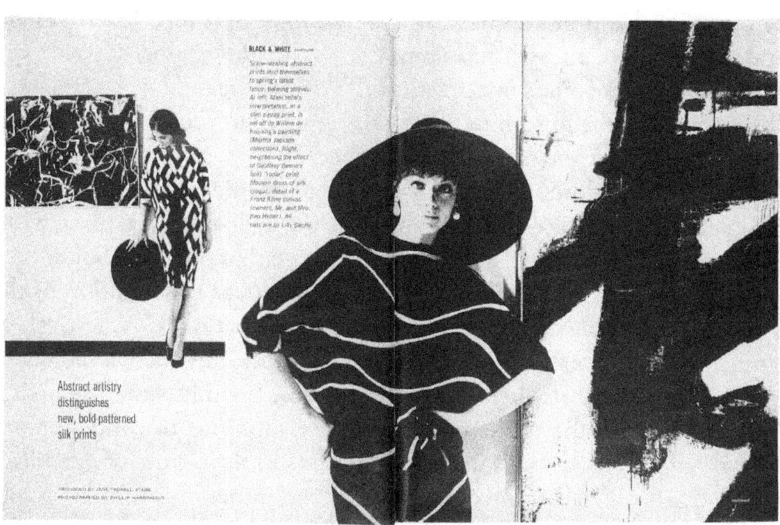

Figure 5.4. Two-page spread from photo feature, "Black and White," *Look* magazine, 28, no. 8 (21 April 1964): 128–29. Photographs by Phillip Harrington.

the Israel Museum. That sense of urgency was due to a variety of issues, few of which had to do with the avant-garde program.[8]

David Finn thought Solomon was a "terrible administrator" and worried about the latter's budget deficits, something Albert List "couldn't stand." Others were unhappy with Solomon for spending "too much time in artists' lofts" scouting new work and not enough managing the museum and fundraising. Magnetic as he was, in Leo Castelli's experience, Solomon held himself "aloof from the collecting world" and its prospective donors. Vera List "strenuously" defended Solomon but failed to persuade others including Finn. Heller was more circumspect. He tried to reconcile the museum's aim of doing both "those things which we call Judaica" and "those things which we call contemporary," with how the "alert, intellectual, sensitive 'advanced Jew' . . . has lived his life." Although Heller found the avant-garde exhibits an "interesting way to express visually parts of our being," fundraising to support them was difficult. The "Judaica Jews couldn't tolerate" the avant-garde program, while "the Jewish people who were modern"—instead of supporting the Jewish museum—preferred backing "the Whitney [Museum] or [Museum of] Modern [Art], perhaps because they did not "want to be too Jewish in their identification." In the face of these problems, Heller acknowledged that the "Seminary tried nobly" to accept the avant-garde exhibits but could not do more to absorb their costs. In the end, Solomon's gifts did not outweigh his limitations, posing a dilemma that for Heller was endemic: "The problem with museums . . . is the philosopher king. If you get the aesthetic man he's not practical. If you get the man who can be the administrator or the fund-raiser he doesn't know Tintoretto from Tiepolo. It's very hard to get the two things together."[9]

By fall 1963, Solomon's position had become untenable. He was given a probationary contract that ran through the following June but without a salary increase. Then an opportunity arose that provided Solomon a graceful way out. He was asked to organize America's contribution to the visual art portion of the Venice Biennale, an international arts festival, in October 1964. The nation's participation was funded by the United States Information Agency (USIA) via institutions like the museum. The invitation was based on the museum's "excellent exhibitions of contemporary art" and Solomon's "outstanding contributions to the stature of American artists." USIA officials wanted him, under the museum's auspices, to assemble an exhibit of that "type and calibre" to represent America at the Biennale. Solomon obtained the board's permission to accept the invitation on the museum's behalf. At the same meeting in which it approved the Biennale plan, the board accepted his resignation effective July 1964. Even as Solomon began working on the Biennale, he continued supervising the museum's exhibitions, balancing avant-garde projects with those of "Judaic interest."[10]

His final avant-garde exhibit, *Jasper Johns*, opened in February 1964 with 174 paintings, drawings, prints, and sculptures, making it the first comprehensive survey of the artist's work. Johns (b. 1930) was a contemporary and intimate friend of Rauschenberg, the two had studios in the same loft building, and like Rauschenberg, Johns was non-Jewish and had a piece in the *New York School, Second Generation* exhibit (Figure 3.12). Sharing to some extent Rauschenberg's interest in popular imagery, Johns pursued the visual culture of everyday life in ways that augured what became Pop Art. Unlike his friend, however, Johns expressed his ideas in works that partook more fully of materials and techniques rooted in the history of Western art, albeit with striking twists. His richly textured paintings were created with the ancient medium of encaustic, which enabled him to build up deeply layered, complex surfaces. During the period surveyed by the museum's exhibit, Johns was creating iconic works that elevated him to among America's best-known and highly regarded artists: targets, American flags, maps of the continental United States, and numerals (Figure 5.5). The exhibition was reviewed widely with some critics juxtaposing his relative youth—he was thirty-three at the time—with the rising prices his work commanded as his following among

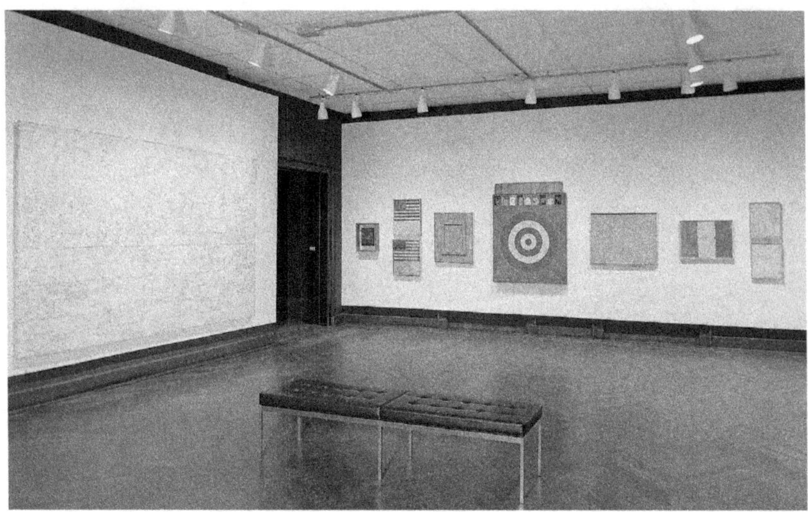

Figure 5.5. Installation view, *Jasper Johns*, ca. February 1964. Photograph by Ambur Hiken. The Jewish Museum, New York/Art Resource, NY.

collectors grew. All in all, the show was regarded as "less audacious" than the Rauschenberg survey, but most reviewers found great promise in his work, several accurately identifying the qualities that would mark him as one of the most influential artists of his generation.[11]

Following the Johns survey was *Thou Shalt Have No Other Gods Before Me*, a scholarly exploration of ancient Near Eastern religions based on 226 objects, nearly all borrowed from fifteen institutions and private collectors (Figure 5.6). Falling somewhere between the museum's secular and religious aims, it consisted of figures, reliefs, divination vessels, and other objects. They represented the variety of ancient religions in Egypt, the eastern Mediterranean, and across the Fertile Crescent, including Anatolia to the north, and east beyond Mesopotamia to Persia (Iran). Among the objects were two Mesopotamian pieces from the Jewish Museum and a Cycladic figure lent by Ben Heller, who proposed the exhibit. *Thou Shalt Have No Other Gods Before Me*, wrote Solomon, comprised "a curious and impressive irony" because it showed that "representations of the divine" existed among all the ancient Near Eastern civilizations except Judaism. Equally ironic was that, of them all, the only surviving one was Judaism, "in which the concept of God rested in abstract ideas" that resisted "reduction to finite, mundane terms"—that is, to figurative representations. Solomon's formulation of "abstract ideas" of God and their irreducibility is reminiscent of Leo Steinberg's invocation of the abstract in his *New York*

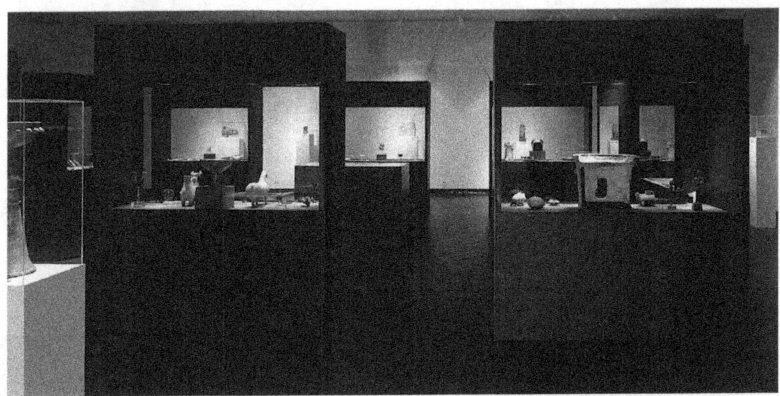

Figure 5.6. Installation view, *Thou Shalt Have No Other Gods Before Me*, ca. May 1964. The Jewish Museum, New York/Art Resource, NY.

School, Second Generation essay. There Steinberg found an "aptness" in the museum's exhibiting abstract art because both "Jewry and modern art are masters of renunciation"; that is, "Jewry survived as an abstract nation, proving, as did modern art, how much is dispensable." But Solomon and Steinberg were saying different things. Steinberg likened abstraction in Judaism—the religion's reduction to essential beliefs, to abstraction in art—the reduction of content to the essentials of form and materials. Solomon interpreted the phenomenon of abstraction in Judaism not as a distillation of religion to pure beliefs, but rather as a way of resisting the creation of figurative representations of God. Nonetheless, Solomon shared with Steinberg an interest in abstraction as a critical modality for exhibiting works lacking visible Jewish content, whether avant-garde or—in this case—ancient.[12]

The debate over balancing avant-garde exhibits with Judaica did not wane after Solomon's departure. Instead, it was revisited in anticipation of finding his successor. Responding to mixed signals from the seminary, Heller inaugurated the discussion by proposing the museum seek greater autonomy from the seminary. Underlying the idea was his conclusion that the museum's attempts at achieving parity between its Judaica and avant-garde exhibits was inherently problematic. Because the avant-garde program had "more sparkle" and would garner more financial support, the museum would eventually be able to function independently if it committed fully to new art. He appreciated, however, that the seminary's sponsoring a program of Judaica *and* avant-garde art was "most appealing." Citing the motivations for Finkelstein's *Eternal Light* broadcasts, Heller argued "all art is involved with interpreting tradition, . . . extending it, . . . creating a new tradition." Because Judaism lacked a "plastic tradition," however, he believed the museum ought to help create one. Yet it would take time before the avant-garde experiment proved to be "in line with tradition [or] helping to make a new one." Accordingly, the museum needed more autonomy and a less "exact percental relationship between . . . Contemporary and Judaica programs." Heller recommended a transition toward more policy autonomy and financial independence that included the addition of non-Jewish museum board members.[13]

Schapiro, now a board member, responded by giving a first-hand account of why the museum turned from prioritizing ritual objects to art and then the avant-garde.

> When the Seminary decided to enlarge the scope of the Museum [after receiving the Warburg mansion], it was guided by the following thought. . . . A collection of Jewish ritual objects has a limited interest to visitors. . . . The habit of regarding the religious world through the printed word, and the deadening effects of modern commercialized taste. . . , have left many Jews insensitive to the visually beautiful, . . . handmade objects . . . from a now remote past. It was hoped that by opening the Museum to art in general and particularly to contemporary art, the interest in . . . ritual objects would be quickened. . . ; they would be seen as works of art as well as historical antiquities.[14]

Having made that decision, however, planners confronted the challenges of achieving this new aim.

> Among the possibilities considered then was the exhibition of works by contemporary Jewish artists . . . concerned with Biblical and other Jewish themes. The restriction . . . seemed narrow and parochial . . . , of judging art only by its relevance to one's religious beliefs and traditions. . . . It would ignore the fact that these same painters and sculptors of Jewish themes produce other works . . . with themes that belong to a common world independent of religious beliefs. . . . [In] welcoming . . . work by contemporary Jewish artists [of all kinds], the Seminary recognized the importance of . . . the modern conception of art as a valid and irreplaceable activity open to the expression of a wide range of experiences, perceptions and ideas.[15]

At this point Schapiro shifted from history to advocacy.

> Existing in a community that strives for the greatest openness to humane values . . . , it is desirable that a Museum dedicated to art should be hospitable to all that is good in contemporary art, while maintaining its original purpose of preserving and making better known . . . objects of Jewish art from the past. A Jewish Museum of Art can no more limit itself to the work of Jewish artists than a Jewish University to the intellectual achievements of Jewish scholars and scientists. It is through the parallel to Jewish colleges, hospitals and cultural centers that one should understand the breadth of the [museum's current] program.[16]

Schapiro anticipated related questions such as: Aren't there "enough museums in New York that show contemporary art?" In response, he argued that while New York had many art museums, too few were presenting avant-garde art at a level comparable to the Jewish Museum. As confirmation of his position, Schapiro pointed to the avant-garde program's "extraordinary" attendance, which had boosted the museum's annual figures from an average of about 88,000 during Kayser's time to around 130,000.[17]

Another rhetorical question he posed was: "Is it wise that an activity that pertains to the whole of society, like contemporary art, be identified" with the seminary? Schapiro too referred to Finkelstein's intergroup and broadcast activities but went further, asserting that the seminary's Jewishness compelled the museum's contemporary art advocacy.

> The fact that Jews have taken the initiative in expanding the Jewish Museum is a sign of the vitality of Jewish association in this country and of its . . . progressive character in matters that affect society as a whole. One can anticipate a future state of affairs in which individuals unite for a common cultural aim without consciousness of their religious or ethnic origins; but as things are today the divisions in society are still such as to make the religious and ethnic association an important ground of constructive cultural activity. This is obvious enough in hospitals, schools, charities, and other public endowments; it would be absurd to object to all these foundations because they might as well have been contributed to society without a Jewish name.

Schapiro persuaded seminary trustees to continue the avant-garde exhibits as before, but finding the right balance between them and Judaic programming remained unresolved.[18]

The status quo left some board members wary of a future change of heart among seminary trustees. Following up on Heller's proposal, the board sought and obtained greater autonomy from the seminary in accordance with new "ground rules." Among them was a stipulation that the "Museum is to be non-sectarian, but respecting all religions." Assertion of the museum's "non-sectarian" status was challenged, however, and Schapiro negotiated a compromise whereby the museum would advance "artistic culture in the Jewish community" by exhibiting "contemporary art, both religious and secular, by Jews and Gentiles." Ideally this approach would also enliven Jewish and non-Jewish interest in the museum's ritual object collections "as works of art as well as historical antiquities." By continuing to function as an *art* museum, with a permanent collection of Judaica and a changing exhibition program prioritizing avant-garde art, it hopefully could serve both the Jewish community and the contemporary art world. If not precisely nonsectarian, the museum could be sectarian but with nonsectarian goals.[19]

The Museum, the Seminary, and Conservative Judaism

Though this understanding smoothed over internal differences, public debate about the Judaica versus avant-garde exhibits continued, sometimes within the art world and sometimes beyond. Emily Genauer (1911–2002), then–chief art critic of the *New York Herald Tribune*, occasionally questioned the appropriateness of a Jewish museum exhibiting avant-garde art, prompting Heller to explain the reasoning behind the program and how it translated Jewish values into art-world benefits. The concerns of another art critic, Katharine Kuh, reached beyond the art world to nettle the seminary's rabbinic constituency. Kuh (1904–94), who then wrote for the nationally distributed *Saturday Review*, came to New York from Chicago, where—as a former gallery owner and curator for the Art Institute of Chicago—she retained a following. In an article assaying New York's "surplus of modern art museums," Kuh attacked what she saw as indistinguishable, mediocre "'hit' shows" mounted by institutions competing for high attendance and financial support. Given the city's hundreds of commercial galleries specializing in contemporary art, Kuh singled out the Museum of Modern Art, the Whitney Museum of American Art, and the Guggenheim Museum as "doubly redundant." The Jewish Museum was not spared. Kuh had expected to see exhibits on Jewish art and history there, "much as Asia House presents the art and culture of the Far East." Instead, it too had jumped on "the modern merry-go-round," as evident with the Rauschenberg and Johns surveys which, she argued, were inappropriate because "neither artist is Jewish, neither deals with Jewish culture." Were the museum to return to its roots, Kuh argued, the museum "would at once justify its name and add a much-needed dimension" to the city's art scene. Or the museum could continue its avant-garde pursuits and change its name, a problem because the Museum of Modern Art had already captured "modern" for its moniker. Perhaps, Kuh concluded, the Jewish Museum should "call itself the Gallery of More Modern Art."[20]

Kuh's article, alongside seminary-newsletter items on the museum, reached Rabbi Samuel H. Dresner who then led a Massachusetts synagogue. Dresner (1923–2000) was ordained in the seminary's rabbinic program and was a rising star in American Conservative Judaism as a civil rights activist and prolific scholar. Bemoaning the deterioration of Jewish religious life amid "the swirling swill of the pleasure-mad" twentieth century, Dresner challenged the Conservative rabbinate, congregations, local and national Jewish funding agencies, and the seminary to undertake a "renewal" of Jewish observance and education. Ever alert to evidence of Jewish-community waywardness, he wondered to a fellow rabbi what the Jasper Johns show had to do with Jewish art or Judaism. Dresner's complaint reached Finkelstein, who explained that the museum would always stress exhibits "of interest to students of Jewish history and the Jewish religion." Yet, he added, the museum also "takes the position that the expression of ideas in art are also part of Judaism." This policy to him was not very different from "our setting up a College of Liberal Arts, in which we taught mathematics, science, and general history on the assumption that a knowledge of all these subjects is worthwhile for a Jew, provided it is combined with knowledge of Judaism itself." Finkelstein still believed the museum could integrate its Judaica and avant-garde programming in mutually generative ways, concluding that, in the future everyone will be grateful for the museum's efforts. For the present he counseled patience. Dresner's critique was not, however, just about the museum, it was about Finkelstein's priorities in general. "This 'episode' of the Jewish Museum," Dresner wrote his colleague, would "damage any further attempt we may make to deepen Jewish life." For him, the museum exemplified a larger problem that Finkelstein overlooked or chose to ignore: the seminary's role in Conservative Judaism.[21]

The seminary's development under Finkelstein and his predecessors was guided by an aspiration they shared to serve American Jews by rising "above the denominational fray of Jewish life," especially the divisions of religious orthodoxy and liberalism. Yet, the seminary's success in preparing and placing rabbis with congregations across America nourished the formation of new associations that gradually narrowed its constituencies into another denomination. The first was founded as the seminary's alumni association in 1901, which renamed itself the Rabbinical Assembly of the Jewish Theological Seminary in 1919. In subsequent decades, it began exerting increasing pressure on the seminary to provide counsel and support over doctrinal matters faced by rabbis, especially those tending their congregations in comparative geographical isolation. The other association, envisioned by Solomon Schechter as a "Conservative Union" to foster communication and coordinate religious standards among congregations, was established in 1913 as the United Synagogue. Together, the Rabbinical Assembly and the United Synagogue grew into pillars of what became Conservative Judaism, providing monetary support for the seminary and, in return, expecting to influence the seminary's educational programs and policies. Finkelstein welcomed the interests of the seminary's organizational counterparts and regarded the seminary's tripartite relationship with them as "unique not only in Jewish history, but in the history of religion generally." Yet he also encountered tensions in that relationship as the Rabbinical Assembly and United Synagogue consolidated their identities, articulated their needs, and attempted to "impose their image" on the seminary. Finkelstein aired their concerns but firmly rebuffed overtures impinging on the seminary's research, teaching, and outreach, steadfast in his conviction that the seminary must remain both an autonomous "umbrella institution" for all Jews and preserve its faculty's intellectual freedom and diversity of views. The rabbis and lay leaders of Conservative Judaism, on the other hand, sought "an institution whose primary allegiance was to the tenets of its faith rather than the norms of higher education."

Over time, the seminary came to rely on the Rabbinical Assembly and United Synagogue for assistance with its growing fundraising needs. That relationship occasionally devolved into recriminations, however, when seminary leaders were embarrassed or annoyed by prominent individuals within these organizations who noisily espoused views that put off wealthy backers. For their part, the rabbis and congregations believed the seminary failed to help nurture the Conservative movement and its "denominational cohesiveness." Hoping the seminary would become Conservative Judaism's "fountainhead," they perceived Finkelstein as all but disdaining the movement's needs. Over time, as the seminary's financial burdens increased and it depended more and more on the Rabbinical Assembly and United Synagogue for fiscal support, it attracted closer scrutiny of its spending priorities. Among them was Finkelstein's emphasis on "'outside' activities" such as the Institute for Religious and Social Studies, *The Eternal Light*, and the museum's avant-garde exhibitions. That questioning irritated Finkelstein, who regarded his Conservative-movement critics as "isolationists" and "myopic," insufficiently appreciative of "the impact of the secular world on . . . Jewish life"—particularly following the Holocaust—and thus the urgency to improve intergroup relations and assert moral leadership in American public affairs. He shared Dresner's concerns about Judaism and Jewish survival, but Finkelstein viewed them in a wider context. Debates over the nature and doctrines of Conservative Judaism, and the seminary's ostensible role in presiding over them, felt less urgent to Finkelstein as he contemplated what seemed to him to be the far graver problems confronting the world as the Cold War deepened. Complaints about the museum's exhibitions were annoying to be sure, but to Finkelstein they amounted to little more than minor skirmishes in an approaching battle over the future of Judaism in America and America's future in the world. For his critics, the exhibitions were symptomatic of problems with his stewardship and the seminary's role in Conservative Judaism.[22]

Ethnography, History, or Art

During these discussions, the museum board sought an interim director to manage day-to-day operations while Solomon—still employed by the museum—fulfilled the Biennale contract; and to buy time as the board searched for his replacement. Hans van Weeren-Griek (1910–91) soon emerged as the top candidate. Born in Florida and trained in the Netherlands, he had worked at several institutions and agencies in America and the Netherlands, most recently as acting director of the Des Moines Arts Center (Iowa). Van Weeren-Griek fit the bill as a professional with extensive experience who was "not interested in long-term assignments." The board hesitated initially, however, because his background was more in educational outreach than contemporary art and he was not Jewish. Yet the contemporary-art program could be sustained with guest curators, board members reasoned. As for his not being Jewish, List felt that was "completely immaterial." Van Weeren-Griek was appointed acting director for a year beginning in March 1964.[23]

The museum was in some disarray when van Weeren-Griek took over and he prioritized balancing the budget, improving collections records, tidying facilities, and adding a member's lounge—hopefully in demand after the imposition of an entrance fee for nonmembers. He also organized an education department and established an ongoing exhibit loan program in collaboration with the American Federation of Arts and the Smithsonian Institution. Van Weeren-Griek maintained the museum's Judaic and avant-garde exhibits, but as poles of a programming continuum. In his foreword to a contemporary sculpture exhibit catalogue, he reiterated the museum's embrace of "the entire range of Jewish history, culture and art" and portrayed the avant-garde program as only the latest expression of the trajectory leading from Judaism's origins to contemporary Jewry. So it was, he declared, that the museum both "cherishes the past and lives in the present." If "the past" was the Judaica collection, its cherishing was now reified with the appointment of a full-time Judaica curator, Tom L. Freudenheim.[24]

Freudenheim began working on a temporary, part-time basis as curatorial assistant in June 1962, his position becoming "permanent" assistant curator the following September. Freudenheim (b. 1937) completed a baccalaureate degree at Harvard and studied at Hebrew Union College—Reform Judaism's rabbinic seminary—before taking the post. From the start, the tasks of updating the museum's permanent collection displays, keeping up with new acquisitions, and responding to information requests was daunting. The museum's Judaica patrons, especially Harry G. Friedman, noticed the problem and lobbied seminary and museum officials to provide staff support for Freudenheim. Before acting, the museum's board asked Abram Kanof, still one of its members, to work with Freudenheim on mapping the improvements more assistance would enable. Freudenheim drafted a plan for Kanof's review that addressed several issues, chief among which was the museum's Judaica collection displays. There were, he believed, three alternatives for the displays. One was an ethnographic arrangement of artifacts "according to the particular ceremonies" and settings in which they were used, the resulting displays constituting "an explanation of Judaism through its objects." The second option presented the same things "according to period and/or country of origin" facilitating stylistic comparisons. The third was a combination of the first two. Freudenheim preferred the second one because he perceived the Judaica program as contributing to the institution's overall "function as an art Museum" by showing Judaism's "relation to the visual arts." He opposed using the collection to merely explain Judaism but acknowledged doing so might be "valuable for Jewish education in a religious-school-manner." That would, however, undercut the museum's effectiveness in relating Judaica to the visual arts. In terms echoing the reasoning behind the avant-garde program, Freudenheim added that a visual-arts emphasis could be enhanced by exhibiting the "ceremonial art of other religions" to explore similarities with and differences from Judaica. Because the museum by then possessed one of the world's leading Judaica collections, it had "a special responsibility . . . in this general field beyond the confines of Judaism."[25]

Kanof opposed Freudenheim's art orientation, preferring instead a "pedagogic function" and countered with principles to guide future planning: "A Judaica program is not concerned . . . with artistic excellence. Judaism is a religion and hence a Judaic program must concern itself with . . . Jewish religious observance, with the actual ritual use of a ceremonial object [and] its historic significance." Kanof thought displays should feature an object's place in "the development of a ritual," "the light it casts on religious history," "its association with an individual, a community, or an event," and be shown alongside others used in the same or related rituals. He also articulated display techniques relevant to his vision. While artworks are best exhibited against "a stark or neutral background," Kanof argued, ritual objects are best shown against "a background which of itself carries significance or mood." To that end, he advocated supplementing their display with "old prints, paintings and minhagim [traditions or customs] books" depicting the objects' ritual uses. In contrasting display techniques for artworks versus objects of ethnographic or historical interest, Kanof astutely captured exhibition fashions of the day. His reference to a "stark or neutral background" for artworks suggests what a little over a decade later would be called the "white cube," a setting that reinforces a work's aura as "art" and isolates it from anything that distracts from its contemplation. Kanof's alternative—the placement of religious artifacts with others used in the same or related rituals, against evocative backgrounds, and augmented with depictions of the ceremonies in which they are utilized—call to mind fully contextualized ethnographic exhibits such as Kayser's "Sabbath Room" (Figure 3.9). The choices Kanof offered, the artifact isolated to heighten its aesthetic appreciation versus the artifact situated with others to communicate its religious use and history, were ordinarily contingent on the types of institutions where they might be practiced. At the time, art museums were most likely the settings where artifacts would be individually spotlighted in "stark or neutral" environments; history or natural history museums were usually where artifacts would be embedded in richly staged historical or ethnographic settings—the latter varying widely from groupings of like things, to extensively documented narratives, to recreations of entire scenes such as period rooms or dioramas. Yet, choosing among these alternatives from the "poetics of museum display" meant deciding how the museum wished to interpret its Judaica collections: as works of art, historical evidence, or ethnographic specimens—or some combination of these alternatives. A sense of the museum's desired and actual audiences would ordinarily contribute to that decision. But at the time the museum was in a period of uncertainty over its most desired audiences, with the seminary and its constituencies comprising one and the New York art world—now ascendant—comprising another. The museum's board members were caught in the middle.[26]

Kanof's and Freudenheim's exchange culminated in a report written by the latter. It reiterated their opposing views, including Freudenheim's preferences he summed up as "We are, in other words, an *art museum*." He cited the museum's prioritization of the avant-garde, now strategically, by linking the Judaica program with it. Freudenheim believed that if the Judaica holdings were properly contextualized, their displays could be melded with the museum's avant-garde shows. That would be achieved by showing a "visual interplay" between "the beautiful in the Jewish visual tradition"—ritual objects, and that "in today's world"—contemporary art. The actual implementation of his scheme was left unexplained, however, and perhaps for that reason or Freudenheim's departure some months later, little came of the report. Then too, despite its interest in doing better by the Judaica collection, the board was preoccupied with finding a new director. How to balance Judaica and avant-garde programming remained an open question.[27]

Notes

1. AKatz to Rabbi Maxwell M. Farber, 14 May 1963, RG 25–4–34, LJTS.
2. "Schedule of Exhibitions" [7 February 1963,] RG 25–7–23, LJTS. For studies of Rauschenberg's work, see "Bibliography," Robert Rauschenberg Foundation, accessed December 2019, https://www.rauschenbergfoundation.org/artist/bibliography-0. AS, introduction to *Robert Rauschenberg* (New York: The Jewish Museum, 1963), [unpaginated]. SSK, ed. *The New York School, Second Generation* (New York: Jewish Theological Seminary of America, 1957), 14; Calvin Tomkins, *Off the Wall: A Portrait of Robert Rauschenberg*, rev. edn. (New York: Picador, 2005), 254–55; and Brian O'Doherty, "Robert Rauschenberg," *New York Times*, 28 April 1963. AS likely learned of Rauschenberg's work via a show at Leo Castelli's gallery around 1958 and mounted a small exhibit of the artist's work shortly thereafter at Cornell; Leo Castelli, oral history interview by Paul Cummings, 14 May 1969 and 8 June 1973, transcript, AAA, SI, 140–41.
3. On the exhibit opening, Tomkins, *Off the Wall*, 190; see also pp. 234–35. For the "real explosion" quote, see Leo Castelli, oral history interview by Paul Cummings, 14 May 1969 and 8 June 1973, transcript, AAA, SI, 142, 111–12. Also on exhibit openings, see Annie Cohen-Solal, *Leo & His Circle: The Life and Work of Leo Castelli* (New York: Knopf, 2007), 333; Grace Glueck, "Art Rite—Opening Night," *New York Times*, 13 December 1964; and [unsigned article,] "How to Attend an Opening," *Time* 93, no. 7 (14 February 1969): 85.
4. Roberta Smith, "Ben Heller, Powerhouse Collector of Abstract Art, Dies at 93," *New York Times*, 4 May 2019. BH was also associated with the Museum of Modern Art and Whitney Museum of American Art. BH and AS knew each other prior to the latter's arrival at the JM; BH, oral history interview by Paul Cummings, 8 January 1973, transcript, AAA, SI, 27, 29, 39–40. See also, BH and Museum of Modern Art, *The Collection of Mr. and Mrs. Ben Heller: An Exhibition . . .* (New York: Museum of Modern Art, 1961). Thomas Lask, "Harry N. Abrams, Publisher, Dies; A Pioneer With Quality Art Books," *New York Times*, 27 November 1979. See also, Harry N. Abrams, oral history interview by Paul Cummings, 14 March 1972, transcript, AAA, SI, [unpaginated]. "The Dedication of the Albert A. List Building of the

Jewish Museum," 17 February 1963, RG 25–7–23, LJTS. BH to Harry Abrams, 20 March 1963, RG 25–4–34, LJTS (emphasis BH's). VL to Mrs. Harry Posner, 5 April 1963, RG 1–216–13, LJTS (emphases VL's). AKatz was appointed to his position about a year earlier; "Arthur Katz Named Executive Vice-President of Jewish Theological Seminary," *Daily News Bulletin* (Jewish Telegraphic Agency) XXVIII, no. 228 (4 December 1961): 4. AKatz to Rabbi Maxwell M. Farber, 14 May 1963, RG 25–4–34, LJTS.

5. Harry N. Abrams to Allen [Alan] M. Stroock, 28 May 1963, RG 25–4–34, LJTS. On MS's formal involvement, see MS to LF, 5 May 1963 and LF to MS, 11 June 1963, MSC, 127:2, CUL and AKatz to MS, 15 October 1963, RG 25–4–34, LJTS. See also, Harry G. Friedman to Alan M. Stroock, 10 July 1963 and Alan M. Stroock to Harry G. Friedman, 15 July 1963, RG 25–4–22, LJTS. Richard Meier, *Richard Meier Architect: 1964–2017*, 7 vols. (New York: Rizzoli International Publications, 1984–2017). Meier studied with AS at Cornell University, and AS had him design the Zagayski exhibit installation; Janet Solinger, oral history interview by Marc Pachter, 7 October 2005, transcript, AAA, SI [unpaginated]; Janet Solinger, oral history interview by Nicki Tanner, 10 May 1993, transcript, UJA-FNYC, I-433, AJHS, 16; AS, introduction to *The Silver and Judaica Collection of . . . Zagayski*, [unpaginated]. Richard Meier, *Recent American Synagogue Architecture* (New York: Jewish Museum, 1963). On exhibit labels, see Ada Louise Huxtable, "Architecture: Designs for American Synagogues," *New York Times*, 5 October 1963. There was a suburban synagogue-construction boom following postwar Jewish migration out of city centers, "baby-boom" growth of Jewish communities, and their increasing prosperity. Lance J. Sussman, "The Suburbanization of American Judaism as Reflected in Synagogue Building and Architecture, 1945–1975," *American Jewish History* 75, no. 1 (September 1, 1985): 31–47. AK, "The Synagogue"; Rabbi Raphael Posner, "The Synagogue in Jewish Law"; and Sidney B. Hoening, Rabbi Seymour Siegel, and Maurice N. Eisendrath, "Statements by Orthodox, Conservative and Reform Rabbis on the Architecture of the Synagogue," in Meier, *Recent American Synagogue Architecture*, 11–18.
6. AS, preface to Meier, *Recent American Synagogue Architecture*, 5. Richard Meier, introduction to Meier, *Recent American Synagogue Architecture*, 7–8, 10. See also, Alfred Werner, "The Living Arts: Art," *American Judaism* 14, no. 1 (Fall 1964): 19, 62.
7. AS, preface and BH, introduction, in BH, *Black and White* (New York: Jewish Museum, 1963), [unpaginated]. B.O.D. [Brian O'Doherty], "This Week Around the Galleries," *New York Times*, 22 December 1963. D. J. [Donald Judd], "Black and White," *Arts Magazine* 38 (March 1964): 65. See also, "Black and White but No Thesis, in New York," *ArtNews* 62, no. 9 (January 1964): 8.
8. AKatz to H. L. C. Jaffe, 31 July 1963, RG 25–4–34, AKatz to Irwin Hersey, 30 September 1963, RG 25–2–9, and AKatz to KK, 12 August 1963, RG 25–4–35, LJTS. See also, AKatz to MS, 10 December 1963, MSC 137:

15, CUL. KK was first approached about the JM at MS's recommendation during the search for SSK. KK, *The Exhibitionist: Living Museums, Loving Museums* (New York: Overlook Press, 2016), 191.

9. VL, oral history interview by Paul Cummings, 9 January 1973, transcript, AAA, SI (unpaginated). DF, oral history interview by Nicki Tanner, 13 February 1990, transcript, UJA-FNYC, I-433, AJHS, 16. Leo Castelli, oral history interview by Paul Cummings, 14 May 1969 and 8 June 1973, transcript, AAA, SI, 147. BH, oral history interview by Paul Cummings, 8 January 1973, transcript, AAA, SI, 41, 43; see also, BH's discussion of the Judaica-versus-avant-garde dichotomy (with the *New York Herald Tribune*'s art critic), BH to Emily Genauer, 26 December 1963, MSC 138:1, CUL.
10. On AS's departure, see Janet Solinger, oral history interview by Nicki Tanner, 10 May 1993, transcript, UJA-FNYC, I-433, AJHS, 19–20 (however Solinger errs on the chronology); Harry N. Abrams to Alan M. Stroock, 28 May 1963, RG 25–4–34, LJTS. Donald M. Wilson (Acting Director, United States Information Agency) to AS, 7 November 1963, RG 25–7–6, and "Agreement and Terms of Grant Between the United States of America and The Jewish Museum," 26 February 1964, RG 25–6–10, LJTS. Minutes, JM Board of Governors, 1 October 1963, and Minutes, JM Board of Governors, "Special Session," 7 October 1963, Alan R. Solomon Papers, 1907–1970, box 1, folder 24, AAA, SI; AKatz to AS, 8 May 1964, RG 25–6–10, LJTS. "The Jewish Museum Announces Resignation of Its Director," 17 January 1964, RG 1–227–25, LJTS. Enzo Di Martino, *The History of the Venice Biennale, 1895–2005: Visual Arts, Architecture, Cinema, Dance, Music, Theatre* (Venice, Italy: Papiro Arte, 2005). AS featured Rauschenberg's work at the Biennale and the artist won the grand prize, boosting his career internationally, Tomkins, *Off the Wall*, 1–11; and Cohen-Solal, *Leo and His Circle*, 286–303.
11. AS, *Jasper Johns* (New York: The Jewish Museum, 1964). Jeffrey S. Weiss, with John Elderfield, *Jasper Johns: An Allegory of Painting, 1955–1965* (Washington, DC: National Gallery of Art and Yale University Press, 2007); Michael Crichton, *Jasper Johns* rev. edn. (New York: Harry N. Abrams, 1994); and Catherine Craft, *Jasper Johns* (New York: Parkstone International, 2012). Johns's dealer, Castelli, discovered the artist's work at the JM; see chapter 3. Castelli also helped AS arrange loans for the exhibit—a few from VL and BH; Leo Castelli, oral history interview by Paul Cummings, 14 May 1969 and 8 June 1973, transcript, AAA, SI, 41, 105–6; the "less audacious" quote is from p. 142. For reviews, see Emily Genauer, "Phenomenal Rise of Jasper Johns," *New York Herald Tribune* (European Edition), 18 February 1964; Sidney Tillim, "Ten Years of Jasper Johns," *Arts Magazine* 38 (April 1964): 22–26; "Art: The Younger," *Newsweek* 63, no. 8 (24 February 1964): 82–83; Dore Ashton, "Acceleration in Discovery and Consumption," *Studio* 167, no. 853 (May 1964): 212–13.
12. BH, oral history interview by Paul Cummings, 8 January 1973, transcript, AAA, SI, 41. AS, preface to *Thou Shalt Have No Other Gods Before Me*, ed.

Ann Farkas (New York: Jewish Museum, 1964), [unpaginated]. For reviews, "Diggings in Turkey Set Back Earliest Date by 1,000 Years," *Canadian Jewish Review* 46, no. 34 (22 May 1964): 8; and "Gods from the Ancient Past," *New York Times*, 3 May 1964. See also, Alfred Werner, "The Living Arts: Art," *American Judaism* 14, no. 1 (Fall 1964): 19, 62. Steinberg, introduction to *The New York School*, 8; see also chapter 3.

13. BH to DF, 6 December 1963, MSC 138:1, CUL. DF to MS, 8 January, and BH to MS, 9 January 1964, MSC 138:1, CUL.
14. BH to MS, 26 March 1964 and MS, Untitled manuscript, 1 April 1964, MSC 138:1, CUL.
15. MS, Untitled manuscript, 1 April 1964, MSC 138:1, CUL.
16. MS, Untitled manuscript, 1 April 1964, MSC 138:1, CUL. On transcending sectarian preferences, fifteen years earlier a *Commentary* editor attributed the community's then "low cultural standards" to sectarian constraints: "The same Jewish group that would feel . . . disgraced if its Mt. Sinai and Beth Israel hospitals were not Class A" nonetheless "tolerates an official Jewish culture that is . . . Class D, more fitting for some backwater denominational sect than for one of the major religio-cultural traditions of the world." Elliot E. Cohen, "The Intellectual and the Jewish Community: The Hope for Our Heritage in America," *Commentary* 8 (1 January 1949): 28.
17. MS, Untitled manuscript, 1 April 1964, MSC 138:1, CUL. Concerning attendance, SSK to SG, 12 January 1956, RG 1–147–15; and "Report for the Board of Overseers, The Jewish Museum," [May 1964], RG 21–4–23, LJTS.
18. MS, Untitled manuscript, 1 April 1964, MSC 138:1, CUL.
19. MS and Hans van Weeren-Griek, Meeting notes, "Organizational relationship between the Jewish Theological Seminary and the Jewish Museum," 24 April 1964, MSC 138:1, CUL. "Report for the Board of Overseers, The Jewish Museum" [May 1964], RG 21–4–23, LJTS. [MS, Ben Heller, Hans van Weeren-Griek], "Statement," 16 May 1964, AF, Box 1, JMA. MS was the principal author, MS, "Statement by Meyer Schapiro," 16 May 1964, MSC 138:1, CUL. MS, Untitled manuscript, 1 April 1964, MSC 138:1, CUL.
20. BH to Emily Genauer, 26 December 1963, Emily Genauer to BH, 29 January 1964, BH to Emily Genauer, 6 February 1964, MSC 138:1, CUL. Robert F. Worth, "Emily Genauer, Critic and Champion of 20th-Century Art, Is Dead at 91," *New York Times*, 25 August 2002. Alan G. Artner, "Chicago Art Curator Katharine Kuh Dies," *Chicago Tribune*, 13 January 1994. Katharine Kuh, "New York's Modern Merry-Go-Round," *Saturday Review* 47, no. 1 (21 March 1964): 25–27. "Asia House" was the first home of the Asia Society, which today has a museum; "Asia Society," *New York Architecture*, accessed March 2020, https://www.nyc-architecture.com/UES/UES049.htm; and "About Asia Society," Asia Society, accessed March 2020, https://asiasociety.org/about.
21. *Encyclopaedia Judaica*, 2nd edn., s.v. "Samuel Hayim Dresner"; Samuel Dresner, "Renewal," *Conservative Judaism* XIX, no. 4 (Summer 1965): 53–69.

Rabbi Samuel H. Dresner to Rabbi Theodore Friedman, 16 March 1964; LF to Rabbi Samuel H. Dresner, 6 April 1965, RG 25–2–9, LJTS.

22. Michael B. Greenbaum, "The Finkelstein Era," in *Tradition Renewed: A History of the Jewish Theological Seminary*, ed. Jack Wertheimer (New York: Jewish Theological Seminary of America, 1997), I:205–16; Michael B. Greenbaum, *Louis Finkelstein and the Conservative Movement: Conflict and Growth* (Binghamton, NY: Global Publications, Binghamton University, 2001), 103–222 (quote is from p. 153); and Jack Wertheimer, "JTS and the Conservative Movement," in Wertheimer, *Tradition Renewed*, II:405–21. Other irritants were the appointment of Reform Jews to the JTS board and invitation of Christian theologians to speak with JTS students; "A Trumpet for All Israel," *Time* 58, no. 16 (15 October 1951): 53. See also, Robert E. Fierstien, ed., *A Century of Commitment: One Hundred Years of the Rabbinical Assembly* (New York: The Assembly, 2000); and Abraham J. Karp, *A History of the United Synagogue of America, 1913–1963* (New York: United Synagogue of America, 1964). Jewish members of the New York art world had other complaints; AKatz to Hans van Weeren-Griek, 30 April and 22 May 1964, and Mrs. I. J. Belmont to AKatz, 18 May 1964, RG 25–2–9, LJTS.

23. On van Weeren-Griek's appointment, see DF to MS, 19 December; and DF to BH, 19 December 1963, MSC 137: 15, CUL. See also, Janet Solinger, oral history interview by Nicki Tanner, 10 May 1993, transcript, UJA-FNYC, I-433, AJHS, 22, 25–28; "Jewish Museum Names New Acting Director," 2 March 1964, RG 25–6–9, LJTS; and Hans van Weeren-Griek, "Art Education through Television," *College Art Journal* 8, no. 4 (1949): 297–98. On the debate over his appointment, see BH to JM Board, 20 January, VL to BH, 22 January, and DF to BH, 27 January 1964, MSC 138:1, CUL. BH to Hans van Weeren-Griek, 5 February 1964, RG 25–6–9, LJTS; BH to JM Board of Governors, 5 February 1964, MSC 138: 1, CUL.

24. "Report for the Board of Overseers, The Jewish Museum" [May 1964], RG 21–4–23, Publicity release, "Jewish Museum Exhibition Program," May 1964, RG 25–3–19, LJTS; see also Nelson Lansdale, "The Jewish Museum," *Philharmonic Hall* (September 1964): 44. LF to Hans van Weeren-Griek, 1 June 1964, RG 1–227–83, and Hans van Weeren-Griek, "Director's Report," 2 June 1964, RG 25–6–9, LJTS. See also, Hans van Weeren-Griek, Acting Director's Report, 15 December 1964, Papers of Tom L. Freudenheim. [Hans van Weeren-Griek, ed.] *Recent American Sculpture* (New York: Jewish Museum, 1964).

25. "Tom L. Freudenheim" (curriculum vitae), accessed April 2020, http://www.culturalconsulting.com/TLFCVMar08.pdf. See also, AKatz to Tom L. Freudenheim, 25 June 1962, RG 25–4–21, and AKatz to Hans van Weeren-Griek, 7 August 1964, RG 25–6–9, LJTS; Tom L. Freudenheim, interview with Jeffrey Abt, 3 April 2020. He was later promoted to associate curator and then curator; VL to AKatz, 22 March 1965, RG 25–4–21, LJTS. Harry G. Friedman to Janet Solinger, 22 January 1964, RG 25–4–22, Harry G.

Friedman to Janet Solinger, 12 May 1964, and LF to Hans van Weeren-Griek, 9 June 1964, RG 1–227–83, LJTS. On Friedman, see chapter 3. [Tom L.] Freudenheim to [Abram] Kanof, "Judaica Program," October 1964, MSC 138:1, CUL.

26. [Abram] Kanof to [Tom] Freudenheim, October 1964, and [Abram] Kanof, "Memorandum presented to Dr. Solomon, and again to Mr. Van Weeren-Griek" [ca. October 1964], MSC 138:1, CUL. Barbara Kirshenblatt-Gimblett, "American Jewish Life: Ethnographic Approaches to Collection, Presentation, and Interpretation in Museums," in *Folklife and Museums: Selected Readings*, ed. Patricia Hall and Charlie Seemann (Nashville, TN: American Association for State and Local History, 1987), 143–62. On comparable concerns in the UK, see Rickie Burman, "Presenting Judaism: Jewish Museums in Britain," in Crispin Paine, ed. *Godly Things: Museums, Objects, and Religion* (London: Leicester University Press, 2000), 136; and Paine, *Religious Objects in Museums: Private Lives and Public Duties* (London: Bloomsbury, 2013), 97–98. Brian O'Doherty, *Inside the White Cube: The Ideology of the Gallery Space* (San Francisco, CA: Lapis Press, 1986). On the poetics of display, see Susan Vogel, "Always True to the Object, in Our Fashion," in *Exhibiting Cultures: The Poetics and Politics of Museum Display*, ed. Ivan Karp and Steven D. Lavine (Washington, DC: Smithsonian Institution Press, 1991), 191–204 and Andrew McClellan, *The Art Museum from Boullée to Bilbao* (Berkeley: University of California Press, 2008), 120–47.

27. Tom L. Freudenheim, "The Jewish Museum, Curatorial Department," December 1964, AF, Box 3, JMA (emphasis Freudenheim's). On Freudenheim's departure, see Tom L. Freudenheim to Hans van Weeren-Griek, 25 May 1965, RG 25–4–21, LJTS. See also, Tom Freudenheim to SH, 16 December 1965, and Tom L. Freudenheim to LF, 30 December 1965, AF, Box 3, JMA.

Chapter 6

Secular Paths through the Avant-Garde, the Lower East Side, and Ancient Israel

Despite irresolution about how best to balance Judaica and avant-garde exhibits, now becoming the museum's "ultimate test," it pressed on—with seminary approval—to mount pioneering contemporary-art exhibits during the mid-1960s, attracting large audiences and critical acclaim. Parallel efforts to display Judaica as art and related explorations of Jewish subjects failed to draw as much popular attention, however. That imbalance shifted when the museum broadened the scope of its Judaic programming, bypassing ritual objects to address topics in the social history of the Jews, modern and ancient with the aid of photographs and documentary materials. Richly evocative, those exhibitions supplanted aesthetic criteria such as craftsmanship or artistic originality with other attributes including ethnicity, nostalgia, and heroism. They drew record-setting numbers of visitors and as much critical approval as the avant-garde shows, but their costs were as high as those of the avant-garde exhibits too, exceeding the museum's fundraising capacity. The Judaica collection remained in the shadows, however, annoying long-term supporters and provoking fresh questions about how best to feature it.[1]

Reaffirming the Avant-Garde

The search for Solomon's successor collapsed over the summer of 1964 after an effort to entice Karl Katz away from the Israel Museum failed. Van Weeren-Griek's able management alleviated the pressure to find a new director, and the board did not settle on one until early the following year. Its choice, Sam Hunter (1923–2014), was then-director of the Rose Art Museum at Brandeis University, which he founded a few years prior (Figure 6.1). Brandeis itself was recently established, in 1948, by the Jewish community as a private, nonsectarian school open to all ethnic and racial minorities in response to lingering discriminatory policies among American higher-education institutions. Of Jewish descent, Hunter earned a bachelor's degree at Williams College, served in the US Navy until 1946, came to New York where he briefly studied painting with Abstract Expressionist Hans Hoffman, and worked as an art critic and editor for the *New York Times*. He belatedly used a Williams College three-year fellowship for art history studies in Italy and, upon returning to New York in 1952, worked for artbook publisher Harry N. Abrams and *Arts Magazine*. Hunter then embarked on a museum career with curatorships at the Museum of Modern Art and Minneapolis Institute of Arts before going to Brandeis. During that period, he also organized contemporary-art exhibits representing the United States at the 1957 São Paulo biennial and 1962 World's Fair in Seattle. Hunter became a prolific writer as well, specializing in twentieth-century and contemporary art, coming to be regarded as "one of the pioneers" of modern-art scholarship and the "first chronicler of artists who . . . proved over time to be the pivotal figures" of the late twentieth century. Athletic, garrulous, and ardent, Hunter possessed an infectious curiosity about contemporary artists and their practices. Known to be "shrewd and incisive but decidedly not doctrinaire," he carried his passions into his work as a curator and museum leader where he could be both tenacious and pragmatic. Like Solomon, Hunter arrived at the Jewish Museum deeply conversant with New York's art world and experienced in institution building; and like Solomon, Hunter lacked experience with Judaica. List, about to become the museum board's chair, recommended Hunter to Finkelstein, highlighting his fundraising success at Brandeis and adding that he possessed "the necessary 'image' in the art world and Jewish Community" for attracting support for the museum. In the appointment letter, Finkelstein underscored Hunter's responsibility for the museum's fiscal health while welcoming the new director's leadership in making the museum an "outstanding contemporary cultural institution."[2]

About a month before arriving, Hunter—wanting to show how "the contrasting claims of Judaica and modernist art can be reconciled"—published his vision for the museum in the *New York Times*. The two interests, he observed, "represent the vision of particular individuals rather than any systematic philosophical position." Hunter set out to forge one built

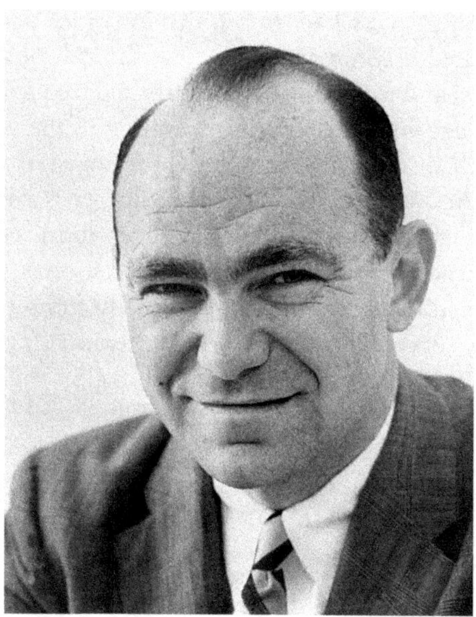

Figure 6.1. Sam Hunter, ca. 1960s. Courtesy of the Robert D. Farber University Archives and Special Collections Department, Brandeis University.

on the museum's foundation of artistic independence, professional standards, and a probing objectivity in its exploration of both the avant-garde and Judaica. Regarding the former-most, the museum was ideally situated because it was not "bound to the past by historic modern collections" like the Museum of Modern Art, the Whitney Museum of American Art, or the Guggenheim. The Jewish Museum offered an alternative as a nimble and more rigorous "proving ground" for new ideas and as a forum for older ideas that warranted further exploration. He also hinted at broadening what "Judaica" could mean by pointing to a planned exhibit of paintings, drawings, and prints related to New York's once-Jewish lower east side.[3]

After arriving in September 1965, however, the avant-garde commanded most of Hunter's attention. Although Judaica was dutifully shown, it was mostly in the form of older and contemporary ceremonial objects in modest exhibits that attracted little attention. He inaugurated his contemporary art programming with a Larry Rivers retrospective Hunter organized while still at Brandeis and that opened there the previous April. Rivers (1923–2002), of Jewish descent, also studied painting with Hans Hoffman—whence Rivers met Hunter—and he took additional courses at New York University, earning an art education degree but never teaching. Rivers had an affinity for older painting traditions and readily acquired a command of their technical means and subjects; and being talented and resourceful, Rivers shifted frequently from style to style. Coming of age with the second generation of the New York school, he spanned the transition from Abstract Expressionism to the mass-culture imagery of Pop Art. Indeed, the breakthrough works of Rauschenberg, Johns, and their successors, would not have been comprehensible without Rivers, who anticipated Pop Art and influenced its evolution. He did so, however, with a historically rich and intellectually complex flair. Auguring developments in subsequent decades, Rivers sometimes ironically and sometimes reverently appropriated iconic works by much earlier artists such as Courbet's *A Burial at Ornans* (1849–1850) and Emanuel Leutze's *Washington Crossing the Delaware* (1851); and he parodied commercial exploitations such as the Dutch Masters cigar brand's use of Rembrandt's *Syndics of the Drapers' Guild* (1662).[4]

The Rivers exhibition featured over 150 paintings, drawings, prints, and sculptures he made between 1950 and 1960, and was accompanied by an enormous installation work he created to augment the Jewish Museum's showing. *Larry Rivers* was a logical follow-on to the museum's retrospectives for Rauschenberg and Johns, and Hunter's estimation of Rivers's work was seconded by critics, a large crowd at the exhibit's opening, and high attendance during its run. As with the Rauschenberg and Johns shows, however, the museum's Judaica advocates were annoyed. But the sources of that aggravation were not the absence of Jewish content or the mystifying nature of the work for the uninitiated. This time they were piqued by images that were all too clear, such as a double portrait of Rivers's mother-in-law in the nude (Figure 6.2) and another of his wife, also in the nude, each startlingly explicit. These and other works sparked a "big hullabaloo" that reached Finkelstein, who called Hunter in to discuss the matter. Claiming he did not want to meddle in "matters of taste," Finkelstein did underscore the museum's role, as a seminary arm, in adhering to the "tenets" of Judaism. Following up on that position, he appointed a committee of three seminary rabbis with whom Hunter was to regularly consult on "the rabbinic-theological aspects" of museum decisions.[5]

The popularity of *Larry Rivers* and subsequent avant-garde exhibits fostered other problems. These ranged from overcrowded openings with visitors smoking in the galleries—violating building safety codes and offending seminary sensibilities—to concern that the museum's Judaica collection was being ignored. New policies and Judaica-collection studies followed but left unresolved the challenge of boosting public interest in

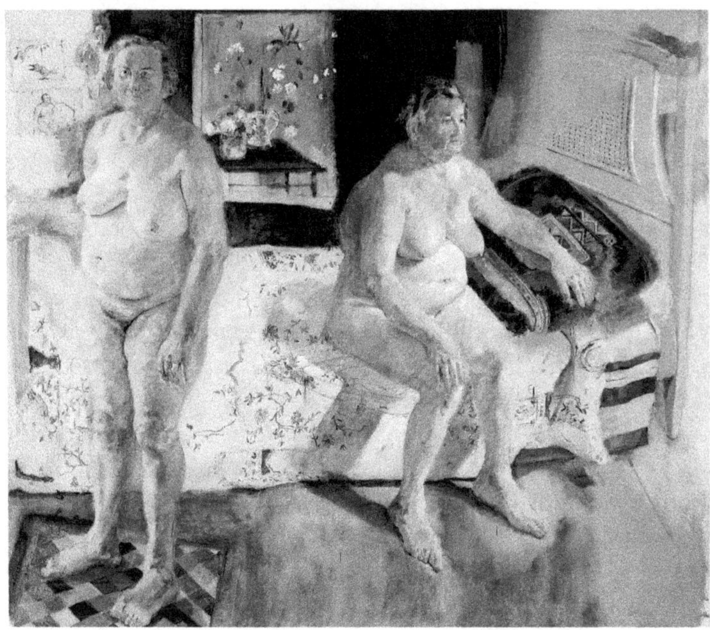

Figure 6.2. Larry Rivers, *Double Portrait of Berdie*, 70 3/4" x 82 ½", oil on canvas, 1955. Gift of an anonymous donor, inv. n: 56.9, Whitney Museum of American Art. © 2023 Estate of Larry Rivers / Licensed by VAGA at Artists Rights Society (ARS), NY. © Whitney Museum of American Art/Licensed by Scala/Art Resource, NY.

Judaica exhibits without losing the avant-garde's enthusiastic audiences. The "strange mixture" of the museum's visitors deepened the challenge:

> There are not only the bohemians, the art students who from one generation to the next come with paint still wet on their jeans, and the college students, tidier usually, armed with notebooks, and the ladies, young and old, out for an afternoon of picture looking and the groups from the suburbs who descend upon each and every museum and gallery, but there are also those one does not see in the other museums so much, the elderly Jewish couples pressing on toward the *kiddush* cups where they stand lost in reflection; the serious [synagogue] Sisterhood ladies on tour, many of them from Orthodox centers, the tourists from St. Paul [Minnesota], from Calgary [Canada], and from Rochester [New York], in the city for a visit, where the Jewish Museum is a must.

The goal of improving Judaica programming and growing its following was not addressed by hiring a curator to replace Freudenheim. Instead, Hunter appointed Allon Schoener to the newly created position of assistant director. Schoener (1926–2021) trained in art history, earning baccalaureate and master's degrees from Yale University, which he augmented with studies at the University of London's Courtauld Institute of Art, before working at the San Francisco Museum of Modern Art and Cincinnati Contemporary Arts Center. Opportunities and interests after his formal training led Schoener to specialize in what, in today's museums, would be called educational outreach. This included the organization of exhibits integrating social history, ethnography, and mass media techniques with the materials and interpretative methods of art museums. Hired primarily to help with museum administration, Schoener voluntarily analyzed the Judaica program, but did not offer any fresh ideas. Though of Jewish descent, his background was not in Judaica.[6]

Prior to Schoener's appointment, Hunter had already signaled his ambitions for the museum's avant-garde exhibits by establishing a new "Curator of Painting and Sculpture" post. He lured a rising star, Trinidad-born Kynaston McShine, for the post from the Museum of Modern Art's circulating exhibitions department. McShine (1935–2018) had served for just six years at MoMA after earning a degree at Dartmouth College and studies at the University of Michigan and New York University's Institute of Fine Arts. Despite his relative inexperience, McShine already evinced a keen eye for the "unexpected . . . as opposed to the academic, the predictable and the institutional." In his offer to McShine, Hunter endorsed an exhibit the new curator was already contemplating on "Environmental Sculpture." Ten months later, in April 1966, the museum presented it as *Primary Structures: Younger American and British Sculptors*, a survey comprised of over fifty works by forty-two artists. McShine chose the title *Primary Structures* to signify sculptures that shared a spare, elemental, and geometric aesthetic—"primary" also referencing the primary colors employed by several of the artists. Many of the sculptures were very large and the expansive galleries of the List addition readily accommodated them, the galleries' featureless, "white cube" environments setting off the works' bold forms and scale (Figure 6.3). The exhibition was arresting as well because of the novelty of materials, facture, and presentation techniques the artists employed. Sculptures were composed of aluminum, fiberglass, Formica, coated glass, fluorescent lights, and fire bricks; many made with industrial fabrication techniques by tradesmen, following artists' instructions; and nearly all the works were displayed without pedestals, instead being placed directly on gallery floors, walls, or suspended from ceilings. These qualities, alongside the artists' claims—and critics' attempts to interpret them—came to be grouped under the umbrella concept of "minimalism." Though some artists rejected the term, it nonetheless stuck, becoming a "tenacious rubric" that has framed the works' reception ever since. *Primary Structures* "broadcast the emergence of minimalism to a

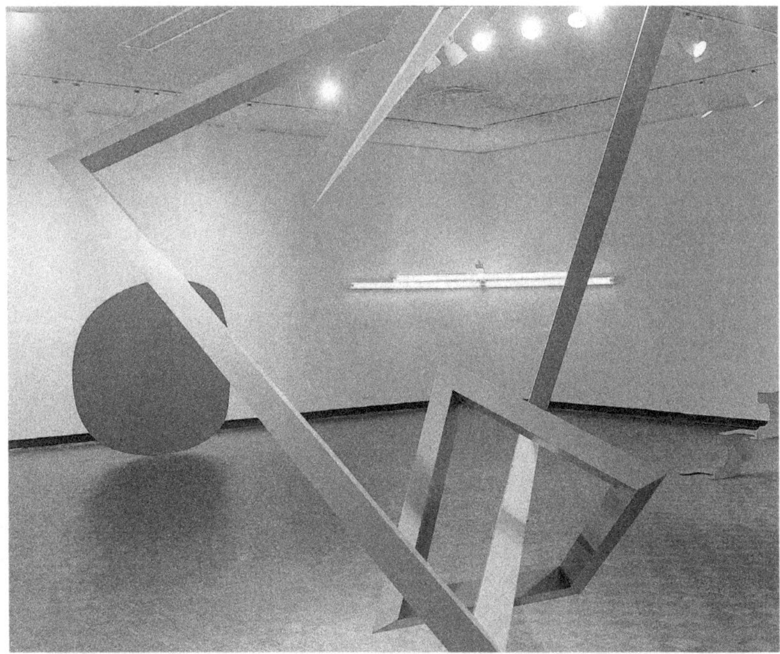

Figure 6.3. Installation view, *Primary Structures: Younger American and British Sculptors*, ca. April 1966. The Jewish Museum, New York/Art Resource, NY.

broader public" and became the most celebrated and influential of the museum's avant-garde exhibitions.[7]

The opening was a notorious and, for some, provocative event. Like preceding ones, it was overcrowded with about twenty-three hundred merrymakers swarming through the museum. Again, there was smoking and drinking throughout; and again, the New York art world was resplendent, dressing up or down, making the opening "unquestionably the zowiest (the with-it set's ultimate accolade) fashion extravaganza in town." There were "long-haired girls in short, short skirts," their "long-haired beaux, most of whom looked as if they had outfitted themselves" in clothes "left at some dry-cleaning establishment in 1946." A few arrived in outfits crafted especially for the exhibit (Figure 6.4). Afterward, Hunter tried to preempt board and seminary complaints by proposing some crowd-control measures. Nonetheless Finkelstein saw the opening as further evidence of the museum straying from seminary values. While he did not ordinarily concern himself with how people dressed, Finkelstein complained to List that he found the attire at the opening disrespectful of "an institution affiliated with the Seminary and housing

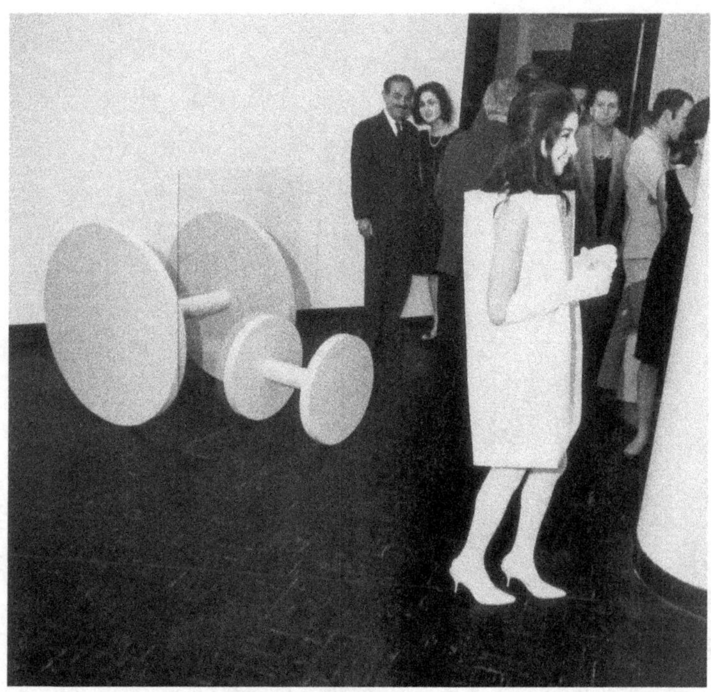

Figure 6.4. Opening reception, *Primary Structures: Younger American and British Sculptors*, 26 April 1966. The Jewish Museum, New York/Art Resource, NY.

religious objects." The stress of stewarding the museum through these straits was too much for her, however, and Albert List persuaded Finn to succeed her as board chair, partly because the latter was also a seminary trustee and better positioned to assure effective communication between it and the museum. This and other changes smoothed over the immediate irritants, and Hunter continued to encourage McShine's avant-garde exhibits, including major retrospectives for Ad Reinhardt (1913–67)—known for his severe, geometric and dark monochromatic paintings; and Yves Klein (1928–62)—remembered for innovations in a variety of media auguring minimal and Pop Art, and for his performance-art projects.[8]

All the while, Hunter looked for ways to improve the Judaica program. Lacking expertise in the field, he sought an advisor to right the program and found one in Avram Kampf (1920–2016). Kampf did graduate work at Columbia University, completed his doctorate at the New School for Social Research, and was a professor at Montclair State University. Kampf's dissertation, on contemporary synagogue art in America, and his subsequent research employed social history alongside art history methodology, indicative of his training with Meyer Schapiro at Columbia. Hunter arranged a one-year, part-time appointment for Kampf starting in spring 1966, as "Consultant in Research and Development." His duties included an immediate personnel matter—recommending a full-time Judaica curator, guiding Judaica-collections management, expanding the museum's service as an "information clearing house" for those building synagogues, and organizing a Judaica exhibit for spring 1967. Museum board members enthusiastically approved Kampf's appointment, viewing him "as something of a Messiah leading them out of the wilderness (avant-garde art?) to the promised land (Jewish culture)."[9]

It soon became apparent, however, that Kampf had his own agenda. He was more interested in pure research—proposing creation of an "Index of Jewish Art" (modeled on the Index of Christian Art at Princeton University) and publishing a journal on Jewish art—than in the day-to-day tasks of curating collections and exhibit planning. Even Finkelstein felt Kampf's priorities "belonged more logically to a university or scholarly institution than to a Museum." As if to prove Finkelstein's point, Kampf proposed the seminary create a "Department of Jewish Art" with full-time faculty and guest lecturers. He argued that it would forge a stronger bond between the seminary and the museum by helping inform rabbis and Jewish educators, in part with courses taught in the museum. Though Finkelstein entertained the proposal, nothing came of it. After several months, Hunter realized Kampf was failing to produce the desired results. Matters came to a head after he recommended a Judaica curator who turned out to be unsuitable. But he was also sidelined by one of the most popular exhibitions in the museum's history, a project that revealed a way for it to serve the Jewish community without relying on ritual objects.[10]

Heritage Rather Than Religion

In Hunter's pre-arrival *New York Times* essay, he—like his predecessors—cited Finkelstein's outreach program as a context for the museum's role in contemporary society. Hunter thought of Finkelstein's initiatives as indicative of how Judaism was reconstructing itself to address the challenges of modern life. A feature of that evolution was the recovery of Jewish cultural history by intellectuals skilled at translating it into "an object of general interest." Hunter had in mind works by Jews other than "academic specialists" or "parochial apologists" who were disseminating heretofore neglected aspects of Jewish literature and history for popular consumption.

The works included the introduction to *A Treasury of Yiddish Stories*, published in English translation in 1953; an anthropological study of life in Eastern European shtetls, *Life is With People*, published in 1952; and the publication, in the late 1940s, of *Tales of the Hasidim* in English translation. Their reception showed a path forward for the museum's Judaica programming, Hunter believed, via a novel phenomenon—a flowering sense of Jewishness not associated with organized religion or its ritual objects. It grew instead out of a broad-based recuperation of the Jewish community's Eastern European past of which each of the works Hunter cited reflected a different facet.[11]

A Treasury of Yiddish Stories, compiled by social and literary critic Irving Howe (1920–93) and Yiddish poet and critic Eliezer Greenberg (1896–1977), is an anthology of works by authors from the mid-nineteenth through the early twentieth centuries. It originated with Howe's uneasy "feelings of 'Jewishness'" and the urge to provide non-observant Jews an alternative to biblical teachings. The result was his "sacred scripture" of proverbs, folk tales, stories, and poems selected from Yiddish literature to furnish a new "creed of secular Jewishness." *A Treasury*'s introduction, to which Hunter referred, elucidates the world of east European Jewry—including the strains of religious and social thought informing their lives—and the evolution of Yiddish as a linguistically distinct fusion of, predominantly, Hebrew and German. Also discussed are the uses of humor, "tradition," and certain memorable characters such as Sholem Aleichem's Tevye the Dairyman, a simple religious man who, buffeted by the winds of change, quarrels with God. The greatest flowering of Yiddish was in Eastern Europe, where it comprised the shared language and ethnic homeland of Jews living in large cities or small villages scattered across a vast region divided among various nations. Its literature expressed the culture of "internally a community, a spiritual kingdom; and externally a society in peril, a society on the margin." That culture, expressed in the word *Yiddishkeit*—meaning both a Jewish way of life and Jewishness—was all but erased during the Holocaust, a remnant surviving on New York's lower east side through which thousands of East European Jewish immigrants passed. Howe and Greenberg, in dedicating their anthology "To the Six Million" (Jews killed in the Holocaust), were responding to that loss. Their work was one of preservation and hopefulness, first in the face of the Holocaust and then in confrontation with the State of Israel's policies discouraging citizens' use of Yiddish as the language of "'dispersion,' stained by exile, defeat, and martyrdom." By the time of *A Treasury*'s publication, Yiddish as a living language had begun to fade. Howe and Greenberg thought of their book as a "saving remnant" intended to engage cosmopolitan Jews otherwise disinterested in *Yiddishkeit*. *A Treasury* was widely read and celebrated, many Jews attributing their knowledge of Yiddish literature to it.[12]

Life is With People: The Jewish Little-Town in Eastern Europe was the first major anthropological study of Eastern European Jewry, in English, when it was published in 1952. It was based on memoirs, histories, previous studies, novels, movies, and interviews with over one hundred immigrants in New York shortly after the Second World War. Intended to record what remained of a culture that had been destroyed during the Holocaust, the project employed salvage ethnography as a means of capturing, via immigrants' memories, a culture that could no longer be observed in situ. The personal testimonies and documents collected, however, represented locales scattered across a broad region. Lacking a structure to shape the evidence into a coherent view, the authors of *Life is With People* drew on the Yiddish literary tradition's "preoccupation with the *shtetl* as the locus of Jewishness" to center their findings. That most of their material came from people who lived in cities or large towns did not matter. The shtetl became for the researchers a distillation of the entire area occupied by Eastern European Jewry, imagined as "a sea of Christian culture dotted with little Jewish islands" where a once "hermetic world was sustained . . . by isolation, hostility, and resistance to change." The shtetl also served as a microcosm wherein the individual threads of many details could be woven into a single tapestry of authentic Jewishness untouched by modernity. Notwithstanding its flaws, however, and perhaps because of them, *Life is With People* was extraordinarily popular. It marked a turnabout in how American Jews regarded their Eastern European origins, inspiring readers demoralized by the Holocaust to take pride in that heritage. *Life is With People* enjoyed a revival in the 1960s after being reissued with a new subtitle, *The Culture of the Shtetl*. One reviewer of the new edition welcomed the insights it provided for American descendants of shtetl Jews, many of whose parents also passed through New York's lower east side.[13]

Tales of the Hasidim, collected by the philosopher and literary scholar Martin Buber (1878–1965), are mostly parables, apothegms, and epigrams of the *zaddikim*—the righteous or saintly leaders of Hasidism. A religious movement that began in eighteenth-century Eastern Europe with roots in Jewish mysticism, Hasidism countered what was perceived as the rigid dogmatism of rabbinic Judaism with spiritual enthusiasm and ecstatic worship. Its adherents, the Hasidim (meaning the devout), preserved these tales by passing them down through the generations, their careful transmission indicative of the potent, almost magical power of each one. Buber's aim in publishing the collection was to introduce readers to the "world of legendary reality" the tales embraced. His very personal culling of this sprawling corpus of Hasidic writings was not a work of historical scholarship, its value residing instead in the way the stories stirred readers. *Tales* found a devoted audience due partly to the vitality and literary grace Buber brought to the collection. But it also offered readers a blend of Jewishness and "spiritual quest" especially beguiling for Jews estranged from institutional Judaism, "a mode of belief" for those in search of "a new way." American author and Pulitzer Prize winner Norman Mailer (1923–2007), writing as a "non-Jewish Jew," rendered a five-part series of appreciative commentaries to selected tales. Like Mailer, the Jews most taken with *Tales* were "those who may be called post-traditional Jews," Jews who either left Judaism or were brought up without its teachings, who now sought to reclaim it without adhering to its religious strictures. Whether taken by Yiddish literature, shtetl culture, or Hasidic tales, these Jews were finding meaning in new forms of Jewishness unencumbered by the religious practices and ritual objects of normative Judaism.[14]

The discovery of the Eastern European past as a source of spiritual and cultural rejuvenation was also a feature of Finkelstein's *The Eternal Light*. Among its hundreds of episodes, more than fifty drew themes from Eastern European history with dramatizations, Yiddish expressions, Hasidic melodies, and references to traditional foods, often portrayed within a "shtetl ideal" of Eastern European Jewry as spiritually prosperous if materially poor. The episodes featured performance versions of Sholem Aleichem stories, most prominently of Tevye the Dairyman, the "archetype of the folksy, good-natured . . . pious but irreverent, half-learned but shtetl-street smart, proud east European Jew." A byproduct was the depiction of a rich folk culture struggling to preserve itself in the face of modernity, a model of meaning and beauty for Jews and non-Jews seeking "new expressions of spirituality." By successfully transcending doctrinal conceptions of Judaism to create a looser category of Jewishness as a cultural commons, the Tevye and *Eternal Light* stories recast Judaism along middle-class lines, "Americanizing Jewishness."[15]

It was the Broadway distillation of the Tevye the Dairyman stories into the Broadway musical *Fiddler on the Roof*, however, that brought Eastern European origins, the shtetl, and *Yiddishkeit* into American popular culture. Although *Fiddler* was not mentioned by Hunter in his *New York Times* essay, it was likely on his mind because *Fiddler* had been drawing adoring, sell-out crowds since its debut in September 1964, ten months before Hunter's piece was published. In *Fiddler*, Tevye's three oldest daughters are to be married off, but only with his permission and in accordance with Jewish law. Yet each of them defies those strictures in different ways.

Aleichem crafted the stories of each to reveal progressively greater threats to Tevye's world, both "external"—by a despotic regime and antisemitism pressing in on his shtetl, and "internal"—by Enlightenment values of individuality and free choice. As *Fiddler* progresses, the first chooses to marry a poor tailor after Tevye had already agreed to her match with the town's prosperous, much-older butcher; the second marries a nonreligious Jewish radical who is soon banished to Siberia; and the third marries a non-Jew. The narrative arc of *Fiddler* shows Tevye struggling not only with the humiliations of poverty and antisemitism, but also with how each daughter's decision presents an ever-greater challenge to his beliefs. *Fiddler* was the quintessence of *Yiddishkeit* recuperated in *A Treasury of Yiddish Stories*, *Life is With People*, and *Tales*. It also transmuted elements of *Yiddishkeit* into a single concept, "tradition," the musical's theme captured in its opening song. "How do we keep our balance?" Tevye says, "That I can tell you in a word—tradition!" Because of it, "everyone knows who he is and what God expects him to do." In distilling Jewish religion, history, and culture into "tradition," the musical transmuted Jewishness into heritage which, as Barbara Kirshenblatt-Gimblet observed, "is not something one does; it is something one has." *Fiddler* concludes with Tevye's family and fellow townspeople being expelled from their shtetl and emigrating to America. In his American audience's imagination, Tevye was "a Jewish Pilgrim, a victim of religious persecution, fleeing intolerant Europe [for] the land of fulfillment" and *Fiddler* was "the Jewish American origin story."[16]

The Lower East Side and Masada

Had Tevye and his family come to America, they likely would have landed in New York and settled on Manhattan's lower east side where, from the 1870s through the 1920s, more Jews lived than anywhere else in America. Through a comparatively small neighborhood, for American Jews it acquired an outsized identity, its location becoming a proper noun—Lower East Side—with iconic features: "Tenements, pushcarts, sweatshops, and synagogues . . . along with pungent smells, loud noises, crowded spaces, and good, rich food. Pious elders, rebellious children, passionate socialists, aggressive union women." Life in the Lower East Side was recalled by those who lived there and shared their memories with children and grandchildren. Those experiences were also captured in innumerable memoirs, novels, documentary photographs, paintings, drawings, and other works done by Jews and others, common themes of which are the travails of immigration, adjustment to a new land, and ultimately success as Jews found their way into American society. So many immigrants passed through the Lower East Side during its more than four decades of densest Jewish settlement, it became something of a "cultural homeland" for American Jews. After the Second World War the distinctly Jewish character of the Lower East Side began dissipating as Jews fanned out to other boroughs and new suburbs while additional minorities moved in. Even so, the Lower East Side remained in the collective memory of assimilated American Jews a sacred site of authentic Jewish culture.[17]

Prior to Hunter's arrival at the museum, the efflorescence of works on Eastern European Jewish culture and its transplantation to New York inspired him to arrange an exhibit of paintings, drawings, and prints on the Lower East Side. Once at the museum, he hired Schoener with the exhibit still in mind and asked him to organize it. Schoener altered and cast a wider net for its contents, however, emphasizing memorabilia over artwork and titling it *The Lower East Side: Portal to American Life*. To implement it, Schoener drew on his educational TV and documentary film experience at the San Francisco Museum of Modern Art. Characterized by Schoener as a multimedia "study," his scheme for *The Lower East Side* included more than 150 photographic enlargements; Yiddish theater posters and programs; enlargements of Yiddish sheet-music covers, letters, and other archival materials; enlarged maps locating synagogues, schools, theaters, and similarly significant sites; and quotations from contemporary literary works. These were arranged as though tracing the immigrant experience from landing in America, to street life, and then into homes, schools, and workplaces. Also included were film and audio recordings playing on continuous loops (Figure 6.5), most of the former compiled from forgotten film footage, the latter of prominent actors from the Yiddish theater's heyday. A film created for the exhibition featured Zero Mostel (1915–77), the actor then playing Tevye in *Fiddler on the Roof*, reading English translations of letters sent to the advice column "Bintel Brief" (Bundle of Letters) of the then–Yiddish newspaper *Forverts* (Forward). The column served immigrants asking day-to-day questions about work and personal matters—relationships, troubled family, marital prospects. The selections read by Mostel offered touching, intimate views of immigrant life and its anxieties, magnifying the exhibition's impact. Schoener hoped the exhibit would rekindle memories for those who once lived in the Lower East Side, flesh it out for those whose elders spoke of it, and inform others. As if to underscore the Lower East Side's transformation into an artifact of memory, Schoener said it "was neither a place nor a time; it is a complex historical idea embroidered with emotional overtones."[18]

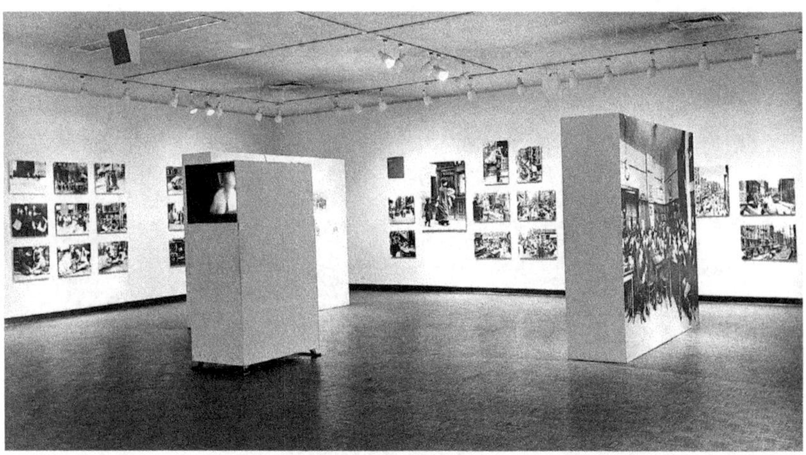

Figure 6.5. Installation view (video monitor in left foreground), *The Lower East Side: Portal to American Life*, ca. September 1966. The Jewish Museum, New York/Art Resource, NY.

A few days prior to the exhibit's opening, word of its subject inspired a journalist's "sentimental journey" through the neighborhood that augured its potential to reconnect many with their roots. Once it opened, a reviewer added that any New Yorkers whose forebears immigrated through the Lower East Side should bring their children "to show them the land of their fathers." Indeed, viewing it became a multigenerational family activity, sometimes with "Grandparents flock[ing] in with grandchildren." Visitors swarmed the exhibit, and it became "what 'Fiddler on the Roof' is to theater." Journalists reported viewers' responses as a topic in its own right. "For most of the parents, and for all of the grandparents, the exhibition [was] an evocation of poignant personal memories. . . . If this urgency of memory lays claim on those who have actually undergone the experience, it has a different imperative, possibly a greater one, for those who come after." A visitor quietly said, "'I worked in a sweatshop until the 1910 cloakmakers' strike,' . . . nodding at a picture of striking workers." Nearby, others studied Yiddish newspaper reports on the 1911 Triangle Shirtwaist Factory fire, where many Jews died. "Some dab at their eyes." One image stuck with many visitors and was highlighted by several critics—the photograph of an impoverished cobbler living in a coal cellar preparing for the Sabbath (Figure 6.6). That it moved so many is indicative of Schoener's skill in selecting and orchestrating memorable works to make *The Lower East Side* one of the most popular exhibitions in the museum's history. It attracted over 150,000 visitors, the demand

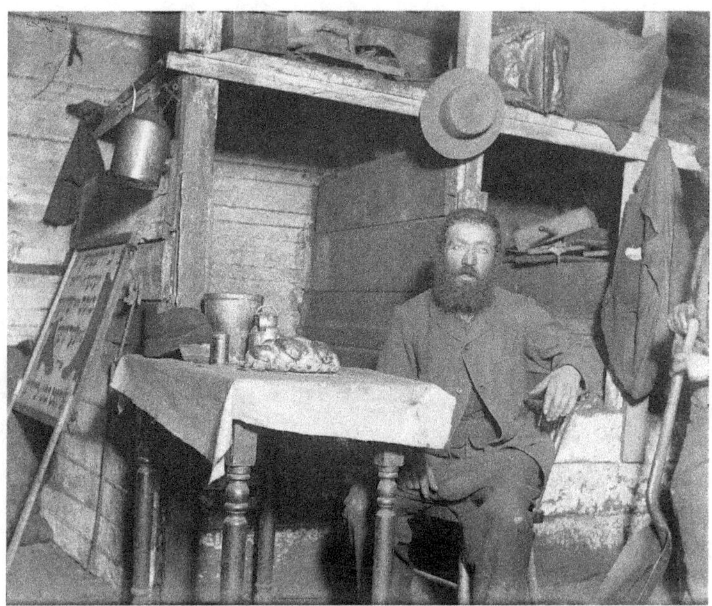

Figure 6.6. Jacob A. (August) Riis, "Ready for Sabbath Eve in a Coal Cellar—a Cobbler in Ludlow Street," ca. 1890. Museum of the City of New York. 90.13.4.291.

leading the museum to extend its hours and the show's duration by an additional week; and to schedule another, longer run the following year. The exhibition contributed to the "sacralization of the Lower East Side" as sharing its stories became "at bottom, a religious act, a ritual exercise in 'feeling Jewish.'" More than any other exhibit in the museum's history, *The Lower East Side* appealed to the many segments of the Jewish community, luring visitors from New York's increasingly distant suburbs as well as its boroughs, the young and old, the religiously observant and the disaffected, the Jewish bourgeoisie and its intelligentsia. The very breadth and passionate response of *The Lower East Side*'s audiences also threw into sharp relief the comparative diffidence with which many responded to the museum's ritual object displays.[19]

Despite *The Lower East Side*'s success, the continuation of avant-garde shows like the Reinhardt and Klein surveys alongside the comparative neglect of the museum's Judaica collection rankled some observers. Hoping that with *The Lower East Side* the museum had finally found the right balance between the avant-garde and Jewish topics, board members were perplexed by the continuing complaints and turned to Finkelstein for guidance. But he was leery of intervening—especially if the board persisted with the avant-garde—believing he could not change minds and to avoid overruling its members causing them to leave. Finn was puzzled by Finkelstein's response because the board nearly unanimously supported robust Judaic programming. Further, the only plan to improve it, the one prepared by Kampf, was found inappropriate by Finkelstein. Ultimately, Finn concluded, the issue was really the museum's leadership, and despite Hunter's willingness to improve Judaica programming, that was no substitute for curatorial expertise with it. Money was another worry. Hunter was careless with spending, had ignored a growing deficit, and was a "sloppy" manager, alarming his board and seminary officials. He was asked to address the issue at a special meeting and complied with an accounting of the museum's financial straits and a plan to assure its fiscal future. Along with budget cuts, Hunter challenged the board to raise more money. He thought the present exhibition policy was fine but acknowledged that having a Judaica curator to succeed Kampf would make a big difference. Yet that would cost even more. Vera List lobbied seminary trustees to stand by the museum, and to calm the waters the Lists made an additional donation to reduce the deficit. In thanking the Lists, Finkelstein pointed to a forthcoming "Masada exhibit" that, like *The Lower East Side*, would help the museum be "accepted in Philistine circles where modern art is not fully appreciated," a cutting reference to fellow Conservative Jews.[20]

"Masada" recalls a seminal event in ancient Jewish history, the meaning of which was magnified by the Holocaust and Israel's birth. It is a small plateau in lower Israel, about forty miles southeast of Jerusalem near the Dead Sea. Less than a half mile long and about one thousand feet wide at its center, Masada's sheer sides on the east rise nearly fifteen hundred feet above the Dead Sea flats and on the west steep inclines separate it from the Judean Desert. Its topography affords commanding views in every direction and ready defense against attacks. Masada may have served as an ancient outpost, but it was the Roman-anointed king of Judea, Herod, who transformed it into a fortified, palatial retreat. Following his death in 4 BCE, Judea descended into chaos, the Jews revolted against Rome, and they were attacked by Roman forces. Around 66 CE nearly a thousand rebels and their families fled to Masada and held out there until 73/74 CE, when they were besieged and eventually defeated by Roman legions. Josephus (Yosef ben Matityahu), who was born to a Jewish family but defected to the Roman side, wrote in his *The Jewish War* (or *Judean War*) and *Jewish Antiquities*, that the rebels, rather than be enslaved by the Romans, ended their resistance by communal suicide. The extent and detail of his writings established Josephus as a formidable source, but gaps and fanciful assertions prompted modern archaeologists to doubt his accuracy. A thorough excavation of Masada with Josephus's account in mind was organized by Yigael Yadin in the early 1960s. Yadin (1917–84) was a charismatic Israeli archaeologist, military commander, and politician who skillfully publicized Israel's archaeological discoveries. After completing his explorations on Masada, Yadin wrote a colorful account, published in 1966, in which he details finds he believed confirmed the Jewish rebels' martyrdom, a conclusion questioned by subsequent scholars. Nonetheless, coming not long after the Holocaust and Israel's statehood in 1948, Yadin's assertion deepened Masada's transformation—for Israelis and the Jewish diaspora alike—into a potent symbol of solidarity and resistance. One manifestation is the oath sworn by Israeli army recruits after climbing the plateau: "Masada will not fall again."[21]

The Jewish Museum's Masada exhibition was organized by Joy Ungerleider who, while accompanying her husband on business trips to Israel, volunteered on Yadin's excavations including those at Masada. Ungerleider (1920–94) was drawn to museum work by her familiarity with biblical archaeology, her family's involvement in the Dead Sea Scrolls discoveries, and its funding of an Israel Museum building to house them. She had earned a bachelor's degree in Hebrew studies from New York University, where she later completed a master's degree in the same field. "Very strong-minded," Ungerleider was establishing herself as a leading Jewish philanthropist who, as an "activist donor," brought a rare combination of "ideas and vigor and money." But it was through her determination and vision that she became known as a "driving force" for the better at the museum and several other institutions she aided or helped steward. When Ungerleider learned in 1966 that Yadin was planning a Masada exhibit in London, she proposed to Finkelstein that it be brought to the Jewish Museum. He agreed provided she chair the effort, including fundraising to meet the high loan fee Yadin stipulated. Ungerleider did so, curating a version of Yadin's exhibition that opened in New York and then traveled to other American venues. Opening in October 1967, *Masada: A Struggle for Freedom* employed the multimedia approach of *The Lower East Side* but went further in its theatricality. In addition to photomurals, film projections, voice recordings, maps, and diagrams, the exhibit contained an eight-by-ten-foot scale model showing Masada's topography, life-size and miniature dioramas (Figure 6.7), and nearly full-scale interior reconstructions of a Herodian temple and rebels' dwelling. Arranged over two floors of the museum, *Masada* told two stories. One was of the archaeological effort; the other of the rebels' lives and the Roman siege that ended them. Hundreds of artifacts were displayed, some featured in the recreated scenes. Among the latter were biblical and other scroll fragments as well as blackened vessels perhaps from the final conflagration. Press coverage

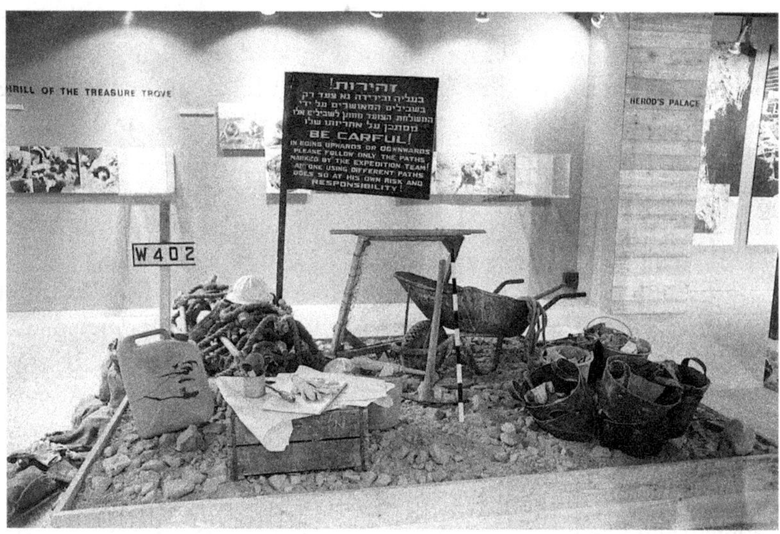

Figure 6.7. Installation view, *Masada: A Struggle for Freedom*, ca. October 1967. The Jewish Museum, New York/Art Resource, NY.

highlighted both stories, but Yadin's claim of having confirmed Josephus's account of the rebels' final hours received the most attention. That ending was dramatized in the exhibit's last alcove. There "psychedelic lights simulating the flames of the fires . . . before the mass suicide" formed the backdrop for an actor's recording of the rebel leader's speech exhorting the others "to die with honor rather than live in captivity."[22]

Masada was even more popular than *The Lower East Side*, attracting a yet larger attendance—nearly two hundred thousand—requiring extended hours to accommodate the demand. Discussions of the exhibit addressed two intertwined resonances the Masada story held for many Jews, the Holocaust and Israel's fraught relations with its Arab neighbors. Some likened the futility of the rebels' resistance against Rome to the Warsaw Ghetto Uprising against the Nazis. When the sixty-four thousand Jews in the ghetto learned of a Nazi plan to deport the able-bodied to forced-labor camps and kill the remainder, a resistance was prepared. The Nazis launched their plan on Passover eve in April 1943 and for nearly a month Jews fought back before the Nazis crushed the rebellion, killing about a fifth of the occupants and deporting the rest. Finkelstein, in an exhibit catalogue essay, analogized the Masada and Warsaw Ghetto stories, as did an *Eternal Light* broadcast, "The Unvanquished." Presented during the Masada exhibition, it told of a Polish archaeologist now living in Israel who, afflicted by the loss of her husband and son in the Warsaw ghetto, was piecing "together not only ancient pottery fragments, but contemporary truths" about freedom and survival. Implicit was another contemporary truth, modern Israel's emergence as an indispensable, last-resort homeland for European Jewry's surviving remnants. But the arousal of Arab opposition by Israel's founding rendered the young nation's geopolitical surroundings precarious and an editorial on *Masada* related the Jews' encirclement by Roman legions to contemporary Israel's being surrounded by hostile Arab armies. By that point, Israel had fought three wars with its neighbors and the most recent, the Six-Day War, took place just four months before *Masada* opened. The war was precipitated by a compact of aggression among countries bordering Israel. Tensions escalated after a naval blockade, massing of armed forces along Israel's borders, and sporadic shelling of Israelis. Israel responded with preemptive air, land, and naval strikes, defeating their opponents in six days. The runup to and aftermath of the Six-Day War galvanized Jewish support worldwide and heightened interest in the Masada story, making the exhibition, according to Ungerleider, "something much bigger."[23]

Victim of Confusion | An Institution Adrift

Until *Masada*, the forewords of the museum's exhibit catalogues were invariably written by its directors or curators. For *Masada*, it was authored by David Finn as board chair, indicative of Hunter's opposition to the exhibit and raising anew doubts about his leadership. Hunter "boycotted" *Masada* because he thought its archaeological content belonged in New York's American Museum of Natural History, not an art museum, even if Jewish. Concerns over Hunter's stewardship continued, and despite the exhibit's success and the Lists' additional funding, the museum was running a steep deficit. Behind-the-scenes conversations about Hunter's performance accelerated, and two weeks after *Masada*'s opening, he resigned. A journalist quoted Hunter as saying the museum's "increasing emphasis on Judaica at the expense of contemporary art" influenced his decision, but the reporter also noted disagreements among board members over the extent to which exhibits of its ritual objects collection, "one of the finest in the world," ought to be prioritized. Finkelstein denied the museum would withdraw entirely from contemporary art, but he thought "a slight change of emphasis" might be in order. Yet he also reaffirmed his belief that the museum should exhibit works of modern art that express "some relationship to Jewish tradition," even if they are "not necessarily creation[s] of Jews."[24]

Hunter's resignation drew sharp reactions from the museum's friends. One saw his departure as marking the avant-garde program's demise and urged Finkelstein to stand by it, doubting "a Jewish Seraglio is either desirable or essential." In response, Finkelstein recalled the museum's founding Judaica purposes but acknowledged the value of its contemporary-art exhibits, adding that he hoped the museum would do more in the future. Arguing the opposite to Finkelstein, Kanof said that although he had supported the Judaica/avant-garde experiment, after five years he concluded that it had failed. Kanof believed there were two reasons, one being the difficulty of finding a modern-art director capable of treating the Judaica fairly. The other was the board. Kanof felt too many of the most recently elected members were chosen for their wealth. Instead of donating more when the avant-garde shows ran deficits, however, they balanced the budget by cutting the Judaica program. Other observers attributed Solomon's as well as Hunter's short tenures to both the board *and* the seminary. One critique, "The Jewish Museum: Victim of Confusion," came from Arthur A. Cohen, guest curator for one of the first exhibitions during Solomon's directorship, *The Hebrew Bible in Christian, Jewish and Muslim Art*. Cohen thought Hunter's exit reflected "the hopeless confusion" besetting the relationship between "the Jew of money" (museum board members) and "cultural institutions of the West" (the museum) and Judaism (the seminary). In the final analysis, Cohen believed the underlying problem was the relationship between Judaism and the visual arts. It was not a "pragmatic" one of artmaking and patronage, but rather an "ideological" one inherent to Judaism's humanist obligation to support expressions "of the human spirit." Unfortunately, that ideology runs afoul of a theological issue: idolatry. Not idolatry of the biblical kind, but of succumbing "to the idolatry of power, prestige, influence, and money"—Jews confusing museum philanthropy with art-world glamour. As confused as the board or seminary might have been in governing the museum, Cohen's analysis was equally tangled, self-contradictory, and absent useful answers—issues pointed out by Finn and Schapiro.[25]

Another response, "The Jewish Museum: An Institution Adrift," came from Avram Kampf, who by then was no longer in the museum's employ. He set the museum in the context of its European antecedents to emphasize certain commonly held values: preserving and promoting Jewish art, serving as an information resource, and producing scholarship. Kampf believed that, already in the 1940s, the museum strayed from those virtues and as a result it lacked the research, publication, and fellowship programs to foster Judaica scholarship, functions Kampf unsuccessfully proposed about a year earlier. That the seminary did not include the study of Jewish art in its rabbinic or teacher-training curriculums, or avail itself of the museum's collections for research, at least partially explained the museum's current predicament. Another issue was the board, in particular Vera List and the others who a decade earlier ushered Kayser out in favor of Solomon. Echoing Cohen, Kampf regarded them as what Alvin Toffler called "cultural consumers" in their uses of newly found affluence: "Among the new American collectors and patrons [were] a number of wealthy Jews who came to the art world in search of an avenue of spiritual adventure, social mobility, and financial investment." Although Solomon's appointment was an attempt to establish an integrated Judaica and avant-garde program, the differences between the two were heightened and a "Janus-faced creature" resulted, "hopelessly divided between the Jewish and the secular." Kampf also saw the board as representing the "kaleidoscope of . . . forces in Jewish life," mirroring schisms in the larger Jewish community as well. Perhaps the museum needed a fresh start, he said, one that would not be found solely in Judaica or in modern art, but only in fusing the two into "a new configuration." Reaching that goal, Kampf warned, will be "the ultimate test."[26]

Notes

1. For ultimate test, see AK, "The Jewish Museum: An Institution Adrift," *Judaism* 17, no. 3 (Summer 1968): 282–98.
2. On KK's recruitment, see KK to MS, 22 August 1964, MSC 138:1 and 22 August 1965, MSC 140:3, CUL. On van Weeren-Griek's work, see "The Jewish Museum, Report for Board of Governors," May 1965, RG 21–5–9, LJTS. On SH, DF to MS, 11 September 1964, MSC, 138: 1, CUL. Publicity release, 17 March 1965, RG 25–5–18, LJTS; "Director of Jewish Museum Named," *New York Times*, 19 March 1965; Roberta Smith, "Sam Hunter, 91, Curator and Museum Founder, *New York Times*, 26 August 2014; see also *Contemporary Authors Online* (Detroit, MI: Gale, 2001), *Biography in Context*, s.v. "Sam Hunter," accessed April 2020, doi: GALE|H1000048418. For quotes on SH, see Sally Yard and Hugh M. Davies, "Sam Hunter (1923–2014), *Artforum International*, accessed March 2023, https://www.artforum.com/passages/sally-yard-and-hugh-m-davies-on-sam-hunter-1923–2014–48585; and Jamie Saxon, "Samuel Hunter, Authority on 20th-Century Art and 'Profound' Mentor, Dies," Office of Communications, Princeton University, accessed March 2023, https://www.princeton.edu/news/2014/07/31/samuel-hunter-authority-20th-century-art-and-profound-mentor-dies. VL to LF, 17 February, LF to SH, 26 February 1965, RG 25–4–27, LJTS.

3. SH, "The Jewish Museum: What Is It, Why Is It, and What Next?" *New York Times*, 8 August 1965.
4. Judaica exhibits presented after SH arrived were: "Jewish Ceremonial Textiles," "Modern Jewish Ceremonial Silver," "Two Centuries of Frankfurt Silver," and "Contemporary Art for the Synagogue," [JM,] "Jewish Museum Exhibitions: 1947–Present," 2 September 2009. See also, Katherine Kline, *Contemporary Art for the Synagogue: The Jewish Museum* [New York: Jewish Museum, 1966]. Barbara Rose and Jacquelyn Days Serwer, *Larry Rivers: Art and the Artist*, foreword David C. Levy (Boston, MA: Little, Brown and Company, 2002); Larry Rivers, *What Did I Do?: The Unauthorized Autobiography*, assisted by Arnold Weinstein (New York: Aaron Asher Books, 1992). See also, Michael Kimmelman, "Larry Rivers, Artist with an Edge, Dies at 78," *New York Times*, 16 August 2002. SH, *Larry Rivers* (New York: October House for Poses Institute of Fine Arts, Brandeis University, 1965). For quotes, see Frank O'Hara, "A Memoir," in SH, *Larry Rivers*, 9, 17; SH, "Introduction," in SH, *Larry Rivers*, 20; Grace Glueck, "Rivers Paints Himself Into the Canvas," *New York Times*, 13 February 1966. Rivers's Jewish background was not mentioned in the catalogue or exhibit reviews, but the JM did field questions about it after the show opened; Janet Solinger (JM Administrator, 1961–1965), oral history interview by Nicki Tanner, 10 May 1993, transcript, UJA-FNYC, I-433, AJHS, 29.
5. SH, *Larry Rivers*. See also, SH, "The Recent Work of Larry Rivers," *Arts Magazine* 39, no. 7 (April 1965): 44–50. On the installation, titled *History of the Russian Revolution*, see T.B.H. [Thomas B. Hess], "Larry Rivers' History of the Russian Revolution," *Art News* 64, no. 6 (October 1965): 36–37, 58. For reviews, see Harold Rosenberg, "Rivers' commedia dell' arte," *Art News* 64, no. 2 (April 1965): 35–37, 62–63; John Canaday, "N.Y. Sees Paintings by Rivers," *New York Times*, 27 September 1965. On attendance, see Grace Glueck, "Rivers Paints Himself Into the Canvas"; and Silvia Tennenbaum, "Jewish Home for the Graven Image," *Midstream: A Monthly Jewish Review* 12, no. 6 (June–July 1966): 17. On the hullabaloo, see DF, oral history interview by Nicki Tanner, 13 February 1990, transcript, UJA-FNYC, I-433, AJHS, 18. LF to SH, 10 October and 8 November 1965, RG 1–232–9, LJTS; see also, Abram Kanof, oral history interview by Judy Tenney, 19 November 1990 and 26 May 1992, transcript, UJA-FNYC, I-433, AJHS, 28–29.
6. On overcrowded openings, see LF to VL, 1 December and VL to SH, 5 December 1965, RG 1–233–23, LJTS. [DF,] "The Jewish Museum: Governing Policies," 8 February 1966, RG 25–4–25, [SH], "The Jewish Museum, Report to Board of Overseers," March 1966, RG 21–5–16, LJTS; and [DF,] "The Jewish Museum: Operating Principles and Procedures" [March 1966,] AF, Box 1, JMA. See also, Arthur T. Jacobs to DF, 22 March 1966, RG 25–4–25, LJTS. On visitors, see Tennenbaum, "Jewish Home for the Graven Image," 17. [SH?,] Untitled report, "Judaica Department," ca. 20 January 1966, RG 1–241–39, LJTS; Abram Kanof to LF, 12 March,

LF to Abram Kanof, 15 March 1966, RG 1–241–39, Minutes, Board of Overseers, 20 March 1966, RG 21–5–14, LJTS. On Schoener's appointment, see Publicity release, 14 January 1966, RG 1–244–53, LJTS; and Janet Solinger, oral history interview by Nicki Tanner, 10 May 1993, transcript, UJA-FNYC, I-433, AJHS, 31; Allon Schoener, oral history interview by Lisa Rubens, 5 December 2007, transcript, Oral History Project, San Francisco Museum of Modern Art and Regional Oral History Office, Bancroft Library, University of California, Berkeley, 37. Allon Schoener to SH, 3 and 12 January 1966, AF, Box 3, JMA; Allon Schoener, "Resume," accessed June 2020, https://allonschoener.net/resume.htm; Gale Literature: Contemporary Authors (2003), *Gale in Context: Biography*, s.v. "Allon Schoener," accessed May 2020, doi: GALE|H1000115905. See also, Alex Vadukul, "Allon Schoener, Curator Whose 'Harlem' Exhibit Drew Outrage, Dies at 95," *New York Times*, 25 April 2021.

7. SH to Kynaston L. McShine, 18 June 1965, RG 25–5–15, LJTS; "Jewish Museum Names Curator," *New York Times*, 7 September 1965. McShine remained at the JM for just three years before returning to MoMA; Roberta Smith, "Kynaston McShine, the Intrepid Curator of Two Historic Art Shows, is Dead at 82," *New York Times*, 15 January 2018; see also, David Frankel and Richard Serra, "Kynaston McShine, 1935–2018," *Artforum International* 56, no. 9 (May 2018): 51. [Kynaston McShine,] *Primary Structures: Younger American and British Sculptors* (New York: Jewish Museum, 1966); republished in a facsimile edition packaged with the catalogue for a follow-up exhibition; [Jens Hoffman,] *Other Primary Structures* (New York: Jewish Museum and Yale University Press, 2014). On McShine's JM work, see Kynaston McShine, oral history interview by Carolyn Lanchner (1932–2016, curator in the Department of Painting and Sculpture, Museum of Modern Art; oral history compiled by David Frankel), 1 April 2010–13 January 2011, transcript, Oral History Program, Museum of Modern Art, 14–16, 19. Brian O'Doherty, *Inside the White Cube: The Ideology of the Gallery Space* (San Francisco: Lapis Press, 1986). On the exhibit, see Bruce Altshuler, "Theory on the Floor: Primary Structures, The Jewish Museum," in *The Avant-Garde in Exhibition: New Art in the 20th Century* (New York: Harry N. Abrams, Inc., 1994), 220–35 (for the "primary colors" reference, p. 227); see also, Phaidon Editors and Bruce Altshuler, eds., *Biennials and Beyond — Exhibitions That Made Art History: 1962–2002* (New York: Phaidon Press Limited, 2013), 51–64. See also, James Meyer, *Minimalism: Art and Polemics in the Sixties* (New Haven, CT: Yale University Press, 2001), 10–30; for closing quote, p. 30.
8. Meyer, *Minimalism*, 153. For reviews, see Grace Glueck, "Anti-Collector, Anti-Museum," *New York Times*, 24 April 1966; Hilton Kramer, "Art: Reshaping the Outermost Limits," *New York Times*, 28 April 1966; Hilton Kramer, "'Primary Structures'—The New Anonymity," *New York Times*, 1 May 1966; Andrew Hudson, "English Sculptors Outdo Americans," *Washington Post*, 8 May 1966; Robert M. Coates, "The Art Galleries: Art and

the Machine," *New Yorker* (21 May 1966): 177–79; M[el] Bochner, "Primary Structures," *Arts Magazine* 40, no. 8 (June 1966): 32–35; "Engineer's Esthetic," *Time* 87, no. 22 (3 June 1966): 64–67; John J. O'Connor, "The Gallery: Exploring Space," *Wall Street Journal*, 6 June 1966; and Corinne Robins, "Object, Structure or Sculpture: Where Are We?" *Arts Magazine* 40, no. 9 (September/October 1966): 33–37. See also, "Shape of Art for Some Time to Come," *Life* 63, no. 4 (28 July 1967): 38–43. On the opening, see Charlotte Curtis, "Art Gallery Hoppers Extend East Side Rush Hour Into the Night," *New York Times*, 27 April 1966. See also, Meyer, *Minimalism*, 10. For context, see *New York: The New York Art Scene*, text by AS (New York: Holt Rinehart Winston, 1967); including a photo of VL on p. 18. SH to VL, 27 April 1966, RG 1–240–5, LJTS. Albert A. List to DF, 29 April 1966, RG 1–240–5, LF to VL, 9 May 1966, RG 1–242–31, and DF to LF, 16 May 1966, RG 1–240–5, LJTS. DF, oral history interview by Nicki Tanner, 13 February 1990, transcript, UJA-FNYC, I-433, AJHS, 21–22, 35; LF to VL, 20 May 1966, RG 1–242–31 and LF to DF, 20 May 1966, RG 1–240–5, LJTS; "Jewish Museum Announces New Board Officers," 30 June 1966, RG 11–44–13, LJTS. Lucy R. Lippard, *Ad Reinhardt: Paintings*, preface SH, (New York: Jewish Museum, 1966). Kynaston McShine, Pierre Descargues, and Pierre Restany, *Yves Klein*, with extracts from Yves Klein's "The monochrome adventure" (New York: Jewish Museum, 1967). See also, Kynaston McShine, oral history interview by Carolyn Lanchner (oral history compiled by David Frankel), 1 April 2010–13 January 2011, transcript, Oral History Program, Museum of Modern Art, 22–23, 40; and John Canaday, "I Got the Yves Klein Blues," *New York Times*, 5 February 1967.

9. Irit Miller, "Avram Kampf (1920–2016)," *Ars Judaica: The Bar Ilan Journal of Jewish Art* 13 (2017): 149–54. AK, "A Study of Contemporary Synagogue Art" (PhD diss., The New School for Social Research, 1962); subsequently published as, AK, *Contemporary Synagogue Art: Developments in the United States, 1945–1965* (New York: Union of American Hebrew Congregations, 1966). DF to SH, 2 May 1966, RG 1–241–20, LJTS; SH to AK, 18 May 1966 and SH, "A Memorandum of Understanding with Avram Kampf" [18 May 1966], AF, Box 3, JMA.
10. Colum P. Hourihane, "The Index of Christian Art," *Grove Art Online* (2013), accessed May 2020, https://doi-org/10.1093/gao/9781884446054.article.T2229108. On AK's unsuitable ideas, see DF to LF, 28 February 1967, RG 1–248–43, LJTS. On the Jewish art department, see AK to DF, 5 October 1966, DF to LF, 24 October 1966, and LF to DF, 31 October 1966, RG 1–240–5, LJTS. SH to DF, 16 January 1967, and [SH], "Judaica Department: Interim Report," 13 February 1967, AF, Box 3, JMA. See also, AK, oral history interview by Nicki Tanner, 24 July 1990, transcript, UJA-FNYC, I-433, AJHS, 9, 16–21 and DF, oral history interview by Nicki Tanner, 13 February 1990, transcript, UJA-FNYC, I-433, AJHS, 42–45. On the curator problem, see Hannah Abrahamson to MS, 21 March 1967, MSC 138:2, CUL.

11. SH, "The Jewish Museum: What Is It, Why Is It, and What Next?" *New York Times*, 8 August 1965. Irving Howe and Eliezer Greenberg, eds., *A Treasury of Yiddish Stories* (New York: Viking Press, 1953), 1–71; Mark Zborowski and Elizabeth Herzog, *Life is With People: The Jewish Little-Town of Eastern Europe*, foreword Margaret Mead (New York: International Universities Press, 1952); Martin Buber, *Tales of the Hasidim: The Early Masters* and *Tales of the Hasidim: The Later Masters*, trans. Olga Marx, 2 vols. (New York: Schocken Books, 1947–1948). SH also cited *Commentary*; and for relevant context, see Marcus Krah, *American Jewry and the Re-Invention of the East European Jewish Past* (Berlin, Germany: De Gruyter Oldenbourg, 2018), 71–95.
12. Edward Alexander, "Irving Howe and Secular Jewishness: An Elegy," *Judaism* 45, no. 1 (Winter 1996): 107–8. Howe and Greenberg, introduction to *A Treasury of Yiddish Stories*, 3, 42–43, 54, 71. David G. Roskies, "The Treasures of Howe and Greenberg," *Prooftexts* 3, no. 1 (January 1983): 110. See also, Krah, *American Jewry*, 224–27; and Norman Podhoretz, "Jewish Culture and the Intellectuals: The Process of Rediscovery," *Commentary* 19, no. 5 (May 1955): 451–57.
13. Zborowski and Herzog, *Life is With People*; Barbara Kirshenblatt-Gimblett, introduction to Mark Zborowski and Elizabeth Herzog, *Life is With People: The Culture of the Shtetl*, reprinted from 1962 edn. (New York: Schocken Books, 1995), ix, xii–xiv, xvi, xxxi–iii, xxxv–xxxix. Zborowski and Herzog, *Life is With People*, 24–25. Mark Zborowski and Elizabeth Herzog, *Life is With People: The Culture of the Shtetl* (New York: Schocken Paperbacks, 1962). Milton Himmelfarb, "Books in Review," *Commentary* 34, no. 4 (1 October 1962): 367–68. On the reception of *Life is With People*, see also, Krah, *American Jewry*, 179–88.
14. Howe and Greenberg, introduction to *A Treasury of Yiddish Stories*, 14–16. Martin Buber, preface and introduction to *Tales of the Hasidim: The Early Masters* (New York: Schocken Books, 1947), ix, 1–3. Paul Mendes-Flohr, "Martin Buber's Reception Among Jews," *Modern Judaism* 6, no. 2 (May 1986): 118. On Buber's handling of the tales, see Gershom Scholem, "Martin Buber's Interpretation of Hasidism" in Scholem, *The Messianic Idea in Judaism and Other Essays on Jewish Spirituality* (New York: Schocken Books, 1971), 228–50; and Gershom Scholem, "Martin Buber's Conception of Judaism" in Scholem, *On Jews and Judaism in Crisis: Selected Essays*, ed. Werner J. Dannhauser (New York: Schocken Books, 1976), 126–71, especially pp. 165–71. Buber, introduction to *Tales of the Hasidim*, 3–5; and Mendes-Flohr, "Martin Buber's Reception Among Jews," 113, 118–19, 124–25. Leslie A. Fiedler, "Books in Review: Hasidim and Modern Jew," *Commentary* 7, no. 2 (1 February 1949): 198. Norman Mailer, "Responses & Reactions," *Commentary* 34, no. 6 (1 December 1962): 504–6, the quote is from p. 506. See also, Mailer, "Responses & Reactions II," *Commentary* 35, no. 2 (1 February 1963): 146–48; "Responses & Reactions III," *Commentary* 35, no. 4 (1 April 1963): 335–37; "Responses & Reactions

IV," *Commentary* 35, no. 6 (1 June 1963): 517–19; "Responses & Reactions V," *Commentary* 36, no. 2 (1 August 1963): 164–65. On the reception of Buber's Hasidic works, see Krah, *American Jewry*, 201–11.

15. Krah, *American Jewry*, 7, 169–78. On the inception and reach of *The Eternal Light*, see chapter 3.
16. Alisa Solomon, *Wonder of Wonders: A Cultural History of Fiddler on the Roof* (New York: Metropolitan Books, Henry Holt and Company, 2013), 155, 212, 214; on "Tradition," pp. 139, 161–63. Seth L. Wolitz, "The Americanization of Tevye or Boarding the Jewish *Mayflower*," *American Quarterly* 40, no. 4 (December 1988): 514–36. Joseph Stein, *Fiddler on the Roof: Based on Sholom Aleichem's Stories*, music by Jerry Bock, lyrics by Sheldon Harnick, directed and choreographed by Jerome Robbins (New York: Crown Publishers, 1964). Barbara Kirshenblatt-Gimblett, introduction, xxxviii. Stein, *Fiddler on the Roof*, 2–3, 145, 151–53. Krah, *American Jewry*, 237, 243. Alisa Solomon, "How 'Fiddler' Became Folklore," *Forward*, 1 September 2006, accessed June 2020, https://forward.com/culture/1710/how-e2-80-98fiddler-e2-80-99-became-folklore/. Some criticized *Fiddler*'s sentimentalization of the shtetl experience; see, for example, Irving Howe, "Tevye on Broadway," *Commentary* 38, no. 5 (1 November 1964): 73–75. For an earlier history of Jews romanticizing life in the old country, see Richard I. Cohen, "Nostalgia and 'The Return to the Ghetto,'" in *Jewish Icons: Art and Society in Modern Europe* (Berkeley: University of California Press, 1998), 154–85.
17. Hasia R. Diner, *Lower East Side Memories: A Jewish Place in America* (Princeton, NJ: Princeton University Press, 2000), 13, 27, 40.
18. SH, "The Jewish Museum," Publicity release, 14 January 1966, RG 1–244–53, LJTS; Allon Schoener, oral history interview by Lisa Rubens, 5 December 2007, transcript, Oral History Project, San Francisco Museum of Modern Art and Regional Oral History Office, Bancroft Library, University of California, Berkeley, 31, 37; on Schoener's multimedia background, pp. 11–14, 17, 21–22, 24–25. Over Schoener's objections, SH insisted the show still include paintings, drawings, and prints portraying life on the Lower East Side, some by Jewish artists and most not, that were displayed in a separate gallery, Allon Schoener, "A Retrospective Walk Through the Harlem On My Mind Exhibition at the Metropolitan Museum of Art, 1969," *The Cosmopolitan Observer* (blog), 30 August 2015, https://thecosmopolitanobserver.blogspot.com/2015/08/a-walk-through-harlem-on-my-mind.html. SH's insistence may have been informed by his earlier book; SH, *Modern American Painting and Sculpture* (New York: Laurel Edition, Dell Publishing Company, 1959), 28–40. Allon Schoener, ed., *The Lower East Side: Portal to American Life (1870–1924)* (New York: The Jewish Museum, 1966), 10, 38–43, 63–65. The artworks are absent from a more extensive book Schoener subsequently published on the show; Allon Schoener, ed., *Portal to America: The Lower East Side, 1870–1925* (New York: Holt, Rinehart and Winston, 1967). Jared Brown, *Zero Mostel: A Biography* (New

York: Atheneum, 1989). Rachel Rojanski, "Forverts/Forward," *Oxford Bibliographies*, Oxford University Press, accessed June 2020, doi: 10.1093/OBO/9780199840731-0194. Isaac Metzker, *A Bintel Brief: Sixty Years of Letters from the Lower East Side to the Jewish Daily Forward*, trans. Diana Shalet Levy (New York: Ballantine Books, 1972). For reviews, see "Jewish Museum Exhibit Recalls New York's Lower East Side," *Jewish Advocate*, 20 October 1966; and Emily Genauer, "Crowds See Jewish Museum's Exhibit on East Side Life," *World Journal Tribune*, 22 September 1966.

19. Harvey Swados, "A Sentimental Journey to the Lower East Side," *New York Times*, 18 September 1966; Richard J. Shepard, "Jewish Museum Depicts a Ghetto," *New York Times*, 21 September 1966 and "Visit to Museum Jogs Memories," *New York Times*, 17 October 1966. On evoking memories, see Robert Alter, "Exhibiting the Lower East Side," *Commentary* 43, no. 1 (January 1967): 69–70. Regarding the cobbler image, see Trude Weiss-Rosmarin, "'Jewish Vogue' Continues in U.S. Culture," *Jewish Advocate*, 2 November 1967; [Editorial], "What We Have Lost," *Jewish Advocate*, 27 October 1966; Alfred Kazin, "The Writer and the City," *Harper's Magazine* 237, no. 1423 (1 December 1968): 110–27; and Alter, "Exhibiting the Lower East Side," 67–71. On attendance, see Shepard, "Visit to Museum Jogs Memories"; Diner, *Lower East Side Memories*, 80; SG to SSK, 26 October 1966, RG 1–241–40, LJTS. "Jewish Museum Extends 'Lower East Side' Show," *New York Times*, 7 October 1966; "Lower East Side Exhibit Reopens at New York's Jewish Museum April 4," *Jewish Advocate*, 16 March 1967; "Jewish Museum Lists Purim Fete Saturday Night," *New York Times*, 26 March 1967. Schoener prepared *Portal to America* for the show's second run. On sacralization and ritual, respectively, see Diner, *Lower East Side Memories*, 79; Jenna Weissman Joselit, "Telling Tales: Or, How a Slum Became a Shrine," *Jewish Social Studies* 2, no. 2 (Winter 1996): 61.

20. DF to LF, 16 February 1967, LF to DF, 21 February 1967, and DF to LF, 28 February 1967, RG 1–248–43, LJTS. On SH's spending, see AKatz to SH, 10 May and SH to AKatz, 1 June 1965, RG 25–4–27, LJTS. Memorandum, SH to DF, 13 March 1967, and Minutes, Executive Committee, JM, 13 March 1967, RG 25–3–2, LJTS. On SH's management, see Janet Solinger, oral history interview by Nicki Tanner, 10 May 1993, transcript, UJA-FNYC, I-433, AJHS, 30. On VL's appeal to the JTS trustees and the Lists' contribution, see DF to VL, 4 April 1967, LF to VL, 6 April 1967, and LF to Albert A. List, 5 April 1967, RG 1–250–55, LJTS.

21. *Encyclopaedia Judaica*, 2nd edn. (2007), s.v. "Masada," by Guy D. Stiebel. See also, Max L. Margolis and Alexander Marx, *A History of the Jewish People* (Philadelphia, PA: Jewish Publication Society of America, 1927), 166–67, 170–71, 203–4; and Jodi Magness, *Masada: From Jewish Revolt to Modern Myth* (Princeton, NJ: Princeton University Press, 2019); on the making of the "Masada myth" and Yadin's role in it, pp. 187–200. Neil Asher Silberman, *A Prophet from Amongst You | The Life of Yigael Yadin: Soldier, Scholar, and Mythmaker of Modern Israel* (Reading, MA: Addison-Wesley

Publishing,1993). Yigael Yadin, *Masada: Herod's Fortress and the Zealots' Last Stand* (New York: Random House, 1966). See also, S. J. Goldsmith, "The Magic of Masada," *Jewish Advocate*, 8 December 1966. Shortly after Yadin's book, Masada began to be used for bar mitzvahs; "Jewish National Fund News," *Jewish Advocate*, 2 March 1967.

22. "Joy Ungerleider-Mayerson," *Jewish Women: A Comprehensive Historical Encyclopedia*, Jewish Women's Achive, by Deborah Lipstadt, 27 February 2009, accessed June 2020, https://jwa.org/encyclopedia/article/ungerleider-mayerson-joy; see also, "Joy Ungerleider-Mayerson, 74; Former Head of Jewish Museum," *New York Times*, 9 September 1994. Quotes are from Richard J. Scheuer, oral history interview by Nicki Tanner, 7 July 1995, transcript, UJA-FNYC, I-433, AJHS, 16; and Stuart Silver, oral history interview by Rosalind Mancher, June and August 1994, transcript, UJA-FNYC, I-433, AJHS, 52. Her first husband, Samuel Ungerleider Jr., died in 1972, and when she married Philip Mayerson in 1976 she altered her last name to Ungerleider-Mayerson. "Samuel Ungerleider Jr. Dead; Pulp and Paper Executive, 55," *New York Times*, 6 June 1972; "Joy Ungerleider Bride of Dr. Philip Mayerson," *New York Times*, 26 November 1976. JU, oral history interview by Judy E. Tenney, 19 December 1989, transcript, UJA-FNYC, I-433, AJHS, 22–23. On housing the Dead Sea Scrolls, see "Shrine of the Book," Israel Museum, Jerusalem, accessed June 2020, https://www.imj.org.il/en/wings/shrine-book. On JU's exhibit work, see Richard J. Scheuer, oral history interview by Nicki Tanner, 7 July 1995, transcript, UJA-FNYC, I-433, AJHS, 9–12; and DF to Edith Levine, 18 October 1966, RG 1–240–5, LF to DF, 21 February, and LF to DF, 11 October 1967, RG 1–248–43, LJTS. See also, DF, oral history interview by Nicki Tanner, 13 February 1990, transcript, UJA-FNYC, I-433, AJHS, 22–25. JU was soon appointed to the JM's board, "Jewish Museum names new Board member," publicity release, 6 December 1966, RG 11–44–13, LJTS.

    The exhibition catalogue was published as *Masada and the Finds from the Bar-Kokhba Caves: Struggle for Freedom*, exhibition coordination by JU (New York: Jewish Museum, 1967). Other exhibit venues were Field Museum of Natural History, Chicago; Dallas Museum of Fine Arts; Detroit Institute of Arts; Museum of the Philadelphia Civic Center; and De Young Memorial Museum, San Francisco. For three exhibit previews by the same author, see Sanka Knox, "Museum to Show Siege of Masada," *New York Times*, 5 June 1967; Knox, "A.D. 72 Revolt Against Rome Restaged in Miniature Show," *New York Times*, 2 October 1967; and Knox, "Masada Display on View Tomorrow," *New York Times*, 11 October 1967. For a thorough description, see David Holmstrom, "The Siege of Masada Retold," *Christian Science Monitor*, 14 October 1967. For the concluding quote, see John Canaday, "Archaeology as Adventure," *New York Times*, 12 November 1967.

23. "The Jewish Museum," Report to Board of Overseers, April 1968, RG 21–6–7, LJTS. *Holocaust Encyclopedia*, United States Holocaust Memorial Museum, s.v. "Warsaw Ghetto Uprising," accessed June 2020, https://en-

cyclopedia.ushmm.org/content/en/article/warsaw-ghetto-uprising. See also, Irving Werstein, *The Uprising of the Warsaw Ghetto, November 1940–May 1943* (New York: W. W. Norton, 1968); and Israel Gutman, *Resistance: The Warsaw Ghetto Uprising* (Boston, MA: Houghton Mifflin, 1994). LF, "Masada and Its Heroes," in *Masada and the Finds from the Bar-Kokhba Caves*, 13, 15. "Eternal Light TV Hanukah Program on Masada Sunday," *Jewish Advocate,* 21 December 1967. [Editorial], "The Jewish Museum's 'Masada,'" *Jewish Advocate*, 28 December 1967. *Encyclopaedia Judaica*, 2nd edn. (2007), s.v. "Six-Day War," by Chaim Herzog. See also, Guy Laron, *The Six-Day War: The Breaking of the Middle East* (New Haven, CT: Yale University Press, 2017). JU, oral history interview by Judy E. Tenney, 19 December 1989, transcript, UJA-FNYC, I-433, AJHS, 44.

24. On the natural history museum comparison and SH's performance, see DF, oral history interview by Nicki Tanner, 13 February 1990, transcript, UJA-FNYC, I-433, AJHS, 25–26. For the boycott quote, see AK, oral history interview by Nicki Tanner, 24 July 1990, transcript, UJA-FNYC, I-433, AJHS, 24. On financial problems, see Corrected meeting minutes, Executive Committee, JM, 24 August 1967, RG 25–2–39, LJTS and Kynaston McShine, oral history interview by Carolyn Lanchner (oral history compiled by David Frankel), 1 April 2010–13 January 2011, transcript, Oral History Program, Museum of Modern Art, 24. On SH's tenure, see LF to VL, 26 September and 11 October 1967, RG 1–250–55, DF to KK, 9 October 1967, RG 1–248–43, LJTS. Milton Esterow, "Director of Jewish Museum Quits in Policy Rift," *New York Times*, 25 October 1967. Another factor in SH's decision may have been health problems. DF mentions a heart attack prior to SH's resignation; see p. 26 of his oral history cited above in this note; see also, DF to Herbert Poster, 4 December 1967, AF, Box 1, JMA. SH went to Princeton University, where he was a faculty member and adjunct curator at its art museum; see cites in note 2 above.
25. John A. Talbott to LF, 11 November, LF to John A. Talbott, 17 November 1967, RG 1–248–43, LJTS. Abram Kanof to LF, 27 October 1967, RG 1–259–14, LJTS. See also, Abram Kanof, oral history interview by Judy Tenney, 19 November 1990 and 26 May 1992, transcript, UJA-FNYC, I-433, AJHS, 23–25, 44–45. On cutting the Judaica budget to cover avant-garde program deficits, see also, Tom L. Freudenheim to LF, 30 December 1965, AF, Box 3, JMA. Arthur A. Cohen, "The Jewish Museum: Victim of Confusion," *Congress Bi-Weekly: A Journal of Opinion and Jewish Affairs* 34, no. 15 (20 November 1967): 7–8. Concerning *The Hebrew Bible* exhibit, see chapter 4. For responses to Cohen, see DF, SH, et alia, "The Function of the Jewish Museum: An Exchange," *Congress Bi-Weekly: A Journal of Opinion and Jewish Affairs* 34, no. 17 (18 December 1967): 2, 21–22. See also, DF to Herbert Poster [editor of the *Congress Bi-Weekly*], 4 December 1967, AF, Box 1, JMA; and MS, "On AA Cohen, (on Jewish Museum)" [ca. December 1967], MSC 137:15, CUL. MS served as a paid consultant for the JM between May 1963 and SH's appointment, when MS resigned the consultancy

and became a JM board member; MS to LF, 5 May 1963, MSC 127: 2, CUL; MS to LF, 19 and 29 April 1965, and LF to MS, 20 and 22 April 1965, RG 1–235–47, LJTS.

26. AK, "Jewish Museum," 282–98. See also, AK, oral history interview by Nicki Tanner, 24 July 1990, transcript, UJA-FNYC, I-433, AJHS, 20–23, 25. Alvin Toffler, *The Culture Consumers: A Study of Art and Affluence in America* (New York: St. Martin's Press, 1964), 34–35, 51–52. For responses to AK, see "Communications," *Judaism* 18, no. 1 (Winter 1969): 103–8. One response was written by SSK but sent by a mentee over the latter's signature; William M. Kramer, "Stephen S. Kayser in Los Angeles: A Personal Memoir," in *Crown for a King: Studies in Jewish Art, History and Archaeology in Memory of Stephen S. Kayser*, ed. Shalom Sabar, Steven Fine, and William M. Kramer (Jerusalem and New York: Gefen Publishing House, 2000), 26.

Chapter 7

The *Jewish* Jewish Museum

The *Lower East Side* and *Masada* exhibitions modeled ways to attract that portion of the Jewish community longing for more engaging shows on Jewish topics. Yet pursuit of similar exhibits was not easy. One impediment was the social history content of those types of projects which ran counter to the museum's identity as an art institution. Meanwhile the avant-garde exhibitions' rising costs in the late 1960s exacerbated tensions when budgets were balanced at the expense of Judaica collection displays and care. Despite the museum's inability to resolve this conflict, it continued tinkering with what types of Judaica exhibits would appeal to Jews on the one hand while probing the boundaries of contemporary art on the other. Alternating between the different kinds of exhibits, or showing them simultaneously, could be dizzying as the museum made "no stops . . . on the express between the antique and pop art, between Persian synagogues and plastic hot dogs." The experimentation endured until deficits at the museum grew so high and patience at the seminary so thin that the museum was all but closed and its mission reset to "all-Jewish" programming. The shift coincided with Finkelstein's retirement, the winding down of his outreach programs, changes in the Jewish community, and a shift in New York's art world as nearby institutions stepped up their avant-garde exhibits rendering those of the museum superfluous.[1]

The Soul Museum

The board commenced its search for Hunter's replacement in 1967 and Karl Katz (Figure 7.1), who was among the candidates before Hunter got the nod, rose to the top. Katz (1929–2017) earned his undergraduate and master's degrees at Columbia University, focusing on art history, archaeology, and Semitic studies. Under Schapiro's mentorship, he nearly completed a doctorate there with a dissertation on Hebrew

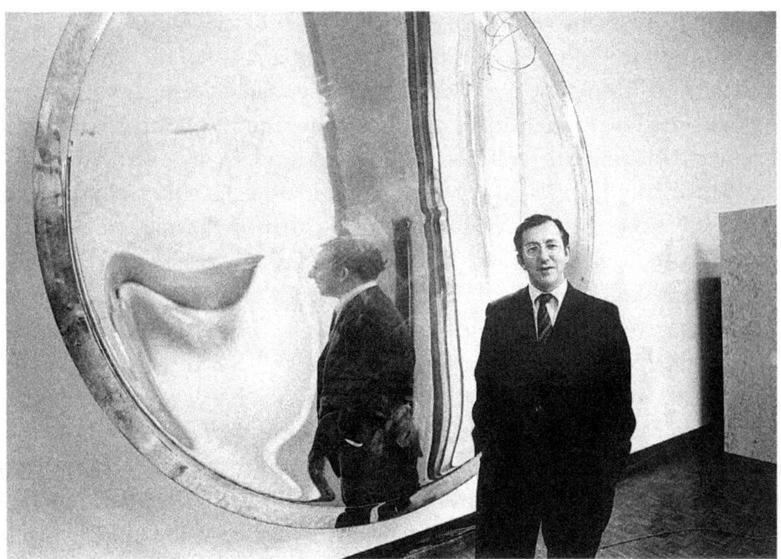

Figure 7.1. Karl Katz, in *Pond* exhibit installation, October 1968. Photograph by Michael Evans. © *New York Times*/Redux.

manuscripts from Yemen, before going into museum work. Katz served in the Metropolitan Museum of Art's education department and then pursued archaeology in Israel, becoming a curator of the Israel Museum's predecessor. He helped lead its expansion into today's institution, rising to chief curator of Judaica, fine arts, and sculpture—including modern art—in the process. Seasoned, idealistic, and ambitious, Katz was the personification of a modern museum professional. He was also as familiar with prominent Jewish opinion leaders and philanthropists—secular and religious, American and Israeli—as he was with the predominant social and cultural issues in contemporary Jewish life. Ebullient and something of a bon vivant, Katz was a persuasive advocate as well, evident in his successful fundraising and board member recruitment in the Jewish community. He longed to return to New York and had remained in touch with Schapiro, Finkelstein, and Finn after Hunter's appointment; and he began campaigning for the directorship after word of Hunter's difficulties got out. Finn was especially interested in Katz because the latter was so experienced with fundraising, Judaica, and comfortable with the seminary—perhaps because Katz attended a yeshiva (a Jewish religious school) in his youth.[2]

But Katz's recruitment was clouded by renewed debates over the Jewish Museum's priorities, List and Kanof being the fiercest combatants, she advocating the avant-garde program, he the Judaica. Finkelstein sought common ground and encouraged a seminary colleague to draft "A Statement of Principles" for their collective consideration. It emphasized the museum's Jewish identity as a seminary unit and its custodial responsibilities for the Judaica. Yet it also recognized modern art, including works "not identifiably Jewish," as representing human values Judaism strives to cultivate. Neither List nor Kanof was persuaded by the statement, or another prepared by Katz. Kanof, annoyed by the impasse, voted "no" on a recommendation to hire Katz. Though he considered Katz to be qualified, Kanof believed they were setting Katz up for failure. It was high time, Kanof argued, for the board to decide once and for all between Judaica and modern art. He would accept either a "Jewish Jewish Museum or a first-class Museum of Modern Art," though he preferred the former, believing there were already plenty of excellent art museums. A decision not to decide resulted. Katz interpreted the outcome differently, however, and thought the museum's next iteration could be a "symbiosis" of its founding purposes and the avant-garde. Those backing his candidacy believed that with his background in archaeology, Judaica, and modern art, Katz was ideally suited to set the museum right and he was offered the post. But in learning of the museum's governance and financial problems during his interviews, Katz cautioned the board that it and he both were taking risks and sought assurances of the board's and seminary's wholehearted backing. They were duly supplied, and Katz accepted the directorship to start in September 1968.[3]

He was welcomed to New York in fall 1968 with interviews by art critics and others curious about his museum plans. He promised "a balancing act," honoring its Judaica commitment while assuring the avant-garde program would continue. That meant keeping "one foot in the third millennium B.C. and the other in 1969." Katz planned to revamp the Judaica collection's display, expanding its historical depth and material breadth from what had been three hundred years of ritual objects, to a survey reaching back several millennia illustrated with archaeological finds, other artifacts, and dioramas. What had formerly been arranged like "European decorative arts" would now represent the sweep of Jewish history "from the patriarchs to the present," across the Middle East, Europe, and America, in a "story-telling way." As for temporary exhibits, Katz's conception of the avant-garde program resembled his predecessors', but his vision for Jewish programming embraced Judaica and sociocultural history as well as exhibits on challenging topics such as "anti-Semitism in art." To avoid the sentimentality and romanticism of *The Lower East Side* or *Masada*, moreover, Katz turned to "conscience" as a basis for rethinking Judaism's visual culture. The museum would now explore the interanimations of Jewish cultural history and social conscience, especially in the modern era. The America to which Katz returned had experienced several years of civil rights marches, the assassinations of Martin Luther King Jr. and Robert F. Kennedy, uprisings in urban centers, and Vietnam War protests. Conscience for Katz meant having the museum become an agent of social change, a stance being discussed among other museum professionals in response to a sense of deepening crisis and despair in America.[4]

Katz's first two exhibitions were *Ingathering: Ceremony and Tradition in New York Public Collections*, predominantly a Judaica loan exhibition, and *Pond* an immersive, multimedia installation project. Each occupied an entire floor of the List Building, *Ingathering* on the first floor, *Pond* on the second. *Ingathering* drew on the collections of twenty-three New York institutions, including the Metropolitan Museum of Art, the Brooklyn Museum, the Pierpont Morgan Library, the American Numismatic Society, and several synagogues, to reify Katz's goal of showing the temporal and geographical reach of Jewish history. The exhibition, which featured nearly 250 works from the lending institutions and twenty-five from the Jewish Museum, was divided into ten sections, from "The Period of Judges, Kings and Prophets, 1200 to 586 B.C.E." to "New York City, 1654–1860." The contents ranged from ancient vessels and coins, to medieval and early Renaissance texts, to ritual objects from the sixteenth through the nineteenth centuries. The New York section was the most varied, containing portraits, synagogue records such as a minute book and cantorial contract, and city plans showing congregations' locations. *Ingathering* arose from Katz's hunch that most of New York's major museums had some Judaica in their collections, his guess based on seeing isolated Jewish objects scattered among museums in America and abroad. Katz likened the phenomenon to the diaspora: "For a Jew, these poignant remnants, stranded among the treasures of alien cultures, are . . . reminiscent of the fate of his own people." *Ingathering* reassembled these artifacts of Judaism's "dispersed culture," echoing the Jewish people's survival by congregating in the diaspora and proving, Katz hoped, that exhibits of such material need not be "gloomy."[5]

Katz commissioned Robert Whitman to create *Pond*. Whitman (b. 1935) studied literature at Rutgers and then art history at Columbia University before turning his energies to creating innovative mixed-media works. He achieved prominence among a handful of artists mounting performance works in lower Manhattan's lofts, leading to his association with the "Happenings Movement" of the late 1950s and early 1960s. Whitman pioneered the incorporation of film footage in such works as well as audio recordings, slides, and live actors in the sometimes elaborate environments he constructed. These techniques were utilized in *Pond*'s creation. In a darkened gallery, he employed shapes of reflective film (Figure 7.1) to create a "warped hall of mirrors" that trembled with electronic sounds and recorded voices; and that flashed with projected images and strobe lights—an "electronic fantasy." One critic, comparing Whitman to "an organist waxing eloquent in some grand cathedral," believed *Pond* was the best installation of its kind yet done. Katz wanted the juxtaposition of *Ingathering* with *Pond* to exemplify his approach to balancing the museum's Judaic and avant-garde programs. He hoped that the two dramatically different exhibits would not only attract two dissimilar audiences, but also pleasantly surprise and engage visitors who came for one and then saw the other. The "cross-pollination" worked, Katz felt, *Ingathering* being "very satisfying to the traditionalists" and when they saw *Pond* "they just [got] turned on"; and when "the contemporary art crowd," attracted by *Pond*, saw *Ingathering* it thought "gee whiz, it's really fascinating" and acquired a "new regard for Jewish culture."[6]

Katz aimed for similar juxtapositions in the future, but that did not quite happen, as he dealt with the vagaries of exhibit scheduling and funding. He compensated by pursuing exhibits on current topics to engage the Jewish community, the contemporary art world, and the wider public, such as *Up Against the Wall*. It opened in December 1968 with nearly one hundred posters, reproductions of graffiti, enlarged photographs, street-sound recordings, and documentary film footage, mainly from the May 1968 student protests in France (Figure 7.2). Sparked by university policies and overcrowding, the protests were joined by French workers and others as demands widened to encompass economic, political, and antiwar issues across France. Most of the posters were created in art schools' print-making studios commandeered by protesters. Katz staged the show as if "a Parisian street scene" with posters crowding gallery walls and recordings of the city's protests playing in the background. Katz went to France to collect posters, record protests, and recruit a "resident revolutionary," a French art student from one of the studios, to advise on the installation and answer visitors' questions. The French materials were supplemented with over twenty posters from Prague student protests in August 1968 against the Soviet-bloc invasion crushing Czechoslovakia's "Prague Spring" democratization. The museum board initially objected to the exhibit over aesthetic concerns—the posters' lack of "style," mediocre drawing, and "haphazard" typography. Katz countered that because Jews were always "at the forefront of liberal movements" and had participated in the civil rights and antiwar protests of the 1960s, the posters were

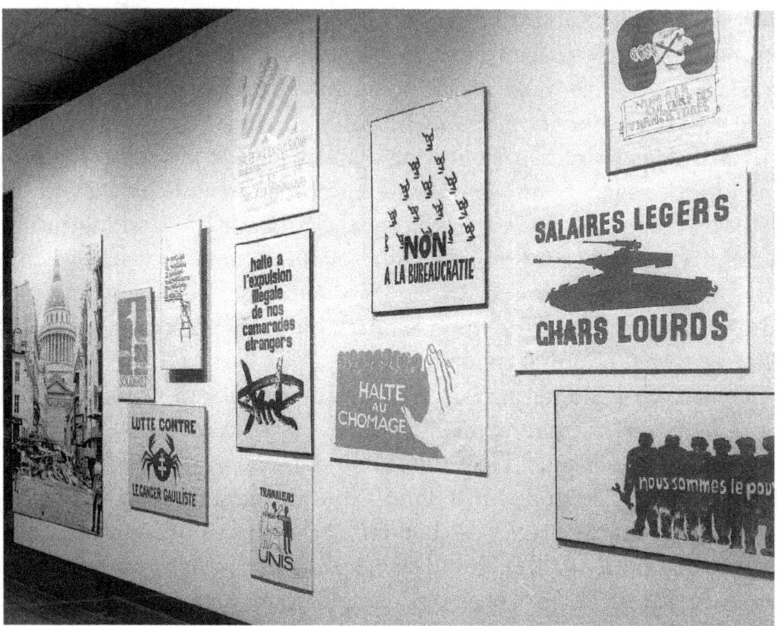

Figure 7.2. Installation view, *Up Against the Wall*, ca. December 1968. The Jewish Museum, New York/Art Resource, NY.

indeed appropriate. What better way, he asked, to affirm Jewish values than to exhibit works conveying "A cry of the students"? The show's attendance was good and critics' responses favorable, one critic observing that the posters' "offhandedness" was more authentic than if they were aesthetically refined. During an interview on *Up Against the Wall*, an enthusiastic seminary official called its host "a Soul Museum," endorsing Katz's emphasis on social conscience as a guiding principle.[7]

Pushing Boundaries: Ethical, Social, Financial

The board's misgivings about *Up Against the Wall* reflected a more general disquiet about Katz's judgment that emerged not long after Katz's arrival. Familiar complaints about the avant-garde shows and the audiences they attracted played a part. So too did Katz's appointment of an "Italian Catholic" woman as the museum's administrative head instead of holding out for a qualified Jew. Then there was an archaeological exhibit, *Riches of Glorious Kingdoms: Precious Objects of Persia*, which Katz presented to put the Jewish holiday of Purim—rooted in the biblical Book of Esther—in historical context. Objecting to his interpretation of the holiday, board members thought "Persia meant Islamic, and ours was a *Jewish* museum." Katz also wanted to open the museum on Saturdays for the first time, despite the day's sanctity as the Jewish Sabbath, because most other museums' attendance was then. Following a policy he helped craft at the Israel Museum, he suggested the Jewish Museum open free of charge, with the sales desk closed, to avoid desecrating the Sabbath by handling money. The admission and guard staff were not Jewish, so no Jews would be compelled to work, and the proposed hours of noon to 5:00 p.m. would minimize conflicts for Jews attending Sabbath morning prayers. His proposal "hit a solid wall of no" at the seminary.[8]

Finances were also an irritant. His exhibitions began running deficits from the start of his tenure, mainly because, as Katz admitted, budgeting was not his "strong suit." He did hold fundraisers, urge more board contributions, and court individual donors. But the nation began sliding into a major recession in 1969 and economic headwinds undercut the museum's outside funding. To help fill the gap, Finn, through his public relations firm, Ruder & Finn, began bringing corporation-sponsored exhibits to the museum. Starting in the 1950s, the firm had urged businesses to cultivate "goodwill" by underwriting art museums' exhibitions. One of its clients was the Mead Corporation, a top producer of paper and packaging goods. Finn steered an international touring exhibit backed by Mead, *European Painters Today*, to the museum for its winter 1969 season. A critic noticed the cozy relationship between Finn, as the museum's board chair, his firm, and its client, but excused it as helping offset museums' insular shows of American art with a survey of European developments. Katz celebrated Mead's sponsorship exclaiming that if the flow of corporations' "big money" continues, "there is no limit to what we can do." The issue came up again, less than a year later, with *A Plastic Presence* (Figure 7.3), sponsored by another of Ruder & Finn's clients, Philip Morris, then the nation's leading cigarette producer. The entanglement of Finn, his firm, and his client in the exhibit was pointedly questioned this time, compelling Katz and Finn to publicly defend the arrangement. The exhibit, which surveyed contemporary artists' experiments in the comparatively new medium of plastics, was found by critics to be "esthetically uneven." But it received more unwelcome attention outside the art world via the mass-circulation monthly *Reader's Digest*. For its "Laughter, the Best Medicine" column, a reader wrote of visiting the exhibit where he "was standing before a large blob of plastic. Two Jewish matrons came up. After a moment of silence, one turned to the other and said in a distressed tone, 'That's Jewish?'"[9]

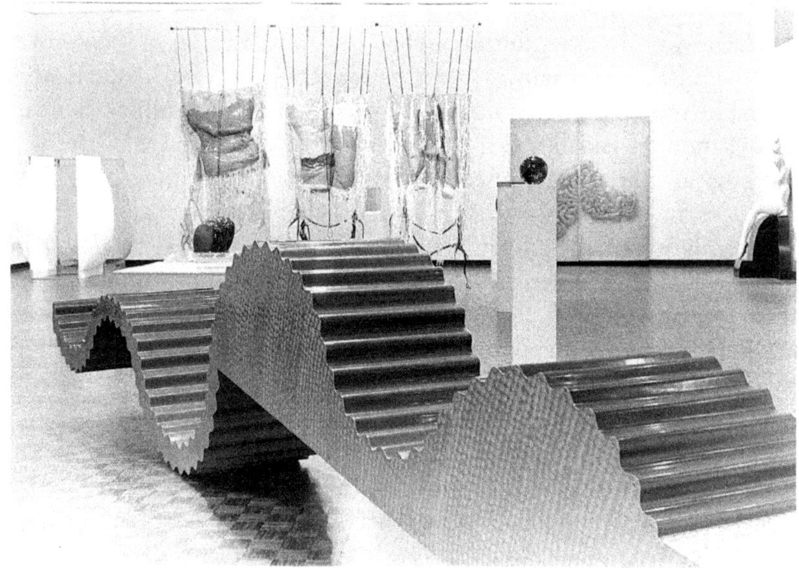

Figure 7.3. Installation view, *A Plastic Presence*, ca. November 1969. The Jewish Museum, New York/Art Resource, NY.

Over the course of 1969 and 1970, Katz hoped to rejuvenate the museum's Judaica collection, then numbering over ten thousand objects, which was in "dire straits." While displays had occasionally been refreshed, the storage facilities reflected decades of haphazard accumulation and neglect. Upgrading both would be costly, however, and board members considered selling "2nd or 3rd rate items or duplications of 1st rate items." Instead, Katz pursued a New York State Council on the Arts grant to fund the collection's reinstallation and care. He proposed showing the objects as integral to Jewish worship in home and synagogue, which entailed expanding the permanent collection's gallery space with displays of ritual objects in relation to Sabbath and holiday uses; life cycle events such as marriage, circumcision, and burial; and Torah reading—together a throwback to Kayser's methods. Katz's installations, however, would be contextualized with "textual material, documents, blow-ups, slides, engravings" and visitors would be assisted with interpretive booklets or "Teleguide [audio/visual] systems." The proposed changes were intended for two audiences: the "knowledgeable viewer" wanting to see more of the collection; and "the Jewishly uneducated, both Jew and non-Jew." As if to endorse Katz's aims, a reviewer for a Lutheran magazine wrote that the museum's emphasis at the time seemed "more artistic than historic. Those of us who know little . . . of these artifacts would . . . like to see more printed historical matter in the displays."[10]

Though Katz was attentive to the permanent collection's display, when it came to addressing Jewish topics he preferred broader explorations including modern Israeli culture. Drawing on his knowledge of the still-young nation, he programmed a major photographic survey of the six decades from Israel's roots in Zionist settlements of the early 1900s to the aftermath of the Six-Day War. The exhibit, *Israel/The Reality*, contained over three hundred black-and-white photographs, most enlarged on panels, by over forty photographers about two-thirds of whom were Israeli. It opened in September 1969 and occupied all three floors of the List addition, the photographs comprising a wide array of subjects. There were images of shipboard immigrants, children exercising, a young woman paratrooper, soldiers during and after the Six-Day War, a kibbutz wedding, a mother nursing, famous personages, a kibbutznik shouldering irrigation pipes into what was once desert, and vivid landscapes. Reviews of *Israel/The Reality* were laudatory and it drew large crowds, the visitors' responses being "one of homage. . . . People come with their families and . . . stand absorbed for minutes at a time" before the photographs. The exhibit was so popular it was presented again nearly two years later.[11]

Perhaps because of *Israel/The Reality*'s success, Katz believed he had sufficient credibility within the Jewish community to pour even more resources into avant-garde exhibits. Their critical praise "went straight to my head," Katz later admitted, "and with every successful show, I wanted to do even bigger, better projects." Nearby art-world rivals such as the Guggenheim Museum, the Whitney Museum of American Art, and the Metropolitan Museum of Art were another motivation. He said it was difficult "to be fiscally conservative when your neighbors were world-class institutions, and spending accordingly. . . . I wanted the Jewish Museum to compete." Driven, Katz pushed ahead with daring shows, eye-catching catalogues, and lavish openings bound to attract media coverage. The museum's avant-garde exhibits from the summer of 1969 through the fall of 1970 were increasingly costly, provocative, or both, the most noteworthy of which were *Inflatable Sculpture*, *Using Walls*, and *Software*.

Inflatable Sculpture consisted of sculptural works made of rubber, translucent polyethylene, or "crystalline vinyl" inflated with air or—for some floating pieces—helium (Figure 7.4). The show featured works by six artists who employed a range of low- to high-tech devices for inflating their pieces, from fans to electronically operated "air jets." *Inflatable Sculpture* was inspired partly by the technologies of space exploration—the first moon landing was in late July 1969, just a few weeks after the

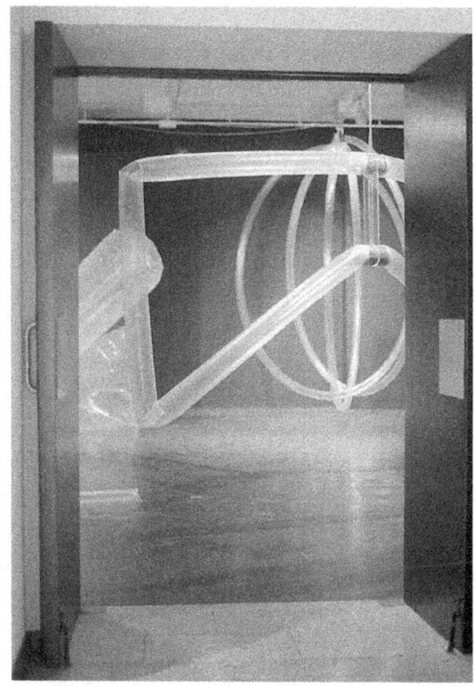

Figure 7.4. Installation view, *Inflatable Sculpture*, ca. July 1969. Photograph by Charles Frazier. The Jewish Museum, New York/Art Resource, NY.

opening—and the ephemeral nature of the disposable materials. Reviewers saw the show differently, however, one describing it as the "summer's sexiest show," hinting at two characteristics of the works: their "tactile skin-like quality" and their "ability to change shape." One installation contained a "Rabelaisian duo of male and female organs. The giant-size phallus goes through stages of tumescence and de-tumescence and the female orifice quivers." Another's similar erection would occasionally "bop the unsuspecting viewer on the head." But most of the pieces evinced a fragility that prompted a critic to wonder if *Inflatable Sculpture* would last the summer. One work did burn in a small fire that began in Katz's office, attributed to a window air conditioner's short circuit.[12]

Using Walls, a two-part exhibit, was organized by Susan Tumarkin Goodman, an assistant curator at the museum since 1967, to survey aspects of contemporary wall art. One part, *Using Walls (Indoors)*, consisted of conceptual and process-oriented works created directly on the museum's interior walls; the other, *Using Walls (Outdoors)*, consisted of public-art projects on New York building exteriors intended to bring "a refreshing, rejuvenating new visual interest" to the city's "grimy corners." For the first, fourteen walls were allocated to fifteen artists—two in collaboration—to create works thereon; the second, displayed in a darkened room, contained light boxes and color-slide projections showing the outdoor works in context. The artists of *Using Walls (Indoors)* altered their designated surfaces with paint, charcoal, pencil, adhesive tape, or fresco treatment; draped acrylic sheets or pasted paper sheets; or they chiseled away the wall plaster to reveal the substrate beneath. The museum was uniquely able to allow its use as "an alternative space," the invasive alterations not posing the type of conflict between "the radical and the establishment" it would at institutions such as the Museum of Modern Art or the Whitney Museum of American Art.[13]

Using Walls was overshadowed, however, by New York's art-world protests against the Vietnam War. They were preceded by demonstrations in the late 1960s but intensified in spring 1970 after America expanded the conflict into Cambodia. On 4 May 1970, the Ohio National Guard shot thirteen student protesters and bystanders on the Kent State University campus, killing four, and demonstrations erupted across the nation. In New York, in solidarity, artists exhibiting in the city's museums and galleries requested that their shows be closed for two weeks, including those in *Using Walls*. Katz not only complied, he also spoke at a public forum organized by artists and New York art-institution employees to oppose the war, economic inequality, and racial and gender discrimination. He declared that museums should do their part by raising social consciousness, his admonition coming at the very moment some museums, including the Metropolitan Museum of Art and the Museum of Modern Art, were targeted by protesters. The Jewish Museum avoided that plight, according to Katz, because he spoke with anyone he could: demonstrators in the street, "student revolutionaries" at Columbia University, editors of the *Evergreen Review*, a countercultural journal. Word of his efforts alongside the museum's avant-garde history, Katz believed, insulated it from conflicts at other institutions. "In the protesters' eyes," he claimed, "the Metropolitan and MoMA were full of stuffed shirts, but the Jewish Museum was . . . their liberal darling." Yet the museum did not entirely escape the activists' scrutiny. Among them were young Jews who attacked what they perceived as Jewish organizations' neglect of their community's needs. Those views were captured in a cartoon that singled out several institutions including the Jewish Museum, the latter for cramming "Jewish art into the basement" and showing instead "'modern art' [and] 'in' things like that" (Figure 7.5). Katz was more bothered, however, by protests over museums' reliance on trustees and corporate backers profiting from the

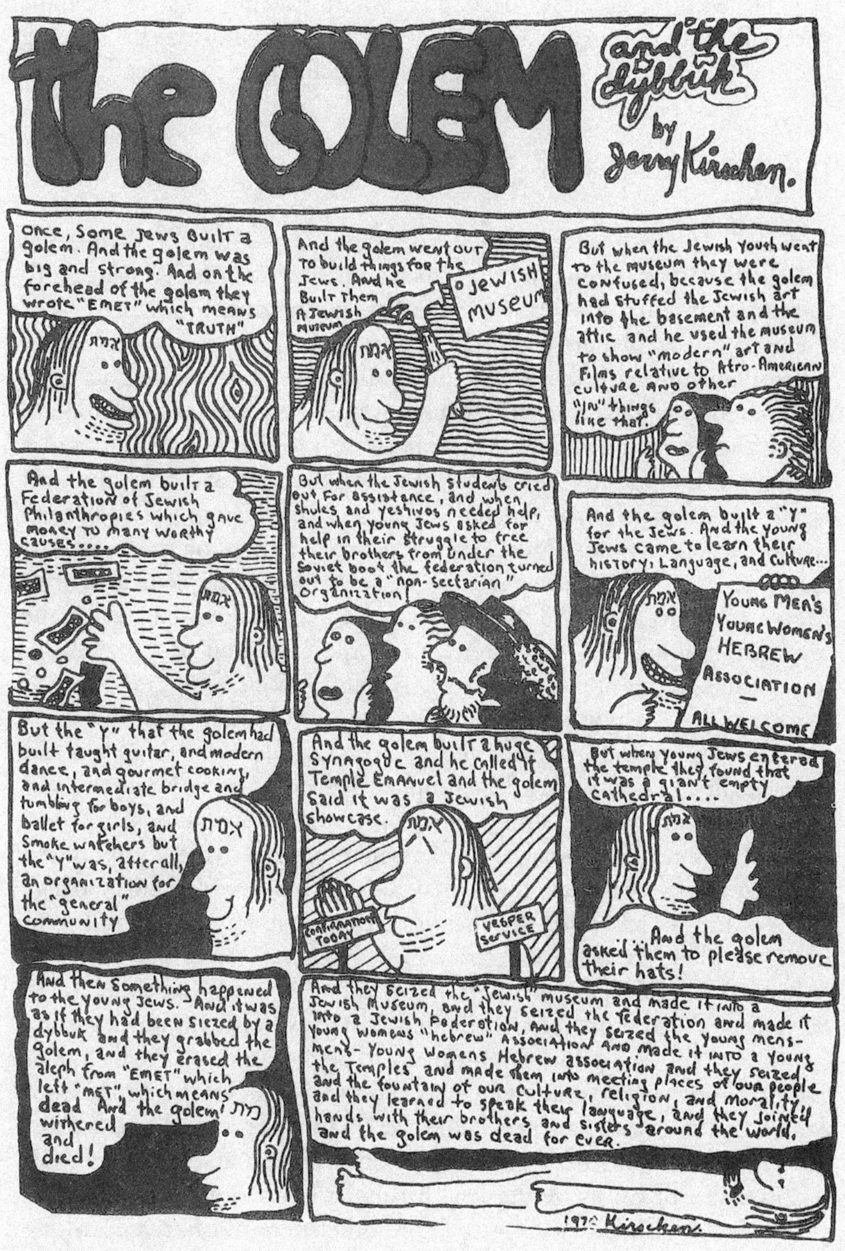

Figure 7.5. "the Golem and the dybbuk," ca. April 1970, by Jerry Kirschen, later published in *Ayin l'tzion* (עין לציון) 6, nos. 2–3 (December 1972–January 1973): 13. Courtesy of Yaakov (Jerry) Kirschen.

war. He was not about to decline corporate backing "just to earn the goodwill of some angry young artists." Katz had to prioritize his funding because he had little choice. A deficit was forcing him to cut staff.[14]

Denouement

Arthur T. Jacobs, the seminary's executive vice president and museum liaison then, was alarmed by the deficit's threat to seminary finances. To impress upon Finn, Finkelstein, and others the gravity of the situation, in August 1970 Jacobs presented alternatives for getting the budget under control including: "Liquidation," "Closing the Museum and using it as a warehouse," "Keeping the Museum open, with a Judaica program only," and "Keeping the Museum open, with a Judaica program and a minimal contemporary program." Each would come at a cost, the least expensive of which was the Judaica/"minimal contemporary" alternative because the avant-garde exhibits generated most of the museum's income. After Jacobs's presentation, he, Finn, and Katz consulted with Meyer Schapiro and the Lists. Schapiro adamantly opposed closing the museum, arguing that the seminary was the custodian of a major collection and responsible for assuring its public access. The group agreed to a "minimal" exhibit scheme emphasizing Jewish and Israeli themes, a more robust fundraising plan, and sale of the museum's "duplicate and poor quality Judaica." Vera List dropped her avant-garde advocacy and endorsed an immediate exhibit series on Jewish contributions to "western civilization." Her shift was an expression of underlying loyalty to the museum come what may, but it may also have been eased by a change in New York's art world: the "death of the avant-garde." According to Irving Sandler, art critic and chronicler of postwar American art, "Not only did Modernism end in 1970, but so did the New York School . . . as *the* fountainhead of major art." Despite List's insistence on quick action, however, there were prior commitments to be met. Katz received a major grant from the New York State Council on the Arts—its largest museum grant to date—based on specified requests. Some fit with the new plans such as refurbishment of Judaica collections display and storage as well as an exhibit of works by the Jewish Russian-born American photographer Roman Vishniac (1897–1990). Another item did not, a year-long "Center for Decentralized Television," an installation of "closed-circuit television" shows of young, New York state filmmakers' works. Katz had also scheduled a corporate-sponsored exhibition on computers and art that was well along and way over budget.[15]

Software—Information Technology: Its New Meaning for Art was organized by a guest curator, Jack Burnham (1931–2019), then a Northwestern University professor and rising theorist on the interanimations of art and technology. American Motors Corporation, once a major automobile manufacturer, sponsored the exhibition at Finn's behest with Ruder & Finn acting as the intermediary. *Software* filled all three floors of the List addition with a variety of computer and other electronic equipment, some interactive or utilized in installations, the works created by twenty-one artists and collectives. Prior to opening, the exhibit was publicized in an industry newsletter noting a special effort to assure the equipment avoided breakdowns that had plagued other computer exhibits. Technical problems did occur, however, and when *Software* opened in September 1970, "'Temporarily Out of Order' was the operative phrase." Reviewers thought it was not so much an art exhibit as "a confusing, capricious and sometimes fascinating" display reminiscent of "futuristic exhibits in old World's Fairs and museums of science and industry." All that suited Burnham, who opposed differentiating between art and non-art. More troublesome were censorship allegations over works Katz threatened to pull: a short film quoting Chinese Communist leader Mao Tse-Tung; "Radio Free Poetry," a hyperlocal broadcast—visitors could hear on transistor radios—of recordings by leading poets, artists, and others including African American activist Eldridge Cleaver (1935–98), who had recently been accused of anti-Zionist remarks; and "A.I.R." (Artist-In-Residence), by the pioneering video and new-media artist Les Levine (b. 1935) that featured continuous-loop TV video recordings of him working, eating, reading, and enjoying several minutes of sexual intercourse. After briefly battling the artists, Katz relented, and the works were presented mostly as intended. But he realized the show may have been too transgressive, "even for the cutting-edge Jewish Museum."[16]

His fears were soon confirmed. While giving Finkelstein and the Smithsonian's director of museums a preview of *Software*, Katz led them past Levine's videos just as a scene of "the artist in his studio, stark naked—with two beautiful women" was running. Finkelstein stormed out saying, "Mr. Katz, . . . this is the end." Soon after, Rabbi Samuel Dresner—who six years prior complained about the avant-garde exhibits—read about the *Software* censorship disputes and resumed his campaign against the program, this time appealing to United Synagogue and Rabbinical Assembly leaders to file a complaint on behalf of Conservative Judaism's faithful. Finkelstein reported the matter to Finn and Albert List just as the two, as seminary trustees, were coping with the museum's out-of-control budget. The trustees issued an ultimatum to the museum's board:

unless it took full fiscal responsibility for the museum, it must immediately become "basically Jewish." Finn at first opposed the demand arguing that Finkelstein's intergroup programs "were not self-paying in any way; were not necessarily Jewish. The Institute of Religious and Social Studies was the only school that taught priests and ministers as well as rabbis. . . . The Jewish Museum was consistent with that tradition." Finn relented, however, and the museum's board members, unable to fund the museum on their own and having already pledged themselves to a similar policy, backed the museum's turn to "all-Jewish" programming.[17]

Software was Katz's "undoing." He resigned effective February 1971, and news of his departure ignited yet another public debate over the museum's future. The coming changes were due to finances, Finn explained, adding that despite the avant-garde program's popularity and critical approval, it was not fiscally viable. He admitted the new all-Jewish policy was "ideological," but claimed it would not limit the museum to "parochial concerns." A Jewish-community paper applauded the change but editorialized it is "easier said than done." Anticipating future exhibits and fearing the adoption of simplistic definitions of relevance, the editors cautioned "kitsch by artists of Jewish descent is not 'Jewish art.'" Arthur A. Cohen, in his essay "Museum or Mausoleum?," doubted it would be less financially burdensome to mount professional, "*effectively* Jewish" exhibits and added that when avant-garde shows ran over budget, nervous backers overlooked the actual problem: museums are costly no matter what they show. To shortchange future Judaica exhibits, he declared, would be to "convert the Jewish Museum into a mausoleum." Meanwhile, hiring Katz's replacement was postponed until the museum's finances were in order. Finkelstein opted for interim management headed by the museum's administrative assistant and a seminary official. Confronted by the seminary's desperate finances and his faculty's opposition to further museum support, Finkelstein feared its closure was a distinct possibility. He appealed to board members for support with only mixed results, the largest gift coming from Vera List, and for nearly two years the museum limped along with a skeletal staff and modest exhibit schedule. The contrast between the museum's tumultuous avant-garde heyday and the tranquility of its all-Jewish turn was so great, some assumed the museum *had* closed. The conclusion of its avant-garde era was sealed with the donation of its art library's "modern portion" to the Guggenheim Museum.[18]

All this coincided with Finkelstein's retirement. Finkelstein was succeeded by Gerson D. Cohen (1924–91), a brilliant and charismatic scholar who received his rabbinic ordination at the seminary and then earned a doctorate in Semitic languages at Columbia University. While Cohen shared aspects of Finkelstein's vision, he shifted the seminary's priorities in ways that reinforced the museum's changes and reflected sociocultural trends affecting both institutions. Cohen preserved some of Finkelstein's outreach efforts, such as the media broadcasts, but devoted more attention to the seminary's constituencies and core mission. Where Finkelstein kept the United Synagogue and Rabbinical Assembly at an arm's length and strove to elevate the seminary above the denominational fray of American Judaism, Cohen repositioned the seminary as Conservative Judaism's "spiritual center." Where Finkelstein pursued intergroup relations across a broad array of institutional and programmatic forums, Cohen concentrated on boosting the seminary's stature in American higher education, initially by establishing curricular relationships with neighboring institutions. The context of these changes was Cohen's emphasis on streamlining the seminary's academic administration and revitalizing its undergraduate, rabbinic, and graduate programs. As Cohen's initiatives proceeded, he spent less and less time on the kinds of outreach to non-Jews and Jews of other denominations Finkelstein prioritized. That inward shift affected the museum as well. Without Finkelstein's backing, the museum had lost not only an indispensable link with a major Jewish institution, but also a thinker whose vision of American intergroup relations provided much of the avant-garde program's rationale. Over the subsequent decade, the museum's governance ties with the seminary were dissolved and it became financially independent, though it remains "under the auspices" of the seminary to this day.[19]

Cultural History, Ethnicity, and Jewish Experience

As the museum adjusted to an "all-Jewish" program, a tenet of its mission since its transformation in the 1940s—that it was an *art* museum—also became an issue. One of the museum's top Judaica donors, Daniel M. Friedenberg, asked for example, "Can a Jewish Museum Live by Art Alone?" Friedenberg (1923–2011) was a Jewish coins and medals collector who, like his father, Samuel, gave hundreds to the museum as well as caring for and writing about them as a part-time, volunteer curator. Having done so from Stephen Kayser's time through Katz's, Friedenberg had an insider's view of the museum's attempts to "ride two horses in tandem," Judaica and the avant-garde. He understood the reasoning behind the avant-garde program, but now that other museums were more actively showing contemporary art, it was time for one focused on Judaism. But Friedenberg was also uncomfortable with the museum's past approach and wondered if there was "enough esthetic material in the Jewish tradition" for a viable museum of Jewish art. Even at the Israel Museum, which by then had "the greatest collection of top-quality Judaica," its visual impact was "disappointing." Although "a Jewish Museum of History is possible," Friedenberg believed, "a Jewish Museum of Art" is not. To prosper, Friedenberg argued, the museum should concentrate "on the religious, economic, political, artistic, and scientific contributions of Jews." He concluded that the museum faced another stark choice: abandon the art emphasis in favor of a sociocultural approach and flourish, or stick with art and fail. A few months later, in December 1971, the museum received a major donation to—as though echoing Friedenberg's ideas—reestablish it as a "Museum of Jewish History and Culture." Joy Ungerleider, who enthusiastically agreed with that aim, was persuaded to serve as acting director during the interim, a step backed by the donors with another gift. By October 1972, she became the permanent director, and upon assuming the position Ungerleider parted with her predecessors who regarded it as "first and foremost, an art museum." Instead, she thought of it as "a history museum and an ethnic museum."[20]

Underlying her approach was growing popular interest in ethnic identity. As Katz left the museum, acknowledging its shift to "all-Jewish" exhibits, he noted that "Increasingly there is a need for ethnic show cases. This could be a great one." By "ethnic show cases," Katz meant museums serving specific ethnic groups, citing the Studio Museum of Harlem as an example. It was established in 1968 to collect and exhibit art by African Americans, artists in the African diaspora, and those from the African continent. The "Jewish" in Jewish Museum was also coming to be seen more as an ethnic than religious attribute, indicative of perceptions informed partly by studies on the interanimations of ethnicity and religion. In 1955, Will Herberg published his groundbreaking *Protestant, Catholic, Jew,* in which he reported a "new form of self-identification and social location" drawing into focus as "the ethnic group." The nomenclature of "ethnic" and "ethnicity" in relation to group identity soon became common in the scholarship of American social scientists and within a decade entered popular discourse. Museum board members also began thinking of Jewishness in those terms, some wanting to emphasize "ethnicity" because it "is so important a part of modern society." Given a widening interest in minority groups, they reasoned, the museum should—on behalf of Jews—model how "a minority culture can present itself" to society.[21]

The ramifications of this change for the museum's ritual objects collection were not clear, however. The elevation of ethnicity as an interpretive modality did not necessarily include religion. How, then, might the museum's Judaica holdings function within its new-found ethnic mission? One possibility resided in the era's workings of "symbolic ethnicity and symbolic religiosity" mapped by Herbert J. Gans. A sociologist of Jewish descent, Gans (b. 1927) started examining contemporary American Jewry while still a doctoral student in the 1950s. He approached it as essentially an ethnic group similar to other American ethnic groups, "but with a culture . . . in the anthropological sense—in which a distinctive religion has been dominant." Gans distinguished, however, between "two aspects of Jewish life, *Judaism* and *Jewishness*." "Judaism" for him possessed two components: "traditional" Judaism and "symbolic" Judaism. He considered traditional Judaism to be a "complex of sacred and secular, ceremonial and everyday codes and behavior patterns." By "Jewishness," Gans meant "one's sense of identity as a Jew, and . . . identification with other members of the Jewish community." The context of his observations was the transition from first-generation Jewish immigrants to a second generation, including the erosion of religious observance among the latter—the religiosity of the first generation became less meaningful for the second generation as it began pursuing markers of prestige valued by its non-Jewish neighbors: joining "country clubs (mostly Jewish)," becoming politically active, and acquiring "cultural capital." This process seeded a new "symbolic Judaism" that was still developing when Gans studied it.[22]

Yet, the second generation's assimilation into American society entailed a need "to assert or confirm [Jewishness], on secular as well as sacred occasions, in various material and non-material ways." For Gans, the forms of this kind of Jewishness became the currency of symbolic Judaism. He described it as symbolic because a major function is "to serve as a symbol for the *expression* of Jewishness." There are three forms: first, a "Jewish 'objects culture' that consists in the collecting and displaying of traditionally Jewish symbols and physical objects"; second, a "new 'Jewish popular culture' that 'Judaizes'" forms of entertainment and foodways; and third, a "problems culture" that expresses Jewishness "by defining cultural problems as moral issues." Within this context, the Jewish Museum could be seen as an institutionalization of symbolic Judaism. But Gans did not find religious identification and expression dissipating after the advent of symbolic Judaism, rather he perceived them evolving into a pair of phenomena: "symbolic ethnicity" and "symbolic religiosity." By symbolic ethnicity, he meant the acquisition and use of "ethnic symbols . . . for the purpose of feeling or being identified with a particular ethnicity, but without participating in an existing ethnic organization." Symbolic religiosity refers to "the consumption of religious symbols apart from regular participation in a religious culture and in religious affiliations" to avoid impeding "secular lifestyles." Especially relevant to the museum's story is Gans's observation that participants in symbolic religiosity "collect religious artifacts," "tune occasionally into religious programming, or take 'tours' that emphasize visits to religious sites." Equally relevant are the ways Gans's respondents reflected the changing landscape of American Judaism shaped, on one hand, by an ebbing of religious identity—such as intermarriage; and on the other, by an efflorescence of Jewish schools, summer camps, and related institutions created to "inform and remind [Jews] of the beliefs and practices of their heritage." That array of organizations, often evincing some measure of secularity, came to represent a Jewish American "civil religion" of shared ethnic and civic values. Functioning outside the ambit of synagogues per se, such settings were the crucible for a "symbiosis" of symbolic religion and symbolic ethnicity. The Jewish Museum, as a secular institution associated with a seminary, reflected that symbiosis, unstable though it was.[23]

The durability of ethnicity itself, especially as a counterpart to religion in Judaism, was uncertain, Gans thought. He believed the end of ethnicity might be delayed through an extended period of "post-symbolic stages," for example, "when ethnicity is remembered in museums." It could also be sustained in other ways, he believed, such as "by visiting ethnic restaurants, . . . music and dance festivals, the ancestral country," or with objects such as family memorabilia or those in museum exhibits. The appeal of the museum's *Lower East Side* and *Masada* exhibits may be attributable to the way each reified symbolic ethnicity. Perhaps, as well, advocates of the museum's ritual-object displays were doing the same for symbolic religion. Writing in the late 1970s, not long after the museum's turn from the avant-garde to all-Jewish programs, Gans suggested that the then-current appetite for ethnic symbols might necessitate sustaining "at least some old cultural practices, possibly in museums," presumably akin to the historic reenactments at heritage sites like Colonial Williamsburg. He imagined organizations attempting to maintain old cultures might garner some support "by supplying ethnic nostalgia" and moreover that "some ethnics may aid such organizations if only to assuage their guilt at having given up ancestral practices."[24]

These phenomena were studied from a historical viewpoint by Eli Lederhendler who, writing about the "urban ethnicity" of New York's Jewish community, framed the topic as a tension between "two utopian ideals": a "cosmopolitan" vision akin to the universalism advanced by Jewish Museum leaders during its avant-garde heyday, and a "tribal" longing they at first rejected as parochial but finally embraced with all-Jewish programs. The former was "a quest for a cosmopolitan paradise [of] unhindered participation in the life of a world-city," the latter one of building a "center that might sustain the entire Jewish people." Differences between the two utopian visions, Lederhendler found, deepened during the post–Second World War era, a story that parallels the museum's trajectory during the same period. They included several crosscurrents: rejection by the city's intellectuals, "at the cutting edge of American political and aesthetic discourse," of much that was "stereotypically Jewish as woefully lacking in breadth or universal reach"; the emergence of a "culture of retrieval" (evident in *The Lower East Side* exhibit); the growing prominence of Jews "actively involved in promoting a specialized religious sphere" (like the seminary), which, "in tandem [is] involved in promoting a separate, secular sphere" (such as the museum), facilitating a "more visible 'organized religion'" *and* a "more far-reaching . . . secularism." For Lederhendler, as the chasm between the two utopian ideals widened, the universalist logic of contemporary Jewish social thought was upended and "the path to the universal" was found to begin in "the most particularist parts of Jewish heritage." Or, as Daniel Friedenberg put it when endorsing the museum's shift to all-Jewish programs, even if the museum's subject matter was Jewish and thereby parochial, it could also be universal via Judaism's humanistic values.[25]

Given these trends, if the Jewish Museum were to continue showing works of art, how might they be selected and interpreted in accordance with its new emphasis on ethnicity? Avram Kampf, who volunteered his assistance in the runup to Katz's departure and became a paid consultant during the aftermath, answered by curating a major exhibition, *Jewish Experience in the Art of the Twentieth Century*. It contained over 260 works by 114 artists grouped into such categories as traditional Judaism, migrations, the Holocaust, and modern Israel. The paintings, drawings, and sculpture it contained ranged from realistic depictions and fanciful scenes by Raphael Soyer and Marc Chagall to abstract expressionist works by Adolph Gottlieb and Mark Rothko. Having "never used the term 'Jewish art'" because he did not believe "there is such a thing, except maybe for ceremonial objects," Kampf cast a wider net to survey works that had "some relevance to Jewish life—even the remotest, even if they reject Jewish life." The exhibit thus comprised a "social matrix" of "life experiences collectively shared, intensified, interpreted and transformed" by the artists. The exhibit also instantiated some avoidances. It was not intended to distill twentieth-century Jewish history as reflected in art, it was not limited to works by artists of Jewish descent, and it did not aim to prove there is "a Jewish art." Instead, it treated works others might consider to be Jewish art as evidence of the "Jewish Experience." The exhibit attracted a fair amount of critical attention. Of the more probing reviews, one of the most sympathetic was by a non-Jew, John Russell (1919–2008), then–art critic for the *New York Times* who applauded Kampf's achievement in identifying a "specifically Jewish awareness." Critics of Jewish descent saw it differently.[26]

One was Harold Rosenberg (1906–78), a leading art critic and thinker of the avant-garde era, who like Clement Greenberg, was a New York art-world presence renowned for his writings on Abstract Expressionism. Rosenberg questioned the very premise of a "Jewish experience." He believed that, to the extent twentieth-century Jews and non-Jews alike struggled with "identity," it was a "condition . . . experienced uniquely by each individual, and cannot be expressed as a common experience." When a Jewish artist explores art and life, moreover, it is to enter the mainstream of art as a universal phenomenon. For that reason, an exhibit that "corrals such artists into a national category violates their aims and falsifies the meaning of their work." Robert Pincus-Witten (1935–2018), a critic, historian, and professor at the City Colleges of New York, also objected to Kampf's use of "Jewish experience," adding that art produced by non-Jews also contributed to "defining the Jewish experience." His main complaint, however, was about Kampf's use of works depicting Judaic imagery, suggesting the exhibit should actually have been called "Jewish Illustration in the Art of the Twentieth Century." Regarding Kampf as "an apologist for retrograde aesthetics," Pincus-Witten also believed that although Kampf's approach was historically useful when addressing depictions of Jewish themes, it falsified abstract works made after the mid-1940s.[27]

Max Kozloff (b. 1933), a prolific historian, critic, and an *Artforum* editor at the time, saw the works in the exhibition as responses to the challenges of modernity along a gradient of ethnically identifiable markers depending on each artist's place "in time and distance, relative to the values of the . . . host culture." Indeed, he added, "we are all . . . on different schedules when it comes to the identities we once had and abandoned, want to keep, or are searching for anew." As a result, Kozloff thought of the exhibit as "a kind of family album" in which scattered members are pictured at various points in life. If one set Kampf's thematic categories aside, Kozloff believed, it was possible to discern the way art can reflect "an ethnic consciousness." He believed that Kampf had dispensed with a historical trajectory in order to explore certain "latent subjects" evident in "recurring states of mind." Unlike Pincus-Witten, Kozloff was not bothered by depictions of Jewish subjects and focused instead on the Judaic "cultural consciousness" present in the works as a "much broader and deeper condition." His reference to cultural consciousness was another way of speaking about ethnicity and identity. The "legacies" of ethnicity, or heritage, were being claimed by many groups, Kozloff added, and such avowals of ethnic identification were arising organically from within communities or in response to stigmatization from outside. At the same time, the pressures of assimilation, also arising naturally from within or being imposed from without, were conflicting with the allure of ethnicity, contributing "an increasing tension to our scene." By presenting the works in *Jewish Experience* not as art per se, but as the residue of Jewish "life experiences collectively shared, intensified, interpreted and transformed," Kampf had rendered that tension apparent.[28]

During its avant-garde period, in 1966, the museum invited Harold Rosenberg to address the question: "Is There a Jewish Art?" He began with a joke: "Is There a Jewish art? First they build a Jewish Museum, then they ask, Is There a Jewish art? Jews!" Continuing in that vein, Rosenberg added, "As to the question itself, there is a Gentile answer and a Jewish answer. The Gentile answer is: Yes, there is a Jewish art, and No, there is no Jewish art. The Jewish answer is: What do you mean by Jewish art?" Turning serious, Rosenberg sorted past explorations of the topic by Jews and non-Jews into several plausible definitions: (1) "art produced by Jews"; (2) "art depicting Jews or containing Jewish subject matter"; (3) "the art of Jewish ceremonial objects"; (4) "Jewish handicraft," that is, "a kind of ceremonial . . . folk art"; (5) "metaphysical Judaica" arising from a unique "Hebrew conception of reality"; and (6) "in a negative sense" stemming from the Second Commandment, "creating objects in the mind and banning physical works of art." Rosenberg was interested in works by living Jewish artists, but the ones he had mind were not by artists "creating as Jews"—making art that was visibly Jewish—but works that were the "closest expression of themselves." "Though not a Jewish art," Rosenberg thought, it is nonetheless "a profound Jewish expression . . . loaded with meaning for all people." These observations derived from his consideration of ethnic identity and its place in the lives of many artists of the era who helped forge "a genuine American art." Rosenberg saw in their commonality a "will" to an American identity, an "aesthetics of self" that included artists of Jewish descent thus freeing them from even needing to ask "whether a Jewish art exists or can exist." In setting aside the necessity for those artists to address the "Jewish art" question, Rosenberg excused others from fretting about it too, including those responsible for the Jewish Museum. But he was preaching to the choir.[29]

Vera List, Ben Heller, and even Abram Kanof, for example, were self-identifying Jews who prioritized personal relationships with art of all kinds, not only what might qualify as "Jewish art" however defined. List acknowledged that Judaica and anything else that "pertained to Jewish interest and Judaism . . . played a necessary role in the museum." But, she added, "as a Jew living today . . . I was also interested in contemporary art—whoever did it—Catholic, Protestant, Jew. It was the aesthetic value—how I reacted to it as a human being. After all, Jews are human and non-Jews also are human. I think man's urge to express . . . is universal and has meaning." Furthermore, List remarked, just as the museum's Judaica collection "reflected the life of Jews, say, in seventeenth-century Italy," she felt the museum "in 1950–1960–1970 should reflect the life of the Jew at that time." Her sense of where artistic meaning might be found, moreover, was not limited to the avant-garde, citing "the Crucifix or some Christian symbol—because of its basic humanitarian content." On a trip to Spain, she saw a painting of Saint Sebastian that deeply affected her, List said, adding it was "so poignant. . . . It's not Christian . . . it's mankind and man's inhumanity to man. It doesn't make any difference if it's Joseph, Moses, Saint Sebastian, or who it is." Heller's interests were similarly broad. He was especially interested in "Indian-Asian art" at the time and thought of viewing it as "a way of our coming to terms with [that] part of the world" and understanding the people who created it as part of "our present existence." While a museum board member, he thought of the Judaica-versus-avant-garde disputes as reflecting divergent aspects of "the involvement of Jews . . . in the way in which the alert, intellectual, sensitive 'advanced Jew' . . . has lived his life so often." Despite differences between the two programs, Heller believed their coexistence expressed in visual terms conflicting "parts of our being that many of us have individually."[30]

Although Kanof much preferred the museum's Judaica programs over the avant-garde, his interpretation of what that might mean was equally liberal. He recalled an exhibit "by a young Catholic artist" of a "series of paintings about Nazism" that Kanof felt could "certainly" be displayed by the museum. It would be appropriate, even though it was neither by a Jewish artist nor addressed Jews and the Holocaust, because the series treated "the fascist, totalitarian aspects of Nazism." Kanof also admired the work of Mark Rothko (1903–70), an avant-garde painter of Jewish descent associated with Abstract Expressionism, citing in particular a group of dark, severe paintings Rothko created in the 1960s for a nondenominational meditation space. Now called the Rothko Chapel, it was built adjacent to the University of St. Thomas in Houston, Texas—a Catholic institution—by the collectors John and Dominique de Menil to serve it and the surrounding community. The de Menils were inspired by a movement to reinvigorate Catholicism, in part through the creation of modern worship spaces and ritual objects, their motivations resembling those which impelled Kanof to establish the Tobe Pascher Workshop at the Jewish Museum. Of the Rothko Chapel, Kanof marveled, "When you go in you're in a place of sanctity. . . . Even though [Rothko's] a master of modern art, there's a religious feeling in his work."[31]

The debates over the museum's mission between the opposing groups represented by List and Kanof can be seen as reflecting the ways that, during the post–Second World War period "American Jews were profoundly divided . . . over the Jewish aspects of their lives." For a while, the differences between the avant-garde and Judaica advocates were veiled by the extraordinary successes of American Jewry during the era. Despite the Depression, the war, and the Holocaust, the community experienced a "golden age" from the late 1940s to the late 1960s marked by prosperity, acceptance, and "the triumph of . . . cultural liberalism" marked in part by the emergence of a new generation of Jewish collectors. People like List, Heller, and Kanof were among those who embraced both "the dignified idealization of their [Jewish] origins in . . . bejewelled spiceboxes and yet [were] sufficiently with it to dig Rauschenberg." Under their leadership, the museum made "no stops . . . on the express between the antique and pop art, between Persian synagogues and plastic hot dogs." While differing in their aims for the museum, List, Heller, and Kanof shared a deep passion for objects of all kinds, respected each other's judgment, and never questioned the Jewishness of those with opposing views. While they welcomed expert determinations of what might qualify as "Jewish art," in the end its definition did not matter because List, Kanof, and the others instead prioritized the art that was most personally meaningful for them and, by assumed proxy, for their contemporaries among Jews and non-Jews alike. Had the objects at the center of their debates not been so readily marshaled into such starkly different categories—on the one hand, the avant-garde, which included a preponderance of works by non-Jews or that lacked visible Jewish content, and on the other, Jewish ritual artifacts—the debates might not have been so fraught. But that range of objects and their reception among "alert, intellectual, sensitive 'advanced Jew[s]'" on both sides reflected, as Silvia Tennenbaum observed in 1966, a "sense of dichotomy which the Jewish Museum . . . inherited from the whole of Jewish experience."[32]

Notes

1. For this chapter's title, Abram Kanof to LF, 23 January 1968, RG 1–259–14, LJTS; and "A Jewish Jewish Museum [emphasis the paper's], 'Art Mailbag,' To the Editor," *New York Times*, 28 February 1971. Quote from Silvia Tennenbaum, "Jewish Home for the Graven Image," *Midstream: A Monthly Jewish Review* 12, no. 6 (June–July 1966): 21.
2. McShine was acting director during the search; Kynaston McShine, oral history interview by Carolyn Lanchner (compiled by David Frankel), 1 April 2010–13 January 2011, transcript, Oral History Program, Museum of Modern Art, 24. KK, oral history interview by Rosalind Mancher, January 1997, transcript, UJA-FNYC, I-433, AJHS, 2–19; see also, Sam Roberts, "Karl Katz: Museum Director and Innovator, Dies at 88," *New York Times*, 12 November 2017; DF, oral history interview by Nicki Tanner, 13 February 1990, transcript, UJA-FNYC, I-433, AJHS, 26–28; Abram Kanof, oral history interview by Judy Tenney, 19 November 1990 and 26 May 1992, transcript, UJA-FNYC, I-433, AJHS, 26–27. KK also hoped to complete his doctorate; KK to MS, 21 May 1966, MSC 140:3, CUL. On campaigning, see KK to LF, 25 May 1967, RG 1–250–16, and DF to KK, 9 October 1967, RG 1–248–43, LJTS.
3. Seymour Siegel, "The Jewish Museum: A Statement of Principles," 1 December 1967, RG 25–4–25, LJTS. Siegel (1927–88), a professor of theology and ethics at JTS, served on a JM advisory committee at the time. See also, Abram Kanof to LF, 7 December 1967, RG 1–250–13, KK, [Principles statement, ca. 5 December 1967,] RG 1–250–16, Abram Kanof to LF, 14 December 1967, LF to Abram Kanof, 15 January 1968, and Abram Kanof to LF, 23 January 1968, RG 1–259–14, LJTS. KK, *The Exhibitionist: Living Museums, Loving Museums* (New York: Overlook Press, 2016), 193–96. See also, KK, oral history interview by Rosalind Mancher, January 1997, transcript, UJA-FNYC, I-433, AJHS, 19–21; Milton Esterow, "Jewish Museum Finds Its New Director, Brooklyn-Born Karl Katz, in Israel," *New York Times*, 3 April 1968.
4. KK, oral history interview by Rosalind Mancher, January 1997, transcript, UJA-FNYC, I-433, AJHS, 21. Grace Glueck, "Fingers, Jackstraws and Lincoln Logs [New Broom]," *New York Times*, 21 April 1968; Glueck, "At Jewish Museum, 3000 B.C. and 1969," *New York Times*, 18 October 1968. See also, KK to MS, 12 September 1968, MSC 140:3, CUL and Minutes, Board of Overseers, 12 January 1969, RG 21–6–10, LJTS. Nicholas Mirzoeff, *An Introduction to Visual Culture*, 2nd edn. (New York: Routledge, 2009). On social activism and museums, see Andrew McClellan, "A Brief History of the Art Museum Public," in *Art and its Publics: Museum Studies at the Millennium*, ed. Andrew McClellan (Malden, MA: Blackwell Publishing, 2003), 23–35.
5. KK, introduction to *Ingathering: Ceremony and Tradition in New York Public Collections* [New York: Jewish Museum, 1969, unpaginated]. On its

inception, see KK, *Exhibitionist*, 197. Grace Glueck, "At Jewish Museum, 3000 B.C. and 1969," *New York Times*, 18 October 1968; and David L. Shirey, "Art: Two in One," *Newsweek* 73, no. 5 (3 February 1969): 36.

6. There was no catalogue for *Pond*. "Robert Whitman," Pace Gallery, accessed July 2020, https://www.pacegallery.com/artists/robert-whitman. KK, *Exhibitionist*, 197–98. Dore Ashton, "New York Commentary," *Studio International* 177, no. 908 (February 1969): 94. "Karl Katz: New York As the World's Art Leader," by Irving M. Levine, *New York Tomorrow, WNYC*, 26 November 1968, NYPR Archive Collections, New York Municipal Archives ID: T5948, accessed August 2023, https://www.wnyc.org/story/karl-katz-new-york-as-the-worlds-art-leader/.
7. Rebecca J. DeRoo, *The Museum Establishment and Contemporary Art: The Politics of Artistic Display in France After 1968* (Cambridge: Cambridge University Press, 2006), 19–60; Keith Reader, with Khursheed Wadia, *The May 1968 Events in France: Reproductions and Interpretations* (New York: St. Martin's Press, 1993); and Kristin Ross, *May '68 and Its Afterlives* (Chicago, IL: University of Chicago Press, 2002). Grace Glueck, "Aux Barricades! With Posters," *New York Times*, 15 December 1968. KK, *Exhibitionist*, 199–200. Harold Rosenberg, "The Art World: Surrealism in the Streets," *New Yorker* XLIV, no. 45 (28 December 1968): 52, 55. Kieran Williams, *The Prague Spring and Its Aftermath: Czechoslovak Politics, 1968–1970* (Cambridge: Cambridge University Press, 1997). Hear also, "Karl Katz: New York As the World's Art Leader," by Irving M. Levine, *New York Tomorrow, WNYC*, 26 November 1968, NYPR Archive Collections, New York Municipal Archives ID: T5948, accessed August 2023, https://www.wnyc.org/story/karl-katz-new-york-as-the-worlds-art-leader/. On attendance, see "The Jewish Museum," Report to Board of Overseers, May 1969, RG 21–6–17, LJTS. On soul museum, see Jack Siegel, "Jewish Museum with a Conscience," *Jewish Advocate*, 19 December 1968.
8. KK, *Exhibitionist*, 199, 200–2 (emphasis KK's). See also, Ruth Salit to KK, 20 November, and KK to Ruth Salit, 26 November 1968, RG 1–259–17, LJTS; and Samuel H. Dresner to KK, 9 December 1968, RG 1–259–17 and "The Jewish Museum," Report to Board of Overseers, May 1969, RG 21–6–17, LJTS. On Sabbath hours, see KK to LF, 4 August, LF to KK, 9 October 1969, RG 1–267–6, and DF to LF, 15 October 1969, RG 1–265–32, LJTS.
9. KK, *Exhibitionist*, 207–8. DF to Albert A. List, 20 December 1968, RG 1–260–3, Arthur T. Jacobs to DF, 11 June 1969, RG 1–265–32, LJTS. *International Directory of Company Histories* (Farmington Hills, MI: St. James Press, 2014); *Business Insights: Essentials*, s.v. "Ruder Finn Group, Inc.," accessed July 2020, doi: GALE|I2501318432. See also, Alvin Toffler, *The Culture Consumers: A Study of Art and Affluence in America* (New York: St. Martin's Press, 1964), 97; chapter 4; and DF, *The Way Forward: My First Fifty Years at Ruder • Finn* (New York: Millwood Publishing, 1998), 4–5, 39–42. Musée des arts décoratifs, *Peintres Européens d'Aujourd'hui/European Painters Today* (Paris: Union centrale des arts décoratifs, 1968). Grace Glueck, "No

More Pecans," *New York Times*, 26 January 1969. David L. Shirey, "Art: Two in One," *Newsweek* 73, no. 5 (3 February 1969): 36. Tracy Atkinson and John Lloyd Taylor, eds., *A Plastic Presence*, 2 vols. (Milwaukee, WI: Milwaukee Art Center, 1969). "Our Heritage, Philip Morris, USA," Altria Group, Inc., accessed July 2020, https://www.altria.com/about-altria/our-heritage?src=top-nav; see also, Richard Kluger, *Ashes to Ashes: America's Hundred-Year Cigarette War, the Public Health, and the Unabashed Triumph of Philip Morris* (New York: Alfred A. Knopf, 1996). DF was aware of cigarette-smoking dangers, Ruder & Finn staff were uneasy about Philip Morris, and DF consulted with LF before accepting it as a client; DF, *Way Forward*, 78. Grace Glueck, "Art Notes: Building the Plastic Image," *New York Times*, 7 December 1969; Grégoire Müeller, "A Plastic Presence," *Arts Magazine* 44, no. 2 (November 1969): 37; Robert Pincus-Witten, "New York," *Artforum* 8, no. 5 (January 1970): 69; and Carter Ratcliff, "New York Letter," *Art International* 14, no. 1 (20 January 1970): 93–94. KK and DF, "Art Mailbag: Are 'Backers' All Bad?" *New York Times*, 4 January 1970. Corporate-sponsorship critiques were relatively new then and they still come up; Michael Kimmelman, "Does It Really Matter Who Sponsors a Show?," *New York Times*, 19 May 1996; and Kimmelman, "Art, Money and Power," *New York Times*, 11 May 2005. See also, Andrew McClellan, *The Art Museum from Boullée to Bilbao* (Berkeley: University of California Press, 2008), 225–32; and Alex J. Taylor, *Forms of Persuasion: Art and Corporate Image in the 1960s* (Berkeley: University of California Press, 2022); for references to Ruder & Finn's work, pp. 55, 67–72, 80–88, 229–33, 258n30. "Laughter, the Best Medicine," in *Reader's Digest* 97, no. 582 (October 1970): 152 ("Contributed by Robert McMillan"). John Heidenry, *Theirs Was the Kingdom: Lila and Dewitt Wallace and the Story of the Reader's Digest* (New York: W. W. Norton, 1993).

10. KK, *Exhibitionist*, 202–3. On the JM's collections management later on, see Paul N. Perrot and Mary Elizabeth King, "American Association of Museums Accreditation Visiting Committee On-Site Evaluation for Museums," 20 August 1979, MSC 137:15, CUL and Mildred S. Compton to JU, 6 December 1979, MSC 137:15, CUL. Meeting minutes, Judaica Committee, JM, 12 February1970, RG 25–2–15, LJTS. On the Arts Council, see Anthony Leonard Barresi, "The History and Programs of the New York State Council on the Arts" (PhD diss., University of Michigan, 1973). KK to Allon Schoener, 13 March 1970, RG 1–274–22, LJTS. Schoener by then was Director, Visual Arts Program, New York State Council on the Arts, Allon Schoener, oral history interview by Laurin Raikin, 1971, transcript, AAA, SI. On "Teleguide systems," see "Man's the Theme, but the Machine Makes Expo Go" [Canadian] *Globe and Mail*, 23 May 1967; Leonard Sloane, "Advertising: Landlord Offers TV as an Extra," *New York Times*, 4 August 1964; and Irwin M. Gross, "Teaching Art Through the Television Medium" (EdD diss., New York University, 1964), 139–50. For the last quote, see Jeanne W. Halpern, "New York's Most Surprising Museum," *This Day* 20 (September 1969): 22.

11. KK, foreword to *Israel / The Reality: People, Places, Events in Memorable Photographs*, ed. Cornell Capa (New York: World Publishing Company in association with the Jewish Museum, 1969), [unpaginated]. "Unique Photo-Essay on Israel Opens Sept. 18 at Jewish Museum," *Jewish Advocate*, 28 August 1969; Grace Glueck, "Israel in Photos: Her People's Joys and Ordeals," *New York Times*, 19 September 1969; and "Israel: The Reality," *Jewish Advocate*, 9 October 1969. On visitors' responses, see Jacob Deschin, "Picture History of Israel," *New York Times*, 28 September 1969. On the exhibit's second presentation, see [JM], "Jewish Museum Exhibitions: 1947–Present," 2 September 2009. There were about thirty thousand visitors, nearly a third of the JM's total attendance in 1969, "The Jewish Museum," Report to Board of Overseers, May 1970, RG 21–6–20, LJTS.
12. KK, *Exhibitionist*, 207–8. Grace Glueck, "One Body, One Voice [Blowups]," *New York Times*, 29 June 1969; Noel Frackman, "Inflatable Sculpture," *Arts Magazine* 44, no. 1 (September/October 1969): 55; Peter Schjeldahl, "When It's All in the Bag," *New York Times*, 13 July 1969. See also, Grace Glueck, ". . . And Carloads of Rockefeller," *New York Times*, 1 June 1969. "Fire at Jewish Museum, Shuts Halls Till Sunday," *New York Times*, 24 July 1969. The damage was mostly in KK's and adjacent offices, which may explain the JM's archival gaps for prior years; KK to LF, 24 July 1969, RG 1–267–6; and "The Jewish Museum," Report to Board of Overseers, May 1970, RG 21–6–20, LJTS.
13. Susan Tumarkin Goodman, introduction to *Using Walls (Indoors)*, ed. Susan Tumarkin Goodman (New York: Jewish Museum, 1970), unpaginated. Catalogue photographs show the artists creating their installations "to give a sense of the process rather than the finished work"; Susan T. Goodman to Jeffrey Abt, 3 August 2020. Goodman, *Using Walls (Outdoors)*. The exhibit also included a "work on the facade" of the JM, Goodman, acknowledgments, in *Using Walls (Outdoors)*, unpaginated. See also, KK, *Exhibitionist*, 226. Grace Glueck, "Art Shows Overflow Jewish Museum," *New York Times*, 14 May 1970. For closing quote, see Julie H. Reiss, *From Margin to Center: The Spaces of Installation Art* (Cambridge, MA: MIT Press, 1999), 86.
14. Thomas M. Grace, *Kent State: Death and Dissent in the Long Sixties* (Amherst: University of Massachusetts Press, 2016). Grace Glueck, "Art Shows Overflow Jewish Museum," *New York Times*, 14 May 1970; Glueck, "Art Community Here Agrees on Plan to Fight War, Racism and Oppression," *New York Times*, 19 May 1970. See also, Lucy R. Lippard, "The Art Workers Coalition: Not a History," *Studio International* 180, no. 927 (November 1970): 171–74. KK, *Exhibitionist*, 208–12, 215. On Columbia, see *A Time to Stir: Columbia '68*, ed. Paul Cronin (New York: Columbia University Press, 2018); on the *Evergreen Review*, see Loren Glass, *Counterculture Colophon: Grove Press, the Evergreen Review, and the Incorporation of the Avant-Garde* (Stanford, CA: Stanford University Press, 2013). On cuts, see Publicity release, 4 June 1970, RG 25–3–1, LJTS.
15. Jacobs (1912–2018) joined JTS in the mid-1960s after working at Jewish welfare, philanthropic, and congregational entities, "Dr. Arthur T. Jacobs,"

The Rye Record, 17 October 2018, accessed August 2020, https://ryerecord.com/dr-arthur-jacobs/. Arthur T. Jacobs to LF, 20 August 1970, RG 5–2–15, LJTS. On VL's loyalty, see Abram Kanof, oral history interview by Judy Tenney, 19 November 1990 and 26 May 1992, transcript, UJA-FNYC, I-433, AJHS, 31, 37; Richard J. Scheuer, oral history interview by Nicki Tanner, 7 July 1995, transcript, UJA-FNYC, I-433, AJHS, 20. Note also, VL's backing of the Tobe Pascher Workshop, Nancy M. Berman, *Moshe Zabari: A Twenty-Five Year Retrospective* (New York: The Jewish Museum, 1986), 4, 16. Irving Sandler, "Epilogue: 1970—The Death of the Avant-Garde," in *American Art of the 1960s* (New York: Harper and Row, 1988), 359–64; the quote is from p. 363 (emphasis Sandler's). On the grant, see KK to Allon Schoener, 13 March 1970, RG 1–274–22, LJTS. See also, "The Jewish Museum," Report to Board of Overseers, May 1970, RG 21–6–20, LJTS. The Vishniac exhibit was October 1971–January 1972; see also Roman Vishniac and Cornell Capa, *The Concerns of Roman Vishniac: Man, Nature, and Science: An Exhibit of Photographs and Films* (New York: International Fund for Concerned Photography, 1971). On the center, see Davidson Gigliotti, "A Brief History of Rain Dance," Radical Software, accessed August 2020, https://www.radicalsoftware.org/e/history.html.

16. Jack Burnham, ed., *Software—Information Technology: Its New Meaning for Art* (New York: The Jewish Museum, 1970). On its inception, see KK, *Exhibitionist*, 215–17, 220. "A Node for Jack Burnham," Robert Horvitz, accessed August 2020, https://horvitz.multiplace.org/burnham/homepage.htm; Jack Burnham, *Beyond Modern Sculpture: The Effects of Science and Technology on the Sculpture of this Century* (New York: George Braziller, 1968); see also, Jack Burnham, *Dissolve into Comprehension: Writings and Interviews, 1964–2004*, ed. Melissa Ragain (Cambridge, MA: The MIT Press, 2015). James S. Olson and Abraham O. Mendoza, "American Motors Corporation," in *American Economic History: A Dictionary and Chronology* (Santa Barbara, CA: Greenwood/ABC-CLIO, 2015), 32–33. On DF's involvement, KK and DF, "Art Mailbag: Are 'Backers' All Bad?" *New York Times*, 4 January 1970. On maintaining equipment, see "Soft Sell," *Industrial Design* 17, no. 7 (September 1970): 17. On out-of-order comment, see Grace Glueck, "Varied Problems Beset Opening of Jewish Museum's 'Software,'" *New York Times*, 18 September 1970. See also, Bitite Vinklers, "Art and Information: 'Software' at the Jewish Museum," *Arts Magazine* 45, no. 1 (September/October 1970): 46–47; and Robert Mallary, "Notes on Jack Burnham's Concepts of a Software Exhibition," *Leonardo* 3, no. 2 (April 1970): 189–90. On world's fairs, see Grace Glueck, "Jewish Museum's 'Software' Confusing," *New York Times*, 26 September 1970. Jack Burnham, "Notes on Art and Information Processing, in *Software*, 10. For other reviews, see John J. O'Connor, "The Gallery: Gerbils and Wheelchairs," *Wall Street Journal*, 4 November 1970; T[homas] B. H[ess], "Editorial: Gerbil Ex Machina," *ARTnews* 69, no. 8 (December 1970): 23; Louis Chapin, "'Software' and Its Herd of Computers," *Christian Science Monitor*, 16 October 1970; Barbara Gold, "Technology

Out of Order," *Baltimore Sun*, 4 October 1970; Barbara Rose, "Art: Culture Collision," *Vogue* 156, no. 6 (1 October 1970): 98; and Carter Ratcliff, "New York Letter: Software," *Art International* XV, no. 1 (20 January 1971): 29. On the films, see Bob Fiore and Barbara Jarvis, "Software Battle," *Artforum* IX, no. 3 (November 1970): 41. Giorno Poetry Systems, "Radio Free Poetry," in *Software*, 50–52. Jacob Zumoff, "Eldridge Cleaver," in *African American Lives*, ed. Henry Louis Gates and Evelyn Brooks Higginbotham (New York: Oxford University Press, 2004), 173–74. Les Levine, "Artist Exposes Himself Electronically: A.I.R. [Artist-In-Residence] 1968–70," in *Software*, 62–63. KK, *Exhibitionist*, 218, 220–21.

17. KK, *Exhibitionist*, 217–20. Samuel H. Dresner to Jack Stein, 22 September, LF to Samuel H. Dresner, 25 September, RG 1–272–24, LF to DF, 28 September, RG 1–273–2, LF to Albert A. List, 28 September, RG 1–274–53, and DF to LF, 8 October 1970, RG 1–273–2, LJTS. The review that set Dresner off was Grace Glueck, "Varied Problems Beset Opening of Jewish Museum's 'Software,'" *New York Times*, 18 September 1970. On JM's finances, see KK, *Exhibitionist*, 221–22; see also, Arthur T. Jacobs to LF, 17 November 1970, RG 25–2–27 and Memorandum, Arthur T. Jacobs to DF, Abram Kanof, VL, et alia, 21 January 1971, RG 25–2–15, LJTS. On DF's opposition, see DF, oral history interview by Nicki Tanner, 13 February 1990, transcript, UJA-FNYC, I-433, AJHS, 31–32.

18. On KK's resignation and next career step, see KK, *Exhibitionist*, 222–23, 237–40; KK, oral history interview by Rosalind Mancher, January 1997, transcript, UJA-FNYC, I-433, AJHS, 23, 29; Sam Roberts, "Karl Katz, Museum Director and Innovator, Dies at 88," *New York Times*, 12 November 2017. For KK's reflections at the time, see Jay Jacobs, "Pertinent & Impertinent: Like a Comet," *Art Gallery Magazine* 14, no. 6 (March 1971): 8–9, 69. Grace Glueck, "Museum Turns to All-Jewish Shows," *New York Times*, 5 January 1971. See also, "No More Avant-Garde," *Washington Post*, 6 January 1971; Richard Taffe, "The New Jewish Museum of New York," *Jewish Advocate*, 18 February 1971. Publicity release, 11 January 1971, RG 25–2–15, LJTS. [Editorial], "Jewish Museum: Parochialism or Self-Respect?" *Jewish Advocate*, 7 January 1971. See also, "Jewish Museum to Abandon Diverse Policy; Katz Resigns," *Jewish Exponent* [Philadelphia], 12 February 1971; and Esther Klein, "The Publisher Speaks," *Jewish Times* [Philadelphia], 25 February 1971. Arthur A. Cohen, "Museum or Mausoleum?" *New York Times*, 7 February 1971 (emphasis Cohen's); on Cohen's previous JM involvement, see chapters 4 and 6. See also, DF to Arthur Cohen, 11 January, and DF to VL, 13 January 1971, RG 1–279–66, LJTS. On museum expenses, see Lawrence Alloway, "Art," *The Nation* 212, no. 4 (25 January 1971): 125–26. For support of the change, see letters under "A Jewish Jewish Museum [emphasis the paper's], 'Art Mailbag,' To the Editor," *New York Times*, 28 February 1971; and Emily Genauer, "Art and the Artist," *New York Post*, 16 January 1971. On the JM's interim administration, see DCK to LF, 23 March 1971, RG 25–5–23, LJTS. On closing

JM and financial straits, see LF to VL, 29 March 1971, RG 1–279–66, and Jerome S. Katzin, "Report on the Fiscal Condition of the Seminary," 30 April 1972, RG 21–7–22, LJTS. On LF's fund-raising, see LF to JM Board of Governors, 31 March, RG 25–2–19, LF to VL [ca. 31 March], RG 25–2–22, LF to VL, 1 April, and VL to LF, 5 April 1971, RG 1–279–66, LJTS; see also, DCK to DF, 4 June, and DF to DCK, 24 June 1971, RG 1–278–4, LJTS. A source of the JM closure misperception was oral-history interviewer Nicki Tanner; see Janet Solinger, oral history interview by Nicki Tanner, 10 May 1993, transcript, UJA-FNYC, I-433, AJHS, 45; Richard J. Scheuer, oral history interview by Nicki Tanner, 7 July 1995, transcript, UJA-FNYC, I-433, AJHS, 15; AK, oral history interview by Nicki Tanner, 24 July 1990, transcript, UJA-FNYC, I-433, AJHS, 26. Among JM staff, only JU got it wrong; JU, oral history interview by Judy E. Tenney, 19 December 1989, transcript, UJA-FNYC, I-433, AJHS, 29–30. The JM mounted about eighteen exhibitions during the period, [JM], "Jewish Museum Exhibitions: 1947–Present," 2 September 2009; see also, "The Jewish Museum," Report to Board of Overseers, May 1972, RG 21–7–22, LJTS. On library donation, see Thomas M. Messer [then–Guggenheim director] to Harriet Catlin, 22 June 1971, RG 25–5–14, LJTS.

19. Israel Shenker, "Rabbi Finkelstein to Retire; Joy of Study Undiminished," *New York Times*, 28 September 1971; and "Noted JTS Leader to Resign," *Jewish Advocate*, 30 September 1971. *Encyclopaedia Judaica*, 2nd edn. (2007), s.v. "Gerson D. Cohen," by Michael Panetz; Raymond P. Scheindlin, "Gerson D. Cohen (1924–1991)," *Proceedings of the American Academy for Jewish Research* 58 (1992): 15–18. Jack Wertheimer, "JTS and the Conservative Movement" and Paula E. Hyman, "The Unfinished Symphony: The Gerson Cohen Years," in *Tradition Renewed: A History of the Jewish Theological Seminary*, ed. Jack Wertheimer (New York: Jewish Theological Seminary of America, 1997), II:426–33 and II:237–47. "The Jewish Museum," Jewish Theological Seminary of America, accessed April 2023, https://www.jtsa.edu/the-jewish-museum/; "About this Site," Jewish Museum, accessed April 2023, https://thejewishmuseum.org/about-this-site.

20. *Encyclopaedia Judaica*, 2nd edn. (2007), s.v. "Samuel Friedenberg," by Cecil Roth; "Samuel Friedenberg, Builder Here, Dies; Donated Collection for the Jewish Museum," *New York Times*, 6 May 1957; Samuel Friedenberg, *Exhibition of Jewish Medals: From the Collection of Mr. Samuel Friedenberg* (New York: The Jewish Theological Seminary, 1940); and LF to Samuel Friedenberg, 28 October, RG 25–1–4, and LF to FSW, 28 October 1947, RG 1–63–17, LJTS. "Daniel M. Friedenberg," *The Oregonian*, 11 September 2011. *Great Jewish Portraits in Metal: Selected Plaques and Medals from the Samuel Friedenberg Collection . . .* (New York: Schocken Books for the Jewish Museum, 1963); Daniel M. Friedenberg, *Jewish Medals: From the Renaissance to the Fall of Napoleon (1503–1815)* (New York: C.N. Potter for the Jewish Museum, 1970); Ya'akov Meshorer and Ira Rezak, *Coins Reveal: The Samuel and Daniel M. Friedenberg Collection of Coins and Medals* (New York: The

Jewish Museum, 1983). Daniel M. Friedenberg, "Can a Jewish Museum Live by Art Alone?" *New York Times*, 29 August 1971. For public responses, "Art Mailbag: Debating a Jewish Museum," *New York Times*, 24 October 1971; for private ones, including AK's, see folder RG 25–5–10, LJTS. On the donations, see David Fogelson to Bernard Mandelbaum, 6 December 1971, RG 25–4–31, Publicity release, 11 February 1972, RG 25–5–26, and Draft publicity release, 18 January 1972, RG 25–4–39, LJTS; Unknown to MS, 10 January 1972, MSC 138: 3, CUL; Gertrude E. Fogelson, oral history interview by Nicki Tanner, 3 July 1991, transcript, UJA-FNYC, I-433, AJHS, 15–17; and David Fogelson to Richard J. Scheuer, 6 November 1972, RG 25–4–39, LJTS. See also, DCK, "Report on . . . Meeting with Mr. & Mrs. [David] Fogelson and Mrs. [Arthur] Liman," 14 June [1972], RG 25–6–1, [Unknown] to DCK, 24 July, DCK to Gerson D. Cohen, 27 July 1972, RG 25–4–32, DCK to AK, 10 August, RG 25–5–15, Gerson D. Cohen to DCK and Harriet Catlin, 18 August, RG 25–4–32, Albert A. List to Gerson D. Cohen, 13 September 1972, RG 25–2–22, LJTS. LF to JU, 20 October 1972, RG 25–6–8, LJTS; see also, JU, oral history interview by Judy E. Tenney, 19 December 1989, transcript, UJA-FNYC, I-433, AJHS, 25–27, 55–56; for the last two quotes, p. 37. On JU, see also chapter 6.

21. Publicity release, 11 January 1971, RG 25–2–15, LJTS. "Studio Museum History," The Studio Museum in Harlem, accessed October 2020, https://www.studiomuseum.org/about; see also, *The Studio Museum in Harlem: 25 Years of African-American Art* (New York: The Studio Museum in Harlem, 1994). Judging by a 1977 survey, there was a blossoming of ethnic-identity museums and repositories in the second half of the twentieth century; Lubomyr R. Wynar and Lois Buttlar, *Guide to Ethnic Museums, Libraries, and Archives in the United States* (Kent, OH: Program for the Study of Ethnic Publications, Kent University, 1978). KK, *Exhibitionist*, 215. Will Herberg, *Protestant, Catholic, Jew: An Essay in American Religious Sociology*, rev. of 1955 edn. (Chicago, IL: University of Chicago Press, 1983), 14. Concerning the uses of "ethnic" and "ethnicity" starting in the 1950s, see also, Nathan Glazer and Daniel P. Moynihan, introduction to *Ethnicity: Theory and Experience*, ed. Glazer and Moynihan (Cambridge, MA: Harvard University Press, 1975), 1–26. See also, Max Weber, "Ethnic Groups," in *Theories of Society: Foundations of Modern Sociological Theory*, ed. Talcott Parsons, Edward Shils et alia (New York: Free Press of Glencoe, 1961), 305–9. Also relevant are Laurence J. Silberstein, "Mapping, not Tracing: Opening Reflection," in *Mapping Jewish Identities*, ed. Silberstein (New York: New York University Press, 2000), 31n14; and Deborah Dash Moore, introduction to *American Jewish Identity Politics*, ed. Moore (Ann Arbor: University of Michigan Press, 2008), 1. On ethnicity at the JM, see "Future Plans for the Jewish Museum," [ca. November 1971,] RG 25–2–1, Draft publicity release, 18 January 1972, RG 25–4–39, LJTS.

22. Stephen Sharot, *Comparative Perspectives on Judaisms and Jewish Identities* (Detroit, MI: Wayne State University Press, 2011), 145, 150. *Contemporary*

Authors Online (Detroit: Gale, 2002), *Biography in Context*, s.v. "Herbert J. Gans," accessed October 2020, doi: GALE|H1000035145. Herbert J. Gans, "American Jewry: Present and Future | Part 1: Present," *Commentary* 21, no. 5 (May 1956): 422, 424–26 (emphases Gans's). On cultural capital, see Pierre Bourdieu, *The Field of Cultural Production: Essays on Art and Literature*, ed. Randal Johnson (New York: Columbia University Press, 1993), 7, 270n24.

23. Gans, "American Jewry: Present and Future": 427–30 (emphasis Gans's). See also, Samuel Heilman, "Jews and Judaica: Who Owns and Buys What?" in *Persistence and Flexibility: Anthropological Perspectives on the American Jewish Experience*, ed. Walter P. Zenner (Albany, NY: State University of New York Press, 1988), 260–79. Herbert J. Gans, "Symbolic Ethnicity: The Future of Ethnic Groups and Cultures in America," *Ethnic and Racial Studies* 2, no. 1 (January 1979): 1–2. Herbert J. Gans, "Symbolic Ethnicity and Symbolic Religiosity: Towards a Comparison of Ethnic and Religious Acculturation," *Ethnic and Racial Studies* 17, no. 4 (October 1994): 578, 582, 585–86. Gans's discussion of generational changes recasts Herberg's summation of "Hansen's Law": "What the son wishes to forget, the grandson wishes to remember"; Herberg, *Protestant, Catholic, Jew*, 30, 186–87, 257. Stephen Sharot, "A Critical Commentary on Gans' 'Symbolic Ethnicity and Symbolic Religiosity' and Other Formulations of Ethnicity and Religion Regarding American Jews," *Contemporary Jewry* 18, no. 1 (December 1997): 26, 27, 30–32, 36. See also, Jonathan S. Woocher, *Sacred Survival: The Civil Religion of American Jews* (Bloomington: Indiana University Press, 1986); and John Stone and Kelsey Harris, "Symbolic Ethnicity and Herbert Gans: Race, Religion, and Politics in the Twenty-first Century," *Ethnic and Racial Studies* 40, no. 9 (2017): 1397–1409.
24. Herbert J. Gans, "Another Look at Symbolic Ethnicity," *Ethnic and Racial Studies* 40, no. 9 (2017): 1410–11. Gans, "Symbolic Ethnicity": 17. "Colonial Williamsburg," The Colonial Williamsburg Foundation, accessed September 2022, https://www.colonialwilliamsburg.org/.
25. Eli Lederhendler, *New York Jews and the Decline of Urban Ethnicity, 1950–1970* (Syracuse, NY: Syracuse University Press, 2001), 9, 13, 16, 63, 65–69, 110, 121; see also references to the JM, pp. 26, 140, 159. Friedenberg, "Can a Jewish Museum Live by Art Alone?" See also, Edward Alexander, "Irving Howe and Secular Jewishness: An Elegy," *Judaism* 45, no. 1 (Winter 1996): 102, 107. Also relevant is a philosophical analysis citing the JM; Arthur C. Danto, "Postmodern Art & Concrete Selves: The Model of the Jewish Museum," in *From the Inside Out: Eight Contemporary Artists*, ed. Susan Tumarkin Goodman (New York: Jewish Museum, 1993), 11–21. Also on Jewish ethnicity as "an inseparable combination of universalism and particularism," see Jack Riemer, "An Essay-Review of the Non Jewish Jew," *Jewish Advocate*, 2 January 1969.
26. AK endorsed Friedenberg's views previously discussed; see folder RG 25–5–10 and "Avram Kampf, 1971: Digest of Opinion on Future of Jewish Museum, Museum Study," April 1971, RG 25–4–32, LJTS. AK was

appointed to a JM part-time position with the donations that brought JU aboard; "Interview with Avram Kampf," 23 December 1971, RG 25–5–24, DCK to AK, 20 June 1972, RG 25–4–32, LJTS; Gerson D. Cohen to DCK, 27 June, RG 25–4–30, [Theodore H. Silbert], "Search Committee," 10 July, RG 25–6–1, Meeting minutes, JM Board of Governors, 10 July 1972, RG 25–2–24, DCK to Martin M. Grabois, 13 July 1972, RG 25–4–32, LJTS; and [Louis Goldenberg] to MS, 18 July 1972, MSC 138:3, CUL. See also, AK to DCK, 13 July, and AK, "Proposal for the Operating Structure and Program for the Jewish Museum for the Next Two Years," [13] July 1972, RG 25–4–30, LJTS; and AK, oral history interview by Nicki Tanner, 24 July 1990, transcript, UJA-FNYC, I-433, AJHS, 24–29. See also, JU, oral history interview by Judy E. Tenney, 19 December 1989, transcript, UJA-FNYC, I-433, AJHS, 47–48. AK, *Jewish Experience in the Art of the Twentieth Century* (New York: Jewish Museum, 1975), 8, 49n1. AK subsequently expanded the material into AK, *Jewish Experience in the Art of the Twentieth Century* (South Hadley, MA: Bergin & Garvey Publishers, 1984). A scholar linked the exhibit with a pair of Soviet Jewry-related JM exhibits mounted three years prior, seeing in them evidence of the JM's shift "from formalist interpretations of art in the 1960s toward socially derived interpretations of art in the 1970s and 1980s"; Maya Balakirsky Katz, "Staging Protest: The New York Jewish Museum and the Soviet Jewry Movement," *American Jewish History* 96, no. 1 (March 2010): 61–78. John Russell, "Art That Tells of the Jewish Experience," *New York Times*, 24 October 1975; William Grimes, "John Russell, Art Critic for The Times, Dies at 89," *New York Times*, 24 August 2008. See also, "Jewish Experience in the Art of the Twentieth Century," *ArtNews* 75, no. 1 (January 1976): 117–18.

27. Harold Rosenberg, "The Art World: Jews in Art," *The New Yorker* LI, no. 44 (22 December 1975): 64–68. Debra Bricker Balken, *Harold Rosenberg: A Critic's Life* (Chicago, IL: University of Chicago Press, 2021). See also, John Russell, "Harold Rosenberg is Dead at 72, Art Critic for the New Yorker," *New York Times*, 13 July 1978; Dore Ashton, "On Harold Rosenberg," *Critical Inquiry* 6, no. 4 (Summer 1980): 615–24; and Mark Godfrey, "'That Oldtime Jewish Sect Called American Art Criticism,'" in *Action/Abstraction: Pollock, De Kooning, and American Art, 1940–1976*, ed. Norman L. Kleeblatt (New York: Jewish Museum and Yale University Press, 2008), 247–65. "Robert Pincus-Witten, Historian, Critic, and Curator Who Coined 'Post-Minimalism,' Has Died," *ArtNews*, 28 January 2018, accessed November 2020, https://www.artnews.com/art-news/news/robert-pincus-witten-historian-critic-curator-coined-post-minimalism-died-9717. Robert Pincus-Witten, "Six Propositions on Jewish Art," *Arts Magazine* 50, no. 4 (December 1975): 66–69. For a somewhat contrary view, see Lawrence Alloway, "Art," *The Nation* 221, no. 17 (22 November 1975): 541–42. On the "concern for Jewish experiences," see also, Matthew Baigell and Milly Heyd, introduction to *Complex Identities: Jewish Consciousness and Modern Art*, ed. Baigell and Heyd (New Brunswick, NJ: Rutgers University Press,

2001), xiv. However, Baigell subsequently rejected the notion in response to two hypothetical questions: "First, what is Jewish about Jewish art and, second, is there something called The Jewish Experience? The answer to the first question is 'nothing,' and to the second, 'no.'" Matthew Baigell, *Jewish Art in America: An Introduction* (Lanham, MD: Rowman & Littlefield, 2007), xiii.

28. Max Kozloff, "Jewish Art and the Modernist Jeopardy," *Artforum* 14, no. 8 (April 1976): 43–47. *Gale Literature: Contemporary Authors* (Farmington Hills, MI: Gale, 2007), *Gale In Context: Biography*, s.v. "Max Kozloff," accessed November 2020), doi: GALE|H1000055760.
29. Harold Rosenberg, "Is There a Jewish Art?" *Commentary* 42, no. 1 (July 1966): 57–60. See also, Kalman P. Bland, *The Artless Jew: Medieval and Modern Affirmations and Denials of the Visual* (Princeton, NJ: Princeton University Press, 2000), 39–40, 53; Margaret Olin, *The Nation Without Art: Examining Modern Discourses on Jewish Art* (Lincoln: University of Nebraska Press, 2001), 160–62, 193; and Godfrey, "'That Oldtime Jewish Sect Called American Art Criticism'," 258–64. For other attempts to define or reflect upon definitions of "Jewish art," see, Joseph Gutmann, "Is There a Jewish Art?," in *The Visual Dimension: Aspects of Jewish Art*, ed. Clair Moore (Boulder, CO: Westview Press, 1993), 1–19; Baigell, *Jewish Art in America*, ix–xxiv; and Samantha Baskind and Larry Silver, introduction to *Jewish Art: A Modern History* (London: Reaktion Books, 2011), 7–14. See also, chapter 3.
30. VL, oral history interview by Nicki Tanner, 27 March 1990, transcript, UJA-FNYC, I-433, AJHS, 11–12, 18–19; see also, VL, oral history interview by Paul Cummings, 9 January 1973, AAA, SI (unpaginated). VL discussed the possible display of Christian imagery at the JM with LF, although the context is unclear; LF to VL, 8 March 1962, RG 1–207–2, LJTS. BH, oral history interview by Paul Cummings, 8 January 1973, transcript, AAA, SI, 21–22, 39–41.
31. Abram Kanof, oral history interview by Judy Tenney, 19 November 1990 and 26 May 1992, transcript, UJA-FNYC, I-433, AJHS, 39–40. On Kanof and the workshop, see chapter 4. On the Rothko Chapel in context, see Pamela G. Smart, *Sacred Modern: Faith, Activism, and Aesthetics in the Menil Collection* (Austin: University of Texas Press, 2010), 21–45; "Much of [the de Menils'] activity was directed toward achieving some kind of rapprochement . . . between the sacred and profane, the transcendental and the secular world," p. 8.
32. Hasia R. Diner, *The Jews of the United States, 1654–2000* (Berkeley: University of California Press, 2004), 259, 305–6. Tennenbaum, "Jewish Home for the Graven Image," 18, 21, 23. Tennenbaum (1936–2013) is best known today as a fiction writer.

Epilogue

Over the following decades, the Jewish Museum stayed the course of its "all-Jewish" mandate by presenting exhibitions rooted in Jewish cultural history such as *Gardens and Ghettos: The Art of Jewish Life in Italy*, in 1989, which adopted a multidisciplinary approach supported with Judaica alongside paintings, drawings, and sculpture. Other shows, like *The Circle of Montparnasse: Jewish Artists in Paris, 1905–1945*, in 1985, reflected the museum's usual art emphasis in a historical survey of paintings, sculptures, and drawings. Occasionally the museum modeled a much broader scope in concept and materials displayed as with *The Dreyfus Affair: Art, Truth, and Justice*, in 1987. Integrating social history and cultural studies, the exhibit contained not only artworks, but also archival materials, documentary photographs, newspapers, and ephemera, among which were antisemitic portrayals. They were marshaled to tell the story of a wrongly accused and ultimately exonerated French officer Alfred Dreyfus, of Jewish descent, during a years-long miscarriage of justice that divided France at the turn from the nineteenth to twentieth centuries. Sometimes the museum stretched the boundaries of what all-Jewish might mean, but never so far or so persistently as during its avant-garde era. For example, there was *Action/Abstraction: Pollock, de Kooning, and American Art, 1940–1976*, a 2008 exhibit centered on two non-Jewish artists but that also included works by artists of Jewish descent and, significantly, was structured around the writings of Clement Greenberg and Harold Rosenberg. When the museum turned to a clearly non-Jewish topic, it was by revisiting its avant-garde heyday as was the case with *Other Primary Structures*, in 2014, inspired by the museum's pioneering 1966 *Primary Structures* exhibition, or *New York: 1962–1964*, in 2022, that used its role—during Alan Solomon's directorship—"as a jumping-off point" to explore New York's 1960s art world. With the benefit of hindsight, it set the artistic innovations of the era in a broader sociocultural context—an exercise in "self-promotional retrospection." That revisiting of the past also resurrected questions raised during Solomon's tenure such as, "Why exactly was [*New York: 1962–1964*] at the Jewish Museum?" As though agreeing with Ben Heller's observation concerning "the alert, intellectual, sensitive 'advanced Jew,'" a writer thought that type of exhibit might represent a "kind of Platonic vision of how to approach a given moment in history as a curious and open-minded Jew." Nonetheless, the museum still "pingpongs between very overtly Jewish exhibits" and those "having only the ghost of a Jewish angle."[1]

The exhibit *Too Jewish? Challenging Jewish Identities* illustrated the museum's continuing challenges. Presented in 1996 and featuring thirty-nine paintings, drawings, prints, mixed media-works, videos, and installations by nineteen artists, it aimed to show how contemporary "Jewish artists" dealt with questions of identity. *Too Jewish?* was divided into sections, one on representations of the Jewish body, another on depictions of Jews in popular culture, and the last on ritual as spiritual practice outside normative Judaism. Most works explored both negative as well as positive stereotypes—often with parody, satire, or irony—with results that were "confrontational, funny, and poignant." The exhibit's context was "a growing awareness of Jewish ethnicity as a missing link in the discourse on diversity and difference" in America. One reviewer noting this, felt *Too Jewish?* set itself apart, however, "from much of the race-based, gender-based and ethnic-based stuff that has swamped the art scene" in the prior decade through the artists' uses of humor and avoidance of "victim art." Because many of the works dealt in the "mired relationship between identity and stereotype," however, they left some questioning the extent to which the exhibit truly challenged "traditional" identity. Daniel A. Segal—a cultural anthropologist and historian—believed *Too Jewish?* in fact "produces and exhibits . . . 'traditional' identities." Rhetorically echoing the exhibit's title, Segal asked "Can You Tell a Jew When You See One?" and focused in part on the curatorial decision to "limit the roster of participation to Jewish artists." Determining the artists' ethnicity or the relevance of their work without resorting to stereotypes was all but impossible, he argued. Verifying the artists' ancestry would only resurrect other racial, ethnic, or religious stereotypes, whether done "bilaterally, as in Nazi racial science, or unilineally as in Orthodox [Jewish] law." To challenge traditional Jewish identity, Segal implied, one must first ascertain what that means.[2]

In aiming to show "Jewish artists" as a "marginalized group worthy of representation within the new identity-based order" of contemporary America, the exhibit relied on stereotypes in two ways: first, as Segal discerned, in the selection of the participating artists; and second, in the artists' methods of addressing questions of identity. By presenting

"Jewishness—that is Jewish difference—in very much the same way that other identity exhibitions present other ethnic and racial identities," the museum added a fresh dimension to its century-old origins in the contact zones of Jewish self-representation. As discussed at the beginning of this book, late-nineteenth-century French, British, and American Jews used their ritual objects to present an autoethnography to their others. Now Jews were utilizing representations of Jewishness—whether theirs or others', often drawn from popular culture—to claim a place in a "new identity-based order." When, about the same time as *Too Jewish?*, James Clifford applied Mary Louise Pratt's notion of the contact zone to museums, he explained how ethnic museums present minority "articulations of a discrete culture and history" in response "to histories of exclusion and silencing." The results often assert a "collective identity" as "a distinctive way of life, tradition, form of art." As though having seen *Too Jewish?*, Clifford added this "is the stuff of contemporary cultural politics, creative and virulent."[3]

For a few of the artists included in *Too Jewish?*, examining "a distinctive way of life" entailed reaching back to Judaism's pre-Enlightenment, pre-emancipation period before it bifurcated into the separate religious and ethnic spheres also considered at this book's beginning. The artists, in approaching Jewishness as a way of life imbued with religiosity, as an interior condition rather than an ethnic marker, nonetheless were creating "work for the secular sphere of [the] gallery." The outcome was, as noted by the exhibit's curator, ironic because "the religious theme or intent inherent in these works" led some of the artists to wonder whether their work was "'too Jewish' to exhibit in [secular] galleries, possibly even Jewish-oriented spaces" like the Jewish Museum. The quandary for such artists lay in determining where else, after all, they might best address Jewishness not as identity but as religious practice. For them, as for one of the exhibit's visitors, their dilemma was one of being "both 'too Jewish' and 'not Jewish enough.'"[4]

In her introductory comment for the *Too Jewish?* catalogue, the museum's director at the time, Joan Rosenbaum, contextualized the exhibition as evincing the "perpetual combination of continuity and change within the realm of Jewish culture." It was a subtle reference to the museum's recent reinstallation of its permanent collection titled *Culture and Continuity: The Jewish Journey*. The display was part of a major enlargement of the museum led by Rosenbaum who, in 1980, succeeded Joy Ungerleider. Rosenbaum (b. ca. 1935) trained in art history at Boston University and Hunter College, later earning a certificate in nonprofit management at Columbia University. She worked as a curatorial assistant at the Museum of Modern Art and directed the museums section of the New York State Council on the Arts before coming to the Jewish Museum. When reviewing arts-council grant applications, Rosenbaum was especially moved by small historical societies' efforts to document local history which she felt paralleled the Jewish community's preservation of its history. Parting from Ungerleider, however, Rosenbaum embraced the museum's redefinition as an art museum starting in the 1950s, but she also believed that while the museum would not be "a religious institution" it could be "a cultural one." Her conception of culture included contemporary art if associated with Jewish life or Judaism and if properly situated within its "political, art historical and societal" contexts. Rosenbaum was inspired by the museum's *Danzig 1939: Treasures of a Destroyed Community* exhibit, presented months before her directorship began. It featured ritual objects from the Jews of Danzig (now Gdańsk, Poland) who, in 1939, fearing a Nazi invasion, deposited the pieces with the museum, stipulating they should remain there in perpetuity unless the community was able to reconstitute itself, which of course never happened. *Danzig 1939* showed Rosenbaum how that kind of project "could appeal, because of its story—though it had religious objects—to secular Jews as well." It also suggested to Rosenbaum a fresh method for reinstalling the museum's Judaica collection.[5]

The collection's display had not been significantly updated in the years after its "all-Jewish" turn, so Rosenbaum's early 1990s plan to enlarge the museum afforded an opportunity to rethink the collection's presentation. The renovation nearly doubled the museum's exhibition space, added visitor amenities, and improved support facilities. It enlarged the museum along Fifth Avenue by filling in the entry plaza on that side, restoring the main entrance back to its original Warburg mansion location on 92nd Street. It also replaced the List wing with a taller addition matching the mansion's height. These changes allowed a seamless extension of the mansion's neo-Gothic exterior along Fifth Avenue (Figure 8.1). The addition also expanded the space for permanent-collection displays on the third and fourth floors—the first two floors reserved for temporary exhibitions as before. The renovated building's inauguration in June 1993 included *Culture and Continuity*, a thematic display of the collection arranged to illustrate how Judaism thrived for millennia despite repeated challenges to its existence. It aimed to show that Judaism's survival was born of the durability of Jewish values and Jews' adaptability in different lands and eras. Three aspects of Jewish experience were threaded through the display: Jews' questioning and reinterpretation of tradition, the interactions of Jews with other cultures, and historical circumstances that transformed

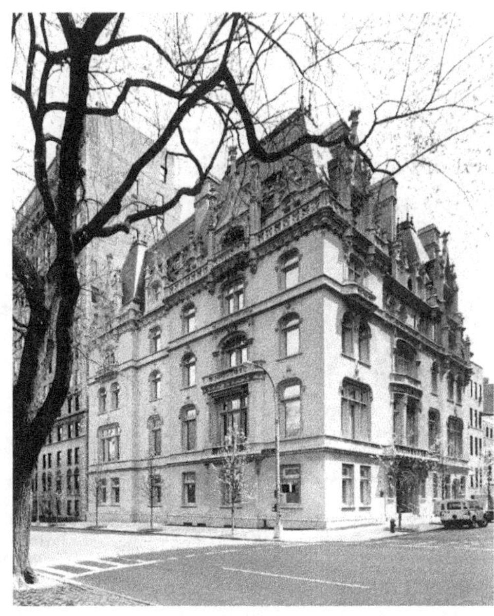

Figure 8.1. Jewish Museum addition (to the left, compare with Figures 3.1 and 4.6), 1993, designed by Kevin Roche (1922–2019) and completed in 1993. The Jewish Museum, New York/Art Resource, NY.

Jewish life. For the most part, *Culture and Continuity* was arranged chronologically and traced about four thousand years of history with nearly one thousand objects—about three times what it showed in the past—supplemented with maps, diagrams, photomurals, an interactive installation, and extensive narrative wall panels and briefer item labels. It was divided into four sections: "Forging an Identity" (on ancient Israel), "Interpreting a Tradition" (on the diaspora, from the Babylonian exile to the early modern period), "Confronting Modernity" (on the period from the Enlightenment and emancipation through the mid-twentieth century), and "Realizing a Future" (on the contemporary era).[6]

Culture and Continuity was a hit with critics and visitors, non-Jews as well as Jews, in part because it lent to its topic "grandeur and particularity." Audience research done after the installation opened showed that while Jewish ritual objects per se are "not a public draw," presenting them in a social or historical context renders them "more attractive to a wider public." At a time when Jewish museums were being established at a rapid pace across America, *Culture and Continuity* elevated its home to the status of the leading museum addressing Jewish culture and history, a position earned by concentrating more on education than aesthetics. With some sections resembling ethnographic displays, as might be found in an anthropology museum, even as others resembled art museum galleries, *Culture and Continuity* succeeded in uniting the museum's "previous incarnations into [one] multi-faceted institution," one that integrated old and new objects in the contexts of history, ritual, and theology. Reviewers also noted the installation's embrace of ethnic identity at a time when public discourse on the topic had become "downright trendy." For hopeful critics and museum professionals, that turn toward parochialism, rather than dividing people, might become a bridge to mutual understanding.[7]

Though more fully exploring its ethnic roots *and* taking up contemporary issues in Jewish culture and society, the museum was unable to escape divisive controversies. Such was the case with its 2002 exhibition, *Mirroring Evil: Nazi Imagery/Recent Art.* It invited visitors to reflect on the nature of evil by addressing the Holocaust's reverberations as perceived by artists a generation or more younger than the Nazis' victims. Most of the artists conveyed their ideas with representations of Nazis and death camps, often via altered forms of mass media—especially films, photographs, toys, and luxury-brand objects. Being conceptual artworks, many relied on parody and satire, forms too easily misread by viewers, even when skillfully explained. Unsurprisingly, given the horrific background of the exhibit's topic, it sparked angry protests from Holocaust survivors, their descendants, and others who felt the exhibit trivialized Nazi atrocities and the suffering they caused. It was thought that after opening *Culture and Continuity*, the museum, from its now more "specialized" position, would be a more effective "crucible for debate." Characterizing the museum as "A Place for Art and Debate" on its centenary in 2004, one critic rhetorically asked, "Why Should It Be Easy?"[8]

Upon Rosenbaum's retirement in 2011 she was succeeded by Claudia Gould. With an art history degree from Boston College and a graduate degree in museum studies from New York University, Gould (b. 1956) rose through curatorial and administrative positions at the Wexner Center for the Arts at Ohio State University, Artists Space in New York, and the Institute of Contemporary Arts at the University of Pennsylvania—all contemporary-art institutions. The Jewish Museum's board was attracted by her expertise in new art and skill in leading wide-ranging interdisciplinary exhibitions, educational programs, and public outreach. A journalist learned that Gould was raised by a Jewish father and Roman Catholic mother, a fact the museum's board chair dismissed as a "nonissue" and that, in an era of interfaith marriages, was an asset in reaching a wider community. Gould later commented that although raised as "culturally

Jewish" she had been unaware of several aspects of Judaism. Until coming to the museum, for example, Gould did not realize that because traditional Judaism is matrilineal, she would not be regarded as Jewish by some. Gould prioritized current art and culture, suggesting that although the museum's mission would remain unchanged, she would draw on her knowledge of contemporary art to also inform historical exhibitions including those of Judaica. Ultimately, she envisioned her programming combining "what went on in the '60s and '70s"—the avant-garde era—with Rosenbaum's emphasis on art's cultural contexts. As for *Culture and Continuity*, Gould intended to "shake things up ever so gently" by reinstalling the permanent collection.[9]

In January 2018, Gould—partnering with senior curator Susan Braunstein—replaced *Culture and Continuity* with *Scenes from the Collection*. The reinstallation was informed by a perception among museum professionals, according to Braunstein, that displays of ritual objects were not "where the excitement lies" and therefore do not draw large audiences, especially more diverse ones, particularly when the objects are conventionally displayed. For those reasons, Braunstein believed, new methods of displaying and interpreting the Judaica appropriate to contemporary interests had to be formulated. As a result, *Scenes from the Collection* was designed to supplant the narrative arc of *Culture and Continuity* with a treatment of the collection as a fortuitous if somewhat random aggregation of diverse objects. The new installation was divided into seven sections, or "scenes," that grouped objects according to arbitrary classifications such as "Constellations," "Taxonomies," "Masterpieces and Curiosities," "Accumulations," and "Signs and Symbols." The introduction to *Scenes* explains that each segment offers "a different filter" for understanding the collection. Although the objects are sometimes arranged in overlapping or linked stories within each segment, even those are "punctuated" with notes on the collection's history. Overall, *Scenes* was also aimed at affirming "universal values . . . shared among people of all faiths and backgrounds." Jewish and non-Jewish viewers would be disappointed, however, if they expected explanatory texts teasing out those universal values. Instead, visitors are cautioned as they enter *Scenes* that the display also embodies changes in curatorial practices designed to break up "artistic canons . . . dominated by the art of Western Europe and North America." This refers primarily to a history of Western museums' displays of non-Western artifacts based on hegemonic values and tastes that in recent decades have been subjected to critical scrutiny. The critique was aimed at encyclopedic art museums and their universalizing approach, however, not ethnocentric museums. It is unclear how a Jewish museum

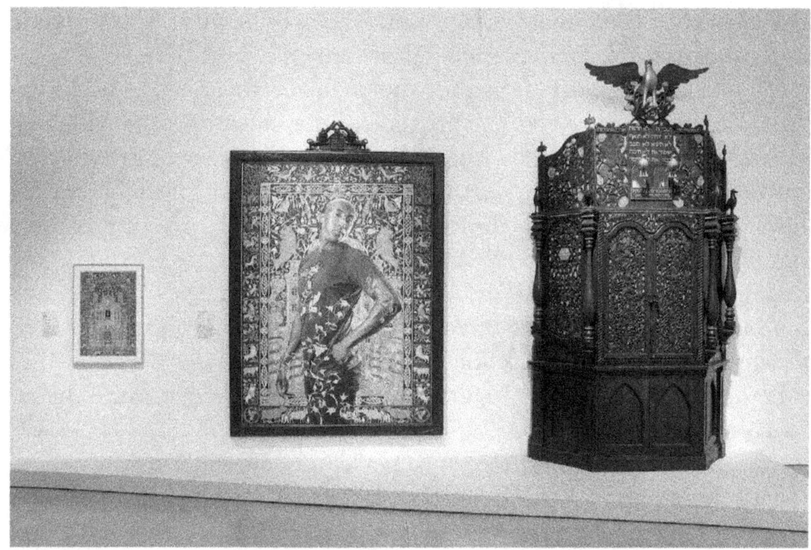

Figure 8.2. Installation view, "Constellations" section of *Scenes from the Collection* galleries, 2018. The Jewish Museum, New York/Art Resource, NY.

displaying Judaica would be positioned to enact those kinds of hegemonies because, after all, it was established by the community that produced the objects it is presenting. In any event, the museum's response to the perceived problem was to dispense with the thematic organization and narrative throughlines of *Culture and Continuity*.[10]

Scenes was also intended to enable a fuller representation of the collection than did *Culture and Continuity* by refreshing sections annually or semi-annually with rotations of different objects through them. The overall effect is limited, however, because *Scenes* is confined to just one floor, unlike its predecessor, which had two floors. Further, because the art works in *Scenes* are generously spaced befitting an art museum (Figure 8.2), other objects—particularly ritual objects—had to be crowded together. Examples of both are in "Constellations," which was conceived to feature a small number of the more compelling works in the collection that represent both "Jewish culture, history, or values" *and* "universal issues of art." The works are arranged, however, without concern for their uses, geographic origins, or chronology. "Taxonomies," which contains well over half of the nearly six hundred objects in *Scenes* (Figure 8.3), offers a mainly typological treatment of diverse objects to highlight the eclecticism and variety of the museum's holdings, likening the results to Renaissance "Cabinets of Wonders" known for combining disparate rarities and oddities. The groupings in "Taxonomies" include ritual objects juxtaposed with a ship model and miniature buildings, ritual objects presented with timepieces and glass vessels, and ritual objects alongside games and pastry molds. In that way, "Taxonomies" not only replicates the arbitrary classifications and randomness of Renaissance-era collections, but also recalls the earliest Judaica displays when plenitude and classificatory expedience shaped displays as in the London 1887 exhibition (Figures 2.3 and 2.5). So too, "Taxonomies" is reminiscent of the museum's displays of the 1930s and 1940s (Figures 2.10 and 3.7), which left a non-Jewish visitor at the time "mystified" by the Judaica, likening the experience to entering a museum of Native American artifacts "set up in a manner understandable only to the Indians themselves."[11]

Other *Scenes* are agglomerations born of curatorial-insider avoidances and conventions. "Accumulations," which for the inaugural display consisted of dozens of stereographs under the theme "Traveling in the Holy Land," was intended to offset the "preciousness" of unique artworks with its assemblage of identically sized, mass-produced images. For "Masterpieces and Curiosities," examples of the former were to be selected for their historical importance, visual allure, and craftsmanship; and the latter because of their eccentricity or singularity. For the inaugural installation, "Masterpieces and Curiosities" featured a "charm bracelet" from a Holocaust survivor imprisoned at the Theresienstadt ghetto and death camp. Attached to the bracelet were monograms, miniature utensils, tiny silhouettes, and other items created by the survivor and others. The display was augmented with other works created at or about Theresienstadt. Interpretive materials explained the bracelet's origins and the items attached to it, as well as other materials in the scene. They did not, however, address the origins and nature of the Holocaust, the place of Theresienstadt in the Nazis' persecution of the Jews, or the larger history of antisemitism. Although "Masterpieces and Curiosities" aimed to show how selected works can reveal "complex histories and rich layers of meaning" when presented in context, much of that context was missing. Instead, the bracelet was treated as a curiosity from a particular site and time. If, as one scholar observed, *Culture and Continuity* had arranged the objects of Judaism into a "chronological tour," *Scenes from the Collection* had arranged them around "exhibition concepts."[12]

Critics were unpersuaded by *Scenes*. Noting it follows a curatorial "vogue for nonchronological hangs" instead of historical narratives, Jason Farago commented that—when effective—the anachronisms show unexpected relationships across time. But they were achieved at the cost of favoring "superficial similarities over historical rigor" because *Scenes*

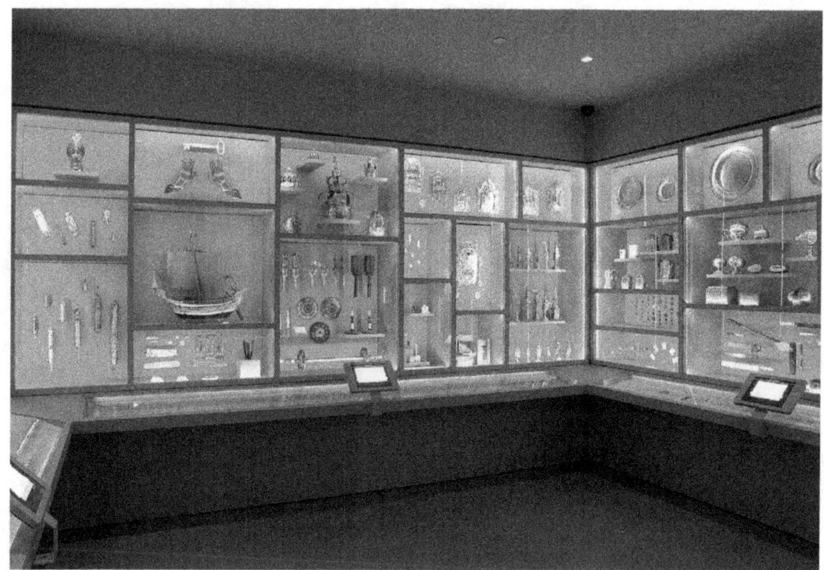

Figure 8.3. Installation view, "Taxonomies" section (east wall) of *Scenes from the Collection* galleries, 2018. The Jewish Museum, New York/Art Resource, NY.

assumes visitors' familiarity with Judaism, thereby dispensing with too much necessary information. Other reviews were even less charitable. Well before *Scenes from the Collection*'s opening, Edward Rothstein had set the stage for such reviews with nearly two decades of essays on the evolution of ethnic identity museums in America. In his formulation, they were created by ethnic groups to serve multiple purposes: presenting the group's accomplishments, countering unfavorable portrayals in encyclopedic museums and popular culture, and as community centers to promote group solidarity. From that perspective, Rothstein saw Jewish museums—which he regarded as ipso facto ethnic identity museums—as racing to the other extreme, becoming the only identity museums "defined by the abnegation" of identity. Among all the Jewish museums he visited, Rothstein discerned a pattern in which the institutions' founding particularism evolved into universalism, endangering the future of Judaism itself. Although Jewish museums succeeded in avoiding the chauvinism too-often evident in other identity museums, that came at a high price. Left unaddressed were vital and informative questions about the nature of Judaism, Jewishness in a secular society, and the role of identity in Jewish survival. As a result, Rothstein argued, Jewish museums had jettisoned the very identity they were created to express and support, suggesting instead that when it comes to Judaism: "The particular is too particular. The Jew is too Jewish. The religion is too religious."[13]

After *Scenes from the Collection* opened, Rothstein returned to many of the same issues, now exemplified, he believed, by the Jewish Museum. His observations came among solicited responses to Menachem Wecker's essay on *Scenes*, "The Wreck of the Jewish Museum." A freelance journalist covering the interanimations of art, culture, and religion, Wecker began the colloquy by arguing that *Scenes*, in failing to address the essential tenets of Judaism, neglected Jews and non-Jews interested in learning about Jewish religion, history, and culture. Indeed, he argued, they would more likely benefit from visiting the Museum of the Bible founded by evangelical Christians in Washington, DC. Wecker's first respondent, Tom Freudenheim, suspected the museum was uneasy with addressing Judaism as a religion and, as a result, *Scenes* neglected the beliefs embodied by the ritual objects it contained. Another respondent, artist and writer Richard McBee, called for a yet firmer emphasis on Jewish cultural history and its current expressions, in part by focusing even more exclusively on contemporary, self-identifying Jewish artists. Rothstein focused on the museum's discussion of Jewish identity in the *Scenes* introductory wall text, highlighting its emphasis on both reflecting Jewish identities in the past and serving as a guide to forming new ones. He, like the others, noted the absence of substantive Judaic contextualization and raised topics left unaddressed: the ways Jews' religious and cultural differences manifested in their ritual objects, the nature of Judaism's sacred holidays and festivals, and how Judaism helped shaped modernity while, in turn, being shaped by it. Rothstein believed the museum had, if anything, distanced itself from the topic of Jewish identity when it literally demolished *Culture and Continuity*, one of the few Jewish museum surveys on Jewish history and religion. The failure of the museum to play a leading role in educating Jews and non-Jews about Judaism was especially painful, he added, at a time when doing so might help combat a rising wave of antisemitism erupting in America in the runup to and following Donald Trump's presidential election.[14]

In its pursuit of "universal values" and "universal issues of art," *Scenes from the Collection* echoed aims of the museum's avant-garde era. Its revitalization of the permanent-collection display, while seemingly forward-looking and professionally fashionable, also reaffirmed the secular underpinnings of museum history. Its display methods and nomenclature—taxonomies, accumulations, masterpieces, and curiosities—were drawn from the origins of museums in their reification of modernity's secularizing ethos. Perhaps inadvertently, *Scenes* vividly reenacts how museums became deracinating machines whereby religious objects were desacralized, arranged, and scrutinized with the presumptive objectivity and universalizing aims of modern knowledge production. It is unsurprising, then, that *Scenes* sparked debates reminiscent of those during the avant-garde era when the museum struggled to balance its Judaica and contemporary-art programs. The results echoed Richard I. Cohen's observation, when recalling the museum's avant-garde era, that "Parochialism, no matter how defined, is for some [their] greatest fear; universalism their never-ending goal." Rothstein, seeing the same pattern, thought it might reflect a deeper problem. When the Jewish Museum and its peers, instead of approaching Judaism as a subject "deserving of the deepest pride and most scrupulous study," sloughed it off, he wondered if "in the face of universalism, Judaism was susceptible . . . of losing itself." In her survey of Jewish museums, Ruth R. Seldin thought that resolving the particularism-versus-universalism issue—to which one might add struggles over religion versus secularism, or ethnicity versus assimilation—would remain problematic "precisely because [they reflect] the tensions and confusion inherent in modern Jewish life." Writing in 2020, about a half century after the termination of the avant-garde program, a critic surveying its history found the museum "still grappling with internal and external debates over whether [it] is 'too Jewish' or 'not Jewish enough.'" As the history of Jewish experiments with public displays reveals, the challenge of striking "just the right balance, to do justice to both aspects" may forever remain an elusive goal.[15]

Notes

1. Vivian B. Mann, ed., *Gardens and Ghettos: The Art of Jewish Life in Italy* (Berkeley: University of California Press, 1989); Kenneth E. Silver and Romy Golan, *The Circle of Montparnasse: Jewish Artists in Paris, 1905–1945* (New York: Universe Books, 1985); *The Dreyfus Affair: Art, Truth, and Justice*, ed. Norman L. Kleeblatt (Berkeley: University of California Press, 1987). *Action/Abstraction: Pollock, De Kooning, and American Art, 1940–1976*, ed. Norman L. Kleeblatt (New York: Jewish Museum and Yale University Press, 2008). On Greenberg and Rosenberg, see respectively chapters 3 and 7. [Kynaston McShine], *Primary Structures: Younger American and British Sculptors* (New York: Jewish Museum, 1966). On that show, see chapter 6. [Jens Hoffman, ed.,] *Other Primary Structures* (New York: Jewish Museum and Yale University Press, 2014). The latter catalogue is accompanied by a facsimile of the now-out-of-print 1966 catalogue. Germano Celant, ed., *New York, 1962–1964* (New York: Jewish Museum | Milan, IT: Skira Editore, 2022). "Exhibition Examines Pivotal Three-Year Period in the History of Art and Culture in

New York City" [publicity release], Jewish Museum, accessed March 2023, https://thejewishmuseum.org/press/press-release/exhibition-examines-pivotal-three-year-period-in-the-history-of-art-and-culture-in-new-york-city. See also, Susan Delson, "A City on the Upswing," *Wall Street Journal*, 9–10 July 2022; Holland Cotter, "In a Manic Era, a Shift in Culture," *New York Times*, 22 July 2022; Karen Wilkin, "'New York: 1962–1964': Present at the Creation," *Wall Street Journal*, 31 August 2022; Jan Avgikos, "New York: 1962–1964," *Artforum International* 61, no. 3 (November 2022): 27. For promotional retrospection, see Suzaan Boettger, "New York: 1962–1964," *Brooklyn Rail*, September 2022, accessed March 2023, https://brooklynrail.org/2022/09/artseen/New-York-19621964. For the last three quotes, see Irene Katz Connelly and Mira Fox, "The Jewish Museum's New Exhibit Is Barely Jewish. Does That Matter?" *Forward*, 17 August 2022, accessed March 2023, https://forward.com/culture/514813/jewish-museum-1962-1964-how-jewish-does-it-need-to-be/. On BH, see chapters 5 and 7.

2. JR, "Director's Statement," in *Too Jewish? Challenging Traditional Identities*, ed. Norman L. Kleeblatt (New Brunswick, NJ: Rutgers University Press, 1996), vii; Norman L. Kleeblatt, preface and "'Passing' Into Multiculturalism," in *Too Jewish?*, ix–x, 3, 5–6, 28. For quoted reviews, see Michael Kimmelman, "Too Jewish? Jewish Artists Ponder," *New York Times*, 8 March 1996; Carol Ockman, "'Too Jewish? Challenging Traditional Identities': Jewish Museum," *Artforum International* 35, no. 1 (September 1996): 106; Christopher Knight, "'Too Jewish?' Good Query; Art Review: Despite the Exhibition's Subtitle, Traditional Identities Are Not Confronted," *Los Angeles Times*, 4 February 1997. See also, Paula Span, "'Too Jewish?' A New York Art Exhibit Asks How That Is Possible," *Los Angeles Times*, 17 March 1996; Frank Rich, "The 'Too Jewish' Question," *New York Times*, 16 March 1996; and Elliott Horowitz, "Too Jewish? And Other Jewish Questions: A Review Essay," *Modern Judaism* 19, no. 2 (May 1999): 195–206. Daniel A. Segal, "Can You Tell a Jew When You See One? or Thoughts on Meeting Barbra/Barbie at the Museum," *Judaism* 48, no. 2 (Spring 1999): 239–40.
3. Kleeblatt, "'Passing' Into Multiculturalism," 5. Segal, "Can You Tell a Jew When You See One?," 240. See chapter 1. James Clifford, "Museums as Contact Zones," in *Routes: Travel and Translation in the Late Twentieth Century* (Cambridge, MA: Harvard University Press, 1997), 213–14, 218.
4. Kleeblatt, "'Passing' Into Multiculturalism," 28. Leslie Camhi, "Jewish Wry," *Village Voice*, 2 April 1996.
5. JR, "Director's Statement," vii. JU left in 1980; JU to MS, 19 December 1979, MSC 137:15 and James L. Weinberg to GDC, 11 April 1980, MSC 138:4, CUL. By then her last name was Ungerleider-Mayerson, see chapter 6. On JR's appointment, see James L. Weinberg to JM Board of Trustees, 9 October 1980, MSC 138:4, CUL and JR, oral history interview by Nicki Tanner, 9 September and 6 October 1999, transcript, UJA-FNYC, I-433, AJHS, 27–31. Publicity release, "After 30 Years of Service, Joan Rosenbaum to Retire as Director of the Jewish Museum in June 2011," 1 December

2010, JM. On JR's historical society, art-versus-history, and Danzig observations, see JR, oral history interview, 21–22, 35, 57. *Danzig 1939, Treasures of a Destroyed Community*, ed. Sheila Schwartz (Detroit: Wayne State University Press for the Jewish Museum, 1980); Ian T. Macauley, "Exhibition on Danzig Set for Jewish Museum," *New York Times*, 16 March 1980. See also chapter 3. Other quotes are from Grace Glueck, "The Jewish Museum Reaches Out," *New York Times*, 4 April 1989.

6. "Jewish Museum to Reopen," *New York Times*, 6 June 1993; and Herbert Muschamp, "Jewish Museum Renovation: A Celebration of Gothic Style," *New York Times*, 11 June 1993. The JM also considered relocating; JR, oral history interview by Nicki Tanner, 9 September and 6 October 1999, transcript, UJA-FNYC, I-433, AJHS, 62–65. Inauguration of the renovated building included two temporary exhibits, *From the Inside Out: Eight Contemporary Artists* and *Collecting for the 21st Century: Recent Acquisitions and Promised Gifts*. *From the Inside Out: Eight Contemporary Artists*, ed. Susan Tumarkin Goodman (New York: Jewish Museum, 1993). On *Culture and Continuity*, JR, oral history interview by Nicki Tanner, 9 September and 6 October 1999, transcript, UJA-FNYC, I-433, AJHS, 59–62. *Culture and Continuity* quotes are from the author's notes and photographs recorded in 2013. The fourth floor of the exhibit was reinstalled in 2000, and the third floor in 2003, prior to an extensive change discussed below.
7. On grandeur, see Roberta Smith, "Jewish Museum as Sum of Its Past," *New York Times*, 11 June 1993. On Jewish ritual objects, see Ena Giurescu Heller, "Religion on a Pedestal: Exhibiting Sacred Art," in *Reluctant Partners: Art and Religion in Dialogue*, ed. Heller (New York: The Gallery at the American Bible Society, 2004), 125. On Jewish museums' proliferation at the time, see Ruth R. Seldin, "American Jewish Museums: Trends and Issues," in *American Jewish Year Book*, vol. 91, ed. David Singer and Ruth R. Seldin (New York: American Jewish Committee, 1991), 71–117. See also, Nancy Frazier, *Jewish Museums of North America: A Guide to Collections, Artifacts, and Memorabilia* (New York: John Wiley & Sons, Inc., 1992). For reviews, see Muschamp, "Jewish Museum Renovation"; Deborah Solomon, "The Gallery: Mansion Site Enlarged, Renovated," *Wall Street Journal*, 11 June 1993. See also, Julia M. Klein, "Provocative Look at Jewish Art, Culture," *Orlando Sentinel* [Florida], 5 September 1993; and Sue Fishkoff, "Picture Perfect: Neither a Traditional Art Museum Nor a History Center . . . ," *Jerusalem Post*, 11 June 1993. On trendiness, see Michael Kimmelman, "A Museum Finds Its Time," *New York Times*, 13 June 1993.
8. Norman L. Kleeblatt, ed., *Mirroring Evil: Nazi Imagery/Recent Art* (New Brunswick, NJ: Rutgers University Press, 2001). Previews clouded the opening with controversy, Lisa Gubernick, "Coming Museum Show with Nazi Theme Stirs New York's Art World," *New York Times*, 10 January 2002; and Edward Rothstein, "Artists Seeking Their Inner Nazi," *New York Times*, 2 February 2002; and protests greeted its opening, Daniel Belasco, "Hot Issues, Cool Art: Jewish Museum's 'Mirroring Evil' Show Finally Opens to Protest,

Curiosity and Yawns," *New York Jewish Week*, 22 March 2002. For other critiques, see Michael Kimmelman, "Evil, the Nazis and Shock Value," *New York Times*, 15 March 2002; Peter Schjeldahl, "The Hitler Show; the Jewish Museum Revisits the Nazis," *New Yorker* 78, no. 6 (1 April 2002): 87; Thane Rosenbaum, "Mirroring Evil: 'Mirroring Evil: Nazi Imagery/Recent Art,'" *Tikkun* 17, no. 3 (May/June 2002): 69. See also, Linda Nochlin, "Mirroring Evil: Nazi Imagery/Recent Art," *Artforum International* 40, no. 10 (Summer 2002): 167–207; James E. Young, "Looking Into the Mirrors of Evil," *Journal of Israeli History* 23, no. 1 (Spring 2004): 157–66; Laura S. Levitt, "Refracted Visions: A Critique of 'Mirroring Evil: Nazi Imagery/Recent Art,'" *Studies in Gender and Sexuality* 6, no. 2 (2005): 199–216 (Levitt also gives some background on the exhibit's planning, pp. 204–6). For a detailed discussion and photos of the exhibit, see Reesa Greenberg, "*Mirroring Evil,* Evil Mirrored: Timing, Trauma, and Temporary Exhibitions," in *Museums After Modernism: Strategies of Engagement*, ed. Griselda Pollock and Joyce Zemans (Malden, MA: Blackwell Publishing, 2007), 104–18. See also, Sarah Boxer, "Man Behind a Museum Tempest: A Curator Defends His Show," *New York Times*, 6 February 2002. On crucible for debate, Michael Kimmelman, "A Museum Finds Its Time." Julie Salamon, "At 100, Still Asking 'Why Should It Be Easy?': The Jewish Museum, a Place for Art and Debate," *New York Times*, 21 January 2004. The article's title question is from a play read by the play's author at a JM event; Tony Kushner, "It's an Undoing World or Why Should It Be Easy When It Can Be Hard?," *Conjunctions* 25 (Fall 1995): 14–32.

9. Publicity release, "After 30 Years of Service, Joan Rosenbaum to Retire as Director of the Jewish Museum in June 2011," 1 December 2010, JM. Kate Taylor, "Jewish Museum Picks Director from Art World," *New York Times*, 23 August 2011; Publicity release, "The Jewish Museum Announces Appointment of Claudia Gould . . . ," 24 August 2011, JM; Allan Kozinn, "A Museum Broadens Its Identity," *New York Times*, 12 February 2013. Gould left the JM in June 2023, Alex Greenberg, "Director of New York's Jewish Museum to Depart After a Decade," *Artnews*, 30 September 2022, accessed March 2023, https://www.artnews.com/art-news/news/claudia-gould-departs-jewish-museum-1234641206/. James S. Snyder (b. 1952), formerly director of the Israel Museum, succeeded Gould in November 2023. Publicity release, "The Jewish Museum Appoints James S. Snyder . . . ," 14 August 2023, JM; Hilarie M. Sheets, "New Museum Director Brings International Experience," *New York Times*, 15 August 2023.
10. Heller, "Religion on a Pedestal," 132. On Braunstein, "Susan L. Braunstein, Senior Curator Emerita," JM, accessed July 2021, https://thejewishmuseum.org/about/staff-profile/susan-braunstein. Publicity release, "Culture & Continuity: The Jewish Journey's Last Day on View . . . ," 12 February 2017, JM; Publicity release, "Scenes from the Collection . . . ," 17 January 2018, Press Office, JM. For installation quotes, see "*Scenes from the Collection*: Wall Texts and Object Labels," JM, accessed July 2021, https://s3.amazonaws

.com/tjmassets/exhibition_pdfs/Scenes_from_the_Collection_Checklist_as_of_1.26.18.pdf. On Western hegemony relevant here, see Sally Price, *Primitive Art in Civilized Places* (Chicago, IL: University of Chicago Press, 1989), especially her chapter "The Universality Principle." See also, Carol Duncan and Alan Wallach, "The Universal Survey Museum," *Art History* 3, no. 4 (December 1980): 448–69; and Andrew McClellan's chapter "Collecting, Classification, and Display," in his *The Art Museum from Boullée to Bilbao* (Berkeley: University of California Press, 2008), 107–54.

11. Perhaps *Scenes from the Collection* was also motivated by a need for more temporary exhibit space. The 1993 building renovation provided "only slightly more changing exhibition space. . . . Everyone wishes we had more." JR, oral history interview by Nicki Tanner, 9 September and 6 October 1999, transcript, UJA-FNYC, I-433, AJHS, 83. The third floor was expanded slightly with the removal of a stairwell; and the fourth floor, once used for *Culture and Continuity*, was reallocated for in-person educational programming and collection storage, Daniela Stigh, Director of Marketing Communications, JM to Jeffrey Abt, 28 July 2021. For installation quotes, "Scenes from the Collection: Wall Texts and Object Labels," JM, accessed July 2021, https://s3.amazonaws.com/tjmassets/exhibition_pdfs/Scenes_from_the_Collection_Checklist_as_of_1.26.18.pdf. The seminal work on Renaissance cabinets, originally published in German in 1908, is Julius von Schlosser, *Art and Curiosity Cabinets of the Late Renaissance: A Contribution to the History of Collecting*, ed. Thomas DaCosta Kaufman and trans. Jonathan Blower (Los Angeles, CA: Getty Research Institute, Getty Publications, 2021). See also, *The Origins of Museums: The Cabinet of Curiosities in Sixteenth- and Seventeenth-Century Europe*, ed. Oliver Impey and Arthur MacGregor (Oxford: Clarendon Press, 1985). Also relevant are Abigail Glogower and Margaret Olin, "Between Two Worlds: Ghost Stories Under Glass in Vienna and Chicago," in *Visualizing and Exhibiting Jewish Space and History*, vol. 26, ed. Richard I. Cohen (Oxford: Oxford University Press, 2012), 217–42; and documentation of the material remnants of Jewish life, in David Altshuler, ed., *The Precious Legacy: Judaic Treasures from the Czechoslovak State Collections* (New York: Summit Books, 1983), 26–27, 39, 167, 181–82. On Native American comparison, see Frances Hawkins to Edward M. M. Warburg, 24 March 1949, RG 1–80–42, LJTS.

12. For installation quotes, see "Scenes from the Collection: Wall Texts and Object Labels," JM, accessed July 2021, https://s3.amazonaws.com/tjmassets/exhibition_pdfs/Scenes_from_the_Collection_Checklist_as_of_1.26.18.pdf. "Theresienstadt Bracelet Texts," JM, accessed July 2021, https://s3.amazonaws.com/tjmassets/press_releases/Scenes_from_the_Collection_MC_Terezin_Bracelet_iPad_FINAL.pdf. The notion of "curiosities" as used by the JM derives from the nomenclature of Renaissance collections; see previous note. Walter Cahn, *Masterpieces: Chapters on the History of an Idea* (Princeton, NJ: Princeton University Press, 1979). On exhibition concepts, see Maya Balakirsky Katz, "'jews': How a Single Painting

in the New York Jewish Museum's Collection Helps Define Jewish Art," *Tablet* [online magazine], accessed December 2020, https://www.tabletmag.com/sections/arts-letters/articles/anastasi-jewish-museum.

13. Jason Farago, "A Museum's Fresh Take on the Whole Megillah," *New York Times*, 25 January 2018. Edward Rothstein, "To Each His Own Museum, as Identity Goes on Display," *New York Times*, 28 December 2010. Edward Rothstein, "The Problem with Jewish Museums," *Mosaic*, 1 February 2016, accessed March 2018, http://mosaicmagazine.com/essay/2016/02/the-problem-with-jewish-museums/. Rothstein's essay focuses on American Jewish museums. In Britain, Jewish museums fully utilize ritual objects and other artifacts to explain Judaism to the general public, in part to "combat prejudice and stereotypes, to promote positive images of Jewish life and people"—acknowledging that Jews are "not only members of a specific religious group, they are also an ethnic and cultural minority." Rickie Burman, "Presenting Judaism: Jewish Museums in Britain," in *Godly Things: Museums, Objects, and Religion*, ed. Crispin Paine (London: Leicester University Press, 2000), 136.
14. Rothstein first addressed *Scenes* in his, "Exhibition Review: A People's History Exiled," *Wall Street Journal*, 23 January 2018. Menachem Wecker, "The Wreck of the Jewish Museum," *Mosaic*, 6 May 2019, accessed September 2019, https://mosaicmagazine.com/essay/arts-culture/2019/05/the-wreck-of-the-jewish-museum/. See also, Menachem Wecker, "The Case for the News Media's Engagement with Museum Religious Exhibits," in *Religion in Museums: Global and Multidisciplinary Perspectives*, ed. Gretchen Buggeln, Crispin Paine, and Brent S. Plate (London: Bloomsbury Academic, 2017), 109–14. Kelly Gannon and Kimberly Wagner, "Museum of the Bible . . . Permanent Collection," *Journal of American History* 105, no. 3 (December 2018): 618–25; and "About, Our Story," Museum of the Bible, accessed July 2021, https://www.museumofthebible.org/our-history. Tom L. Freudenheim, "The Jewish Museum's Discomfort with Religion," *Mosaic*, 13 May 2019, accessed September 2019, https://mosaicmagazine.com/response/arts-culture/2019/05/the-jewish-museums-discomfort-with-religion/. Richard McBee, "There's Plenty of Significant Contemporary Jewish Art Hiding in Plain Sight," *Mosaic*, 24 May 2019, accessed September 2019, https://mosaicmagazine.com/response/arts-culture/2019/05/theres-plenty-of-significant-contemporary-jewish-art-hiding-in-plain-sight/. Edward Rothstein, "The Dismantling of Jewish Identity," *Mosaic*, 20 May 2019, accessed September 2019, https://mosaicmagazine.com/response/arts-culture/2019/05/the-dismantling-of-jewish-identity/. Regarding "new" antisemitic problems at the time of Rothstein's essay, see Johnny Diaz, "Anti-Semitic Incidents Surged in 2019, Report Says," *New York Times*, 12 May 2020.
15. Richard I. Cohen, "Between Encyclopedias and Museums: Modes of Jewish Empowerment and Visibility," in *Simon Dubnow Institute Yearbook*, vol. 9, ed. Dan Diner (Göttingen: Vandenhoeck & Ruprecht, 2010), 468. Also relevant, but phrased as "apologetics" versus "a more universalistic approach,"

is Cohen, "The Visual Revolution in Jewish Life—An Overview," in *Visualizing and Exhibiting Jewish Space and History*, 8–20. For the too-Jewish quote, see Arthur Lubow, "How New York's Jewish Museum Anticipated the Avant-Garde," *New York Times Style Magazine*, 26 July 2020. Seldin, "American Jewish Museums," 85.

Acknowledgments

The questions that led to this book arose during my formative years as I began pursuing interests in both art making and Judaism. These intensified at different times and proceeded at different tempos, sometimes intersecting and sometimes diverging. One period of intersection was during the four summers from 1966 to 1969 when I participated in and then helped lead arts festivals held at the Kutz Camp Institute in upstate New York about forty miles from Manhattan. They were organized by the National Federation of Temple Youth, a program of Reform Judaism's congregational arm, to help advance the creative and performing arts among Jewish high-school students selected from around the country. The environment was conducive to thinking imaginatively about the relationship between the arts and Judaism, and among my mentors at the time were Henri and Melanie Bouton who, alas, are no longer with us. Being close to New York City, I often availed myself of its opportunities, occasionally with guidance from my late Aunt Irmgard (Abt) Sherman who lived there and told me about the Jewish Museum. Like visitors quoted in this book, I was struck by its exhibits of avant-garde art and found its Judaica displays comparatively uninteresting.

My next sustained involvement with art and Judaism came in the mid-1970s. With the encouragement of Rabbi Barry Cytron, then of Tifereth Israel Synagogue in Des Moines, Iowa, I was paid to create a slide collection on what today would be called Jewish visual culture for the synagogue's educational programs. The project required my combing many publications to find and photograph images of exemplary works including ritual objects, synagogue architecture, and paintings and sculptures by Jewish artists. The latter especially had me questioning what works qualified as "Jewish" and thus relevant for the collection. Aspects of that inquiry echoed in conversations with another mentor, artist Jules Kirschenbaum, about Jewish mysticism, its vivid imagery, and religious doubt. It was not until a couple of decades later, after my career in museums and collections—and studies of their history, that I thought back to my Jewish Museum visits, now with far more background in the formation and workings of museums. Reading about the museum's avant-garde era evoked a sense of familiarity because it unfolded during the period when I came of age. What others described in retrospect was in some ways my lived experience. Further, I could see that the best publications on the museum were written in the context of Jewish studies rather than the history of museums and thus overlooked important aspects of the story. It was at the intersection of museum culture and Judaism that I found an opportunity for a fresh look.

The transformation of these observations into a book began with a seed grant from Wayne State University, my institutional home. The grant came during an initiative supporting research in the arts spearheaded by Gloria Heppner, for whose understanding and foresight I am deeply indebted. The grant enabled some years of archival research in out-of-town repositories requiring travel that in turn necessitated a heap of paperwork. The late Marie Persha and then Ted Duenas in my department handled it and myriad related bureaucratic impediments with aplomb. Much of my research was in the archives of the Jewish Theological Seminary where I was graciously assisted by Sarah Diamont and Warren Klein in the beginning, and later on, by Mordecai Schwartz and Andrew Katz. Extensive research was also conducted at the Jewish Museum, where I was welcomed with the very perceptive counsel of Ruth Beesch and assisted in the museum's archive by Barbara Packer. In the museum's rich photography archives, I profited from the thoughtfulness and generously shared knowledge of Katherine Danalakis and Ellen Croisier. So too, Bruce Nielsen at the Katz Center for Advanced Judaic Studies, Kislak Center, at the University of Pennsylvania was unfailingly helpful. Of equally great assistance, though mediated though online forms, were the dedicated interlibrary-loan staff members of Wayne State University and the University of Michigan whose persistence uncovered numerous obscure but essential sources.

Along the way, I had the good fortune to learn from a community of wise and learned scholars. At the outset, among the peer reviews of my seed-grant proposal was one from the late Ivan Karp whose counsel and sagacity were indispensable. As my work proceeded, I profited from the selfless support and kind advice given by Bruce Altshuler, Ray Silverman, and the late Vivian Mann. I am also indebted to Barbara Kirshenblatt-Gimblett, Deborah Dash Moore, Ivan Gaskell, and my colleague Dora Apel for their insights. Tom Freudenheim and Susan Tumarkin Goodman, who both served as curators at the Jewish Museum, graciously shared their knowledge and offered important correctives as I sought to fill gaps in the museum's history. A crucial turning point in my research came with a fellowship at the Frankel Institute for Advanced Judaic Studies at the University of Michigan under the theme Secularization and Sacralization. Adroitly guided by head fellow, Scott Spector, the year teemed with thought-provoking discussions arising from workshop papers and casual conversations. Among my fellow fellows, I gained greatly from the critiques and suggestions offered by Scott, Ariel Mayse, Marc Caplan, Jessica Dubow, and Miriamne Krummel. During that year, I enjoyed the research assistance of Aubree Sepler, who tenaciously searched for and skillfully assembled an array of information, posing generative questions all along the way. As the manuscript for this book neared its final stages, it was mightily improved with probing comments from Connie Webber. Timely support from the Frankel Center for Judaic Studies at the University of Michigan covered the cost of indexing this book during another glorious year at the Frankel Institute, this time with the theme of Jewish Visual Cultures. I am also grateful to the anonymous readers of Berghahn Books for their very useful observations, and among them I am especially indebted to Laura Leibman and Richard I. Cohen who disclosed their identities. The product of years of archival research, this book also benefitted over time from conversations with many others, whose names I never learned or unfortunately have forgotten, following conference papers, in archives, or elsewhere as people learned of this project. Finally, I thank the staff at Berghahn for its guidance throughout and especially Lizzie Martinez who stewarded this book through the production process with patience and understanding.

It saddens me that my Aunt Irm was not around to read the manuscript for this book. Having lived in New York for a long time and being an astute observer of its cultural life and Jewish community—she worked for the United Jewish Appeal—Irm was an informed and unstinting critic who did not let family sentiment get in the way of seasoned provocations. Fortunately, I still have the good-natured and always savvy pokes served up by Mary Paquette-Abt and our children Uri and Danya to assure I pursue my projects with humility.

Selected Bibliography

Archival Sources

American Jewish Historical Society
Archives of American Art, Smithsonian Institution
Archives, Jewish Museum
Library, Herbert D. Katz Center for Advanced Judaic Studies, Kislak Center for Special Collections, Rare Books and Manuscripts, University of Pennsylvania
Rare Book and Manuscript Library, Columbia University Libraries
Smithsonian Institution Archives
Special Collections, The Library of the Jewish Theological Seminary

Most of the archival materials on the JM's history for the period addressed in this book are in the Special Collections, The Library of the Jewish Theological Seminary. Some, especially those concerning exhibitions and collections, are in the Archives, Jewish Museum. A portion of the museum's archives from the mid-1940s through mid-1969 were lost in a museum-office fire: KK to LF, 24 July 1969, RG 1–267–6, LJTS; "The Jewish Museum," Report to Board of Overseers, May 1970, RG 21–6–20, LJTS; and Stanley J. Schacter to MS, 4 June 1985, MSC 138: 4, CUL.

Selected Published Sources

The following are limited to primary sources, significant secondary sources, and substantially relevant contextual works.

Asterisks designate catalogues for exhibits mounted by or shown at the Jewish Museum. Some exhibits during this period were not accompanied by catalogues. There is no single comprehensive and publicly available list of the museum's exhibits. Two helpful, if partial, publicly available lists relevant to this book are "The Jewish Museum, Exhibitions of Contemporary Art, 1947–90," in Goodman, *From the Inside Out*, 8–9; and "Appendix: A Partial Exhibition List from March 1957 to February 1971," in Tu, "History of the Jewish Museum," 104–8.

Abrahams, Joseph B. "The Buildings of the Seminary." In Adler, *Abstract of the Report*, 65–72.

Adler, Cyrus. *Abstract of the Report . . . to the Board of Directors of the Jewish Theological Seminary of America*. Pamphlet [New York: Jewish Theological Seminary of America, January 1934.]

———. "Address Delivered at the Opening of the Semitic Museum." In *The Semitic Museum of Harvard University*, 14–18. Cambridge, MA: Harvard University, 1903.

———. "Address of the President." *Publications of the American Jewish Historical Society* 9 (1901): 1–12.

———. "Americana at the Anglo-Jewish Exhibition." *Publications of the American Jewish Historical Society* 1 (1893): 109–10.

———. "The Beginnings of Semitic Studies in America." In *Oriental Studies Published in Commemoration of the Fortieth Anniversary of Paul Haupt*, edited by Cyrus Adler and Aaron Ember, 317–28. Baltimore, MD: Johns Hopkins University Press, 1926.

———. "The Collection of Religious Ceremonial Objects." *Report of the U.S. National Museum, Annual Report of the Board of Regents of the Smithsonian Institution . . . for the Year Ending June 30, 1893.* House of Representatives, 53d Congress, 2d Session, Mis. Doc. 184, Part 2 (1895), 136–37.

———. "Dr. Cyrus Adler's Address." In *Oriental Studies Published in Commemoration of the Fortieth Anniversary of Paul Haupt*, edited by Cyrus Adler and Aaron Ember, xviii–xix. Baltimore, MD: Johns Hopkins University Press, 1926.

———. *I Have Considered the Days*. Philadelphia: The Jewish Publication Society of America, 1941.

———. *Lectures, Selected Papers, Addresses by Cyrus Adler*. Edited by Edward D. Coleman and Joseph Reider. Philadelphia: Privately printed, 1933.

———. "Museum Collections to Illustrate Religious History and Ceremonials." *Report of the U.S. National Museum, Annual Report of the Board of Regents of the Smithsonian Institution . . . for the Year Ending June 30, 1893.* House of Representatives, 53d Congress, 2d Session, Mis. Doc. 184, Part 2 (1895), 757–68.

———. "Museums of Art, History, and Science." *Library Journal* 23 (August 1898): 95–96.

———. "[Open Letter] Sources of American Jewish History." *The Menorah* V (July–December 1888): 191–93.

———. "A Proposed American Jewish Historical Exhibition." *The American Jewish Year Book* 5662 (1901): 104–8.

———, ed. *The Jewish Theological Seminary of America: Semi-Centennial Volume*. New York: Jewish Theological Seminary of America, 1939.

Adler, Cyrus, and I[mmanuel]. M. Casanowicz. *Biblical Antiquities: A Description of the Exhibit at the Cotton States International Exposition, Atlanta, 1895*. Washington, DC: US Government Printing Office, 1898.

———. *The Collection of Jewish Ceremonial Objects in the United States National Museum*. Washington, DC: US Government Printing Office, 1908.

———. *Descriptive Catalogue of a Collection of Objects of Jewish Ceremonial Art Deposited in the U.S. National Museum by Hadji Ephraim Benguiat*. Reprinted from Report of the US National Museum [Smithsonian Institution] for 1899. Washington, DC: US Government Printing Office, 1901.

Albert, Phyllis Cohen. "Ethnicity and Jewish Solidarity in Nineteenth-Century France." In *Mystics, Philosophers, and Politicians: Essays in Jewish Intellectual History in Honor of Alexander Altmann*, edited by Jehuda Reinharz and Daniel Swetschinski, 249–74. Durham, NC: Duke University Press, 1982.

———. "Israelite and Jew: How Did Nineteenth-Century French Jews Understand Assimilation?" In *Assimilation and Community: The Jews in Nineteenth-Century Europe*, edited by Jonathan Frankel and Steven J. Zipperstein, 88–109. Cambridge: Cambridge University Press, 1992.

Allwood, John. *The Great Exhibitions*. London: Studio Vista, 1977.

Altshuler, Bruce. "Theory on the Floor: Primary Structures, The Jewish Museum." In *The Avant-Garde in Exhibition: New Art in the 20th Century*, 220–35. New York: Harry N. Abrams, Inc., 1994.

Arthur, Chris. "Exhibiting the Sacred." In Paine, *Godly Things*, 1–27.

*Atkinson, Tracy, and John Lloyd Taylor. *A Plastic Presence*. 2 vols. Milwaukee, WI: Milwaukee Art Center, 1969.

Baigell, Matthew. *Jewish Art in America: An Introduction*. Lanham, MD: Rowman & Littlefield, 2007.

Baigell, Matthew, and Milly Heyd. Introduction to *Complex Identities: Jewish Consciousness and Modern Art*, edited by Matthew Baigell and Milly Heyd, xiii–xvii. New Brunswick, NJ: Rutgers University Press, 2001.

Balken, Debra Bricker. *Harold Rosenberg: A Critic's Life*. Chicago, IL: University of Chicago Press, 2021.

Baskind, Samantha, and Larry Silver. Introduction to *Jewish Art: A Modern History*. London: Reaktion Books, 2011.

Batnitzky, Leora. *How Judaism Became a Religion: An Introduction to Modern Jewish Thought*. Princeton, NJ: Princeton University Press, 2011.

Benguiat, Mordecai. "A Jewish Museum in America." In Mann, *Jewish Texts*, 158–60.

Bennett, Tony. *The Birth of the Museum: History, Theory, Politics*. London: Routledge, 1995.

Berger, Maurice, and Joan Rosenbaum. *Masterworks of the Jewish Museum*. New York: Jewish Museum, 2004.

Berger, Natalia. *The Jewish Museum: History and Memory, Identity and Art from Vienna to the Bezalel National Museum, Jerusalem*. Leiden, NL: Brill, 2018.

Berkowitz, Jay R. *The Shaping of Jewish Identity in Nineteenth-Century France*. Detroit, MI: Wayne State University Press, 1989.

Berman, Lila Corwin. *Speaking of Jews: Rabbis, Intellectuals, and the Creation of an American Public Identity*. Berkeley: University of California Press, 2009.

Berman, Nancy M. "Visions, Revisions, and Reverberations: The Evolving Hebrew Union College Skirball Museum." In *New Beginnings: The Skirball Museum Collections and Inaugural Exhibition*, edited by Grace Cohen Grossman, 17–25. Los Angeles: Skirball Cultural Center, 1996.

Beuttler, Fred. "For the World at Large: Intergroup Activities at the Jewish Theological Seminary." In Wertheimer, *Tradition Renewed*, II:162–232.

Biale, David. *Not in the Heavens: The Tradition of Jewish Secular Thought*. Princeton, NJ: Princeton University Press, 2010.

Bilski, Emily D. "Seeing the Future Through the Light of the Past: The Art of The Jewish Museum." In *The Jewish Museum of New York*, by Vivian B. Mann with Emily D. Bilski, 8–21. New York: Scala Books, 1993.

Birmingham, Stephen. *"Our Crowd": The Great Jewish Families of New York*. New York: Harper & Row, 1967.

Birnbaum, Pierre. "Between Social and Political Assimilation: Remarks on the History of Jews in France." In Birnbaum and Katznelson, *Paths of Emancipation*, 94–127.

Birnbaum, Pierre, and Ira Katznelson, eds. *Paths of Emancipation: Jews, States, and Citizenship*. Princeton, NJ: Princeton University Press, 1995.

Bland, Kalman P. *The Artless Jew: Medieval and Modern Affirmations and Denials of the Visual.* Princeton, NJ: Princeton University Press, 2000.

Bloch, Joshua. "Alexander Marx ז"ל (1878–1953)." *Publications of the American Jewish Historical Society* 43, no. 4 (June 1954): 241–52.

Bloom, Alexander. *Prodigal Sons: The New York Intellectuals & Their World.* Oxford: Oxford University Press, 1986.

Boyarin, Jonathan. "The Other Within and the Other Without." In *The Other in Jewish Thought and History: Constructions of Jewish Culture and Identity*, edited by Laurence J. Silberstein and Robert L. Cohn, 424–52. New York: New York University Press, 1994.

Branham, Joan R. "Sacrality and Aura in the Museum: Mute Objects and Articulate Space." *Journal of the Walters Art Gallery* 52/53 (1994/1995): 33–47.

Brenner, David A. *Marketing Identities: The Invention of Jewish Ethnicity in* Ost und West. Detroit, MI: Wayne State University Press, 1998.

Brooks, Mary M. "Seeing the Sacred: Conflicting Priorities in Defining, Interpreting, and Conserving Western Sacred Artifacts." *Material Religion: The Journal of Objects, Art, and Belief* 8, no. 1 (March 2012): 10–29.

Brown, Milton W. "An Explosion of Creativity: Jews and American Art in the Twentieth Century." In Kleeblatt and Chevlowe, *Painting a Place in America*, 22–27.

Buckser, Andrew. "Secularization, Religiosity, and the Anthropology of Jewry." *Journal of Modern Jewish Studies* 10, no. 2 (July 2011): 205–22.

Buggeln, Gretchen. "Museum Space and the Experience of the Sacred." *Material Religion: The Journal of Objects, Art and Belief* 8, no. 1 (2012): 30–50.

Buggeln, Gretchen, Crispin Paine, and Brent S. Plate, eds. *Religion in Museums: Global and Multidisciplinary Perspectives.* London: Bloomsbury Academic, 2017.

Burman, Rickie. "Presenting Judaism: Jewish Museums in Britain." In Paine, *Godly Things*, 132–42.

*Burnham, Jack, ed. *Software—Information Technology: Its New Meaning for Art.* New York: The Jewish Museum, 1970.

Burris, John P. *Exhibiting Religion: Colonialism and Spectacle at International Expositions, 1851–1893.* Charlottesville: University Press of Virginia, 2001.

Bürger, Peter. *Theory of the Avant-Garde.* Translated by Michael Shaw. Theory and History of Literature. Minneapolis: University of Minnesota Press, 1984.

Cantor, Geoffrey. *Religion and the Great Exhibition of 1851.* Oxford: Oxford University Press, 2011.

*Capa, Cornell, ed. *Israel / The Reality: People, Places, Events in Memorable Photographs.* New York: World Publishing Company in association with the Jewish Museum, 1969.

Casanova, José. "The Secular and Secularisms." *Social Research* 76, no. 4 (Winter 2009): 1049–66.

*Celant, Germano, ed. *New York, 1962–1964.* New York: Jewish Museum | Milan, IT: Skira Editore, 2022.

Çelik, Zeynep, and Leila Kinney. "Ethnography and Exhibitionism at the Expositions Universelles." *Assemblage* 13 (December 1990): 34–59.

[Center of Jewish Art, Hebrew University]. *The World Directory of Jewish Museums.* Jerusalem: Eliezer Fisher, Ltd., 1994.

Chernow, Ron. *The Warburgs: The Twentieth-Century Odyssey of a Remarkable Jewish Family.* New York: Random House, 1993.

Clifford, James. "Museums as Contact Zones." In *Routes: Travel and Translation in the Late Twentieth Century*, 188–219. Cambridge, MA: Harvard University Press, 1997.

Clifton, James. "Truly a Worship Experience? Christian Art in Secular Museums." *RES: Anthropology and Aesthetics* 52 (Autumn 2007): 107–15.

*Cohen, Arthur A. *The Hebrew Bible in Christian, Jewish and Muslim Art*. New York: Jewish Museum, 1963.

———. "The Jewish Museum: Victim of Confusion." *Congress Bi-Weekly: A Journal of Opinion and Jewish Affairs* 34, no. 15 (20 November 1967): 7–8.

———. "Museum or Mausoleum?" *New York Times*, 7 February 1971.

Cohen, Naomi W. *Encounter with Emancipation: The German Jews in the United States, 1830–1914*. Philadelphia, PA: Jewish Publication Society, 1984.

Cohen, Richard I. "Between Encyclopedias and Museums: Modes of Jewish Empowerment and Visibility." In *Simon Dubnow Institute Yearbook*, vol. 9, edited by Dan Diner, 459–72. Göttingen: Vandenhoeck & Ruprecht, 2010.

———. "An Introductory Essay: Viewing the Past." In *Art and Its Uses: The Visual Image and Modern Jewish Society*, vol. 6, Ezra Mendelsohn, gen. ed., edited by Richard I. Cohen, 3–8. Oxford: Oxford University Press, 1990.

———. *Jewish Icons: Art and Society in Modern Europe*. Berkeley: University of California Press, 1998.

———. "The Visual Revolution in Jewish Life—An Overview." In Cohen, *Visualizing and Exhibiting*, 3–24.

———, ed. *Visualizing and Exhibiting Jewish Space and History*. Oxford: Oxford University Press, 2012.

Coolick, Gayle Meyer. "The Public Career of Cyrus Adler." PhD diss., Georgia State University, 1981.

Corbey, Raymond. "Ethnographic Showcases, 1870–1930." *Cultural Anthropology* 8, no. 3 (August 1993): 338–69.

Cottington, David. *The Avant-Garde: A Very Short Introduction*. Oxford: Oxford University Press, 2013.

Dalin, David G. "The Patriarch: The Life and Legacy of Mayer Sulzberger." In Friedman, *When Philadelphia Was the Capital*, 58–74.

Danto, Arthur. "Body and Soul." *The Nation* 279, no. 3 (19–26 July 2004): 40–43.

———. "Postmodern Art & Concrete Selves: The Model of the Jewish Museum." In Goodman, *From the Inside Out*, 11–21.

Dellheim, Charles. *Belonging and Betrayal: How Jews Made the Art World Modern*. Waltham, MA: Brandeis University Press, 2021.

Desvallées, André, and François Mairesse. "Musealisation." In *Key Concepts in Museology*, 50–52. Paris, FR: Armand Colin, 2010.

Deutsch, Yaacov. "Polemical Ethnographies: Descriptions of Yom Kippur in the Writings of Christian Hebraists and Jewish Converts to Christianity in Early Modern Europe." In *Hebraica Veritas? Christian Hebraists and the Study of Judaism in Early Modern Europe*, edited by Allison P. Coudert and Jeffrey S. Shoulson, 203–4. Philadelphia: University of Pennsylvania Press, 2004.

Dicker, Herman, ed. *The Mayer Sulzberger-Alexander Marx Correspondence, 1904–1923*. New York: Sepher-Hermon Press, 1990.

———. *Of Learning and Libraries: The Seminary Library at One Hundred*. New York: Jewish Theological Seminary of America, 1988.

Diner, Hasia. "Like the Antelope and the Badger: The Founding and Early Years of the Jewish Theological Seminary, 1886–1902." In Wertheimer, *Tradition Renewed*, I:1–42.

———. *The Jews of the United States, 1654–2000*. Berkeley, CA: University of California Press, 2004.

———. *Lower East Side Memories: A Jewish Place in America*. Princeton, NJ: Princeton University Press, 2000.

Dinnerstein, Leonard, and Gene Koppel. Introduction to *Nathan Glazer: A Different Kind of Liberal*, edited by Dinnerstein and Koppel, v–vii. Tucson: University of Arizona, 1973.

Dresner, Samuel. "Renewal." *Conservative Judaism* XIX, no. 4 (Summer 1965): 53–69.

Endelman, Todd. "Jewish Self-Identification and West European Categories of Belonging: From the Enlightenment to World War II." In *Religion or Ethnicity? Jewish Identities in Evolution*, edited by Zvi Gitelman, 104–30. New Brunswick, NJ: Rutgers University Press, 2009.

Epstein, Helen. "Meyer Schapiro: 'A Passion to Know and Make Known.'" *Art News* 82, no. 5 and 6 (May and Summer 1983): 60–85, 84–95.

Erickson, Ruth. *30 Years of New Year Graphics from the Jewish Museum: The Albert and Vera G. List Graphics Commissions*. Essay by Jane Kent. Burlington, VT: Burlington City Arts, 2006.

Erlande-Brandenburg, Alain. "The Isaac Strauss Collection." In *Jewish Treasures from Paris: From the Collections of the Cluny Museum and the Consistoire*, compiled by Victor A. Klagsbald. Jerusalem: Israel Museum, 1982.

*Farkas, Ann, ed. *Thou Shalt Have No Other Gods Before Me*. New York: Jewish Museum, 1964.

Feiner, Shmuel. *Haskalah and History: The Emergence of a Modern Jewish Historical Consciousness*. Translated by Chaya Naor and Sondra Silverston. Oxford: Littman Library of Jewish Civilization, 2002.

———. *The Jewish Enlightenment*. Translated by Chaya Naor. Philadelphia: University of Pennsylvania Press, 2004.

———. *The Origins of Jewish Secularization in Eighteenth-Century Europe*. Translated by Chaya Naor. Philadelphia: University of Pennsylvania Press, 2010.

Feldman, Jeffrey David. "Exhibiting Judaica or Jewish Exhibitionism: A Comparison of Two Nineteenth-Century Exhibitions." Master's thesis, St. Cross College, Oxford University, 1993.

Feuchtwanger-Sarig, Naomi, Mark Irving, and Emil Schrijver, eds. *Jewish Art in Context: The Role and Meaning of Artifacts and Visual Images*. Studia Rosenthaliana. Louvain, Belgium: Peeters, 2014.

Finn, David. *The Way Forward: My First Fifty Years at Ruder • Finn*. New York: Millwood Publishing, 1998.

Finn, David, Sam Hunter, Percival Goodman, et al. "The Function of the Jewish Museum: An Exchange." *Congress Bi-Weekly: A Journal of Opinion and Jewish Affairs* 34, no. 17 (18 December 1967): 2, 21–22.

Fisher, Philip. *Making and Effacing Art: Modern American Art in a Culture of Museums*. Oxford: Oxford University Press, 1991.

Fishof, Iris. *From the Secular to the Sacred: Everyday Objects in Jewish Ritual Use*. Jerusalem: Israel Museum, 1985.

Frankel, Jonathan. "Assimilation and the Jews in Nineteenth-Century Europe: Towards a New Historiography?" In *Assimilation and Community: The Jews in Nineteenth-Century Europe*, edited by Jonathan Frankel and Steven J. Zipperstein, 1–37. Cambridge: Cambridge University Press, 1992.

Frauberger, Heinrich. "The Need to Collect Images of Jewish Art." In Mann, *Jewish Texts*, 156–58.

Frazier, Nancy. *Jewish Museums of North America: A Guide to Collections, Artifacts, and Memorabilia*. New York: John Wiley & Sons, 1992.

Freudenheim, Tom L. "The (Jewish) Jewish Museum." *Moment* 2, no. 2 (November 1976): 27–29, 51–52.

———. "The Jewish Museum's Discomfort with Religion." *Mosaic*, 13 May 2019, https://mosaicmagazine.com/response/arts-culture/2019/05/the-jewish-museums-discomfort-with-religion/.

Friedenberg, Daniel M. "Can a Jewish Museum Live by Art Alone?" *New York Times*, 29 August 1971.

Friedman, H. G. "Letter to Dr. Alexander Marx Concerning the H. G. Friedman Collection of Judaica, 24 December 1941." In Mann, *Jewish Texts*, 163–66.

Friedman, Murray, ed. *When Philadelphia Was the Capital of Jewish America*. Philadelphia: Balch Institute Press, 1993.

Gamilly, Hector. "L'Exposition Des Arts Rétrospectifs, Au Trocadéro." *L'Exposition es Paris: Journal Hebdomadaire* 39 (December 1878): 307–8, 312.

Gans, Herbert J. "American Jewry: Present and Future | Part 1: Present." *Commentary* 21, no. 5 (May 1956): 422–30.

———. "Another Look at Symbolic Ethnicity." *Ethnic and Racial Studies* 40, no. 9 (2017): 1410–17.

———. "Symbolic Ethnicity and Symbolic Religiosity: Towards a Comparison of Ethnic and Religious Acculturation." *Ethnic and Racial Studies* 17, no. 4 (October 1994): 577–92.

———. "Symbolic Ethnicity: The Future of Ethnic Groups and Cultures in America." *Ethnic and Racial Studies* 2, no. 1 (January 1979): 1–20.

Gaskell, Ivan. "Sacred to Profane and Back Again." In *Art and Its Publics: Museum Studies at the Millenium*, edited by Andrew McClellan, 149–62. Oxford: Blackwell Publishing, 2003.

Gitelman, Zvi. "Conclusion: The Nature and Viability of Jewish Religious and Secular Identities." In *Religion or Ethnicity? Jewish Identities in Evolution*, edited by Zvi Gitelman, 303–22. New Brunswick, NJ: Rutgers University Press, 2009.

Glazer, Nathan. *American Judaism*. Chicago, IL: University of Chicago Press, 1957.

Glazer, Nathan, and Daniel P. Moynihan. Introduction to *Ethnicity: Theory and Experience*, edited by Glazer and Moynihan, 1–26. Cambridge, MA: Harvard University Press, 1975.

Glogower, Abigail, and Margaret Olin. "Between Two Worlds: Ghost Stories Under Glass in Vienna and Chicago." In Cohen, *Visualizing and Exhibiting*, 217–42.

Godfrey, Mark. "'That Oldtime Jewish Sect Called American Art Criticism.'" In Kleeblatt, *Action/Abstraction*, 247–65.

Golub, Jacob S. *The Jewish Museum*. New York: Jewish Education Committee of New York, [ca. 1949].

*Goodman, Susan Tumarkin, ed. *From the Inside Out: Eight Contemporary Artists*. New York: Jewish Museum, 1993.

*———. *Using Walls (Indoors) and Using Walls (Outdoors)*. 2 vols. New York: Jewish Museum, 1970.

Goodwin, George M. "A New Jewish Elite: Curators, Directors, and Benefactors of American Art Museums." *Modern Judaism* 18, no. 1 and 2 (February and May 1998): 47–49, 119–52.

Graetz, Michael. *The Jews in Nineteenth-Century France: From the French Revolution to the Alliance Israélite Universelle*. Translated by Jean Marie Todd. Stanford, CA: Stanford University Press, 1996.

Greenbaum, Michael B. "The Finkelstein Era." In Wertheimer, *Tradition Renewed*, I:162–232.

———. *Louis Finkelstein and the Conservative Movement: Conflict and Growth*. Binghamton, NY: Global Publications, Binghamton University, 2001.

Greene, Virginia. "'Accessories of Holiness': Defining Jewish Sacred Objects." *Journal of the American Institute for Conservation* 31, no. 1 (Spring 1992): 31–39.

Greenhalgh, Paul. *Ephemeral Vistas: The Expositions Universelles, Great Exhibitions and World's Fairs, 1851–1939*. Manchester, UK: Manchester University Press, 1988.

Grimes, Ronald L. "Sacred Objects in Museum Spaces." *Studies in Religion/Sciences Religieuses* 21, no. 4 (1992): 419–30.

Gross, William L. "Catalogue of Catalogues: Bibliographical Survey of a Century of Temporary Exhibitions of Jewish Art." *Journal of Jewish Art* 6 (1979): 133–57.

Grossman, Grace Cohen. *Jewish Museums of the World*. New York: Universe Publishing, 2008.

Grossman, Grace Cohen, and Richard Eighme Ahlborn. *Judaica at the Smithsonian: Cultural Politics as Cultural Model*. Washington, DC: Smithsonian Institution Press, 1997.

Guilbaut, Serge. *How New York Stole the Idea of Modern Art: Abstract Expressionism, Freedom, and the Cold War*. Translated by Arthur Goldhammer. Chicago, IL: University of Chicago Press, 1983.

Gurock, Jeffrey S. *Jews in Gotham: New York Jews in a Changing City, 1920–2010*. New York: New York University Press, 2012.

Gutmann, Joseph. "Is There a Jewish Art?" In *The Visual Dimension: Aspects of Jewish Art*, edited by Clair Moore, 1–19. Boulder, CO: Westview Press, 1993.

———. "Jewish Art and Jewish Studies." In *The State of Jewish Studies*, edited by Shaye J. D. Cohen and Edward L. Greenstein, 193–211. Detroit, MI: Wayne State University Press for JTS, 1990.

———. *Jewish Ceremonial Art*. New York: Thomas Yoseloff, 1964.

———. "The Kirschstein Museum of Berlin." *Jewish Art* 16/17 (1990/1991): 172–76.

———. "Prolegomenon" and "The 'Second Commandment' and the Image in Judaism." In *No Graven Images: Studies in Art and the Hebrew Bible*, edited by Gutmann, xi–lxiii, 3–16. New York: KTAV Publishing House, 1971.

Heimann-Jelinek, Felicitas. "Inventory of the Sabbath Room." In *Rabbiner - Bocher - Talmudschüler: Bilder Des Weiner Malers Isidor Kaufmann, 1853–1921*, 147–63. Vienna: Jüdisches Museum der Stadt Wien, 1995.

Heimann-Jelinek, Felicitas, and Wiebke Krohn, eds. *The First Jewish Museum*. Vienna, Austria: Jüdisches Museum der Stadt Wien, 2005.

*Heller, Ben. *Black and White*. New York: Jewish Museum, 1963.

Heller, Ena Giurescu, ed. *Reluctant Partners: Art and Religion in Dialogue*. New York: The Gallery at the American Bible Society, 2004.

Herberg, Will. *Protestant, Catholic, Jew: An Essay in American Religious Sociology*. Revision of 1955 edn. Chicago, IL: University of Chicago Press, 1983.

Hiesinger, Kathryn B., Celia Cullen Martin, and Felicitas Thurn-Valsassina. "On the Mountain Top, All Paths Unite: Private Banking and Art Collecting in America After the Civil War." In Weber, *Jüdische Sammler*, 69–81.

Hinsley, Curtis M. "The World as Marketplace: Commodification of the Exotic at the World's Columbian Exposition, Chicago, 1893." In Karp and Lavine, *Exhibiting Cultures*, 344–65.

Holloway, Steven W. "The Smithsonian Institution's Religious Ceremonial Objects and Biblical Antiquities at the World's Columbian Exposition (Chicago, 1893) and the Cotton States and International Exposition (Atlanta, 1895)." In *Orientalism, Assyriology and the Bible*, edited by Steven W. Holloway, 95–138. Sheffield, UK: Sheffield Phoenix Press, 2006.

Hödl, Klaus. "The Turning to History of Viennese Jews: Jewish Identity and the Jewish Museum." *Journal of Modern Jewish Studies* 3, no. 1 (March 2004): 17–32.

*[Hoffman, Jens, ed.] *Other Primary Structures*. New York: Jewish Museum and Yale University Press, 2014.

Howe, Irving. *The End of Jewish Secularism*. New York: Hunter College, City University of New York, 1995.

*Hunter, Sam. *Larry Rivers*. New York: October House for Poses Institute of Fine Arts, Brandeis University, 1965.

———. "The Jewish Museum: What Is It, Why Is It, and What Next?" *New York Times*, 8 August 1965.

Hyman, Paula E. *The Emancipation of the Jews of Alsace: Acculturation and Tradition in the Nineteenth Century*. New Haven, CT: Yale University Press, 1991.

———. *The Jews of Modern France*. Berkeley: University of California Press, 1998.

Israel, Matthew. "A Magnet for the With-It Kids." *Art in America* 95, no. 9 (October 2007): 73–83.

Jacobs, Joseph, and Lucien Wolf, eds. *Catalogue of the Anglo-Jewish Historical Exhibition*. Edition de luxe. London: F. Haes, 1888.

The Jewish Museum. New York: Jewish Museum, 1947.

Joselit, Jenna Weissman. "By Design: Building the Campus of the Jewish Theological Seminary." In Wertheimer, *Tradition Renewed*, I:271–92.

———. "Telling Tales: Or, How a Slum Became a Shrine." *Jewish Social Studies* 2, no. 2 (Winter 1996): 54–63.

———. *The Wonders of America: Reinventing Jewish Culture, 1880–1950*. New York: Hill and Wang, 1994.

Joskowicz, Ari, and Ethan B. Katz, eds. *Secularism in Question: Jews and Judaism in Modern Times*. Philadelphia: University of Pennsylvania Press, 2015.

Kaganoff, Nathan M. "AJHS at 90: Reflections on the History of the Oldest Ethnic Historical Society in America." *American Jewish History* 71, no. 4 (June 1982): 466–85.

*Kampf, Avram. *Jewish Experience in the Art of the Twentieth Century*. New York: Jewish Museum, 1975.

———. "The Jewish Museum: An Institution Adrift." *Judaism* 17, no. 3 (Summer 1968): 282–98.

Kanof, Abram. "The Tobe Pascher Workshop, 1956–1986." In Nancy M. Berman, *Moshe Zabari: A Twenty-Five Year Retrospective*, 6. New York: The Jewish Museum, 1986.

Kaplan, Louis. "Reframing the Self-Criticism: Clement Greenberg's 'Modernist Painting' in Light of Jewish Identity." In Soussloff, *Jewish Identity*, 180–99.

Karp, Abraham J. "Louis Finkelstein (1895–1991)." In *American Jewish Year Book*, edited by David Singer and Ruth R. Seldin, 527–34. New York: American Jewish Committee and Jewish Publication Society, 1993.

Karp, Ivan, Christine Mullen Kreamer, and Steven D. Lavine, eds. *Museums and Communities: The Politics of Public Culture*. Washington, DC: Smithsonian Institution Press, 1992.

Karp, Ivan, and Steven D. Lavine, eds. *Exhibiting Cultures: The Poetics and Politics of Museum Display*. Washington, DC: Smithsonian Institution Press, 1991.

Katz, Karl. *The Exhibitionist: Living Museums, Loving Museums*. New York: Overlook Press, 2016.

*———, ed. *Ingathering: Ceremony and Tradition in New York Public Collections* [New York: Jewish Museum, 1969].

Kaufmann, David. "Etwas von Jüdischer Kunst." In *Gesammelte Schriften*, edited by M. Brann, 3: 150–53. Frankfurt, Germany: Kommissions-Verlag von J. Kauffmann, 1908–15.

Kayser, Stephen S. "After Displacements I Find Coherence Again." In *The Hour of Insight: A Sequel to Moments of Personal Discovery*, edited by R. M. MacIver, 41–50. New York: Institute for Religious and Social Studies, Jewish Theological Seminary, 1954.

———. "Defining Jewish Art." In *Mordecai M. Kaplan Jubilee Volume*. 2 vols., Moshe Davis, English volume, 457–67. New York: Jewish Theological Seminary of America, 1953.

[———.] *Designing of Modern Jewish Ceremonial Art* [New York]: Jewish Museum, 1953.

———. Introduction to *Jewish Ceremonial Art*, edited by Stephen S. Kayser. Philadelphia, PA: Jewish Publication Society of America, 1955.

*———. *The Jewish Museum: 1947, 1957* [New York]: [Jewish Museum, Jewish Theological Seminary], 1957.

———. "The Jewish Museum After Ten Years." *Adult Jewish Education: A Quarterly Journal* (Spring 1957): 6–9.

*———, ed. *The New York School, Second Generation*. New York: Jewish Theological Seminary of America, 1957.

———. "Visual Arts in American Jewish Life." *Judaism: A Quarterly Journal* 3, no. 4 (Fall 1954): 437–45.

Kelly, Alison. "St. Mungo Museum of Religious Life and Art, Glasgow." *Material Religion: The Journal of Objects, Art, and Belief* 1, no. 3 (2005): 435–37.

Kirshenblatt-Gimblett, Barbara. *Destination Culture: Tourism, Museums, and Heritage*. Berkeley: University of California Press, 1998.

———. Introduction to *Life is With People: The Culture of the Shtetl*. Reprinted from 1962 ed., with a foreword by Margaret Mead, by Mark Zborowski and Elizabeth Herzog, ix–xlviii. New York: Schocken Books, 1995.

Kirshenblatt-Gimblett, Barbara, and Jonathan Karp. Introduction to *The Art of Being Jewish in Modern Times*, edited by Kirshenblatt-Gimblett and Karp, 1–19. Philadelphia: University of Pennsylvania Press, 2008.

Klagsbald, Victor A. *Jewish Treasures from Paris: From the Collections of the Cluny Museum and the Consistoire*. Jerusalem: Israel Museum, 1982.

*Kleeblatt, Norman L., ed. *Action/Abstraction: Pollock, De Kooning, and American Art, 1940–1976*. New York: Jewish Museum and Yale University Press, 2008.

*———. *The Dreyfus Affair: Art, Truth, and Justice*. Berkeley: University of California Press, 1987.

*———. *Mirroring Evil: Nazi Imagery/Recent Art*. New Brunswick, NJ: Rutgers University Press, 2001.

*———. *Too Jewish? Challenging Traditional Identities*. New Brunswick, NJ: Rutgers University Press, 1996.

*Kleeblatt, Norman L., and Susan Chevlowe, eds. *Painting a Place in America: Jewish Artists in New York, 1900–1945 -- A Tribute to the Educational Alliance Art School*. New York: The Jewish Museum, 1991.

Kolb, Leon. "The Vienna Jewish Museum." In *The Jews of Austria: Essays on Their Life, History, and Destruction*, edited by Josef Fraenkel, 147–59. London: Vallentine Mitchell and Company, 1967.

Kong, Lily. "Re-Presenting the Religious: Nation, Community and Identity in Museums." *Social & Cultural Geography* 6, no. 4 (August 2005): 495–513.

Korey, Michael. "Displaying Judaica in 18th-Century Central Europe: A Non-Jewish Curiosity." In Cohen, *Visualizing and Exhibiting*, 25–54.

Krah, Marcus. *American Jewry and the Re-Invention of the East European Jewish Past*. Berlin, Germany: De Gruyter Oldenbourg, 2018.

Krautheimer, Richard. "On Collecting for the New Jewish Museum, New York." In Mann, *Jewish Texts*, 166–69.

Kuspit, Donald. "Critics, Primary and Secondary." In *American Art in the 20th Century: Painting and Sculpture, 1913–1993*, edited by Christos M. Joachimides and Norman Rosenthal, 145–49. Munich: Prestel, 1993.

———. "Dialectical Reasoning in Meyer Schapiro." *Social Research* 45, no. 1 (Spring 1978): 93–129.

———. "Identity in Modern Art." In Mann, *Jewish Texts*, 152–55.

———. "Meyer Schapiro's Jewish Unconscious." In Soussloff, *Jewish Identity*, 200–17.

———. "Meyer Schapiro's Marxism." *Arts Magazine* 53, no. 3 (November 1978): 142–44.

Lederhendler, Eli. *New York Jews and the Decline of Urban Ethnicity, 1950–1970*. Syracuse, NY: Syracuse University Press, 2001.

Liberles, Robert. "Postemancipation Historiography and the Jewish Historical Societies of America and England." In *Reshaping the Past: Jewish History and the Historians*, edited by Jonathan Frankel, 45–65. Oxford: Oxford University Press, 1994.

Liesville, A.-R. de. *Coup-d'Oeil Général sur l'Exposition Historique de l'Art Ancien (Palais Du Trocadéro)*. Paris: Honoré Champion, 1879.

Limouze, Dorothy. "Introduction: The History of the Warburg Gift." In *The Felix M. Warburg Collection: A Legacy of Discernment*, 9–22. Poughkeepsie, NY: Loeb Art Center, Vassar College, 1995.

Lubow, Arthur. "How New York's Jewish Museum Anticipated the Avant-Garde." *New York Times Style Magazine*, July 23, 2020, https://www.nytimes.com/2020/07/23/t-magazine/jewish-museum-new-york.html.

Maggen, Michael. "The Conservation of Sacred Materials in the Israel Museum." In *Conservation of Living Religious Heritage: Papers from the ICCROM 2003 Forum on Living Religious Heritage, Conserving the Sacred*, edited by H. Stovel, N. Stanley-Price, and R. Killick, 102–6. Rome: ICCROM, 2005.

*Mann, Vivian B., ed. *Gardens and Ghettos: The Art of Jewish Life in Italy*. Berkeley: University of California Press, 1989.

———. *Jewish Texts on the Visual Arts*. Cambridge: Cambridge University Press, 2000.

*Mann, Vivian B., and Richard I. Cohen, eds. *From Court Jews to the Rothschilds: Art, Patronage, and Power, 1600–1800*, New York: The Jewish Museum, 1996.

**Masada and the Finds from the Bar-Kokhba Caves: Struggle for Freedom*. Exhibition coordinated by Joy G. Ungerleider. New York: Jewish Museum, 1967.

McClellan, Andrew. *The Art Museum from Boullée to Bilbao*. Berkeley: University of California Press, 2008.

*[McShine, Kynaston.] *Primary Structures: Younger American and British Sculptors*. New York: Jewish Museum, 1966.

*Meier, Richard. *Recent American Synagogue Architecture*. New York: Jewish Museum, 1963.

Mendes-Flohr, Paul. "Fin-de-Siècle Orientalism, the *Ostjuden* and the Aesthetics of Jewish Self-Affirmation." In *Divided Passions: Jewish Intellectuals and the Experience of Modernity*, 77–132. Detroit, MI: Wayne State University Press, 1991.

Metzler, Tobias. "Jewish History in the Showcase." *Museological Review* 12 (2007): 101–11.

Meyer, Michael A. *Jewish Identity in the Modern World*. Seattle: University of Washington Press, 1990.

———. *The Origins of the Modern Jew: Jewish Identity and European Culture in Germany, 1749–1824*. Detroit: Wayne State University Press, 1967.

Miller, Julie. "Planning the Jewish Museum, 1944–1947." *Conservative Judaism* 47, no. 1 (Fall 1994): 60–73.

Miller, Julie, and Richard I. Cohen. "A Collision of Cultures: The Jewish Museum and the Jewish Theological Seminary, 1904–1971." In Wertheimer, *Tradition Renewed*, II:310–61.

Minkoff, N. B. "Authority on Jewish Art." *B'Nai B'Rith Messenger* 52, no. 7 (1 October 1948): 31–32.

Mintz-Manor, Limor. "Between Neighbors and Strangers: Representations of the Indigenous People of America and Construction of Jewish Identity in Early Modern Western Europe." *Jewish History* 36, no. 3–4 (December 2022): 265–95.

Mitchell, W. J. T. "Schapiro's Legacy." *Art in America* 83 (April 1995): 29, 31.

Moore, Deborah Dash. *At Home in America: Second Generation New York Jews*. New York: Columbia University Press, 1981.

———. Introduction to *American Jewish Identity Politics*, edited by Deborah Dash Moore, 1–20. Ann Arbor: University of Michigan Press, 2008.

Morris, Bernice, and Mary M. Brooks. "Jewish Ceremonial Textiles and the Torah: Exploring Conservation Practices in Relation to Ritual Textiles Associated with Holy Texts." In *Textiles and Text: Re-Establishing the Links Between Archival and Object-Based Research*, edited by Maria Hayward and Elizabeth Kramer, 244–48. London: Archetype Publications, 2006.

Mosquera, Gerardo. "Meyer Schapiro, Marxist Aesthetics, and Abstract Art." *Oxford Art Journal* 17, no. 1 (1994): 76–80.

Motherwell, Robert. *The School of New York*. Beverly Hills, CA: Frank Perls Gallery, 1951.

Mulas, Ugo. *New York: The New York Art Scene*. Text by Alan Solomon. New York: Holt Rinehart Winston, 1967.

*Musée des arts décoratifs. *Peintres Européens d'Aujourd'hui/European Painters Today*. Paris: Union centrale des arts décoratifs, 1968.

Nelson A. Rockefeller, Lewis L. Strauss: Remarks at the Dedication of the Jewish Museum. . . . New York: Jewish Theological Seminary of America, 1947.

Neuman, Abraham A. *Cyrus Adler, a Biographical Sketch*. New York: American Jewish Committee, 1942.

O'Donnell, C. Oliver. *Meyer Schapiro's Critical Debates: Art Through a Modern American Mind*. University Park: Penn State University Press, 2019.

Oko, Adolph S. *A History of the Hebrew Union College Library and Museum*. Cincinnati: Hebrew Union College Press, 1944.

Olin, Margaret. *The Nation without Art: Examining Modern Discourses on Jewish Art*. Lincoln: University of Nebraska Press, 2001.

———. "Violating the Second Commandment's Taboo: Why Art Historian Meyer Schapiro Took on Bernard Berenson." *Forward* 98 (4 November 1994): 23.

O'Neill, Mark. "Making Histories of Religion." In *Making Histories in Museums*, edited by Gaynor Kavanagh, 188–199. London: Leicester University Press, 1996.

Orzech, Charles D. *Museums of World Religions: Displaying the Divine, Shaping Cultures*. New York: Bloomsbury Academic, 2020.

Paine, Crispin, ed. *Godly Things: Museums, Objects, and Religion*. London: Leicester University Press, 2000.

———. "Religion in London's Museums." In Paine, *Godly Things*, 151–70.

———. *Religious Objects in Museums: Private Lives and Public Duties*. London: Bloomsbury, 2013.

Paul Romanoff, Ph.D.: Scholar, Lecturer, Archaeologist. Promotional brochure. New York: Art Lecture Bureau, 1936.

Pieren, Kathrin. "Migration and Identity Constructions in the Metropolis: The Representations of Jewish Heritage in London Between 1887 and 1956." PhD diss. University of London, 2011.

———. "Negotiating Jewish Identity Through the Display of Art." *Jewish Culture and History* 12, nos. 1 and 2 (Summer/Autumn 2010): 281–96.

———. "The Role of Exhibitions in the Definition of Jewish Art and the Discourse on Jewish Identity." *Ars Judaica: The Bar Ilan Journal of Jewish Art* 13 (2017): 73–90.

Pincus-Witten, Robert. "Six Propositions on Jewish Art." *Arts Magazine* 50, no. 4 (December 1975): 66–69.

Podhoretz, Norman. "Jewish Culture and the Intellectuals: The Process of Rediscovery." *Commentary* 19, no. 5 (May 1955): 451–57.

Politzer, Heinz. "The Opportunity of the Jewish Museum: How Best to Encourage Art?" *Commentary* 7, no. 6 (June 1949): 589–93.

Porter, Judith R. "Secularization, Differentiation, and the Function of Religious Value Orientations." *Sociological Inquiry* 43, no. 1 (January 1973): 67–74.

Pratt, Mary Louise. "Arts of the Contact Zone." *Profession* (1991), 33–40.

———. *Imperial Eyes: Travel Writing and Transculturation*, 2nd edn. New York: Routledge, 2008.

Purin, Bernhard. "Isidor Kaufmann's Little World: The 'Sabbath Room' in the Jewish Museum of Vienna." In *Rabbiner - Bocher - Talmudschüler: Bilder Des Weiner Malers Isidor Kaufmann, 1853–1921*, 129–45. Vienna: Jüdisches Museum der Stadt Wien, 1995.

Raz-Krakotzkin, Amnon. "Secularism, the Christian Ambivalence Toward the Jews, and the Notion of Exile." In Joskowicz and Katz, *Secularism in Question*, 276–98.

Robinson, Ira, ed. *Cyrus Adler, Selected Letters*. 2 vols. Philadelphia: Jewish Publication Society of America, 1985.

———. "Cyrus Adler and the Jewish Theological Seminary of America: Image and Reality." *American Jewish History* 78, no. 3 (March 1989): 363–81.

———. "Cyrus Adler: President of the Jewish Theological Seminary, 1915–1940." In Wertheimer, *Tradition Renewed*, I:104–59.

———. "Cyrus Adler, The Philadelphian." In Friedman, *When Philadelphia Was the Capital*, 92–105.

Romanoff, Paul. "The Rediscovery of Jewish Art." *Reconstructionist* 1 (1935): 13–16.

Rosenbach, A. S. W. "The Seminary Museum." In Adler, *Jewish Theological Seminary*, 144–53.

Rosenbaum, Joan. "Director's Statement." In Kleeblatt, *Too Jewish?*, vii.

———. Foreword to Goodman, *From the Inside Out*, 5.

Rosenberg, Harold. "The Art World: Jews in Art." *The New Yorker* (22 December 1975): 64–68.

———. "Collective, Ideological, Combative." In *Art News Annual XXXIV*, edited by Thomas B. Hess and John Ashbery, 74–79. New York: Macmillan Company, 1968.

———. *Discovering the Present: Three Decades in Art, Culture, and Politics*. Chicago, IL: University of Chicago Press, 1973.

———. "Is There a Jewish Art?" *Commentary* 42, no. 1 (July 1966): 57–60.

Rosenfeld, Gavriel D. "Defining 'Jewish Art' in *Ost und West*, 1901–1908: A Study in the Nationalisation of Jewish Culture." *Leo Baeck Institute Yearbook* 39 (1994): 83–110.

Rosensaft, Jean Bloch. "HUC-JIR's Museums: Laboratories for Learning." *The Chronicle*, no. 66 (2005): 27–28.

Roth, Cecil. Introduction to *Catalogue of the Permanent and Loan Collections of the Jewish Museum, London*, edited by R[ichard] D. Barnett, xii–xix. London: Harvey Miller, 1974.

———. *Jewish Art: An Illustrated History*. Rev. edn. Bezalel Narkiss. Jerusalem, Israel: Massada Press, 1971.

Rothstein, Edward. "The Dismantling of Jewish Identity." *Mosaic*, 20 May 2019, https://mosaicmagazine.com/response/arts-culture/2019/05/the-dismantling-of-jewish-identity/.

———. "The Problem with Jewish Museums." *Mosaic*, 1 February 2016, http://mosaicmagazine.com/essay/2016/02/the-problem-with-jewish-museums/.

———. "To Each His Own Museum, as Identity Goes on Display." *New York Times*, 28 December 2010.

Sabar, Shalom, Steven Fine, and William M. Kramer, eds. *A Crown for a King: Studies in Jewish Art, History and Archaeology in Memory of Stephen S. Kayser*. Jerusalem and New York: Gefen Publishing House, 2000.

Saltzman, Lisa. "To Figure, or not to Figure: The Iconoclastic Proscription and Its Theoretical Legacy." In Soussloff, *Jewish Identity*, 67–84.

Samuels, Maurice. "David Schornstein and the Rise of Jewish Historical Fiction in Nineteenth-Century France." *Jewish Social Studies: History, Culture, Society* n.s. 14, no. 3 (Spring/Summer 2008): 38–59.

Sarna, Jonathan D. "Cyrus Adler and the Development of American Jewish Culture: The 'Scholar-Doer' as a Jewish Communal Leader." *American Jewish History* 78, no. 3 (March 1989): 382–94.

———. "The Making of an American Jewish Culture." In Friedman, *When Philadelphia Was the Capital*, 145–55.

Schapiro, Meyer. "[Contribution to 'Symposium' on] Religion and the Intellectuals III." *Partisan Review* 17, no. 4 (April 1950): 331–39.

———. "The Last Aesthete." *Commentary* 8, no. 6 (December 1949): 614–16.

———. "The Liberating Quality of Avant-Garde Art." *Art News* 56, no. 4 (Summer 1957): 36–42.

———. "Mr. Berenson's Values." *Encounter* 16 (April 1961): 57–65.

———. "The Nature of Abstract Art." *Marxist Quarterly* 1, no. 1 (January–March 1937): 78–97.

———. "On the Humanity of Abstract Painting (1960)." In *Modern Art: 19th & 20th Centuries, Selected Papers*, 227–32. New York: George Braziller, 1978.

———. "Race, Nationality and Art." *Art Front* 2 (March 1936): 10–12.

———. "Religious Imagination and the Artist." *ARC Directions* 7 (Fall 1969): 1–4.

———. "The Social Bases of Art." In *First American Artists' Congress Against War and Fascism*, 31–37. New York, 1936.

———. "The Younger American Painters Today." *The Listener* 55, no. 1404 (26 January 1956): 146–47.

Schapiro, Meyer, and Lillian Milgram Schapiro with David Craven. "A Series of Interviews (July 15, 1992–January 22, 1995)." *RES: Anthropology and Aesthetics* 31 (Spring 1997): 159–68.

Schiavo, Laura. "What to Do with Heritage: The Museum of Jewish Ceremonial Objects, 1931–43." In *Radical Roots: Public History and a Tradition of Social Justice Activism*, edited by Denise D. Meringolo, 395–426. Amherst, MA: Amherst College Press, 2021.

*Schoener, Allon, ed. *The Lower East Side: Portal to American Life (1870–1924)*. New York: The Jewish Museum, 1966.

———. *Portal to America: The Lower East Side, 1870–1925*. New York: Holt, Rinehart and Winston, 1967.

*Schoenberger, Guido, and Tom L. Freudenheim, eds. *The Silver and Judaica Collection of Mr. and Mrs. Michael M. Zagayski*. New York: Jewish Museum, 1963.

Schorsch, Ismar. "The Emergence of Historical Consciousness in Modern Judaism." In *Leo Baeck Institute Yearbook XXVIII* (1983): 413–37.

———. *From Text to Context: The Turn to History in Modern Judaism*. Hanover: University Press of New England, 1994.

*Schwartz, Sheila, ed. *Danzig 1939, Treasures of a Destroyed Community*. Detroit, MI: Wayne State University Press for the Jewish Museum, New York, 1980.

"Section Française." *L'Exposition Universelle de 1878 Illustrée*, no. 153 (August 1878): 788.

Segal, Daniel A. "Can You Tell a Jew When You See One? or Thoughts on Meeting Barbra/Barbie at the Museum." *Judaism* 48, no. 2 (Spring 1999): 234–41.

Seldin, Ruth R. "American Jewish Museums: Trends and Issues." In *American Jewish Year Book*, vol. 91, edited by David Singer and Ruth R. Seldin, 71–117. New York: American Jewish Committee, 1991.

Shandler, Jeffrey, and Elihu Katz. "Broadcasting American Judaism: The Radio and Television Department of the Jewish Theological Seminary." In Wertheimer, *Tradition Renewed*, II:364–401.

Shapira, Elana. "Jewish Patronage and the Avant-Garde in Vienna." In Weber, *Jüdische Sammler*, 219–35.

Sherman, Daniel J., and Irit Rogoff. "Introduction: Frameworks for Critical Analysis." In *Museum Culture: Histories, Discourses, Spectacles*, edited by Daniel J. Sherman and Irit Rogoff, ix–xx. Minneapolis: University of Minnesota Press, 1994.

Shiner, Larry. "The Concept of Secularization in Empirical Research." *Journal for the Scientific Study of Religion* 6 (Autumn 1967): 207–20.

*Silver, Kenneth E., and Romy Golan. *The Circle of Montparnasse: Jewish Artists in Paris, 1905–1945*. New York: Universe Books, 1985.

Smith, Graeme. *A Short History of Secularism*. London: I. B. Tauris, 2008.

*Solomon, Alan. *Jasper Johns*. New York: The Jewish Museum, 1964.

*———. Preface to Farkas, *Thou Shalt Have No Other Gods Before Me*. New York: Jewish Museum, 1964.

*———. *Robert Rauschenberg*. New York: [Jewish Museum], 1963.

*———. *Toward a New Abstraction*. New York: Jewish Museum, 1963.

Solomon, Alisa. *Wonder of Wonders: A Cultural History of* Fiddler on the Roof. New York: Metropolitan Books, Henry Holt and Company, 2013.

Sorkin, David. *Jewish Emancipation: A History Across Five Centuries*. Princeton, NJ: Princeton University Press, 2019.

Soussloff, Catherine M., ed. *Jewish Identity in Modern Art History*. Berkeley: University of California Press, 1999.

Stein, Joseph. *Fiddler on the Roof: Based on Sholom Aleichem's Stories*. By Jerry Bock, lyrics by Sheldon Harnick, directed by Jerome Robbins. New York: Crown Publishers, 1964.

Steinberg, Leo. "Contemporary Art and the Plight of the Public." *Harper's Magazine* 224, no. 1342 (March 1962): 31–39.

———. Introduction to Kayser, *The New York School*, 4–8.

Stenne, Georges [David Schornstein]. *Collection de M. Strauss. Description des objets d'art religieux hébraïques: Exposés dans les galeries du Trocadéro, à l'Exposition Universelle de 1878*. Poissy: Typographie de S. Lejay et Cie, 1878.

Stern, Selma. *The Court Jew: A Contribution to the History of the Period of Absolutism in Europe*. Translated by Ralph Weiman. Philadelphia, PA: Jewish Publication Society of America, 1950.

Stolarska-Fronia, Małgorzata. "Jewish Art Collectors from Breslau and Their Impact on the City's Cultural Life at the End of the 19th and the Beginning of the 20th Century." In Weber, *Jüdische Sammler*, 237–53.

Ström, Helena Wangefelt. "How Do Museums Affect Sacredness? Three Suggested Models." *ICOFOM Study Series: Museology and the Sacred* 47, no. 1–2 (2019): 191–205.

Sulzberger, Mayer. "January 20, 1904. To Doctor Cyrus Adler. . . ." In *Biennial Report, The Jewish Theological Seminary of America*, 49–50. New York: [Jewish Theological Seminary of America], 1906.

Swatos Jr., William H., and Kevin J. Christiano. "Secularization Theory: The Course of a Concept." *Sociology of Religion* 60, no. 3 (Autumn 1999): 209–28.

Taylor, Alex J. *Forms of Persuasion: Art and Corporate Image in the 1960s*. Oakland: University of California Press, 2022.

Thompson, Jack C. "On Restoring Sacred Objects." *Leather Conservation News* 14, no. 2 (1998): 1–6.

Thompson, James, and Susan Raines. "A Vermont Visit with Meyer Schapiro (August 1991)." *Oxford Art Journal* 17, no. 1 (1994): 2–12.

Toffler, Alvin. *The Culture Consumers: A Study of Art and Affluence in America*. New York: St. Martin's Press, 1964.

Tomkins, Calvin. *Off the Wall: A Portrait of Robert Rauschenberg*. Rev. edn. New York: Picador, 2005.

Tu, Hsiao-Ning. "The History of the Jewish Museum in New York with an Emphasis on 1963–1971." Master's thesis, City College of New York: City University of New York, 1996.

Tuchman, Maurice, ed. *New York School, The First Generation: Paintings of the 1940s and 1950s*. Rev. edn. Greenwich, CT: New York Graphic Society Ltd., 1971.

*[van Weeren-Griek, Hans, ed.] *Recent American Sculpture*. New York: Jewish Museum, 1964.

von Schlosser, Julius. *Art and Curiosity Cabinets of the Late Renaissance: A Contribution to the History of Collecting*. Edited by Thomas DaCosta Kaufmann. Translated by Jonathan Blower. Los Angeles, CA: Getty Research Institute, 2021.

Verstegen, Ian. *Meyer Schapiro's Critical Debates: Art Through a Modern American Mind*. University Park, PA: Penn State University Press, 2019.

Vogel, Susan. "Always True to the Object, in Our Fashion." In Karp and Lavine, *Exhibiting Cultures*, 191–204.

Warburg, Edward M. M. *'1109': The Warburg House*. 2nd revised edn. New York: Jewish Museum, 2008.

Warburg, Frieda Schiff. *Reminiscences of a Long Life*. New York: Privately printed at the Thistle Press, 1956.

Weber, Annette, ed. *Jüdische Sammler und Ihr Beitrag Zur Kultur der Moderne*. Heidelberg: Universitätsverlag Winter, 2011.

Weber, Max. "Ethnic Groups." In *Theories of Society: Foundations of Modern Sociological Theory*, edited by Talcott Parsons, Edward Shils, and et alia, 305–9. New York: Free Press of Glencoe, 1961.

Wecker, Menachem. "The Wreck of the Jewish Museum." *Mosaic*, 6 May 2019, https://mosaicmagazine.com/essay/arts-culture/2019/05/the-wreck-of-the-jewish-museum/.

Weinland, Martina, and Kurt Winkler. *Das Jüdische Museum Im Stadtmuseum Berlin: Eine Dokumentation*. Berlin: Nicolai, 1997.

Wenger, Beth S. *History Lessons: The Creation of American Jewish Heritage*. Princeton, NJ: Princeton University Press, 2010.

Wertheimer, Jack, ed. *Tradition Renewed: A History of the Jewish Theological Seminary*. 2 vols. New York: Jewish Theological Seminary of America, 1997.

Wettstein, Howard. Introduction to *Diasporas and Exiles: Varieties of Jewish Identity*, edited by Howard Wettstein, 1–17. Berkeley: University of California Press, 2002.

Wharton, Annabel Jane. "JEWISH ART, Jewish Art." *Images: A Journal of Jewish Art and Visual Culture* 1, no.1 (January 2007): 1–7.

Wischnitzer, Rachel. "Jewish Art in New York: A Study in Two Parts." *Hadassah Newsletter*, June–July 1947, 8–10.

Wisse, Ruth R. "The New York (Jewish) Intellectuals." *Commentary* 84, no. 5 (November 1987): 28–38.

Wolf, Lucien. "Origin of the Jewish Historical Society of England." In *Transactions, Jewish Historical Society of England*, vol. VII, 206–21. Edinburgh & London: Ballantyne, Hanson & Co., 1915.

Wolitz, Seth L. "The Americanization of Tevye or Boarding the Jewish *Mayflower*." *American Quarterly* 40, no. 4 (December 1988): 514–36.

Wynar, Lubomyr R., and Lois Buttlar. *Guide to Ethnic Museums, Libraries, and Archives in the United States*. Kent, OH: Program for the Study of Ethnic Publications, Kent University, 1978.

Zborowski, Mark, and Elizabeth Herzog. *Life is With People: The Culture of the Shtetl.* With a foreword by Margaret Mead. New York: Schocken Paperbacks, 1962.

———. *Life is With People: The Jewish Little-Town of Eastern Europe*. Foreword by Margaret Mead. New York: International Universities Press, 1952.

Zipperstein, Steven J. "*Commentary* and American Jewish Culture in the 1940s and 1950s." *Jewish Social Studies* n.s. 3, no. 2 (Winter 1997): 18–28.

Index

Note: Page numbers in bold refer to figures.

Printed in the USA
CPSIA information can be obtained
at www.ICGtesting.com
JSHW011507290124
56245JS00005B/168